Viola Vista by Ben Carl Riley

THE HISTORY OF THE VIOLA

by

Maurice W. Riley

Library of Congress Card Number 79-66348

ISBN: 0-9603150-0-4
       0-9603150-1-2

FOREWORD

The theme, of course, is the Viola, and who can expound that theme more ably than Maurice Riley? Time has taught me that when a man troubles himself to search the record, as he has done, with perseverance and a burning desire to expose it, there results what we have here—a true story, a history, in this case of '*Cinderella No More*', as Tertis so cogently observed. And we violists can be duly grateful to Maurice Riley for having undertaken, and for having so ably fulfilled his mission. The style, of fluent line and continually arresting the readers' attention, disguises the immense labor, and profound enquiry that must have gone into the writing of the *History*. Violists and, indeed, all lovers of stringed instruments owe Maurice Riley a debt of no mean proportions. The Viola, so long neglected by performers and historians, has found its Macaulay at last! And the story, unfolded in the pages that follow, knows exactly where to begin and where to end. It is a tidy narrative and has no loose ends. He has a wonderful way with facts, has Maurice Riley; he is never boring or drily didactic; he is always cultivated yet free of affectation, his exposition many sided and he has a cunning way of handling his material. Henry James tells us that the historian wants more documents than he can really use. I have no way of perceiving how many documents passed through Riley's hands, or crossed his desk, but I am persuaded that he made full use of them. Nothing has been wasted. We are told that the rudest work that tells a story or records a fact is better than the richest without meaning. Here is no such work, and here is richness full of meaning! Let the reader be thankful for it, it becometh him well. Riley has a rare perception of the apt phrase to buttress the telling, and no one can read his pages without the profit that accrues from this ability.

It is a foolish thing to make a long prologue, and it would be unbecoming to go through these chapters one by one pointing out the excellencies of each. Only the reader can be the judge, but I am compelled to be confident of a verdict most favorable.

William Primrose . . . 1979.

v

PREFACE

After World War II, while doing research at the University of Michigan under the direction of Dr. Louise Cuyler for a dissertation in Musicology entitled *The Teaching of Bowed Instruments from 1511 to 1756*, it became evident to me that very little material could be found concerning the viola. The history of the violin, cello, and double bass had a voluminous literature extending back to the earliest printed treatises dealing with musical instruments. The viola, on the other hand, had been sadly neglected. Very little material about it was included in the standard histories or reference books dealing with the violin family.

This dearth of information about the viola prompted me to begin then to collect information with the intention of writing a history of the instrument. By 1970 I had gathered all of the material that seemed to be available from sources in the United States. In 1971, my wife, Leila, and I made the first of four trips to England and Europe to continue the research in the libraries and museums, particularly in the cities of Cremona and Brescia, where many of the great violas had been made. It was equally important to meet violists and scholars who were conversant with various aspects of the viola's history and the music written for the instrument. Many of these people shared their knowledge, or suggested clues, which led to ultimate solutions to problems related to my research. Grateful recognition for their help is included in the section entitled "Acknowledgements."

During the school year of 1975–76, Eastern Michigan University, where I had taught violin and viola since 1947, granted me a year's sabbatical. It was during this year that I began the serious work of putting together the many parts of information that had been gathered during the preceding years. In 1977, after retiring from my position at the University, I was able to give full time to the project that had been developing through the years.

This history of the viola recognizes: (1) the luthiers who developed the instrument; (2) the composers who wrote innovative solo, ensemble, and orchestral literature for it; (3) the violists who, through their dedication and devotion during the last 400 years, have sought to bring the instrument into a position of equality with the violin and the cello; (4) the teachers who have inspired and guided young musicians to improve their skills and become proficient performers; (5) the numerous arrangers who through the years have attempted to fill the great void in the viola literature by adapting compositions originally written for the violin, cello, clarinet, and other instruments; and (6) the many competent editors who through their perserverance and aptitude for research have brought to light many long forgotten works that have vastly enriched the viola literature.

This is not a history of the *viola d'amore*, although that instrument has long been related to the viola, and its similarity of size and pitch range has made it a logical choice for many violists to play as a second instrument. The *viola d'amore* has a separate history and a separate identity in its own right.

Tunings are furnished for many of the instruments discussed in the text. Throughout the book, the octave is indicated by the standard system that follows

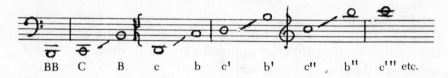

BB   C   B   c   b   c'   b'   c''   b''   c''' etc.

With this system, the present-day viola tuning would be indicated as c, g, d', a'.

The viola's history does not follow a systematic succession of events with the same continuity that prevailed for the volin. There are gaps. This book, therefore, is not the chronicle of an orderly sequence of events; it frequently skips from one country to another to pick up the thread of progress, albeit, sometimes ever so small. Not all of the events in the history of the viola will appear to have equal significance to those in the histories of the violin and the cello. In retrospect, however, many of these seemingly insignificant events are now taking on increased importance.

What began as a projected final chapter to be entitled "Important Violists," gradually expanded into the "Appendix I, Short Biographies of Violists." Initially a limited number of questionnaires was mailed to known violists throughout the world. Many who returned their questionnaires suggested the names of other violists who should be included. Over a period of four years (1976–79) the list finally exceeded 300. Regrettably, some did not return their questionnaires. There are no doubt others who were unintentionally omitted, who should have been included.

Information concerning the present state of the viola in the contemporary world of music has been greatly enriched by the appearance in 1976 of Franz Zeyringer's exhaustive *Literatur für Viola* (3rd edition), as well as by the printings earlier of Lionel Tertis' two autobiographies, *Cinderella No More* (1953) and *My Viola and I* (1974); also by the recent Russian biography, *Vadim Borissovsky, the Founder of the Soviet Viola School* (1977), and by the autobiography of William Primrose, *Walk on the North Side: Memoirs of a Violist* (1978). These books also point to the further need for a comprehensive history of the viola.

The increasing importance placed on the viola by contemporary composers, particularly in the steadily expanding solo repertoire, and also in chamber music and orchestral works, makes it evident that a corresponding musicological literature is now essential for the instrument. The objective of this book is to be a part of this needed literature. No pioneering work of this type can be definitive, but perhaps this book will open the way for other more specialized and more exhaustive studies related to the viola.

ACKNOWLEDGEMENTS

The author gratefully recognizes the invaluable assistance furnished by business firms, institutions, and many individuals who through their generous help and cooperation made possible the completion of this book.

Firms that furnished photographs and important information relating to the viola were: Bein & Fushi, Chicago; Jacques Français, New York City; William E. Hill & Sons, Havenfields, Great Missenden, Buckinghamshire, England; William Moennig & Son, Philadelphia; William Salchow, Ltd., Bowmaker, New York City; Kenneth Warren & Son, Chicago; and Oscar Shapiro, Rare Book Dealer, Washington, D.C.

Institutions that furnished photographs, microfilm, and other materials were: The Library of Congress, The New York Public Library, The University of Michigan Library, Bibliothèque National in Paris, The British Museum Library Reference Division, The Detroit Institute of Art, The New York Metropolitan Museum of Art, Das Germanisches Nationalmuseum in Nürnburg, Die Musikabteilung der Stadtbücherei in Mannheim, and Det Kongelie Bibliotek in Copenhagen.

Among the owners and luthiers who supplied photographs of, and information about their instruments were Otto Erdesz, Paul Doktor, Dr. Jan James, Louis Kievman, Virginia Majewski, Capt. Edgar K. Thompson, Walter Trampler, Roelof Weertman, and Bernard Zaslav.

For information and assistance regarding particular subjects, the author is most appreciative to the following: Harold D. Klatz of Chicago: Chicago violists; John White of London: contemporary English violists; Eduardo R. Dali of Buenos Aires: Argentine violists; Ron Golan of Geneva, Switzerland: Israeli violists; the late Robert Courte of Ann Arbor, Michigan: Belgian and French violists; Thérèse Collette of Paris: French violists; Hedwig Biggle of Ypsilanti, Michigan: Polish violists; Madame Alexandra de Lazari-Borissovsky of Moscow: Russian violists. The following violists and musicologists from West Germany are also included in this listing: Dietrich Bauer of Kassel: supplied many leads related to German violists and German viola music; Prof. Dr. Wolfgang Sawodny of Oberelchingen bei Ulm: furnished lists of *Quartets* for violin (flute or oboe), 2 violas, and cello (bass), and 18th century *Sonatas* for the viola; Dr. V. Klingmüller of

Mannheim: supplied materials relating to the Mannheim 18th century viola compositions; Walter Lebermann of Bad Homburg: generously shared his rich knowledge of 18th century viola music, including his research on the Stamitz family. Austrian violists were likewise helpful: Prof. Karl Trötzmüller of Vienna: furnished information and documents regarding Paul Hindemith; Prof. Franz Zeyringer of Pöllau: gave assistance in many areas; his definitive *Literatur für Viola* was used constantly as a source of documentation.

From Italy, Brenda Bork of Cremona: furnished material related to the Amati family; and from the Netherlands, Amalie Du Ry of Velp: photographs of the statue of Gasparo da Salò in Salò, Italy.

In the United States, there were many who contributed their knowledge and help, including: Herbert K. Goodkind, author of the *Violin Iconography of Antonio Stradivari:* Stradivari violas; Eric Chapman, President of the Violin Society of America: contemporary luthiers and their violas; Albert Mell, editor of the *Journal of the Violin Society of America:* interest and encouragement in the writing of this book; Louis Kievman: many letters and the information he shared; Dr. Myron Rosenblum, President of the American Viola Society: his rich knowledge of the viola was shared innumerable times when problems arose, through a six-year correspondence that was always friendly and rewarding; William Salchow, eminent New York bowmaker: invaluable assistance with Chapter VIII, "Viola Bows."

The author wishes to thank Leonard Mogill, Joseph de Pasquale, Dr. Vladimir Sokoloff, and Thérèse Rochette for their assistance in gathering material about Louis Bailly.

I wish to acknowledge valuable advice pertaining to stylistic writing offered by Dr. Robert A. Warner, Curator of the Stearns Instrument Collection, University of Michigan. Grateful appreciation is extended to Mr. Wallace Bjorke, Head Librarian of the University of Michigan School of Music, for permission to use musical excerpts from the scores to the following operas: Jean-Baptiste Lully, *Cadmus* (1673); Antonio Sacchini, *Oedipe à Colone* (1786); Luigi Cherubini, *Les deux Journées* (1800); Etienne-Nicolas Méhul, *Uthal* (1806); and Gasparo Spontini, *La Vestale* (1807).

The author is indeed indebted to over 300 violists who returned questionnaires, which furnished the substance of the Appendix I of this book, which is entitled "Brief Biographies of Violists."

I especially wish to express my gratitude to that nimble-witted Scotsman, Dr. William Primrose, who first by his viola performances, and then by his correspondence and friendship, has been a fountainhead of inspiration. He always answered my questions with more information than was expected; but then this up-right man always has given more to everyone, audiences in particular, than was expected.

Very special gratitude is due for the generosity of Dr. Fred G. Walcott, Professor Emeritus of English, English Literature, and Education, of the University of Michigan, and long-time string quartet colleague of the author, who read the manuscript of the entire text, and made innumerable corrections and suggestions for improving the style and the exposition.

I cannot refrain from mentioning the support and inspiration I have received from our three sons, all professional musicians: George, violinist; Ben Carl, cellist; and John, violist. Ben Carl did the artwork, and John did much of the photography for this book. And above all, I am indebted to my dear wife, Leila, whose help, encouragement, faith, hard work, and love made it all possible.

CONTENTS

LIST OF PLATES

LIST OF EXAMPLES

CHAPTER I

THE VIOLA IN
THE 16TH CENTURY

Origin and Evolution of the Viola

Three questions relating to the viola that until quite recently have been unanswered concern: (1) the place and date where the violin family originated; (2) the names of the first luthiers to make instruments in the violin pattern; and (3) the precedence of the viola or the violin.

Writers dealing with the history of stringed instruments have suggested that Gasparo da Salò of Brescia, or Gaspar Duiffoprugcar of Lyons, or Andrea Amati of Cremona was the earliest luthier to make violins. Did any of the three actually invent the violin? Were the first instruments of this form actually violas, as has long been believed by many writers? Was Amati an apprentice of da Salò?

Recent research by Carlo Bonetti *(La Genealogia degli Amati-Liutai e il Primato della Scuola Liutistica Cremonese),*[1] Emile Leipp *(The Violin),*[2] Emanuel Winternitz *(Gaudenzio Ferrari, His School and the Early History of the Violin),*[3] and David Boyden *(The History of Violin Playing from its Origins to 1761),*[4] has done much to clarify the issues and unravel the problems mentioned above.

Bonetti found that Andrea Amati was born twenty to thirty years earlier than the musical histories and musical dictionaries had previously recorded. Leipp assembled all of the documents and research available concerning Gaspar Duiffoprugcar, and was able to explain the contributions of this craftsman in the early development of the violin. Winternitz, because of the lack of written evidence relative to

---

[1]Carlo Bonetti, "La Genealogia degli Amati-Liutai e il Primato della Scuola Liutistica Cremonese", *Bollettino Storico Cremonese*, Series II, Anno III, Vol. VII (Cremona, 1938).

[2]Emile Leipp, *The Violin* (Toronto: University of Toronto Press, 1969).

[3]Emanuel Winternitz, *Gaudenzio Ferrari, His School and the Early History of the Violin* (Milano: Varallo Sesia, 1967).

[4]David Boyden, *The History of Violin Playing from Its Origins to 1761* (London: Oxford University Press, 1965).

1

the beginnings of the violin family, turned to Italian paintings of the early 16th century, and particularly those of Gaudenzio Ferrari, to find pictorial evidence that would help to solve the enigma. Boyden assembled all of the known literary information along with the evidence depicted in the paintings of Ferrari and others, thus supplying the missing parts to the puzzle, and then proceeded to draw sound scholarly conclusions.

Gaudenzio Ferrari

Emanuel Winternitz, Emeritus Curator of Musical Instruments at the Metropolitan Museum of Arts, has done very significant research on the possible origins of the violin family. He suggested that early 16th century Italian paintings furnish one of the best sources of information, and in particular the paintings of Gaudenzio Ferrari (c. 1480–1546).[5] Ferrari was a "true Renaissance man" in that he was a painter, sculptor, and architect; and, in addition, he was a fine musician, a performer on the lira and the lute, as Winternitz has proved. Furthermore, Winternitz suggested that Ferrari was probably a builder of instruments and perhaps experimented with the emerging form of the instrument that was to become the violin.[6]

Ferrari's center of artistic activity began north and west of Milano several years before Andrea Amati (born between 1500 and 1511– d.1580?) was building violins in Cremona, and several decades before Gasparo da Salò (1540–1609) was producing stringed instruments in Brescia.

Perhaps the earliest known painting of a violin appears in Ferrari's "La Madonna degli Aranci" (Madonna of the Orange Trees), painted 1529–30, on the wall in the Church of St. Christopher in Vercelli, a town forty miles west of Milano. (A copy, in color, appears as the frontispiece to David Boyden's *History of Violin Playing from Its Origins to 1761*.) Equally important is a fresco painted (1535–6) in the cupola of the Santaria in Saronno, a city thirty miles north of Milano. There, as the Mother Mary is depicted entering Heaven, she is surrounded by an assembly of eighty-seven angels, sixty-one of them playing, or assisting in playing, musical instruments. Among the instruments depicted are early forms of the violin, viola, and cello (see Winternitz, Plate 38;[7] Boyden, Plate 10). In addition to the fresco in

---

[5]Winternitz, *op. cit.*, pp. 10–24.

[6]*Ibid.*, p. 18.

[7]*Ibid.*; and Emanuel Winternitz, *Musical Instruments and their Symbolism in Western Art* (New York: W. W. Norton, 1967); and Boyden, *op. cit.*, p. 120.

Saronno, of particular interest are the paintings of a tenor in the Muso Borgogna at Vercelli and the very large tenor in the outside facade fresco of "Madona di Loretto" in Roccapietra by members of the Ferrari School (see Winternitz, Illustrations 6 and 16).

Some of Ferrari's bowed instruments appear to be distantly related to prototypes of the violin family. Such an instrument is the one in "Child with Viol" (Plate 1).[8] Although this instrument does not have a violin shape, it does have 4 strings, f holes, and a scroll, several of the characteristics that were to differentiate the violin family from other bowed instruments. "Child with Viol" is apparently of secular origin, with no religious connotation, and therefore it is probably a likeness to an instrument familiar to Ferrari.

The multiplicity of types and shapes of bowed instruments depicted in Ferrari's paintings suggests that luthiers in northern Italy were doing a considerable amount of experimentation during the first quarter of the 16th century. Ferrari's paintings suggest that the violin form developed before, or during, this period.

The violin form, as we know it, was a refinement of the various shapes that the luthiers of northern Italy, and elsewhere, had been making. The ultimate violin design resulted from the luthiers' quest to create an instrument that incorporated three qualities: (1) a greater acoustical potential than other existing bowed instruments; (2) a model that was esthetically attractive; and (3) an instrument that could be held and played with maximum ease.

In all probability the ultimate violin design evolved side by side with some of the other forms illustrated in Ferrari's paintings; and the other models were gradually discarded in favor of the one that met the most favorable acceptance by buyers and performers. Winternitz gave a most interesting and informative review of Ferrari's works, and concluded that Ferrari must have been one of the earliest luthiers to experiment with, and to make, instruments in a form similar to the contemporary violin.

Andrea Amati, an Apprentice of Gasparo da Salò?

Carlo Bonetti, as early as 1938, proved that Andrea Amati was born not later than 1511 and perhaps as early as 1500/5.[9] Bonetti's research was not generally known until David Boyden, in 1965, gave

---

[8]Ferrari's "Child with Viol," tempera on panel, is the property of the Detroit Institute of Arts, a gift of Mr. and Mrs. Trent McMath.

[9]Bonetti, *op. cit.*, pp. 15–16.

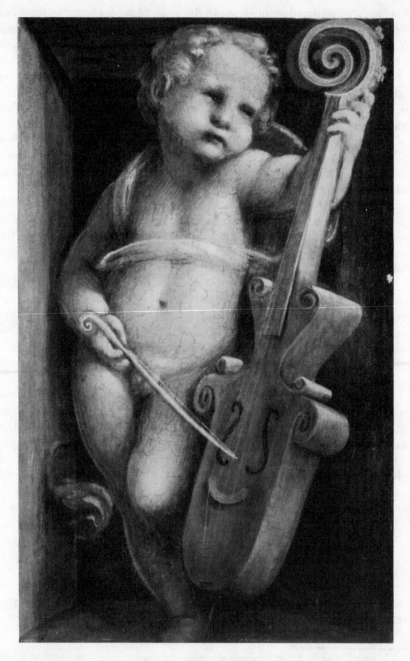

Plate 1. Gaudenzio Ferrari, Italian c.1480/81–1546: *Child with a Viol,*
used with permission of the Detroit Institute of Arts, Gift of Mr. and Mrs. Trent McMath.

due credit to him in his *History of Violin Playing from its Origins to 1761*, and used Bonetti's valuable findings in arriving at new conclusions regarding Amati's contributions to the early development of the violin. Winternitz' research and interpretation of the Ferrari paintings constitute an invaluable clue to the place and time of the emergence of the violin family. Both Winternitz and Boyden concluded that the violin was probably not invented, but rather was the culmination of a gradual evolution in which various forms were utilized until the ideal one appeared.[10]

Regardless of whether there was an "inventor" of the violin, Bonetti laid to rest the long-mistaken relationship of Andrea Amati and Gasparo da Salò. It is now apparent that Amati was born 29 to 40 years before da Salò and therefore could not have been his apprentice. Many writers of the history of stringed instruments have suggested that da Salò was the earliest maker of instruments in the violin form. On the contrary, it is quite probable, in view of Bonetti's research, that Amati and perhaps other luthiers also were making violins before da Salò was born.[11]

Boyden[12] and Kolneder[13] both furnish chronological outlines of the known evidence related to the origins of the violin family in the first half of the 16th century. These outlines clearly show that the production of violins was not unique to Andrea Amati and Gasparo da Salò, and, furthermore, that the instruments of this family were probably played prior to the productive periods of these luthiers. An official document from the treasury of Savoy, dated December 17, 1523, records payment for services of violinists at Vercelli, the same town where Ferrari's first painting of a violin appeared in 1529/30. The earliest known extant violin, according to Kolneder, is one made by Peregrino Zanetto, in Brescia, in 1532.[14]

Gaspar Duiffoprugcar

The status of Gaspar Duiffoprugcar (1514–72) as one of the earliest makers of violins has been defended and disputed by writers for the past two centuries. The contentions center around the famous

---

[10]Boyden, *op. cit.*, pp. 17–30.

[11]For a more detailed account of Andrea Amati's and Gasparo da Salò's contribution to the viola, see Chapter II.

[12]Boyden, *op. cit.*, pp. 21–9.

[13]Walter Kolneder, *Das Buch der Violins* (Zurich: Atlantis, 1972), pp. 270–4.

[14]Kolneder's reference, p. 270, to the earliest extant violin may have been one made by Zanetto da Montichiaro (c.1488–c.1568).

portrait engraved by Woeiriot in 1562 (see Leipp, p. 30, or Boyden, Plate 9). In this picture Duiffoprugcar is surrounded by stringed instruments of all types: assorted sizes of lutes, viols, and two instruments that appear to be violins of an early form. One of these is an alto or tenor of primitive type and resembles several of the instruments in earlier paintings by members of the Ferrari School.

Leipp has done extensive research into the background and lifestyle of Duiffoprugcar, as well as the influence that the environment of the city of Lyons might have had on this luthier.[15] There can be no question that Duiffoprugcar was a highly talented craftsman who produced stringed instruments of quality.

There are, however, three factors, not mentioned by Leipp, that would seem to negate the Lyons master's claim to being the first, or even one of the first makers of the violin: (1) Woeiriot's portrait includes several instruments that could be classed as precursors of the violin, but none that are actually models of the instrument as we know it today; (2) there is no pattern or form extant today called the Duiffoprugcar model; and (3) there are no known existing authentic violins, violas, or cellos made by this eminent maker. On the other hand, there are authentic instruments of the violin family in existence today made by Andrea Amati and Gasparo da Salò.

Written Evidence in the Early 16th Century

Printed evidence concerning the early development of the violin family is limited to a few treatises which furnish information that is somewhat lacking in clarity. Several writers, chiefly the Italians, Lanfranco (1533)[16] and Ganassi (1542–3),[17] and the German, Agricola (1528),[18] describe three-stringed and four-stringed instruments, without frets, and tuned in fifths, which may have been violins or their prototypes. It remained for the Frenchman, Jambe de Fer, in his book, *Epitome Musicale* (1556),[19] to furnish descriptions that definitely applied to violins. He furnished the French names and tunings for all members of the violin family:

---

[15]Leipp, *op. cit.*, pp. 27–31.

[16]Giovanni Lanfranco, *Scintille di Musica* (Brescia, 1553).

[17]Silvestro Ganassi, *Regola Rubertina* (2 vols., Venice, 1542–3).

[18]Martin Agricola, *Musica Instrumentalis Deudsch* (several editions, Wittemberg, 1528–9 to 1545).

[19]Philbert Jambe de Fer, *Epitome musical des tons, sons et accords, es voix humaines, fleustes d'Alleman, fleustes a neuf trous, Violes et Violins . . .* (Lyon: du Bois, 1556), p. 63.

Dessus	:				g	d'	a'	e''

Haute-Contre:		c	g	d'	a'
Taille	:	c	g	d'	a'

Bas	:	BB♭	F	c	g

Jambe de Fer's terms are equivalent to the names for vocal parts: the *dessus* (soprano) was played by the violin; the *haute-contre* (alto) was played by the small viola; the *taille* (tenor) was played by the large viola; and the *bas* (bass) was played by the cello. Jambe de Fer's *bas* is tuned one whole step lower than our present cello. Pitches at that time were relative. Jambe de Fer directed the violinist to tune the *E* string as high as he dared: "Now, then, you are in tune if your string does not break."[20]

Did the Viola Precede the Violin?

It has generally been alleged that the viola evolved as parent member of the violin family, preceding the violin and cello. The principal theories supporting this hypothesis can be summarized briefly as follows:

1. The *lira da braccio*[21] is believed to be the chief ancestor of the violin family because of its *f* holes and shape, as shown by Praetorius in his *Syntagma Musicum*[22] (Plate 2, No. 5). Praetorius furnished also a brief accompanying description:

> The small lyra is like the tenor viola da braccio, and is called Lyra da braccio. It has seven strings, two of them off the fingerboard and the other five lying on it.

The tuning range given by Praetorius was, d d' g g' d' a' d''.[23] Numerous writers have suggested that the viola, because its size, shape, and accordatura were similar to those of the *lira da braccio*, would logi-

---

[20]*Ibid.*, p. 64.

[21]Also spelled *lire da braccio, lyra de bracio,* and *lyra da braccia.* For additional information see Emanuel Winternitz, "Lira da Braccio," *Die Musik in Geschichte und Gegenwart,* Vol. VIII.

[22]Michael Praetorius. *Syntagma Musicum . . .,* Vol. II, *De Organographia* (First and Second Parts of the 1618–19 Editions published in Wolfenbüttel; English translation by Harold Blumenfeld, Kassel: Bärenreiter, 1962), p. 49.

[23]*Ibid.*, p. 26

Plate 2. Michael Praetorius: Wood-cut of Bowed Instruments.

cally have been the first instrument to have been made in the evolutionary process.

2. The musical demands of the early 16th century made the alto-tenor the most important member of the various stringed instrument families (rebecs, fidels, lutes, viols), and as a result the viola would have been the instrument luthiers first produced as they turned to the new family.

3. The word *viola* is the original term used in Italy for the entire violin family. The etymology of the names of the violin family can be explained as being the typical derivatives in the Italian language. Derivatives of the generic Italian word *viola* were formed by using *viol(a)* as a stem: *viol* plus the diminutive *in* equals *violin* or small viola; *viol* plus the augmentative *on* equals *violon* or large viola (bass viol); *violon* plus *ello* (smaller than) equals *violon(c)ello*—the *c* is added for the sake of euphony—literally, a small bass viol. Since the alto-tenor member of the family retained the original name, it might follow that it was the first instrument of the new design.[24]

4. Today there are more 16th century violas extant than there are violins or cellos.

The four arguments listed have been repeated many times by writers as seemingly uncontestable proof that the viola was the original member of the violin family. Recent research appears to refute these contentions. The opposing arguments are listed in the same order:

1. Not all *lira da braccios* did have *f* holes (see Plate 3). Also, Boyden pointed out that "the *lira da braccio* was not the only ancestor of the violin and the tuning of the *lira da braccio* can be equated just as well with the violin as with the viola."[25] Likewise, the apparent similarity in size of the *lira da braccio* and the viola is not tenable evidence, since some *lira da braccios* were 38 cm. (15 in.) in length, almost a violin dimension.

2. The premise that the alto-tenor was the first member of the violin family, owing to the musical demands of the early 16th century, has been challenged by the exhaustive research of Boyden and Winternitz. One of the main functions of music at that time was to match the ranges of the human voices—to accompany or to double singing parts in a supportive role.

---

[24]Dennis Stevens in his chapter, "A Short History" (which is part of the book, *Violin and Viola*, by Yehudi Menuhin and William Primrose, pp. 195–8) traces the terminology and philology of the names of the various members of the violin family and its precursors through the Middle Ages and Renaissance in a fascinating and illuminating manner.

[25]Boyden, *op. cit.*, p. 15.

Plate 3. Giovanni Andrea of Verona: Lira da Braccio, 1511,
in the Kunsthistorisches Museum, Vienna.

3. The assumption that the alto-tenor is the oldest member of the violin family because in Italy its name, *viola*, was a generic term originally applied to all members of the violin and the viol families carries a certain amount of logic, but has not been proved.

4. The fact that there are more 16th century violas extant than violins and cellos could be due to the fact that: (a) violas were used less in the 17th and 18th centuries than the violins and cellos;[26] so therefore, they could have survived the attrition that was inevitable for instruments that were in constant use; (b) many of the 16th century violas were really tenors and were too difficult to play as *viola da braccia* (arm violins). Consequently, many of them were packed away, or displayed as antiques until a future time when a luthier or "restorer" would cut them down to a convenient size.

Conclusion

Pictorial and literary evidence indicates that the violin, viola, and cello in all probability evolved together as a family of instruments. There was no spontaneous genesis of the viola or violin as an instrument, rather several instruments of that shape had their origin around or shortly before 1500. Then a gradual evolution of the shape and dimensions took place. The violin family, in its present forms, appears to have evolved very early in the 16th century, probably in northern Italy, where Andrea Amati, Gasparo da Salò, and other luthiers refined the instruments into their lasting forms.

The violin family pattern was not invented by any one craftsman, but developed gradually from the experiments of numerous luthiers working with various forms until the ideal model was found. Andrea Amati was among the first to arrive at the format of the violin family, as we know it today.

The available evidence might suggest that the viola may or may not have preceded the violin; in all probability it appeared as a member of the new family group of bowed instruments, emerging concurrently with the violin and cello.

---

[26]See Chapter III for description of the decreasing need for violas in the 17th century because of the change from five- to four-part harmony, and the growth of the trio sonata into the most popular form of chamber music.

CHAPTER II

EARLY CREMONESE AND BRESCIAN VIOLAS

Cremona and the Amatis

Andrea Amati was one of the first luthiers to make violas. He constructed them in small and in large dimensions. The production of both small (alto) and large (tenor) violas was prompted by the demands of instrumental music in the 16th century. Frequently instrumentalists joined singers and doubled voice parts, the violins taking the high soprano parts, and the cello playing the bass line. This left the middle range of *alto* and *tenor* to be carried by the violas.

Very few of Andrea's instruments exist today, but among those extant are a few violas. Most of these are of the large model. The fact that Andrea Amati was famous and well known in his own time is attested to by the demand for his instruments as far away as Paris, France. Thirty-eight instruments of the violin family were ordered from Andrea Amati (c.1565) by Charles IX of France (1550–74) for the court musicians. The order specified the following instruments:

> 12 small-pattern violins
> 12 large-pattern violins
> 6 tenors (violas)
> 8 basses (cellos)

The body length of small-pattern violins, at that time, varied from 33 cm. (13 in.) to 35.24 cm. (13 7/8 in.); large-pattern violins varied from 35.5 cm. (14 in.) to 36.8 cm. (14 1/2 in.). Franz Varga suggests that the small violins were probably used in the dance orchestras which played for court balls, and the large violins were used by chamber music groups.[1] To conform with the musical practice described by Jambe de Fer in 1556,[2] it is probable that several of the

---

[1]Franz Varga, *Violins and Violinists* (New York: MacMillan, 1950), p. 31.
[2]Jambe de Fer, *op. cit.*, p. 63.

tenors would have been of small pattern (*hautcontre* or alto) and several of the large pattern (*taille* or tenor).

The instruments made for the French court were ornamented on the backs with paintings of the royal coat-of-arms, and with the motto *Pietate et Justitia* (Compassion and Justice) painted on the ribs. Music was a very important part of the religious life of the French court, and these instruments were also used to accompany voices during chapel services.

At the time Andrea Amati was commissioned to make these instruments, the young king was only fifteen years old. It is likely that the instruments were ordered under the influence of his mother, Catherine de' Medici (1519–89), the regent, who was actually ruling France at that time.[3] Catherine de' Medici brought with her from Florence her taste for the arts, and for all forms of beauty and luxury. She built and decorated the Tuileries in Paris, and gave, as frequently as civil war permitted, sumptuous feasts *à l'Italienne* at Fontainebleau, in the Louvre, and in the Tuileries. For these extravaganzas, she imported Italian dancers in 1554, and Italian violinists in 1555.[4] The musicians needed the finest Italian instruments on which to produce their music. Catherine, being from north central Italy, would doubtlessly have been cognizant of Amati's fine reputation, and true to the Medici tradition, would have insisted on having the best instruments obtainable. But instruments of the violin family must have been known and played in the French court prior to this purchase. The musicians probably doubled on viols and violins as the need demanded. When additional performers were required, they were imported from Italy.[5]

The Amati collection of instruments was kept in the Royal Chapel at Versailles until the October Revolution of 1789, when most of these masterpieces were destroyed by the insanely angry mob. David Boyden, in the *Catalogue of the Hill Collection,* described two of the instruments, a violin (1564) and a viola (1574), that survived the Revolution. Both are now in the Ashmolean Museum, at Oxford University. The viola, according to Boyden:

---

[3]Catherine de' Medici (1519–89) married the Dauphin in 1533. Her husband ascended the throne as Henry II in 1547. In 1559 Catherine's oldest son became king, as Francis I. Following his death in 1560, the next oldest son was crowned as Charles IX. In 1574, the next son in line was named king as Henry III (1551–89). Henry IV (1553–1610), a protestant and son-in-law of Catherine, became king in 1589.

[4]Angene Feves, "Italian Dance Masters at the French Court," *Pro Musica Magazine* (January–February, 1976), pp. 3–6.

[5]*Ibid.*

. . . is a magnificient instrument in a perfect state of preservation with a beautiful tone of extraordinary depth. The table is made of pine of varying grain, varnished a rich golden-brown color, the two-piece back, sides and head being of small-figured maple. . .[6]

From the remaining description, the following dimensions are particularly pertinent:[7]

Body length	— 47.0 cm.	(18 1/2 in.)
Upper bout	— 22.9 cm.	(9 in.)
Middle bout	— 15.7 cm.	(6 3/16 in.)
Lower bout	— 27.0 cm.	(10 5/8 in.)
Ribs (upper)	— 3.8 cm.	(1 1/2 in.)
Ribs (lower)	— 4.0 cm.	(1 5/8 in.)
String length	— 40.3 cm.	(15 7/8 in.).

The body length of 47 cm. (18 1/2 in.) indicates that this viola was of the large pattern. It has not been cut down, as have so many large violas (see Plate 4 for *Viola Dimensions Nomenclature*).

The Stanley Solomon Amati Viola

Of the few Andrea Amati violas extant, most were once the property of the French court. One that was not is now owned by Stanley Solomon (Plate 5). Presently, the instrument has a body length of 43.3 cm. (17 1/16 in.). The original instrument, a tenor-viola, probably had a body length of more than 45.7 cm. (18 in.). This is borne out by its full and open sound. It is used regularly by its owner, the Canadian violist, Stanley Solomon.[8] The Hill Certificate describes the instrument:

Andrea Amati of Cremona, and dates from c.1580. The head, which matches the instrument admirably, is of somewhat later date. The back is in one piece of plain wood cut on the slab. The sides are marked by a faint small curl. The table is of pine of slightly wavy grain of medium width. The varnish is a golden-brown color. This instrument is a characteristic example of the maker's work, but has been somewhat reduced in size to 433 mm. (17 1/16 in.) in length of body. The table of this viola has been restored. The instrument is in a very fair state of preservation and is in sound condition.

---

[6]David D. Boyden, *The Hill Collection* (London: Oxford University Press, 1969), p. 18.
[7]*Ibid.*, p. 19.
[8]For more about Stanley Solomon, see Appendix I.

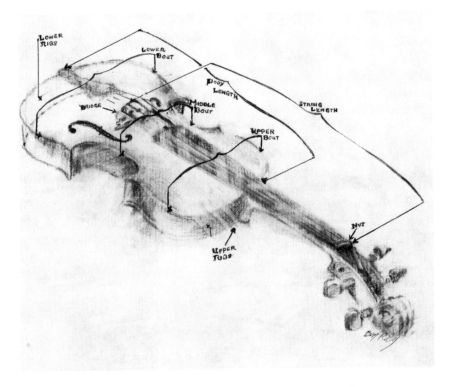

Plate 4. Viola Dimensions Nomenclature by Ben Riley

The dimensions of the Andrea Amati viola are:

Body length — 43.3 cm. (17 1/16 in.)
Upper bout — 20.5 cm. (8 1/16 in.)
Middle bout — 14.0 cm. (5 1/2 in.)
Lower bout — 24.5 cm. (9 5/8 in.).[9]

An Andrea Amati Viola

The viola shown in Plate 6 is believed to be the work of Andrea Amati, except for the ribs. The most dependable appraisers are sometimes hesitant to state with full assurance that an instrument that is

---

[9]Measurements furnished by William Moennig and Son of Philadelphia.

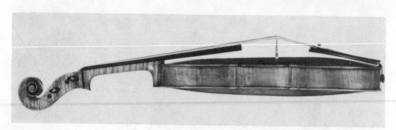

Plate 5. The Solomon Andrea Amati Viola.
Photographs furnished by William Moennig & Son, Philadelphia.

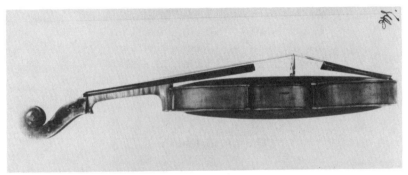

Plate 6. An Andrea Amati Viola

over 400 years old is definitely the work of a particular maker. Emil Herrmann, who sold and certified this instrument, told the purchaser that in his opinion the instrument is the work of Andrea Amati. The certificate is worded in a more cautious manner:

> The viola is an Italian instrument of the school of Andrea Amati, of Cremona, with the exception of the ribs which have been replaced. It bears a label of Andrea Amati, 1567.
> The back is formed of one piece of rather plain curly maple, and the scroll to match. The table is of spruce of medium wide grain in center and much finer on the flanks. The varnish is of a dark golden-brown color.

Everyone who has played or heard this instrument played vouches for its beautiful tone. It is not one of the violas ordered by the French Court. Its dimensions are:

Body length — 40.7 cm. (16 in.)
Upper bout — 18.5 cm. (7 1/4 in.)
Middle bout — 13.4 cm. (5 1/4 in.)
Lower bout — 23.1 cm. (9 in.)
Upper ribs   — 3.4 cm. (1 11/32 in.)
Lower ribs   — 3.5 cm. (1 3/8 in.).

The Amati Family

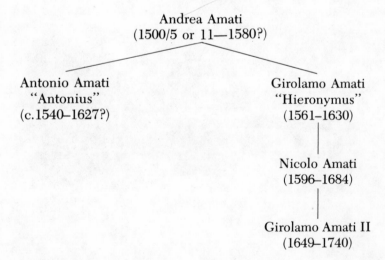

Andrea Amati
(1500/5 or 11—1580?)

Antonio Amati
"Antonius"
(c.1540–1627?)

Girolamo Amati
"Hieronymus"
(1561–1630)

Nicolo Amati
(1596–1684)

Girolamo Amati II
(1649–1740)

Andrea Amati's reputation as a maker of fine stringed instruments was perpetuated by his sons, Antonio (c.1540–1627?) and Girolamo

(1561–1630), better known by their Latinized names, Antonius and Hieronymus, and by Andrea's grandson, Nicolo (1596–1684), the son of Girolamo. The fourth generation was represented by Nicolo's son, Girolamo II (1649–1740), whose instruments, although well made, did not attain the fame of the masterpieces made by the three earlier generations of Amatis.

Antonius and Hieronymus Amati worked in their father's shop up to the time of his death (c.1580). Several instruments ascribed to the last years of Andrea's life present identification problems to even the most knowledgeable appraisers of old Italian stringed instruments. It is difficult, if not impossible, for the experts to say with certainty which instruments were entirely or partly made by Andrea and to what extent the two sons were involved during the late period of Andrea's life. The Trampler viola was probably made, or at least begun, during this time (c.1570–c.1580). It shows the unmistakable influence, if not the actual craft, of Andrea's genius.

The Walter Trampler Amati Viola

A viola of unsurpassed beauty and exquisite tonal qualities is the one owned by Walter Trampler, the eminent viola virtuoso (Plate 7). Wurlitzer, through their expert Simone F. Sacconi, certified the instrument as being the work of Antonious and Hieronymous Amati c.1620. However, Jacques Français, of New York City, and Charles Beare, of London, feel persuaded that it is the work of Andrea Amati, or that Andrea started production of the viola, and the brothers completed it. If the latter is true, then work on the instrument must have started before 1580.

The instrument, in mint condition, presently has a body length of 44.45 cm. (17 1/2 in.), but was cut down c.1800, from its original size, which was more than 47 cm. (18 1/2 in.). It has a golden yellow varnish. Painted on the ribs is the Latin inscription "*Non AEtesin Homine sed Virtus Consideramus*" (or the last word may be "*Considerant*"—the last four letters have been worn off). A literal translation is: "Consider not age in man, but the complete man" (*Virtus* means a man's total intellectual, moral, ethical, and physical assets). Trampler prefers the translation, "Judge a man by what he is, not by his age."

Mr. Trampler not only generously furnished the photographs of his Amati for this book, but permitted the author to take the following measurements of this masterpiece:

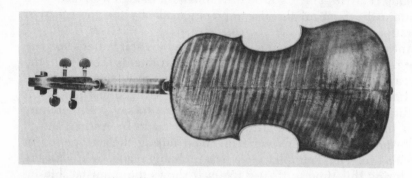

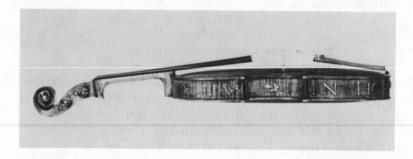

Plate 7. The Trampler Amati Viola.
Photographs furnished by Walter Trampler.

Body length — 44.45 cm. (17 1/2 in.)
Upper bout — 21.59 cm. (8 1/2 in.)
Middle bout — 15.24 cm. (6 in.)
Lower bout — 27.62 cm. (10 7/8 in.)
Upper rib   — 4.45 cm. (1 3/4 in.)
Lower rib   — 4.76 cm. (1 7/8 in.).

Mr. Trampler uses this viola regularly for his concert performances and for the many recordings he makes. The instrument has
beautiful sonority in all registers.

The Brothers-Amati Violas

Ernest Doring, who observed many Amati instruments during his
tenure with the William Lewis & Son store in Chicago, in a monograph, *The Amati Family,* described and furnished photographs of
several Brothers-Amati violas.[10] Included are two large-pattern violas:
one made in 1592, with a body length of 45.2 cm. (17 13/16 in.); and
one dated 1620, with a body length of 45.09 cm. (17 3/4 in). Doring
also included a photograph of another viola, made in 1619, which was
originally of large pattern, but which had been cut down by shortening the center, a practice Doring plainly disdained. His book also
contains material about an un-cut viola, made in 1616, with a body
length of 41.28 cm. (16 1/4 in.). This latter dimension was to become a
fairly common viola length during the remainder of the 17th and early
part of the 18th centuries.

Two excellent violas, the ex-Curtis (Plate 8) and the ex-William
Primrose Amati (Plate 9),[11] illustrate the beautiful design of the An-
tonius and Hieronymus model. The ex-Curtis (now the "George
Brown") Amati has a body length of 42.2 cm. (16 5/8 in.). The ex-
William Primrose Amati, made c.1600, was cut down sometime
around 1800. Its present measurements are:

Body length — 39.8 cm. (15 11/16 in.)
Upper bout — 19.6 cm. (7 3/4 in.)
Middle bout — 13.8 cm. (5 1/2 in.)
Lower bout — 24.6 cm. (9 5/8 in.).

---

[10]Ernest N. Doring, *The Amati Family* (Chicago: William Lewis & Son, n.d.), pp. 21–22. (This
book is a compilation of articles published earlier in the magazine *Violins and Violinists*, from
January, 1942 to July, 1943.)

[11]Photographs furnished by William Moennig & Son of Philadelphia.

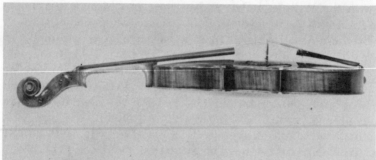

Plate 8. The Ex-Curtis Institute Brothers-Amati Viola.
Photographs furnished by William Moennig & Son, Philadelphia.

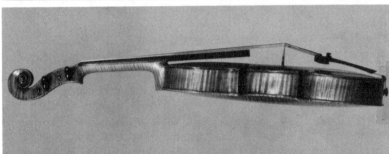

Plate 9. The Ex-Primrose Brothers-Amati Viola.
Photographs furnished by William Moennig & Son, Philadelphia.

Primrose's father bought this viola for 80 pounds, and had a great regard for it.[12] Today it is valued at many times 80 pounds. In 1951 Primrose sold this instrument to the well known San Francisco violist, Ferenc Molnar.

The Henry IV Amati Viola c.1590

Antonius and Hieronymus Amati were commissioned by Henry IV of France, better known as Henry of Navarre, to make at least five instruments for the French court.[13] Two of these instruments survived the ravages of the French Revolution, a violin and a viola, both highly ornamented. The violin is described in great detail, including photographs and history, in the *Lyon & Healy Catalogue* of 1924. The viola is presently the property of Captain Edgar K. Thompson, USN Retired, an amateur violist and chamber music enthusiast of Washington, D.C.

The Henry IV viola is a robust instrument of red-brown color. Covering most of the one-piece maple back is a painting of the armorial bearings of Henry IV, supported on each side by an angel (Plate 10). At each end of the back is a gold letter 'H' surmounted by the crown of France. Both designs are topped by laurel leaves. Geometrically spaced throughout the back are six flambeaux. Painted on the maple ribs is the Latin inscription, *"DVO PROTEGI TVNVS"* (God preserve my tone). This motto progresses around the sides from left to right. The unornamented spruce top has an open and well-defined grain. The present body length is 42.2 cm. (16 1/2 in.), but according to the Hill papers was probably 45.72 cm. (18 in.) or longer before it was cut down sometime around 1800. Alfred Hill, who signed the *Hill Certificate*, wrote, " . . . I consider it a very interesting example of Amati workmanship, a great rarity, and from the tonal point of view, an excellent instrument."[14]

---

[12]See Chapter XV

[13]Henry IV of Navarre (1553–1610) ruled France from 1589 to 1610, first of the Bourbon line, married to Margaret, daughter of Catherine de' Medici. The marriage was annulled in 1600 owing to lack of children. At this time he married Marie de' Medici, with whom he had six children, the beginning of the Bourbon line.

[14]It is not known by what miracle of fortune the Henry IV viola survived the French Revolution. According to the Hill papers, George Herbert, a distinguished amateur musician of London, acquired it early in the 19th century. After his death in 1890, it was sold to the English collector, Miss E. A. Willmott, who kept it for 40 years, then sold it to Hill and Sons. In 1935 it was sold to Antonio Antoncich of Valparaiso, Chile, a well-known collector in South America. Although not a performer, Antoncich built up an outstanding collection, including the Antonius Guarnerius Viola, later to be known as the "William Primrose." Following Antoncich's death, the estate sold the Henry IV viola to Captain Thompson.

Plate 10. The Captain Thompson Brothers-Amati Viola. Photographs furnished by Kenneth Warren & Son, Chicago.

In a lecture delivered September 15, 1977, to the class at the Kenneth Warren and Son School of Violin Making, the school's founder, Kenneth Warren, Sr., referring to the Henry IV viola, stated:

> The subject of our discussion this morning has to do with a viola of noble heritage, that being the Family of the Amati of Cremona. This instrument should be regarded as an outstanding example of Cremona craftmanship.

Warren made it plain that it is the viola's quality per se, and not the ornamentation, that makes it a great instrument:

> While we can admire the ornamentation found on certain instruments, the speaker feels that inscriptions, paintings, and devices inlaid or painted in no way add to the quality and value of these instruments.

The author had the privilege of seeing and playing this instrument twice and can confirm that it is an exceedingly beautiful instrument and has exceptional tonal qualities. The owner, Captain Edgar K. Thompson, also permitted the author to measure the viola, which has the following dimensions:

String length	— 37.0 cm.	(14 1/2 in.)
Body length	— 42.2 cm.	(16 1/2 in.)
Upper bout	— 20.0 cm.	(7 7/8 in.)
Middle bout	— 12.9 cm.	(5 1/16 in.)
Lower bout	— 24.3 cm.	(9 9/16 in.)
Upper rib	— 3.6 cm.	(1 13/32 in.)
Lower rib	— 3.7 cm.	(1 15/32 in.).

Nicolo Amati (1596–1684), perhaps the greatest luthier of his clan, made a very small number of violas because of the lack of demand for these instruments during his lifetime.[15] Those he made are mostly of the large pattern. Henley mentioned only two:[16] one dated 1620, with a beautifully emblazoned back, which was reduced in size in 1811 by John Dodd; and the other, which had belonged to James Goding, of London, was sold by auction for 45 guineas in 1857. This scant information is all that is furnished by Henley, and is indicative of the general decline in the production of violas during the 17th century, a trend not limited to the works of Nicolo Amati, but rather to the output among all Italian luthiers.

---

[15]The reason for the declining rate of viola production is discussed in Chapter III.

[16]William Henley, *Universal Dictionary of Violin and Bow Makers* (Brighton, Sussex: Amati Publishing Co., Ltd., 1960), Vol. I, p. 32.

Hieronymus Amati II (1649–1740) made very few violas; those he produced, however, demonstrate the Amati family heritage of genius. An outstanding example is the instrument owned and played by the contemporary American virtuoso, Toby Appel. It is a 45.09 cm. (17 3/4 in.) viola made in 1705, which is in mint condition.

The City of Brescia

Brescia, a city 48 1/4 km. (30 mi.) north of Cremona, had been famous for the fine quality of lutes and rebecs produced in its ateliers as early as 1450. While the first two generations of Amatis were bringing fame to Cremona by the excellence of their instruments, Brescia also was enjoying the prestige of several outstanding luthiers who worked there. Which 16th century Brescian craftsman first made instruments of the violin pattern is not known. It could have been any of the following: Giovani G. della Corna (c.1484–c.1548), Zanetto Montichiaro (c.1488–c.1568), his son Pellegrino di Zanetto (c.1520–c.1603), or Girolamo Virchi (c.1523–1573). If any of these makers produced violas, they are now extremely rare or have not yet been identified. Gasparo Bertolotti, however, an apprentice of Girolamo Virchi, did make violas, violins, cellos, and basses that have survived.

Gasparo da Salò

Gasparo Bertolotti (1540–1609) is better known as Gasparo da Salò, a name indicating that he had originally lived in Salò, a small village, on Lake Garda, about 24 km. (15 mi.) northeast of Brescia. He opened his own shop in Brescia c.1560. Several of his violins and cellos survive today. A few of his gambas and contrabasses are extant and are in great demand, as are his small and large violas, which are rapidly approaching parity of market price with the great instruments made in Cremona in the 17th and early 18th centuries.

Antonio Maria Mucchi, in 1940, after years of painstaking research, published a significant work on the life and work of da Salò, entitled *Gasparo da Salò, la vita e l'opera 1540–1609.*[17]

[17]Antonio Maria Mucchi, *Gasparo da Salò, la vita e l'opera 1540–1609* (Milano: Ulrico Hoepli, 1948). Mucchi's book was published to honor the 4th Centennial of Gasparo da Salò, under the joint auspices of the Municipality and the University of Salò, and the Municipality and the University of Brescia. The American Violin Society plans to bring out an English translation of this important book, which has long been out of print.

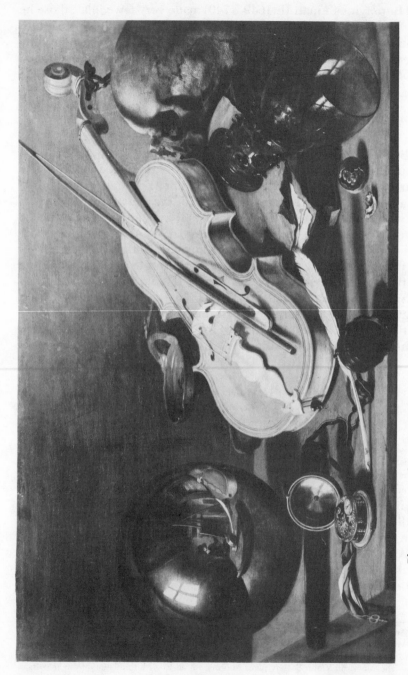

Plate 11. Pieter Claesz: *Still Life* (c.1628) Showing an Instrument of the Brescian School. Used with the permission of the Germanisches Nationalmuseum, Nürnberg.

In an appendix entitled, "Elenco di instrumenti attribuiti a Gasparo" (Catalogue of Instruments Attributed to Gasparo), Mucchi listed 21 violins, 15 violas, 4 cellos, 12 *bassetti* and *contrabassi*, 8 viola da gambas, and 1 lute. These were the instruments known to Mucchi through his research up to 1940. It is significant that he inserted the word "attributed" in the title of this appendix, indicating the difficulty, if not impossibility, of authenticating instruments that are over 400 years old.[18] This does not mean that all of the present-day "Gasparo Violas" not listed in Mucchi's treatise are suspect.[19]

Mucchi illustrated the unfortunate practice of mutilating great instruments by including a photograph of one of da Salò's *Lira da braccios* that was "transformed" into a viola.[20]

Of the 15 violas mentioned by Mucchi, nine were in museums or private collections. Only six violas were in circulation as active concert instruments.

Gasparo apparently experimented with various patterns while continuing to make instruments of the violin type. At least three examples of da Salò instruments called the *Lira-Viola* are extant: in the Ashmolean Museum at Oxford, in the Geiser Collection in Leningrad, (Plate 12), and in the Conservatoire Museum in Brussels.

Mucchi furnished the following measurements of small and large da Salò Violas:[21]

Small Pattern:
 Body length — 40.7 cm. (16 1/32 in.)
 Upper bout — 19.5 cm. (7 11/16 in.)
 Lower bout — 24.5 cm. (9 5/8 in.)
 Upper ribs — 3.8 cm. (1 1/2 in.)
 Lower ribs — 4.0 cm. (1 9/16 in.).

Large Pattern:
 Body length — 44.45 cm. (17 1/2 in.)
 Upper bout — 21.91 cm. (8 5/8 in.)
 Lower bout — 25.72 cm. (10 1/8 in.)
 Upper ribs — 3.81 cm. (1 1/2 in.)
 Lower ribs — 3.96 cm. (1 9/16 in.).

The above dimensions furnished by Mucchi represent the small and large da Salò instruments he had seen. Among other Gasparo

[18]*Ibid.*, Appendix.
[19]See "Mistaken Identification of Violas" section in this Chapter.
[20]Mucchi, *op. cit.*, Tavola XXVII.
[21]*Ibid.*, p. 182.

Plate 12. Gasparo da Salò: Viola-lira
Geiser Collection, Leningrad.

violas, not known to Mucchi, three have particularly interesting measurements: the Kievman Viola (Plate 18) is 39.53 cm. (15 9/16 in.) in length, which is 1.17 cm. (7/16 in.) shorter than Mucchi's small viola. The ex-Bailly-ex-de Pasquale Viola (Plate 16) is essentially the same length as Mucchi's large model. However, the Borissovsky da Salò viola, mentioned later in this chapter, is 46 cm. (18 1/8 in.) in body length.

Robert E. Andrews, the owner of an inherited Gasparo cello, developed an insatiable curiosity about the maker and his productions. This resulted in four years of research, and the writing of a book.[22] Andrews subtitled his monograph on da Salò, "A brief account of his life and of some of the instruments he made." Andrews drew most of his biographical material from Mucchi's book, and this part of the book can be assumed to be accurate; however, the second part, which pertains to the instruments made by da Salò, must be approached with caution. Andrews listed 26 violas, and furnished information regarding their owners. For some of the instruments he gave the dimensions, color of varnish, and other descriptive material. But some of these instruments may not be authentic da Salòs.

Mucchi's research turned up letters and tax records which indicate that some of Gasparo's instruments were sold in France. It is not clear whether these instruments were sold to the French court or to individual buyers. Nor do the records specifically mention the sale of violas. In *Item 2* of Gasparo's 1588 tax return, he explains a debt resulting from a decline in his French business:

> I am a debtor to Rdo. P. D. Gabriel, monk in Sto. Piero for L.60 for the same amount lent me because my art is not going [as well] in France as usual.[23]

It is little wonder that Gasparo's export business to France had fallen off. France had become embroiled in a disastrous strife, known as the War of the Three Henrys, which came to an end with the assassinations of Henry II and Henry III.

In *Item 1* of Gasparo's 1588 tax return, it is evident that he made instruments for special orders:

> I am debtor to M. Antonio di Franzosi of Venice for 102 lire, 10 soldi, for a deposit on a contract which the late M. Simon, his father-in-law, gave me for making a pair of violins, but because of the unexpected death of the said M. Simon, the deposit has remained with me and I have not given them the instruments, so that the said M. Antonio demands the said deposit.[24]

[22]Robert E. Andrews, *Gasparo Bertolotti da Salò* (Berkeley, California: pub. by author, 1953).
[23]Mucchi, *op. cit.*, p. 62 (Trans. by Andrews, *op. cit.*, p. 57).
[24]*Ibid.*, p. 55.

The fact that Gasparo made instruments for special orders perhaps explains why his violas rarely have the same dimensions. The buyers may have ordered particular sized instruments to best fit their personal needs. An equally probable factor, resulting in different dimensions for the da Salò violas, could be the maker's ambition to produce a better sounding instrument by experimenting with different measurements. This insatiable desire to improve one's productions is basic to a craftsman's art—a form of genius so apparent in Gasparo's violas.

Walter Hamma, the internationally famous dealer and appraiser of stringed instruments, gave the following evaluation of Gasparo da Salò's instruments:

> His work is rather robust and flatly constructed, the outlines raw and not symmetrical. The long f holes are wide open and nearly vertical, the tables nearly always wide-grained, and the backs of maple cut on the slab. His scrolls are rather large and coarse, and the varnish, although thin and dark, is good quality. He made, as was common at that time, two models, a large one and a small one. This applies also to his violas which are particularly sought after.[25]

Gasparo violas are not only desirable because of their antiquarian value, but more importantly because of their mellow and resonant tone. These violas are particularly prized as quartet instruments. Ottokar Nováček (1866–1900), Louis Bailly (1882–1974), and Vadim Borissovsky (1900–1972), three great quartet violists, owned and played da Salòs (see Louis Bailly violas, Plates 14–16).[26] Borissovsky, the famous Russian violist, owned and played a marvelous da Salò that is 46 cm. (18 1/8 in.) in length. Irving Ilmer, formerly violist of the Fine Arts Quartet, played a da Salò, which had previously belonged to the renowned Germain Prevost, who had played it in the Belgian Pro Arte Quartet.

The Allan Harshman Gasparo da Salò Viola

This da Salò viola was sold in December, 1964, by William Moennig & Son to Allan Harshman, eminent violist of Los Angeles (Plate 13). It has both a Hill and a Wurlitzer certificate. Moennigs date it c.1560. This would place it in da Salò's early period, shortly after he set up his shop in Brescia. The photographs of this viola

---

[25]Walter Hamma, *Meister italienischer Geigenbaukunst* (München: Schuler Verlagsgesellschaft MHB, 1976 [4th printing of 1965 Ed.; original work printed in 1931]), p. 563.

[26]For a more detailed description of these instruments, see Maurice W. Riley, "Louis Bailly's Two Gasparo da Salò Violas," *Journal of the Violin Society of America*, III, No. 3 (1977), pp. 50–57.

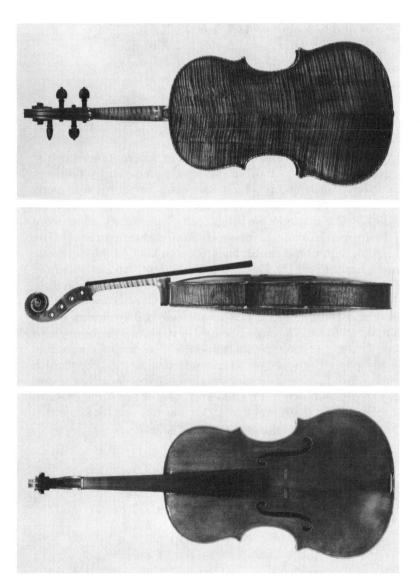

Plate 13. The Harshman Gasparo da Salò Viola.
Photographs furnished by William Moennig & Son, Philadelphia.

illustrate the rugged beauty and massive proportions of Gasparo's early works. It has the dimensions:

> Body length — 44.2 cm. (17 3/8 in.)
> Upper bout — 21.8 cm. (8 9/16 in.)
> Middle bout— 16.6 cm. (6 1/2 in.)
> Lower bout — 27.9 cm. (11 in.).

The Louis Bailly da Salò Violas

Two Gasparo da Salò violas were owned at different times by the famed quartet violist Louis Bailly. The first, purchased by Bailly in 1908, was a large instrument which had been cut down to a body length of 43.8 cm (17 1/4 in.). The photograph of the top (Plate 14) shows wide holes and single purfling, both characteristic of many of da Salò's instruments made in his early and middle periods.[27] The enlarged photograph of the center back shows a knot on the right side of the middle bout (Plate 15). Da Salò was apparently more concerned with the acoustical properties of the wood than with its appearance. Scratched on the back is the name and date of a German owner of the viola: Kirchmayr Rhetor, 1757. The scroll lacks the symmetry of the Cremona makers, but has a rugged beauty of its own. The three views of the viola (Plate 14) show an instrument that is in amazingly fine condition, although it is now over four hundred years old. The varnish is of medium dark-brown. The tone quality is exceptionally big and beautiful. The present owner, Virginia Majewski of Los Angeles, California, purchased the instrument in 1939, and has used it since that time in her performances and recordings.[28]

The dimensions of this viola are:

> String length — 37.9 cm. (14 15/16 in.)
> Body length — 43.8 cm. (17 1/4 in.)
> Upper bout   — 19.45 cm. (7 21/32 in.)
> Middle bout — 13.97 cm. (5 1/2 in.)
> Lower bout   — 25.8 cm. (10 5/32 in.)
> Top ribs   — 3.2 cm. (1 1/4 in.)
> Bottom ribs — 3.34 cm. (1 5/16 in.).

---

[27]Photographs of the ex-Bailly-Majewski da Salò viola were taken by David Rivinus, associate to Michael and Rena Weisshaar of Los Angeles, California.

[28]Maurice W. Riley, "Louis Bailly's Gasparo da Salo Violas," *Journal of the Violin Society of America*, III, 3 (Summer, 1977), pp. 50–57.

Plate 14. The ex-Bailly Majewski da Salò Viola.
Photographs furnished by Virginia Majewski, Los Angeles.

Plate 15. The ex-Bailly Majewski da Salò Viola:
Enlargement of Center Back. Photograph furnished by Virginia Majewski, Los Angeles.

The second Bailly instrument, named by Moennigs as the ex-Bailly-ex-de Pasquale da Salò, is typical of that maker's grand model (Plate 16).[29] It has not been cut down. The varnish is reddish-brown. The top is of two pieces of spruce. The back is of two pieces of maple, cut on the slab.[30] Louis Bailly acquired this viola in 1928 and used it until his retirement.[31] It was purchased in 1955 by Joseph de Pasquale, the distinguished principal violist of the Boston Symphony and the Philadelphia Orchestra. In 1971 it was purchased by Scott Nickrenz of Boston, who plays it in his solo and chamber music performances. The measurements of this instrument are:[32]

---

[29]Photographs of the ex-Bailly-de Pasquale da Salò furnished by William Moennig and Son.

[30]For a more detailed description of this instrument see Maurice W. Riley, *op. cit.*

[31]Purchased in 1928 from Rudolph Wurlitzer. Earlier owners were H. C. Silvestre & Charles Maucotel, Lionel Tertis, and William E. Hill and Sons.

[32]This instrument has been certified by W. E. Hill & Sons (1928), Emil Herrmann (1955), and William Moennig & Son (1970).

Plate 16. The ex-Bailly ex-de Pasquale da Salò Viola.
Photographs furnished by William Moennig & Son, Philadelphia.

String length — 39.0   cm. (15 3/8 in.)
Body length   — 44.8   cm. (17 9/16 in.)
Upper bout   — 20.95 cm. (8 1/4 in.)
Middle bout   — 12.7   cm. (5 in.)
Lower bout   — 25.4   cm. (10 in.).

The Nathan Gordon da Salò Viola

Another remarkable example of the Brescian maker's genius is the instrument owned by Nathan Gordon, principal violist of the Detroit Symphony Orchestra (Plate 17).[33] Certified by Kagan and Gaines of Chicago, this instrument has been used as a model for several fine instruments made in the 20th century by Roelof Weertman.[34] The dimensions of this viola are:[35]

Body length   — 43.6 cm. (17 3/16 in.)
String length — 37.4 cm. (14 3/4 in.)
Upper bout   — 20.5 cm. (8 1/16 in.)
Middle bout   — 13.5 cm. (5 5/16 in.)
Lower bout   — 25.3 cm. (9 5/8 in.).

The Louis Kievman da Salò Viola

Da Salò probably made fewer small than large violas. Almost all of his instruments extant are of the large pattern.[36] An exception is the beautifully ornamented small viola belonging to the Los Angeles violist, Louis Kievman (Plate 18). The Kievman da Salò has a double purfling on both the top and the back, and the back is additionally ornamented with a cloverleaf inlay. This remarkable instrument has been certified by both Hill and Wurlitzer. The Hill certificate reads:

---

[33]Drawings of the Gordon da Salò furnished by Roelof Weertman, of Falmouth, Massachusetts.

[34]Nathan Gordon frequently plays a Weertman copy of his da Salò.

[35]Dimensions are from Roelof Weertman, *Violin Building My Way* (Falmouth, Mass.: Published by the author, 1974), *Appendix*. Mr. Weertman is an expert at making duplicates of old Italian masterpieces. He has made several copies of the Nathan Gordon da Salò in different body lengths, and also copies of the Scott Nichrenz (ex-Bailly-ex-de Pasquale) da Salò viola. Weertman has also made copies of other instruments for such artists as Gordon Staples, concertmaster of the Detroit Symphony; Leslie Parnas, concert cellist; and Mischa Mischakoff, famous concertmaster of the NBC Symphony and other orchestras.

[36]The reasons why so few small-size early Cremonese and Brescian violas exist today are discussed at the end of this section of the chapter in "The Survival of Large Violas."

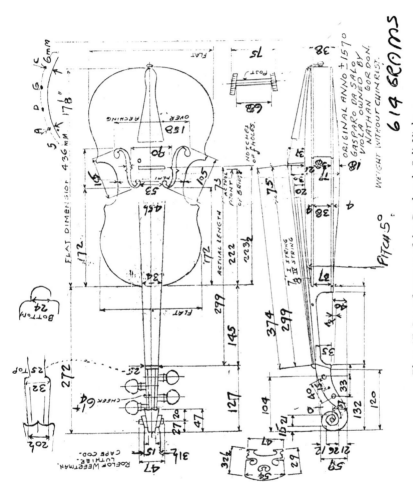

Plate 17. Specifications of the Gordon da Salò Viola.
Drawn and Furnished by the American Luthier, Roelof Weertman, of Falmouth, Massachusetts.

Plate 18. The Kievman da Salò Viola.
Photographs furnished by Louis Kievman, Los Angeles.

Rudolph Wurlitzer
Cincinnati, Ohio
U.S.A.

Dear Mr. Wurlitzer,

    The history of your Gasparo viola, as far as is known to us, is brief.
It was bought by my father from Zach sen. of Vienna, about 1875, who stated
that he had recently purchased it in Italy. My father sold it to Mr. J. S. Cooke of
Liversedge, Yorks, who retained possession of the instrument for some years and
then sold it to Mr. R. D. Waddell of Glasgow.

    This viola is a most interesting example of the maker, inasmuch as it is the
only one of relatively small dimensions we have ever come across, for it has never
been reduced in size and is as it was originally made.

—Alfred Hill, March 29, 1924

Wurlitzer kept it in his private collection until 1936, when it was
sold to a private collector. It was loaned to Mr. Kievman when he was
a member of the Music Art Quartet. In 1955, it was sold to Kievman.
The dimensions of the Kievman da Salò are:

Body length — 39.53 cm. (15 9/16 in.)
Upper bout — 19.69 cm. (7 3/4 in.)
Middle bout — 13.97 cm. (5 1/2 in.)
Lower bout — 24.61 cm. (9 11/16 in.)

In 1906 the city of Salò honored its great native son by placing a
bust of Gasparo, by the Italian sculptor, Angelo Zanelli, in the Municipal Building (Plate 19). Engraved below the bust is the inscription:
"Gasparo da Salò inventor of the violin 1542–1609" [sic].

In the city of Brescia, where Gasparo worked for almost fifty
years, a plaque on the outside of St. Joseph's Church, where he is
buried in an unknown grave, reads:

GASPARO da SALÒ

A master of the art of violin making
Always endeavoring to produce
More perfect models until at last
He gave almost a soul and life
Itself to the modern violin, which was
His own invention [sic].

He was buried in this church.
Born in Salò in 1542   Died in Brescia in 1609[37]

---

[37]Translation by Andrews, *op. cit.*, p. 69.

Plate 19. Bust of Gasparo located in the Salò Municipal Building.
Photographs furnished by Amalie Du Ry of Velp, Netherlands.

The street beside the church where the plaque appears is appropriately called *Via Gasparo da Salò*. The well-intentioned plaque, like the bust mentioned above, although justly honoring Gasparo, contains two historical errors: first, as proven by Mucchi, da Salò was born in 1540, not 1542; and second, as shown in Chapter I, Gasparo was not the inventor of the violin, but many da Salò enthusiasts will always affectionately consider him "the father of the viola."

Mistaken Identification of Violas

The fame of Gasparo violas and their scarcity have resulted in the existence of an ever-increasing number of fraudulent instruments. Of the many violas containing da Salò labels, few can be assumed to be genuine.[38]

---

[38]Louis Kievman, the well-known violist and expert on da Salò violas, in a letter to the author writes, "There are only 10 or 12 Gasparo violas extant, and over a hundred of them are here in Los Angeles."

During the 19th and early 20th centuries, many of the old Italian instruments were sold by dealers who lacked the knowledge to correctly identify the maker. Sometimes an instrument did not contain the original label, or perhaps the label named a maker unknown to the dealer. There was a widespread practice of substituting facsimile labels of the more prestigious and better known luthiers, to insure sale of instruments at more favorable prices. Instruments made in Cremona shops had an international reputation—hence the names Amati, Guarneri, Stradivari, and others were substituted for the original maker's label in violins, violas, and cellos.[39]

The city of Brescia, likewise, was known for having been the home of Gasparo da Salò and Paolo Maggini. The Brescian models were usually easy to distinguish from the Cremonese, but to identify the exact maker was not always possible. So if the rightful maker happened to be less well known than Gasparo da Salò, dealers sometimes substituted a da Salò facsimile label. There was an unfortunate trend to identify all instruments made in Brescia, and instruments from other cities which had characteristics of the Brescian models, as the products of Gasparo da Salò.

According to Jacques Français, the respected New York dealer, many of the leading dealers in Europe, England, and the United States inadvertently became part of a chain of "experts," who sometimes based their certification on an earlier certification by another reputable appraiser. Mistaken identifications were compounded from one dealer to the next. To illustrate this unfortunate practice, Français mentioned two instruments documented in his own archives, violas formerly attributed to Gasparo da Salò. The viola in the possession of P. Amran of Tokyo, Japan, bearing a label, "Gasparo da Salò," is actually, according to Français, an instrument made by Luigi Mariani of Pesaro, in the latter part of the 16th century (Plate 20). The Français documents contain the following description of the viola;

> This instrument, a very rare specimen of this maker, ranks with the best of Gasparo da Salò, for workmanship and exceptional tonal quality. The top is made of four pieces of native spruce with a straight and well-marked grain. The back is made of two pieces of plain maple; the sides and scroll of matching maple. The varnish is of a dark red-brown color. The dimensions:
>
> Body length — 42.3 cm. (16 21/32 in.)
> Upper bout — 20.3 cm. (8 in.)
> Middle bout — 14.7 cm. (5 3/4 in.)
> Lower bout — 24.6 cm. (9 22/32 in.).

---

[39]This practice was not limited to Brescian and Cremonese instruments. Cellos made by Matteo Goffriller (1690–1742), of Venice, were attributed to Carlo Bergonzi, and even Stradivarius, in order to sell them at higher prices.

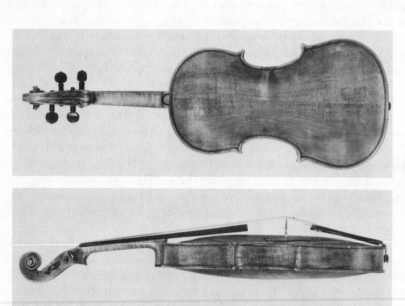

Plate 20. Luigi Mariani of Pesaro Viola.
Photographs furnished by Jacques Français, New York City.

As a second example, Français cited the viola owned by Dr. Steven Warnick of Connecticut, which bears a label, "Gasparo da Salò," but which is actually, Français maintains, the work of Antonio Mariani (early 17th century), with the exception of the scroll (Plate 21). The Français certificate of March 30, 1974, reads:

> This instrument is a rare and handsome specimen of the maker's work and in an excellent state of restoration, with first class tonal quality. It is the same instrument described as a Gasparo da Salò in the Lyon and Healy 1929 Catalogue, reproduced in color.

The Français papers add that the top is made of four pieces of spruce with a fine grain. The back is made of two pieces of maple out of the half slab, and the sides of matching maple. The maple scroll is a very fine reproduction made by Rene Morel. The varnish is of an orange-brown color. The dimensions are:

> Body length — 41.5 cm. (16 11/32 in.)
> Upper bout — 18.5 cm. (7 9/32 in.)
> Middle bout — 13.8 cm. (5 7/16 in.)
> Lower bout — 23.2 cm. (9 1/8 in.).

In addition to the Mariani violas, other makers' instruments have sometimes been mistakenly identified as being the work of da Salò. Among the luthiers who may have had this unfortunate designation are Pellegrino de Zanetto (c.1522–1615) and Gian Battista Doneda (c.1525–1610). Violas made by Gasparo's apprentices have sometimes been the victims of the practice of labelling all Brescian instruments as da Salòs. Among Gasparo's more talented students were: his son, Francesco Bertolotti (1564–1614); Giacomo LaFranchini (15??–?), who worked for da Salò for over twelve years, and after Gasparo's death, worked for Maggini; Giovita Rodiani (c.1545–died after 1624), may have been apprenticed to da Salò, at least he was a contemporary luthier in Brescia who used Gasparo's model, then later used Maggini's.

The violas made by all of the above makers have several things in common that can influence and deceive all but the most discerning eyes of the most assiduous experts. These instruments are four hundred years old; they frequently have been modeled after the da Salò pattern; and the f holes are more perpendicular to the instruments' length than Cremonese models. Two attributes that are not exclusive to Brescian models are sometimes wrongly used as a means of identification for da Salò instruments, namely, double purfling, and carved heads in place of the usual scroll. Double purfling was more consis-

Plate 21. Antonio Mariani of Pesaro Viola.
Photographs furnished by Jacques Français, New York City.

tently used by Maggini than by Gasparo. Carved heads were an affectation, occasionally substituted for the scroll, and were probably commissioned by a prospective buyer, or were included to make the instrument bring a higher price.

The Survival of Large Violas

Most of the genuine da Salò violas that are extant were originally of the large pattern (tenors). Many of these instruments were cut down in the early 19th century to make them easier to play.

Very few of the small-pattern da Salò violas (altos) have survived. This is because they were in almost constant use from the time they left the master's shop. The number of small da Salò violas was reduced by the wear and tear of being played upon, by unfortunate accidents, by the destruction that followed in the wake of the incessant wars that plagued Europe from 1600 on, and by the inevitable attrition destined for such fragile and vulnerable objects as stringed instruments.

On the other hand, the large violas (tenors) were used less and less in the 17th and 18th centuries, as five-part writing gradually gave way to four-part harmonization.[40] With the eventual elimination of Viola II and Viola III parts (French style),[41] the need for large tenors steadily decreased. Also there was the physical factor related to the difficulty of playing the large tenors. Given a choice, most performers who were playing an accompanying part would choose a small-size viola.

The greater use of the small da Salò violas contributed to their attrition, while more of the large da Salòs, through lack of use, survived into the 20th century because they were kept in cases, closets, and vaults, or otherwise protected.

Giovanni Paolo Maggini

Among da Salò's several outstanding apprentices who carried on the Brescian tradition of excellence in instrument making was Gio-

---

[40]This change from five- to four-part writing extended over a period roughly 1600 to 1750; although in some of Bach's Cantatas, Viola I and Viola II parts are found. And even as late as c.1785, Mozart scored for Viola I and II in the orchestral accompaniment to the *Concertante for Violin and Viola in E♭*, K.364.

[41]See Chapter IV for a discussion of the French style of harmonization.

vanni Paolo Maggini (1580–1632). Maggini apprenticed with Gasparo
from 1598 to 1604. There can be no question concerning the positive
influence da Salò had on his most talented pupil; Maggini, however,
did not continue to use da Salò models after leaving Gasparo's shop,
but almost immediately developed his own patterns and dimensions.

Today Maggini violas are almost as scarce as da Salò violins.
Henley estimates that there are only nine Maggini violas extant.[42]

Margaret L. Huggins' monograph on Maggini contains much
valuable information about his innovations and contributions to the
violin family.[43] Some of the characteristics peculiar to Maggini's instruments, as described by Huggins, are: (1) the arching rises immediately from the inner line of purfling; (2) the sides are set closer to the
edges of the top and back than models by other makers; (3) the lower
circles of the f holes are [usually] smaller than the upper ones; (4) the
scroll is from one-fourth to one-half turn shorter than that of other
makers; (5) the purfling is either single or double, more often double;
(6) on the top, beneath the fingerboard, the inner line of purfling is
omitted; (7) Maggini labels are never dated and are placed near the
center of his instruments (Plate 22).[44]

It was Huggins' opinion that both Andrea Guarneri and Stradivari
based their viola models on those of Maggini. Particularly pertinent to
this conclusion is her observation that instruments of Maggini's late
period show features of the "long Strad." She went so far as to contend
that Maggini initiated the "modern viola," and perhaps she was a bit
overly prejudiced when she wrote, "Maggini showed greater fore-
thought and knowledge of viola construction than any other maker."[45]

Hamma's comments on Maggini and his work are equally complimentary. Hamma maintained that Maggini was

> . . . the most celebrated master of the Brescian school, whose creations both in
> workmanship and tonal respects far surpassed those of his contemporaries. He
> used two models, a large and small one, but built mostly a large wide type of
> strongly rounded contours. The arching is full but not too high with practically no
> hollowing of the edges, and there is often double purfling and embellishment.
> The f holes are slender and upright, and sometimes wide open. The varnish
> mostly a beautiful brownish yellow or reddish brown is of the finest quality and
> appearance. His works are rarely met with. Tonally they are mostly very good, if
> somewhat dark in sound.[46]

---

[42]Henley, op. cit.,

[43]Margaret L. Huggins, Gio: Paolo Maggini, His Life and Work (London: W. E. Hill & Sons,
1976, Reprint of the 1892 Ed.). The title page makes it clear that the book is essentially by the Hills:
"Compiled and edited from material collected and contributed by William Ebsworth Hill and his
sons, William, Arthur, & Alfred Hill."

[44]Ibid., pp. 62–63.

[45]Ibid., p. 72. The reader should remember that Huggins' opinions are really those of the
famous Hill family.

[46]Hamma, op. cit., p. 451.

Plate 22. A Paolo Maggini Viola.
Photographs furnished by William Moennig & Son, Philadelphia.

Around the beginning of the 19th century, two brothers, members of a family named Dumas, acquired a set of Maggini instruments: a violin, a tenor, a cello, and a double bass. The Dumas brothers, who lived in an old chateau near Lyons, were amateur musicians and friends of Beethoven.[47] The Dumas "tenor" was a product of Maggini's second period (after 1615) and is the most famous of this maker's surviving violas. Huggins stated that the Dumas tenor will bear comparison with productions of the greatest makers. She added that, if compared to violas of Andrea Guarneri and Stradivari, it will be seen that Maggini was ahead of his time. The Dumas tenor has beautiful golden-brown varnish and the usual double purfling, but does not have other ornamentation. The model is similar in many respects to the "long Strad," which did not appear until about eighty years later.

Huggins listed the following Maggini measurements (presumably of the Dumas viola):[48]

Body length — 42.7 cm. (16 13/16 in.)
Upper bout — 20.64 cm. (8 1/8 in.)
Lower bout — 25.08 cm. (9 7/8 in.)
Upper ribs — 3.49 cm. (1 3/8 in.)
Lower ribs — 3.65 cm. (1 7/16 in.).

After Maggini's death in 1632, no worthy successor appeared in Brescia to continue the high standards attained by him and his teacher, Gasparo da Salò. In 1907 a monument was erected in Brescia to honor Maggini.[49] The city of Brescia always retained its fame for the fine stringed instruments made there from 1450 to 1632, but after 1632, the neighboring city of Cremona became the undisputed world capital of the luthier industry.

[47]Huggins, op. cit., p. 65.
[48]Ibid., pp. 69–70, 72.
[49]Ibid., p. 83.

CHAPTER III

THE VIOLA AND ITS MUSIC IN ITALY DURING THE BAROQUE ERA

The Viola

Italy was not only the principal supplier of violinists to most of the capitals of Europe in the 17th century, but it also carried on a flourishing trade in stringed instruments. Cremona was the undisputed world center of the manufacture of instruments of the violin pattern. Families of luthiers such as Amati, Bergonzi, Grancino, Guadagnini, Guarneri, Ruggieri, and ultimately Stradivari, to name only a few, had their homes and shops in Cremona. Other Italian cities had their own schools of violin making, often including members of the Cremona families who had migrated throughout the Italian peninsula. Among the literally hundreds of other families who practiced their luthier trade in Italian cities were: Tononi in Bologna; Carcassi, Grancino, and Testore, in Milano; Gagliano in Naples; Tecchler in Rome; Goffriller and Seraphin in Venice; Bertolotti, Maggini, Rogeri, and Zanetto in Brescia.

Early in the 17th century, most of the Italian luthiers were making lutes, viols, and violins. There was, however, a gradual decrease in the market for viols and lutes, accompanied by an ever increasing sale for violins, cellos, and basses. Violas were in short demand for two reasons: (1) the gradual change after 1600 from five-part to four-part harmony, thus eliminating one of the inner parts played by the viola; and (2) the emergence of the trio sonata as the most popular form of chamber music in the 17th century, music which usually featured two violins, to the virtual exclusion of the viola.[1]

---

[1] See "Italian Baroque Music for the Viola" for a more detailed discussion of this subject, in this chapter.

The Hills, in their book on Stradivari, gave a general accounting of the status of the production of violas from c.1660 to 1750:

> Before 1660 we find the makers—Zanetto, Gasparo, Maggini, the Amati, and others—frequently constructing the large viola, but very rarely the small one. From 1660 to 1700 the small viola was superseding the large one, though fewer violas of any kind were then made. Between 1700 to 1750 there was almost a cessation of viola-making in all countries; this coincides with the dearth of chamber music composed at this period in which the viola was given a part.[2]

Apprentices of Nicolo Amati

According to Bonetti, documents show that Antonio Amati sold out to his younger brother Girolamo (Hieronymus) in 1588;[3] instruments coming out of the shop, however, including violas, continued to bear the double name of Antonius and Hieronymus on the label until well into the 1620's. The Brothers-Amati partnership was definitely broken with the death of Antonio, at a date that is unknown but which was not later than 1627. Girolamo, his wife, and two daughters fell victim to the deadly plague which wiped out half the population of Cremona in 1630. At that time Nicolo, son of Girolamo, became head of the Amati atelier. The fame of the Amati name and the ever-increasing demand for Amati instruments prompted Nicolo to accept more apprentices than was usual at that time. Among his many talented students were his son, Girolamo II, Francesco Ruggieri, Giovanni Rogeri, Andrea Guarneri, and Antonio Stradivari. The latter two, Guarneri and Stradivari, after completing their apprenticeships, made violas despite the ever-decreasing demand for these instruments.

---

[2]W. Henry Hill, Arthur F. Hill, and Alfred E. Hill, *Antonio Stradivari*, His Life and Work (1644–1737) (London: William E. Hill & Sons, 1902), p. 100.

[3]See David D. Boyden, *The History of Violin Playing from Its Origins to 1761*, p. 109, Footnote 3.

The Guarneri Family

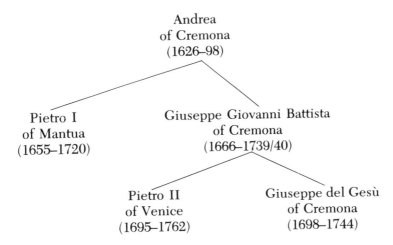

Andrea
of Cremona
(1626–98)

Pietro I
of Mantua
(1655–1720)

Giuseppe Giovanni Battista
of Cremona
(1666–1739/40)

Pietro II
of Venice
(1695–1762)

Giuseppe del Gesù
of Cremona
(1698–1744)

There were many luthiers in the 17th and 18th centuries whose last name was Guarneri. Five of these belong among the top makers of all time. The violins of Giuseppe del Gesù rank with the very finest of those produced by Stradivari. The violas made by Andrea, though few in number, compare favorably with the best crafted by Stradivari.

Andrea Guarneri

Andrea Guarneri (1626–98) apprenticed with Nicolo Amati from c.1638 to c.1645; and then as a master craftsman, he continued to work in Nicolo's shop until 1654, when he launched his own separate career as a luthier. His long association with Amati influenced his creations, many of which have a similar pattern to those of his master. This is particularly true of his violins. As the Hills point out, however, there were "two not unimportant deviations: firstly, his admirable conception of a smaller-sized viola; secondly, his smaller proportioned violoncello, both representing progressive innovations."[4]

Commenting on the small number of Andrea Guarneri violas known to them, the Hills described briefly three of the four they had seen: These violas were about 41.3 cm. (16 1/4 in.) in body length. They were made in 1676, 1690, and 1697.[5]

[4]W. Henry Hill, Arthur F. Hill, and Alfred E. Hill, *The Violin Makers of the Guarneri Family* (London: William E. Hill & Sons, 1931), p. 10.

[5]*Ibid.*, pp. 14–15.

The Hills, in their appraisal of the 1676 viola, wrote this evaluation: "In our opinion this viola is worthy of taking rank amongst the greatest, and it stands for Andrea's highest achievement."[6] The Hill book on the Guarneri Family carries full-page color photographs of this glorious instrument.[7]

The 1690 viola, the Hill book says, compares favorably with the 1676 masterpiece. The 1697 instrument was made one year before Andrea's death. In the opinion of the Hills, this instrument was largely the work of Andrea's talented son, Giuseppe (1666-1739/40). By that time the demand for violas had practically ceased; and according to the Hills, neither Giuseppe, known as "Joseph Guarnerius filius Andrea,"[8] nor his brother Pietro, known as "Peter Guarnerius of Mantua," made any more violas.

The even more famous sons of Giuseppe, Pietro, known as "Peter Guarnerius of Venice" (1695-1762), and Giuseppe, known as "Guarnerius del Gesù" (1698-1744), made few if any violas.

The 1697 viola was formerly called the "Lord Harrington Guarneri," but now is known as the "Primrose Guarneri." It is one of the most famous violas extant. In a letter to William Primrose, dated October 16, 1958, William E. Hill & Sons wrote regarding this instrument:

> It is quite a fine example of the maker whose violas are extremely rare; we have not come across more than three in the whole course of our experience. We would add that we recognize in this instrument the handiwork of Andrea's son Joseph, concerning whose cooperation with his father we comment upon in our work on the life of the Guarneri family.
>
> We congratulate you on becoming the possessor of this unique instrument, the tone of which is of the finest. It may interest you to learn that it was greatly admired by Mr. Kreisler [Fritz Kreisler], when he was here some years ago.
>
> Yours sincerely,
> sgt: A Phillips Hill.[9]

Early in the 19th century, this Guarneri viola was a part of the Gillott Collection. When that collection was sold at a Christie's Auction in 1872, the Earl of Harrington, upon the advice of William E. Hill, purchased the instrument. Later in the 1920's, the Hills purchased this instrument from the Harrington estate and sold it in March

---

[6]*Ibid.*, p. 14.
[7]*Ibid.*, pp. 24–25.
[8]*Ibid.*, p. 15.
[9]The Hill letter was furnished to the author by Robert Bein & Geoffrey Fushi of Chicago, who are preparing an illustrated monograph on the Primrose Andrea Guarneri viola to be published in the near future.

Plate 23. The Primrose Andrea Guarneri Viola.
Photographs furnished by Bein & Fushi, Chicago.

of 1925 to the famous collector, Antonio Antoncich of Valparaiso, Chile. When the Antoncich estate was liquidated, Rembert Wurlitzer acquired the viola and sold it to William Primrose in 1955. Primrose described its fine tonal quality in his autobiography.[10]

This beautiful viola is in an exceptionally fine state of preservation (Plate 23). The back is of maple, one piece cut on the slab, showing prominent slab markings and small knot formations in the upper area. There is an original added wing at each upper and lower flank, indicating the high regard Andrea had for the acoustical properties of this wood—splicing to complete the viola dimensions. The top is cut from two pieces of spruce, with a broad grain at the center, narrowing and then broadening again at the outer flanks. The sides are of maple cut on the slab, with medium-narrow wavy flames. The scroll is original, and of quarter-cut maple with regular narrow flames. The varnish is original, and of a golden-orange color.[11] The dimensions are:

Body length — 41.3 cm. (16 1/4 in.)
Upper bout — 19.3 cm. (7 25/32 in.)
Middle bout — 13.4 cm. (5 1/4 in.)
Lower bout — 24.5 cm. (9 17/32 in.).

This great instrument was recently sold for an undisclosed amount, but what is believed to be the highest price ever brought by a viola.

During Andrea's lifetime the demand for violas steadily decreased, and the sale of tenors (large violas) was almost non-existent. Luthiers probably made tenors, if at all, only on special order, or prearranged sale. When asked if he had ever seen a tenor-size viola made by Andrea Guarneri, Jacques Français, the New York dealer, replied that he had seen only one, the tenor presently owned by Laurence Witten, of Southport, Connecticut.

Members of the Guarneri Family, other than Andrea, made few violas. However, two Guarneri violas, not known to the Hills when they wrote their book in 1931, have appeared. One of the most fascinating is the instrument owned and played by the famous artist-violist, Paul Doktor. It is attributed to one of Andrea's sons, Pietro Giovanni Guarneri of Mantua. According to the Australian luthier,

---

[10]William Primrose, *Walk on the North Side: Memoirs of a Violist* (Provo, Utah: Brigham Young University Press, 1978), pp. 166–7.

[11]From the Rembert Wurlitzer certificate, April 13, 1955, which was furnished to the author by Robert Bein & Geoffrey Fushi of Chicago.

Lloyd Adams, this instrument was originally a tenor, with a body length of over 43.2 cm. (17 in.). Sometime in the 19th century, it was cut down to less than 40.6 cm. (16 in.). Presently, there is a label inside (supposedly a repair label) which reads:

Giovanni Grancino in Contrada
Largha di Milano al segno
della Corona 1685.[12]

At the time it was cut down and the label placed in the instrument, the original carved head was removed and a scroll put in its place.

Eventually the viola was purchased by Professor Richard Goldner of Bellingham, Washington, who decided to have it restored to a larger body-length of 41.3 cm. (16 1/4 in.). For this difficult assignment, he selected the talented Australian luthier, Lloyd Adams. Adams worked on this restoration for over two years, carefully selecting the wood to match the original and attaching the necessary extensions by grafting wings to the upper and lower bouts, and lengthening the top and bottom plates. This arduous operation required great patience and skill to match the grain in the wood of the extensions with the original plates. Then finally Adams did a masterful job of duplicating the original reddish-brown varnish on the new areas in such a way that the restoration can not be detected. To make sure that the new extensions would not weaken the instrument and that the tension of the strings and pressure of the bridge could be sustained, Adams added a piece of slender oval shaped wood (5 by 9 mm.) in the center of the viola, between neck and button. This ingenious device does not impair the sound, and protects the shape of the body against the stresses inherent in stringed instruments. Adams did not change the width of the ribs, leaving them as they were, with an upper measurement of 3.2 cm. (1 1/4 in.), and the lower 3.3 cm. (1 5/16 in.).

When Paul Doktor first saw the instrument, he immediately made the decision to purchase it. After he bought it, he decided to have the ribs widened to better conform with the aesthetic appearance and to give it more resonance. For this remodeling he secured the services of Joseph Settin in 1960, who built the specified higher ribs. Doktor now plays his enlarged Guarneri viola for his concert and recording engagements (see Plate 24). Present dimensions of the instrument are:

---

[12]In a letter to the author, dated September 25, 1978, Paul Doktor points out that both the label and the date are suspect, since Grancino would have been only 15 years old in 1685.

Plate 24. The Doktor Pietro Guarneri Viola.
Photographs furnished by Paul Doktor, of New York City.

```
Body length  — 41.3 cm. (16  1/4 in.)
Upper bout   — 19.7 cm. ( 7  3/4 in.)
Middle bout  — 13.3 cm. ( 5  1/4 in.)
Lower bout   — 24.6 cm. ( 9  3/4 in.)
Upper ribs   —  3.6 cm. ( 1 13/32 in.)
Lower ribs   —  3.7 cm. ( 1 15/32 in.)
String length — 37.3 cm. (14  3/4 in.)
```

Doktor also owns and plays a viola made by Lloyd Adams, which has almost the same measurements.

Another Guarneri viola, not mentioned by the Hills, is an instrument made by Petrus Guarnerius of Venice. Made between 1739 and 1762, it originally had a body length of over 41 cm. (16 5/32 in.) before it was cut down. Its present dimensions are:[13]

```
Body length  — 39.75 cm. (15  5/8 in.)
Upper bout   — 19.   cm. ( 7  1/2 in.)
Middle bout  — 12.6  cm. ( 5     in.)
Lower bout   — 29.9  cm. ( 9 13/32 in.).
```

Stradivari Violas

In 1902, the Hills wrote that they had been able to account for only ten violas made by Stradivari.[14] They had heard of one other viola, a possible eleventh, made in 1695. Ernest Doring, in his book, *How Many Strads* (1945), listed eleven violas.[15] William Henley, in *Stradivari: His Life and Instruments* (1961), increased the total to fifteen.[16] Herbert Goodkind's monumental treatise, *Violin Iconography of Antonio Stradivari, 1644–1737*, states in the Preface that there are seventeen violas; in the statistical summaries at the conclusion of his book, however, he enumerated eighteen in chronological order.[17] Three of these instruments are lost, or at least their present whereabouts are unknown.

---

[13]Photographs and a description of the Petrus Guarnerius viola appear in the *Alte Meistergeigen Beschreibungen-Expertisen, Band 1 Venezianer Schule* (Frankfurt am Main: Verlag das Musikinstrument, 1977), pp. 121–23.

[14]Hill, *Antonio Stradivari, His Life and Work (1644–1737)*, p. 94.

[15]Herbert Goodkind, *Violin Iconography of Antonio Stradivari, 1644–1737* (New York: published by the author, 1972), p. 14. Goodkind cites Doring and Henley.

[16]*Ibid.*

[17]*Ibid.*, p. 723.

Stradivari made over eleven hundred instruments during a long productive lifetime of ninety-three years (1644–1737). Goodkind, through his arduous research, has been able to account for seven hundred twelve (712) of them. Over four hundred have not been found. How many of these were destroyed by fire, vandalism, or carelessness? How many were lost through plundering and looting during the many European wars? How many were stolen by thieves who did not know how difficult it would be to dispose of a masterpiece and in desperation destroyed the evidence that would have led to their incarceration? These are questions that may never be answered. The likelihood of more of these priceless instruments being found becomes increasingly remote.

Based on Goodkind's inventory of Stradivari's total surviving instruments, the percentage of violas is only 2.5%. This surprisingly low figure probably corresponds with the decreasing demand for violas during Stradivari's lifetime.

Chronological List of Known Stradivari Violas[18]

1672 — *Mahler,* small Amati pattern (41.12 cm., 16 3/16 in.)

1687 — *King James II,* Monza

1690 — *Medici-Tuscan,* "*Contralto*" (40.64 cm., 16 in.)

1690 — *Medici-Tuscan,* "*Tenore*" (47.8 cm., 18 13/16 in.)

1695 — *Hill & Sons* (probably lost)

1696 — *Achinto,* Adam

1696 — *Spanish Court,* small model with ornamental inlay

1696 — *Spanish Court,* large model with ornamental inlay (probably of same dimensions as the *Tuscan Tenore*)

1696 — *Camposelice,* Vormbaum

---

[18]List compiled from: Goodkind, *op. cit.,* p. 723; Hill, *op. cit.,* pp. 84–108; and Anna Puccianti, *Antonio Stradivari,* English translation by Salvatore Coco (Cremona: International State School of Lute making, 1959), pp. 15–23.

1700 — *Corsby*, Nichols

1701 — *Macdonald*, one of the most famous of all Stradivari violas
(41.12 cm., 16 3/16 in.)

1710 — *de Boulogne*, A. Bruni, some experts question whether
this instrument ever existed

1715 — *Castelbarco*, Cooper

1715 — Russian Government

1721 — *Carli*, Paganini

1723 — *Gillott*, de Janze, Paganini

1727 — *Cassavatti*, Durand

1731 — *Paganini*, Vuillaume, Joachim, the viola that was the inspiration for Berlioz' *Harold en Italie*

1734 — *Gibson*, *St. Senoch*

Among the special orders for violas from Stradivari, mentioned by
the Hills, the following are of interest:

1685 — Two violas ordered for the court orchestra of the Duke of
Savoy

1690 — Two violas, one large and one small, ordered for the
Medici family in Florence

1707 — Two violas, one large and one small, for the Spanish
Court.[19]

Today there is no trace of the violas ordered for the Duke of
Savoy, if indeed they were ever made. On the other hand, the order
for the Medici is well documented. On September 19, 1690, Stradivari
received a letter from the Marquis Bartolomeo Ariberti, which read in
part:

---

[19]Hill, Antonio Stradivari . . ., *op cit.*, p. 94.

Plate 25. The Stradivari "Tuscan Tenore" made for the Medici Court, 1690.

> I have presented the Prince of Tuscany with the two violins and the cello just
> three days ago, and I can assure you that he has been so pleased with them that I
> could have never expected such great satisfaction. All his virtuous people (and he
> has many at his court) have approved the instruments, judging them perfect . . . I
> beg you to begin, as soon as possible, the manufacture of two violas, a *tenore* and a
> *contralto*. They are needed to complete the consort.[20]

Models for these violas, in the Stradivari archives of the Dalla Valle
Collection, are dated October 4, 1690, the date Stradivari probably
began work on the production of the Medici *tenore* and *contralto*.

These five Stradivari instruments were accurately described in
1700 in an inventory of instruments belonging to His Serene High-
ness Ferdinand, the Prince of Tuscany.[21] They were still at the Medici
Court in 1716.[22] Later, probably during the French invasion, two violins and the *viola contralto* disappeared. Recently one of the violins,
the famous "Tuscan," was given back to Italy. The *viola tenore* (Plate
25) and the cello are now on display in the *Museo del Conservatorio
di Musica Luigi Cherubini* in Florence.[23] The dimensions of the
Tenore are: length, 47.8 cm. (18 13/16 in.); upper bout, 21.9 cm. (8 5/8
in.); lower bout, 27.2 cm. (10 3/4 in.).

Leto Bargagna, in 1911, wrote this description of the Medici
Tenore:

> It is a stupendous instrument, one of the most perfect works made by Stradi-
> vari; it fills everyone fond of lutes with astonishment. I think we will never see
> anything finer. Even its exaggerated shape confers on the instrument a special
> majesty and extraordinary character. The yellow-golden varnish shines and
> gleams with lights which seem as though they are springing out of a living being.
> The whole manufacture is perfect, its design superb, the proportions of each
> single part are harmoniously matched.[24]

Members of the faculty of the *Conservatorio Cherubini* frequently play this masterpiece in concerts. Guest artists are invited,
from time to time, to play it. In 1954 Paul Doktor, the world famous
violist, played it in a concert which included music by Ariosti, Marcello, Vivaldi, Tartini, Nardini, and Locatelli.[25]

The *Tuscan Contralto*, now in the collection of Mrs. Cameron
Baird, is in the Library of Congress, and is available for use by artist
violists.

---

[20]Puccianti, *op. cit.*, pp. 15–16.

[21]*Ibid.*, p. 16.

[22]*Ibid.*, p. 16.

[23]*Ibid.*, p. 17.

[24]*Ibid.*, p. 17–18.

[25]See, *The Way They Play; Book I* (Neptune City, N.J.: Paganiniana Publications, 1972), p. 223,
for a photograph of Paul Doktor playing the Medici Tenor.

The two violas commissioned, according to the Hills, in 1707, for the Spanish court, if made, have been lost or destroyed. The two Spanish Court Violas made in 1696, however, exist today in Madrid. Herbert Goodkind, in a letter to the author dated May 30, 1976, wrote:

> The large 1696 Spanish Court viola made by Stradivari still exists. It reposes in El Placido Royal in Madrid, together with two Strad violins of 1707, and one cello of 1696. All four instruments are decorated—painted and/or inlaid with embellishments; the smaller viola, illustrated in *Iconography* on page 265, was somehow separated from this group at some previous time.

The famous Macdonald Strad viola, 1701, is presently played by Peter Schidlof in concerts given by the Amadeus Quartet.

The Library of Congress, in Washington, D.C., owns the 1727 *Cassavatti* Strad viola. It is available to soloists or string quartets that perform at the Library.[26]

Paganini's purchase of, and great admiration for, his Strad viola of 1731 (made when the great luthier was 86 years old) prompted the violinist to commission Berlioz to write a concerto for the viola. In response, Berlioz composed *Harold in Italy;* a work, however, that did not please Paganini, and which he did not play.[27] The Paganini viola is now owned by the Corcoran Gallery in Washington, D.C., and is part of the "Paganini Quartet" of Strad instruments.

The Gibson Strad viola, 1734, is perhaps the only Strad viola with the back cut on the slab. The dimensions are:

Body length — 40.95 cm. (16 1/8 in.)
Upper bout — 18.26 cm. (7 3/16 in.)
Lower bout — 24.   cm. (9 7/16 in.)

This viola was named for George Gibson, prominent English violist, who played it in Joseph Joachim's Quartet, when Joachim was in London. In recent years, it was played by William Primrose. Rolf Habisreutinger, of Flawil, Switzerland, has placed this viola, along with his nine other Strads, under the control of a foundation, which he established for permanent ownership.[28]

Present Values of Stradivari Violas

Deborah Rankin, a business and financial reporter for the *New York Times,* in a recent article entitled, "Early Violins, the Latest

---

[26]Goodkind, *op. cit,* p. 767.
[27]For more about Paganini and his viola, see Chapter XI.
[28]Goodkind *op. cit.,* p. 748.

Collectibles," described the rapidly rising prices of fine quality stringed instruments.[29] To gather information for her article, she interviewed several experts, including Jacques Français, the New York dealer. They discussed the Sotheby auction held in November of 1978, where the Baron Rothschild Stradivari cello brought $287,000, and the Yehudi Menuhin Guarneri del Gesù violin sold for $221,800. She reported that "a very important Stradivari violin, that would have sold for $35,000 in 1950, would sell today for $300,000, according to Français."

"Strad violas and cellos," Ms. Rankin continued, "command even higher prices, because there are fewer of them left." To corroborate her statement, she quoted Graham W. H. Wells, head of the Sotheby musical instrument department in London, who, commenting on these astronomical prices, stated, "Strad violas are like absolute gold-dust. A really fine Strad viola is worth a great deal more than its equivalent in a violin."

After discussing the inflated prices of instruments and bows made by other makers, Ms. Rankin concluded that the purchase of fine old stringed instruments constitutes more than acquiring a collector's item; barring possible fraud, the purchaser will probably be making a very good investment.

Dwindling Sales of Other Makers

As sales slackened, luthiers made fewer and fewer violas. Some of the most outstanding makers, including Joseph Guarneri del Gesù and Carlo Bergonzi, made no violas. The Hills illustrated this trend by citing an instrument made by David Tecchler (1666–1743), in which the maker wrote on the margin of the label for a viola made in 1730, "La terza viola." In forty years of constructing instruments, he had made only three violas![30]

The slow market for violas in Venice in the first half of the 18th century is confirmed by the production of Domenico Montagnana (1683–1756), who is believed to have made only three.[31] Another illustration of the decrease in viola production is evidenced by the total output of Johannes Baptiste Guadagnini (1711–1786), whose well-

---

[29]Deborah Rankin, "Early Violins, the Latest in Collectibles," *The New York Times* (January 14, 1979), Section 3, p. 2.

[30]Hill, Antonio Stradivari . . ., *op. cit.*, pp. 107–8.

[31]Lionel Tertis owned and played a Montagnana viola of 43.5 cm. (17 1/8 in.), which now belongs to Bernard Shore; the Chicago Symphony owns one, played by the Principal Violist, Milton Preves; the present location of the third is unknown to this writer.

travelled career included periods at Piacenza (1740–49), Milano (1750–58), Cremona (1758–9), Parma (1759–71), and finally Turin (1771–86). It is significant that in all of this time, he is known to have made only nine violas.[32]

The Bernard Zaslav J. B. Guadagnini Viola

A beautiful example of Guadagnini's Turin period is the ex-Villa viola (1781), now in possession of Bernard Zaslav, violist of the Fine Arts String Quartet[33] (Plate 26). This instrument was first owned by Signor Maurizio Villa of Turin; it next passed into the hands of Alfred Hobday of Bayswater, England; then Emil Ferir of Boston; next to William Feiffer of Detroit, and presently it is owned and played by Zaslov.

The Hill certificate,[34] made out to Alfred Hobday, Esq., and dated January 14, 1930, describes the viola as follows:

> The back, in two pieces, is of plain wood cut partly on the slab; that of the sides, cut on the quarter, is marked by somewhat handsome curl, the head being plain; the table of pine of fairly regular and moderately open grain, and the varnish, of soft texture, is of a red-brown color. This viola is an excellent example of the Turin period of the maker's work.

Bernard Zaslav has added this to the description:

> The modern adaptation of the neck was done in 1889 by Stephano Scarampella, whose label is also in the instrument. The excellent tonal quality of this viola is attested to by everyone who has heard it.[35]

The dimensions of this viola are:

Body length   — 40.16 cm. (15 13/16 in.)
Upper bout   — 18.42 cm. (7 1/4 in.)
Middle bout   — 13.34 cm. (5 1/4 in.)
Lower bout   — 23.18 cm. (9 1/8 in.)
Upper ribs   — 3.49 cm. (1 3/8 in.)
Lower ribs   — 3.65 cm. (1 7/16 in.)
String length — 36.83 cm. (14 1/2 in.)

---

[32]See Ernest N. Doring, *The Guadagnini Family of Violin Makers* (Chicago, 1949), photograph p. 284, text p. 285.

[33]In residence at the University of Wisconsin, Milwaukee.

[34]The Hill papers which accompany their Certificate of the ex-Villa viola include a letter to Mr. Hobday, which states ". . . Signor Maurizio Villa had in his possession a small collection of instruments concerning which he published a book, *I Mei Violini*, in 1888, few copies of which are extant. Your viola figures as an illustration therein."

[35]From a letter to the author dated November 26, 1978.

Plate 26. The ex-Villa Zaslav J. B. Guadagnini Viola.
Photographs furnished by Bein & Fushi, Chicago.

The body length of Guadagnini violas is almost a half-inch (1.27 cm.) shorter than those made by Andrea Guarneri, the length considered by many experts as the ideal measurement. Zaslav maintains that the beautiful sound of his instrument demonstrates that a viola's length is not the determining factor in its tonal sonority. He contends that the design, selection of wood, varnish, and attention to all of the many minute details related to making a viola constitute the factors that will determine the tonal quality. The resonant tone in all registers of Guadagnini violas seems to substantiate Zazlav's theory.

Music for the Viola

The first known published instrumental ensemble music to have a part specifically assigned to the viola appeared in 1597 in a work entitled *Sonata pian'e forte*,[36] one of sixteen pieces from the first book of *Sacrae Symphoniäe* by Giovanni Gabrieli (1557–1612). The *Sonata pian'e forte*, according to Gustave Reese,[37] was innovative in that it not only was one of the earliest known pieces to contain dynamic indications but was also among the earliest to designate precise instrumentation. Gabrieli's score calls for two "choruses": the first "chorus" (*Coro* I) contains a *zinc* or *cornetto* and three trombones; the second "chorus" (*Coro* II) is orchestrated for *violino* and three trombones. There can be no question that Gabrieli's *violino* part was for the viola since its range descends to the open C string (see Ex. 1). Boyden suggested that the word *violino* was a Venetian term, since it was used by Zarlino and Gabrieli, both Venetians.[38]

Ex. 1. Giovanni Gabrieli: *Sonata pian'e forte*

Violino (viola)

Bars 27-29   Bars 38-39   Bars 75-76, etc.

One *violino* against a *cornetto* and six trombones would appear to make a very unbalanced ensemble. Several factors should be considered, however, before a judgment is made regarding Gabrieli's ability as an orchestrator. The *zinc* or *cornetto* was a wooden instrument with a cup mouthpiece. It produced a much softer and less

---

[36]See A. T. Davidson and W. Apel (editors), *Historical Anthology of Music*, I, 1946, No. 173.
[37]Gustave Reese, *Music in the Renaissance* (New York: W. W. Norton, 1954), p. 551.
[38]D. Boyden. *History of the Violin*, p. 42.

strident sound than the modern cornet or trumpet. The tone-color and volume of the trombone at that time was more like the subdued sound of the medieval *sackbut* than the modern 20th century trombone. It was used to accompany voices in the church service at St. Mark's Cathedral, where Gabrieli played the first organ. Furthermore, Gabrieli probably intended the *violino* part for a large viola, which would have had more resonance than the modern instrument. Boyden also contended that Gabrieli may have doubled the *violino* part with more than one viola.[39]

The Italian Trio Sonata

The trio sonata, according to Erich Schenk, had its origin in northern Italy in the Lombard-Venetian School, centered around Venice, Brescia, Milano, Bergamo, and Verona.[40] Schenk cited early instrumental trios by Bianchieri (1601), Bellanda (1607), S. Rossi (1607), Gagliarde (1608), and B. Marini (1617); works that were the forerunners to later more highly-organized forms.

By the middle of the 17th century, composers farther south had adopted the trio sonata form, which was introduced to Modena by M. Uccellini in 1641 and to Bologna by M. Cazzati in 1657. From these cities, interest in the form spread throughout Italy, including Rome. It was in Rome in the 1680's that the trio sonata got its greatest impetus through compositions by Archangelo Corelli (1653–1713). Corelli wrote 48 trio sonatas which were published in four sets of twelve:

Op. 1 — *12 Suonate a tre, due violini e violoncello, col basso per l'organo.* Rome, 1681.

Op. 2 — *12 Suonate da camera a tre, due violini, violoncello e violone o cembalo.* Rome, 1685.

Op. 3 — *12 Suonate a tre, due violini e arciliuto, col basso per l'organo.* Rome, 1689.

Op. 4 — *12 Suonate a tre, due violini e violone o cembalo.* Rome, 1694.

Many composers of Italy, Germany, France, and England used the Corelli works as models for some of their compositions.

---

[39]*Ibid.*, p. 83.

[40]Erich Schenk, *The Italian Trio Sonata* (Köln: Arno Volk, 1955), p. 5.

The viola was not included as a participant in the trio sonata, which was usually written for two violins, or two flutes, or two cornettos, or two oboes and continuo. The title did not imply that performance was limited to three players; in fact, four or more instrumentalists would ordinarily be involved. The continuo, or figured bass, was performed by a keyboard instrument (harpsichord or organ), with a gamba, cello, bassoon, double bass, or bass lute usually doubling the bass line. The continuo did not imply the inclusion of the viola as it usually did in orchestral scores.

The omission of the viola from the trio sonata was an unfortunate development that retarded the progress of this instrument in many ways. Not only was the viola usually excluded from the most popular and most prevalent form of instrumental chamber music of the Baroque era, but also composers were failing to recognize it as a solo instrument.

The cello, on the other hand, was always welcomed as a part of the continuo. Late in the 17th century composers began to write solo pieces for the cello. Doménico Gabrielli (c.1640–90) composed two sonatas for cello and figured bass, probably before 1685, and in 1689, he produced *Ricercari per violoncello solo*. Gambatista degli Antonii composed his *Ricarate per violoncello*, Op. 1, in 1687; and Giovanni Battista Bononicini (c.1670–1747) wrote his *Sonatas per 2 violoncellos*, c.1695.

The Violin as a Solo Instrument

Early in the 17th century the preference of the Italians for the violin as a solo instrument precluded the choice of the viola by composers for their works. Three of the leading violin virtuosi, Marini, Fontana, and Farina, composed their own works, and were instrumental in popularizing the violin, almost to the exclusion of the viola and cello, as solo instruments.

Bagio Marini was born in Brescia in 1597, and died in Venice in 1665. His *Affetti musicali*, Op. I, includes the first known solo violin sonata.

Giovanni Battista Fontana, who was born in Brescia late in the 16th century, and who flourished from c.1610 until his death in 1630, was known as '*da Violini*.' His compositions exploited the pitch and technical range of the violin to a greater extent than most of the works written later in the 17th century by other composers.

Carlo Farina was born late in the 16th century in Mantua. His fame as a soloist resulted in his being invited to Dresden, where he became court violinist from 1625 to 1632, and later he held a similar appointment in Danzig, 1636–37. Thereafter, he returned to Italy. The date of his death is unknown. His most famous composition, *Capriccio stravagante* (1627), is probably the earliest program piece for the violin family featuring imitations of the mewing of cats, the barking of a dog, the crowing of cocks, the clucking of hens, and the sound of a drum and a trumpet.

Many fine Italian composer-violinists added to the quantity and quality of violin solo literature throughout the 17th century, a movement that culminated later in the works of Giuseppe Torelli (c.1650–1708), Archangelo Corelli (1653–1713), and Antonio Vivaldi (c.1675–1741). None of these masters composed any known solo works for the viola.

Viola Solo Literature

The first solo pieces for the viola were probably borrowed or adapted from the plentiful supply of compositions for the viola da gamba. Such borrowing was commonplace in the 17th and early 18th centuries. Very few works were written specifically for the viola as a solo instrument, probably because there were very few demands for viola solos. Zeyringer[41] mentions a *Viola Sonata* by the Venetian organist, Massimiliano Neri of 1651; and a work published in 1644 by the Florentine organist, Nicholaus à Kempis, *Sonata for Violin and Viola;*[42] and a *Sonata for Viola* by Carlo Antonio Marino, which appeared late in the 17th century.[43]

As mentioned earlier, the paucity of solo compositions for the viola in the 17th century can be attributed to the Italian predilection for the violin as a solo instrument. Gradually the cello took on more and more status as a solo instrument, and by the end of the century it had acquired a substantial solo literature. The viola, however, continued to be considered an accompanying instrument. It remained for the Germans and the Austrians in the 18th century to exploit the potential of the viola as a solo instrument.

The Viola in the 17th Century Italian Orchestra

There was no standardized instrumentation in the Italian Baroque orchestra of the early 17th century. The viola was sometimes

---

[41]Franz Zeyringer, *Literature für Viola* (Hartberg: Julius Schönwetter, 1976). p. 51.

[42]A modern edition of the Kempis duet was published in Berlin: Sirius-Verlag, n.d.

[43]A modern edition of the Marino work published in Vienna: Doblinger, 1960.

assumed to be a part of the continuo (figured bass) group. Occasionally there was a written part for the viola, which was usually divided into Viola I (alto) and Viola II (tenor) parts. The use of this instrument, however, varied from place to place, and from composer to composer. The continuo part might include a viola or violas, if the performing group was large enough to support the additional accompaniment; and if the continuo went below C, the violist would play an octave higher.

Early in the 17th century some composers were already writing special parts for the viola. Lorenzo Allegri (c.1573–1648) wrote a suite entitled, *Primo Ballo*,[44] scored for Violins I, II, and III, Viola (alto clef), Cello or Viola II (bass clef), and Continuo. The range of the Viola II part never goes below C, and the score designation suggests that the part could be played by either cello or viola, probably a large viola (tenor). Giacomo Carissimi (1604–1674) omitted violas in his oratorios, the orchestration being limited to two violins and continuo.

But the great bulk of orchestral music, outside of the opera, was the *Concerto grosso*, a format that evolved throughout the 17th century, and was finally codified by Corelli, Vivaldi, and others around 1700. Corelli's *12 Concerti grossi*, Op. 6, served as models for Locatelli, Geminiani, and even Handel, who heard these works when he was in Rome in 1709. The Corelli *Concerti grossi* were scored for *Concertante* (solo group) of 2 violins, cello, and keyboard; and a *ripieno* (orchestral group) composed of Violin I, Violin II, Viola, Cello, and Continuo.[45]

Not all composers followed Corelli's instrumentation, as can be seen by a perusal of the *Christmas Concertos* of Francesco Manfredini (1688–17?), Giuseppe Torelli (c.1650–1708), Giuseppe Valentini (c.1681–c.1740), Pietro Locatelli (1693–1764), and Giuseppe Tartini (1692–1770). In the 12 Concerti grossi of Corelli's Op. 6, only No. 8, had a title, *"fatto per le notte di Natale,"* indicating that it was to be performed on Christmas Eve. Other composers followed Corelli's lead and wrote Christmas Concertos. Torelli's *Christmas Concerto* (c.1700) was scored for 2 solo violins, and a *ripieno* of Violin I, Violin II, Viola, and Continuo. Valentini's work (1701) is for Violin I, Violin II, and Continuo, no solo instruments and no violas. Manfredini (1718) used the same instrumentation as Torelli. Locatelli

---

[44]This work appears in Herman Beck's *Anthology of Music, The Suite* (Cologne: Arno Voolk Verlag, 1966), pp. 76–80.

[45]The keyboard part of the *Concertante* group was usually played by a harpsichord for *Concerti grossi da camera*, and by organ for *Concerti grossi da chiesa*. The *Continuo* consisted of keyboard, cellos, gambas, and double bass, depending on availability.

Ex. 2.

Concerto grosso F moll.
(Aus „Concerti grossi", Op. 1; 1721.)*)

Pietro Locatelli (1693-1764).

(1721) scored for a solo group of Violin I, Violin II, Viola I, Viola II, and Cello; the *ripieno* group included Violin I, Violin II, Viola I, Viola II, Cello, and Continuo. Although the material is frequently doubled, Locatelli's writing for four parts was innovative (see Ex. 2). The example cited, in the second movement *(Grave)*, shows the independence of the viola parts in both the *Soli* (Concertino) and the *Tutti* (Ripieno), as contrasted with the filling-in material, typical of most compositions of that time. The Klavier part, realized from the continuo, and the dynamic markings, were added by Arnold Schering, the editor. The first modern printing of Locatelli's *Christmas Concerto* was by C. F. Kahnt, of Leipzig, in 1919. Tartini's *Sinfonia Pastorale* (before 1740) included two solo violin parts in the *concertante*, with a *ripieno* instrumentation similar to Corelli's.

A comparison of the above selected works does not indicate a trend in the scoring for the viola, but rather the diversification in its use by Italian composers from c.1700 to c.1740.

The Viola in Early Opera

Opera was introduced to the Western World in the city of Florence by performances of *Dafne* (1597) and *Euridice* (1600). The new art form, which combined music with theatrical representation, met with enthusiastic response. These initial attempts in opera were produced by the Florentine *Camerata*, a society of writers, poets, musicians, and scholars who were attempting to produce dramas in the same manner that they believed the ancient Greek plays had been performed.

The musical part of these and subsequent operas combined the efforts and talents of composers, singers, dancers, and instrumentalists. The instrumentalists and the instruments they played were cast in new roles that were to exert a tremendous impact on their futures. The instrumentalists had to improve and expand their performance techniques to meet the challenges of the opera's orchestral scores; by the same token, all present-day orchestral instruments owe much of their physical development and improvement to the demands and uses required by opera composers. Many of the instruments used in the early 17th century operas have been superseded by louder and more resonant instruments, a requirement necessitated when opera moved from the locale of the private salon to the much larger public theaters. The harpsichords, viols, lutes, recorders, cornettos, sackbuts and other baroque instruments were gradually replaced by the derivative instruments that we know today. The violin family ultimately replaced the lutes and viols and became the nucleus of the opera orchestra.

The almost immediate acceptance of opera as a popular form of entertainment soon resulted in performances in Mantua, Rome, Venice, and other Italian cities. After the opening of the first public opera house in Venice in 1637, the future success of opera was assured.

Monteverdi, himself a violinist from the city of Cremona, was perhaps the first to realize the resources and potential of the violin and to exploit it in his operas. In his first opera, *Orfeo*, presented in Mantua in 1607, he included parts in the score for a complete family of strings. In a succession of operas during the next thirty-three years, Monteverdi experimented with various instruments and combinations of instruments in an attempt to find instrumental color that would enhance the dramatic action on the stage. He found that the violin was one of the instruments that best suited his musical requirements. In his *Il ritorno d'Ulisse* (Ulysses' Homecoming), produced in Venice in 1641, Monteverdi scored parts for Violin I and II, Viola I and II, and Continuo.[46]

The use of the viola by other composers in the early and middle 17th century is difficult to trace accurately. Many of the early scores do not include specific parts for the viola. The viola, if used at all, was probably a member of the continuo group, in which case it would usually play an octave higher than the gamba, or cello, or bass viol.

Adam Carse traced the instrumentation of early opera orchestras and furnished lists of the various groups that played for particular performances.[47] He found that in operas premiered between 1600–50 the term *violins* is frequently found in the score, but the other string parts are usually assigned to lutes and viols; or, as in many scores, it cannot be definitely determined whether the parts were intended for a specific instrument or if they were to be played by strings and winds in unison. This ambiguity might also be due to the fact that it was easier to assign parts after the composer found out which instruments were available.

In the second half of the 17th century, there was a definite trend for Italian opera composers to write, as Monteverdi had done in 1641, in five parts for the string choir: Violin I and II, Viola I and II, and Continuo.

---

[46]Heinrich Besseler, *Zum Problem der Tenorgeige* (Heidelberg: Müller und Thiergarten, 1949), p. 8.

[47]Adam Carse, *The History of Orchestration* (London: Kegan Paul, Trench, Trubner & Co., Ltd., 1925), pp. 38–54.

One of the leading opera composers of the mid-17th century was Marc' Antonio Cesti (1623–1669), who had studied with Carissimi in Rome. But unlike his teacher, who was mainly a composer of oratorios, Cesti turned to the secular opera as a means of expression. His travels took him to Florence, Vienna, and Venice, where his operas were performed with great success. One of his operas, *La Serenata* (1662), included the following directions for instrumentation in the manuscript score:

> The Symphonies should be played in the French manner, by doubling the parts: six violins, four altos [violas], four basses [cellos], and one contrabass, one spinet *aigue* [an octave higher than standard pitch], a harpsichord, one theorbo, and one chitarrone.[48]

Cesti recommended that the accompaniment of arias be limited to a spinet with two registers, a theorbo, and a contrabass. The chorus, of eight voices, was to be accompanied by the same group, plus a bass viol and a spinet *aigue*. He concluded by saying that the *Sonatas* should be played by the entire orchestra.[49]

Cesti's reference to performing in the French manner has two connotations: (1) that there would be more than one player for each of the violin, viola, and cello parts; and (2) that there would be at least two separate parts for the violas.

Hellmuth Wolff,[50] who did extensive research in early Venetian opera, found that the viola was used in several ways in the late 17th century. He explained that the viola:

> ... was introduced into the orchestra of the 17th century as a kind of "filling-up" instrument. At first it was used as a subordinate instrument to support the second violins or the bass (in the higher octave), but was already also given its own part in Venice or appeared doubled (with two obbligato parts) in the opera orchestra.

Wolff cited specific operas and furnished musical examples in an appendix to his book[51] to illustrate the new uses and devices employing the viola as a solo, and as an accompanying instrument. Antonio Draghi, in his opera *Creso* (Vienna, 1678), used two violas effectively

---

[48]*The Larouse Encyclopedia of Music*, ed. by Geoffrey Hindley London: Hamlyn Publishing Group, 1971), p. 160.

[49]See Ch. IV, for more on the French instrumentation in the 17th century.

[50]See *Preface* to the full score to Georg Philipp Telemann's *Viola Concerto in G Major*, published by Bärenreiter.

[51]Hellmuth Christian Wolff, *Die venezianische Oper in der zweiten Hälfte des 17. Jahrhunderts. Ein Beitrag zur Geschichte der Musik und des Theatres in Zeitalter des Barock* (Berlin: Verlagsgesellschaft, 1937).

in the Concertante for the *Ritornello* of Act III;[52] and he used a viola quintet for accompaniment to an aria in Act II.[53]

Although most composers were scoring for two viola parts, Carlo Pallavincini, in his opera *Messalina* (Venice, 1680), reduced the viola to a single part, thus giving it more prominence than most composers had done previously. This is particularly true, according to Wolff, in the *Sinfonia* to *Messalina*.[54]

Two concertante violas were used for their emotional tone-color in the "Lament-Arias" of Pietro Andrea Ziani's *Il Candaule* (Venice, 1679), and also by Carlo Francesco Pollaroli in his opera, *Ororio* (Venice, 1692).

According to Wolff, the first appearance of the viola as a solo instrument, playing a "Sonata," occurred in *Le promesse degli Dei* (Venice, 1697), an opera by F. T. Richter.

The influence of Ventian opera not only touched Vienna, but reached as far north as Hamburg, where opera flourished at the beginning of the 18th century. The viola was given even more recognition in Hamburg operas than it had previously received in Venice.[55] Meanwhile Italian opera composers gave less attention to the viola, allowing it to return to the anonymity of a continuo instrument.

---

[52]*Ibid.*, Appendix, No. 19.
[53]*Ibid.*, No. 14.
[54]*Ibid.*, No. 67.
[55]See Ch. VI for more about the viola in Hamburg operas.

CHAPTER IV

THE VIOLA IN FRANCE AND ENGLAND DURING THE 17TH AND 18TH CENTURIES

The Viola in French Orchestras

Father Marin Mersenne, of the Franciscan Order of Minims, a correspondent with many of the greatest scientists of his era and a fellow student and friend of Descartes, published an encyclopedic treatise entitled, *Harmonie Universelle* (1636).[1] This included *Traité des instruments,* which illustrated and described all musical instruments used in France in the early 17th century. In *Livre IV* of the *Traité*, the section about stringed instruments, Mersenne was lavish in his praise of the violin and its potential:[2]

> ... And those who have heard the 24 Violons du Roy[3] swear that they have never heard anything more ravishing or more powerful [resonant]. Thus, this instrument is the most proper of all for playing for dancing as it is ideal for ballet and everything else. The beauties and graces that are practiced on it are so great in number that it can be preferred to all other instruments, since the varieties of bowing are so delightful sometimes that one regrets to hear the end, particularly when the performance includes left hand trills *(tremblements)* and mordents *(flattments)*, which lead the listeners to agree that the violin is the king of instruments.

In 1556 Jambe de Fer had listed the *haute contre* and *taille* as the French names of the alto (small viola) and tenor (large viola). Eighty years later, in 1636, Mersenne added a third member to the alto-tenor group, namely, the *quinte* or *cinquiesme*. This appears in his description of *les 24 Violons du Roy*, where he listed the number of players on each of the five parts in the king's ensemble.[4]

---

[1]Marin Mersenne, *Harmonie Universelle* ... (Paris: S. Cramoisy, 1636–37). The part pertinent to this study appears in the section entitled *Des instruments a chordes,* pp. 177–228, of *Livre quatriesme* of the *Traité des instruments.*

[2]*Ibid.*, p. 177.

[3]The *24 Violons du Roy* were established as the official court orchestra by Louis XIII in 1626.

[4]Mersenne, *op cit.*, p. 185.

78

6 *Dessus*	(Violins)
4 *Haute-Contre* or *Haute-Contre Taille*	(Violas and Tenors)
4 *Taille*	
4 *Quinte* or *Cinquiesme*	
6 *Basse*	(Cellos)

Mersenne, commenting on the three alto-tenor parts in *les 24 Violons du Roy*, stated that "the instruments of the middle" *(les parties du milieu)*, the *haute-contre, taille,* and *quinte,* although of different sizes, were tuned in unison to c g d' a'.[5] His grouping, "the instruments of the middle," was also referred to by other writers as "the filling-in instruments" *(les parties du remplissage).*[6]

The importance placed on the viola in the French court at that time is evidenced by the assignment of twelve, or one-half of the players in *les 24 Violons du Roy,* to the viola-tenor section. The three-part inner harmony produced by the assorted sizes of violas must have been one of the principal contributing factors to the "ravishing" and "powerful" sound described by Mersenne.

Following his listing and description of the instrumentation of *les 24 Violons du Roy,* Mersenne added that a different nomenclature prevailed for "the instruments of the middle" in ordinary ensembles outside the court.[7] The two outside parts, he explained, retained the same names, *dessus* and *basse*; however, the three inner parts [alto-tenors] were assigned the names *quinte, haute-contre,* and *taille,* resulting in the following designated order of parts:

Dessus:	Violin (soprano range)
Quinte or *Cinquiesme:*	Small Viola (high alto range)
Haute-Contre:	Large Viola (low alto range)
Taille:	Tenor (tenor range)
Basse:	Cello (bass range)

The *Dessus* part was written on the French violin clef (G clef on the bottom line); the *Quinte* on the soprano clef; the *Haute-Contre* on the mezzo-soprano clef; the *Taille* on the alto clef; and the *Basse* on the bass clef (Ex. 3).

The confusion of nomenclature for the three-part "instruments of the middle," as suggested by Mersenne's two different sets of terms,

---

[5] *Ibid.,* p. 180.
[6] James R. Anthony, *French Baroque Music* (New York: W. W. Norton, 1974), p. 10.
[7] Mersenne, *op. cit.,* pp. 186–9.

Ex. 3. Marin Mersenne: Clefs used by members of the violin family.

| Dessus | Quinte or Cinquiesme | Haute-Contre | Taille | Basse |

can best be clarified by reference to Michel Corrette (1709–95), composer and writer of music instruction books. In his *Méthode d'Alto,* published in 1782, or earlier, he explained that in Lully's time, opera music included three separate viola parts, entitled, *haute-contre, taille,* and *quinte,* all written on C clefs, with C located on the first, second, and third lines respectively. Corette used the same name-order for the three middle parts that Mersenne gave in his first list, the one associated with the music of the French court (Ex. 4).

Ex. 4. French court nomenclature and appropriate clefs for the violin family in Lully's time.

| Dessus | Haute-Contre | Taille | Quinte | Basse |

Many of the French opera and ballet scores of the 17th century do not specify the instrumentation, but use the word *violons* to indicate all of the string parts except the *basse-continue* as shown in the *Cadmus* score (see Ex. 5). If Corette's designations are used, the top staff of the *Cadmus* score would be for the *dessus;* the second staff from the top would be for the *haute-contre;* the third, the *taille;* and the fourth, the *quinte.*

Curt Sachs made it clear that the French terms *quinte, cinquiesme, haute-contre,* and *taille* designated parts, and are not the names of instruments.[8]

Jean-Baptiste Lully (1632–87), a very talented Italian violinist, dancer, composer, and impresario, arrived in Paris when he was only fourteen years old. By use of his talent, personality, ambition, and

---

[8]Curt Sachs, *The History of Musical Instruments* (New York W. W. Norton, 1940), p. 362.

Ex. 5. First page of score to the opera *Cadmus* (1673). Music by Jean-Baptiste Lully, libretto by Philippe Quinault.

scheming, he rapidly rose to the very top of the French court music. Dissatisfied with the attitude and sloppy playing of *les 24 Violons du Roy*, in 1656 he obtained permission from Louis XIII to organize an additional, smaller, and more select group, known as *les Petite Violons du Roy*.[9] This ensemble (comprised of seventeen string players, later enlarged to twenty-one, and by 1686, to twenty-four) was expertly trained by Lully to achieve his rigid performance standards. The King was so pleased with Lully's work that, in 1661, he named Lully *Surintendent de la Musique de la Chambre*. Lully's string or-

---

[9]James R. Anthony, *op. cit.*, pp. 8, 10.

chestra was so disciplined in bowing, in uniformity of fingerings, and in the playing of ornaments that this group became the envy of all the courts of Europe.

Lully's bowings, tempos, and ornamentations, although not written in the music, were a legacy that came to be called the French style (*à la Françoise*). The Lully influence went beyond the borders of France, so much so that the most authoritative descriptive account of the Lully style was written by the German organist and composer, Georg Muffat (c.1645–1704), who studied and observed Lully's music for six years in Paris. He recorded his observations in a preface ("La Premières observations sur la manière de jouer les airs de Ballets à la Françoise selon la méthode de feu Monsieur de Lully") to his two volume publication of his own suites for string orchestra, written in imitation of Lully's style.[10] The instrumentation, however, was for Violin I and II, Viola I and II, and Bass, which was a departure from Lully's older scoring for one violin and three viola parts. Muffat had probably witnessed Lully's experimentation with the use of two violins and two violas in the string choir.

There appears to have been no set instrumentation in French court orchestra music until almost the middle of the 18th century, when many scores began to specify two violin parts and either one or two viola parts. Jean-Marie Leclair (1697–1764) scored his *Concerti grossi* for three violins, viola, cello, and organ.

In the French scores of the late 17th and early 18th centuries, there is sometimes confusion regarding which parts are for violins and which are for violas. Adam Carse took the position that Lully's operas were scored for first and second violin, and first and second viola.[11] Jürgen Eppelsheim, however, who researched Lully's works for his doctoral dissertation, concluded that the second voice of a four- or five-part string choir "could well have been played on a viola, and not on a violin."[12]

Lully's colleagues and successors, Marc-Antoine Charpentier (1634–1704) and Paschal Colasse (1649–1709), continued to use five string parts in their operas, but the trend was already turning away

[10]Georg Muffat, *Florilegium primum* (Augsburg, 1695); and *Florilegium secundum* (Passau, 1698). Reprinted in Vol. I, 2 and Vol. II of *Denkmäler der Tonkunst in Oesterrich* (Vienna, 1894, 1895). Muffat's material on performance practice according to the Lully style is also contained in Vol. I of *Oeuvres completes de J. B. Lully 1632–1687*, edited by Henry Prunieres (Paris: Editions de la Revue Musicale, 1930–39).

[11]Adam Carse, *op. cit.*, p. 71.

[12]Quoted by Andrew D. McCredie, *Instrumentarium und Instrumentation in the North German Baroque Opera* (Published Ph.D. Dissertation, Hamburg University, 1964), p. 255. Eppelsheim's book is listed in the Bibliography of this book.

from this instrumentation. By the middle of the 18th century French orchestral music was more and more conforming to the generally accepted four-part writing of Violin I, and II, Viola, and Cello; and with a few rare exceptions, *les parties du milieu*, with the multiple viola parts, were a thing of the past.

The Viola in the Second-Half of the 18th Century

There was little French interest in the viola as a solo instrument until Karl and Anton Stamitz, the two German virtuosos from Mannheim, performed in Paris at the *Concerts Spirituels* in 1772, 1774, and 1778, and also published several compositions *d'Alto*.[13] At the same time composers of Parisian operas were giving more attention to the viola's tonal qualities as a means of heightening dramatic situations on the stage.[14] In c.1782, Michel Corrette published the first *Méthode d'Alto*, in response to an interest in, and a need for, an instruction manual for the instrument.[15] This was followed by a succession of printed tutors in Paris, signalling a new era of development for the viola, and its music, in the 19th century.

The Viola in 17th Century England

In England the viola was called the *tenor* or *mean(e)*. The name *tenor* indicated that it had the same range and usually doubled as the human tenor voice. The term *mean(e)* was used in England during the 15th through the 17th centuries to refer to instruments that played the middle parts.[16] Even after the large-size violas had become obsolete, the term *tenor* continued to be used and has persisted in England to the present day.

In 17th century England the very large tenors were sometimes tuned an octave lower than the violin. The smaller tenors were tuned to the same pitches as the present-day viola.

The violin was known in England as early as the latter part of the reign of Queen Elizabeth I (c.1600). By 1641 fourteen violinists were listed in the Royal Band, which numbered fifty-eight musicians. As early as the Commonwealth (1653), violinists were arriving in Eng-

---

[13]See Chapter VI, "Viola Music In Germany During the 18th Century."
[14]See Chapter VII, "The Viola in Opera in the Late 18th and Early 19th Centuries."
[15]See Chapter IX, "Instruction for the Viola."
[16]The term *mean(e)* was also used to indicate the two middle strings of lutes and viols.

land from the Continent. In a contest the English violinist, Davis
Mell, was defeated by the Swedish violinist, Thomas Baltzar. The
viola and other members of the violin family, however, did not enjoy
as much attention or success in England in the first half of the 17th
century as they did in Italy, Germany, and France. The popularity of
the viols did not leave much room for the other bowed instruments.
Furthermore, the internal political and religious strife, along with a
succession of wars, did little to nurture the growth of the arts.

Ultimately the general unrest in England led to the execution of
Charles I (1649) and the accession of Oliver Cromwell as Lord Pro-
tector of the Commonwealth (1653–58). Music was not stamped out by
the rigid policies of the Commonwealth, nor was it encouraged. Viol
music continued to flourish as the most acceptable form of string music.

Charles II (1630–85), forced into exile during the Commonwealth, was recalled to the throne in 1660. He had spent part of his
exile as a guest at Versailles, where he was greatly impressed with the
luxurious life at the French court, and, among other things, with the
presentation of opera, ballet, and other musical offerings. The instrumental music at Versailles had particularly impressed the new English monarch. As one of the ways of emulating the French court, he
activated two groups of his own, *The 24 Violins of the King*, patterned
after *les 24 Violons du Roy*, and a more selected group, *The Four and
Twenty Fiddlers* as his *Private Musick*, in imitation of Lully's *les
Petite Violons*.

Although Charles II did not introduce the violin family into England, his court orchestras gave a significant impetus to the promotion
of interest in instruments that had previously been held in low regard
by many of the discerning lovers of serious music. At the same time,
many amateurs of good taste were beginning to turn to the violin as an
instrument to play for their own enjoyment. No longer was this instrument to belong solely to the professional, who played for dancing,
or who was a member of a court ensemble.

The tenor was belatedly recognized as a respectable instrument,
as is attested by the succession of editions of a treatise published by
John Playford (1623–1686). The first edition of this work, entitled *A
Brief Introduction to the Skill of Musick, for Song & Viol*, published
in 1654, did not contain even a mention of the violin family. A third
enlarged edition, however, entitled *An Introduction to the Skill of
Musick*, brought out in 1658, contains a new added section, "Brief
Introduction to the Playing of the Treble Violin." This important addi-

tion constituted the first known printed English tutor for the violin.[17] But this edition did not include instructions for the viola or cello. The twelfth edition (1694) did contain some material about the viola; an enlarged chapter included brief but timely mention of the viola for those who might want to play it in consort with the violin and cello. Following his directions for tuning the violin, Playford continued:

> Having thus given you the Tuning of the *Treble-Violin*, it will be very necessary here to set down the Tuning of the *Tenor-Violin* and the *Bass-Violin*, being both used in consort. The *Tenor* or *Mean* is a larger Violin than the Treble, and is tuned five notes lower than the Treble; and the Cliff [sic] is put sometimes on the middle, and sometimes on the second line.

Playford's example (see Plate 27) not only supplements the above paragraph, but also was intended to demonstrate part of his method for tuning the tenor.

Theater music in England did not furnish the opportunities to violists that were to be found in the opera scores of Venice, Paris, Hamburg, and other centers of culture during this period. Although Matthew Locke (1632–77), in his operas *Psyche* (1673) and *The Tempest* (1675), did score for four-part string choirs, the tenor part, little more than a harmonic filler, was written in the mezzo-soprano clef. Henry Purcell (c.1659–95), in *Dido and Aeneas* (c.1677), wrote for violins I and II, viola and bass; and in *King Arthur* (1691) he used violins I and II, violas I and II, and bass in the Overture. In this latter opera, Purcell did not restrict the viola to doubling the tenor part, but gave occasional freedom that the viola had not previously enjoyed in English works. This is particularly true in the accompaniments to the choruses of *Dido and Aeneas.*

The viola was not included in the *Trio Sonata*, the new popular ensemble music form, that was first exported from Italy and then adopted by Purcell and other English composers as a format for many of their own compositions.[18] The result was decidedly favorable to increasing the popularity of the violin, accompanied by a corresponding decrease in the use of the viola.

The Viola in England During the 18th Century

In England during the 18th century, very little music was composed for the viola, or *tenor*. Francesco Geminiani (1687–1762),

---

[17]*An Introduction to the Skill of Musick* appeared in nineteen numbered editions and five or six unnumbered editions between 1654 and 1730.

[18]See "The Trio Sonata" in Chapter III.

the Skill of Muſick.

A BRIEF
INTRODUCTION
To the Playing on the
Treble-Violin.

THE *Treble-Violin* is a chearful and ſprightly Inſtrument, and much practiſed of late, ſome by Book, and ſome without; which of theſe two is the beſt way, may eaſily be reſolved: To learn to Play by *Rote* or *Ear*, without Book, is the way never to Play more than what may be gain'd by hearing another Play which may ſoon be forgot; but on the contrary, he which

F 4   Learns

An Introduction to

Having thus given you the *Tuning* of the *Treble-Violin*, it will be very neceſſary here to ſet down the Tuning of the *Tenor-Violin*, and the *Baſs-Violin*, being both uſed in Conſort. The *Tenor* or *Mean* is a larger *Violin* than the *Treble*, and is Tuned five Notes lower than the *Treble*; and the *Cliff* is put ſometimes on the middle, and ſometimes on the ſecond Line.

Example.

Tuning the Tenor-Violin.

Firſt String. 2d String. 3d String. 4th String.

A la mi re. D la ſol re. G ſol re ut. C fa ut.

Tuning the Baſs-Violin.

Firſt String. 2d String. 3d String. 4th String.

G ſol re ut. C fa ut. FF fa ut. BB mi.

Thus (after the plaineſt method I could) I have ſet down ſeveral *Rules* and *Directions* for the *Treble-Violin* by way of *Fretting*, which I have known uſed by ſome Eminent Teachers on this Inſtrument as the moſt facile and eaſie to Initiate their Scholars; and alſo *Directions* for Pricking down *Leſſons* in *Letters*; Yet I do not approve of this way of Playing by *Letter*, ſave only as a Guide to young Practitioners, to bring them the

more

Plate 27. Title Page of Playford's Instructions for "Playing on the Treble-Violin," and Page mentioning the *Tenor-Violin.*

William Herschel (1738–1822), William Flackton (1709–1793), and Benjamin Blake (1751–1827), nevertheless, did write significant works for the viola.

Francesco Geminiani, born in Italy and a student of Corelli, spent most of his adult life in London. His *Concerti Grossi* are of particular interest for violists, for he not only included the viola in the *ripienos*, but also in the *concertinos* of his Op. 7 (1746). The viola solo parts, it is true, made only modest technical demands and were musically unpretentious compared to the solo material assigned to the violins and cello. But these works must have met with some degree of success, because Geminiani later revised his *Concerti Grossi*, Op. 2, to include viola parts in the *concertinos*.

William Herschel, the renowned astronomer, was born in Hanover, Germany, in 1738. His parents took him to England in 1757, where he lived the rest of his life. Herschel's accomplishments in science, and particularly in the field of astronomy, have almost obscured the fact that he was also a musician. He actually began his adult life as a professional musician, being at the same time an amateur astronomer. At age 14 he played both the violin and the oboe, the latter well enough to be accepted into the band of the Hanoverian Guards. When his family moved back to Hanover, he decided to remain in England and try to make a career as a composer and organist. His most important position was as organist and choir director of the Octagon Chapel Church in Bath. For the next few years he held this position in the church, gave a few private lessons, composed, and at the same time pursued his second interest, astronomy.[19]

Before he adopted astronomy as a full-time profession, he wrote, among many other compositions, three concertos for viola:

Viola Concerto in C Major (no place or date indicated on the Ms).
Viola Concerto in D Minor, Maidstone, August, 1759.
Viola Concerto in F Major, London, October, 1759.

The *Concerto in F Major for Viola, Strings, and Cembalo* was performed at the Fifth International Viola Congress held in Rochester, New York, in 1977, with the solo part played by Robert Coleman, accompanied by the United States Chamber Orchestra, Lt. Lowell E. Graham, conductor. The overall reaction was one of mixed responses. Everyone was surprised to learn that the eminent astronomer had written 18 symphonies and 11 concertos—three of them for the viola,

---

[19]The event that catapulted Herschel into international fame as an astronomer was his discovery of the eighth planet, Uranus, on the night of March 13, 1781, a discovery that had eluded all of the professional astronomers, who supposedly had better telescopes than Herschel's home-made one.

one of which they had just heard. Otherwise the work was not particularly impressive. Most of the auditors would probably have agreed with Vincent Duckles,[20] who commented that the *Concertos* are not mature works, but are, nevertheless, significant. It was Duckles' opinion that the two *Viola Concertos* composed in the fall of 1759 lack depth and demonstrate technical shortcomings, but are impressive by their power and integrity.

Duckles saw in the scores some influence of the North German school, which culminated in the works of C. P. E. Bach. Duckles evaluated the Herschel *Concertos* as being ambitious works, experimental in the then new expressive *emfindsamer Stil*, but far removed from the rococo *galant*.

Herschel should not be condemned if his compositions lack polish and artistry. Rather he should be credited with having been the earliest known musician in England to write concertos for the viola.

William Flackton (1709–1793) was born and died in Canterbury, England, where he was an organist and composer of sacred music, and perhaps an amateur violist. His interest in the viola was demonstrated by the fact that one of his earliest sets of compositions, *Opus 2*, included works for the instrument. His *Opus 2* originally included six *Sonatas:* three for *Tenor and Continuo,* and three for *Cello and Continuo.*[21] The publication date is not known; the Baroque style of the works, however, and also the early opus number suggest a date not later than 1760, and possibly as early as 1740. The *Opus 2* eventually met with enough success to induce Flackton to add two more *Sonatas,* one for *Tenor* and one for *Cello,* which he published in 1770. These four *Sonatas for Tenor and General Bass* of *Opus 2* are the earliest known *Viola Sonatas* published in England:

> *Sonata in C Major,* No. 4, n.d.
> *Sonata in D Major,* No. 5, n.d.
> *Sonata in C Major,* No. 6, n.d.
> *Sonata in C Minor,* No. 8 (1770).

The format of the first three works is a mixture of church and chamber sonata; each has three movements, beginning with a slow one, followed by a fast one, and then concluding with a double *Minuetto.* The *Minuettos* are in two parts: *Minuetto I* is in the key of the other

---

[20]Vincent Duckles, "William F. Herschel's Concertos for Oboe, Viola, and Violin," *Festschrift Otto Eric Deutsch zum 80 Geburststag* (Kassel: Bärenreiter, 1963), pp. 66–74.

[21]A work of Flackton's in similar Baroque style was published by Walsh in 1758: *Six Sonatas for 2 Violins and Continuo.*

P R E F A C E.

THESE Solos for a Violoncello were compofed originally for the Ufe of a young Gentleman, and are now publifhed on a Prefumption of their Utility to all young Practitioners in general.

The Solos for a Tenor Violin are intended to fhew that Inftrument in a more confpicuous Manner, than it has hitherto been accuftomed; the Part generally allotted to it being little more than a dull Ripiano, an Acceffory or Auxiliary, to fill up or compleat the Harmony in Full Pieces of Mufic ; though it muft be allowed, that at fome particular Times, it has been permitted to accompany a Song, and likewife to lead in a Fugue; yet even then, it is affifted by one, or more Inftruments in the Unifons or Octaves, to prevent, if poffible, its being diftinguifhed from any other Inftrument ; or, if it happens to be heard but in fo fmall a Space as a Bar or two, 'tis quickly over-powered again with a Crowd of Inftruments, and loft in Chorus.

Such is the Prefent State of this Fine Toned Inftrument *, owing, in fome Meafure, to the Want of Solos, and other Pieces of Mufic, properly adapted to it †.

The Author takes this Opportunity of acknowledging his particular Obligations to Mr. ABEL, for infpecting this Work in Manufcript before it went to the Prefs; the Publication of which, it is hoped, may be productive of other Works of this Kind from more able Hands ‡, and eftablifh a higher Veneration and Tafte for this excellent, tho' too much neglected Inftrument.

The greateft Mafters allow the Tenor Violin to have a particular Delicacy of Tone.
† *Upon Enquiry at all the Mufic Shops in London for Tenor Solos, none were to b found, neither was it known by them that any were ever publifhed.*
‡ *Since this Work was printed, feveral Publications have appeared, intitled, Quar tettos and Quintettos, wherein a much greater Regard is paid to the Tenor than ufua and confidering the prefent growing Attention given to it, by the moft eminent Compofer little Doubt is to be made of feeing it foon rank amongft the firft Clafs of Inftruments.*

Plate 28. William Flackton: Preface to *Solos for a Tenor Violin*.
Courtesy of The British Library

movements; *Minuetto II* is in the parallel minor key. *Sonata No. 8 in C Minor* is in four movements: *Adagio, Allegro, Siciliano,* and *Minuetto.* All movements are in the tonic key except the *Siciliano,* which is in the dominant key of G Minor.

Flackton's *Preface* to the original edition of *Opus 2,* including his footnotes, is given in its entirety because of the important information it furnishes regarding viola music in London at that time (see Plate 28):[22]

It is of interest that the second footnote of the "Preface" states that there was no printed solo music for viola available in London. Flackton decided to remedy this situation "and establish a higher Veneration and Taste for this excellent, tho' too much neglected Instrument."

English interest in the viola is further demonstrated by the publications of Benjamin Blake. His compositions included three albums, each with *Six Duets for Violin and Tenor,* published in 1780, 1782, and 1785; a *Duo for Violin and Tenor,* Op. 7, 1790; and *3 Solos for Tenor and Cello,* Op. 9, c.1795.

English Luthiers

Few violas were made by English luthiers in the 18th century. The best instruments came from the shops of Daniel Parker (1705–61), Peter Wamsley (1715–51), Benjamin Banks (1727–95), and William Forster (1739–1808). All made their instruments in London except Banks, who opened his shop in Salisbury after having apprenticed in London.

Parker's earliest productions were modeled after Amati; then he became the first English maker to fashion his instruments on the Stradivari pattern.

---

[22]The Mr. Abel mentioned by Flackton in his "Preface" was Carl Friedrich Abel (1725–87), violist and renowned virtuoso of the viola da gamba. Abel's musical training had been with his father and with J. S. Bach. He went to London in 1759, where he later was employed as chamber musician to Queen Charlotte in 1765. Copies of the original publication are in the British Museum Library and in the Library of the Conservatorio St. Cecilia in Rome. Modern editions of the Flackton *Sonatas* have been published by Doblinger, edited by Renzo Sabatini (1960), and by Schott, edited by Walter Bergman (1942 and 1966).

Wamsley copied Stainer patterns when he first opened his atelier, but soon changed to Strad patterns. His few remaining violas are much sought after.

Banks, who had apprenticed with Wamsley, made several large-sized violas, which had excellent sonority of tone. They were modeled after works of Stainer and also the "grand pattern" of Nicolo Amati. The violas made by his sons, Benjamin II and James, were not the equal of those made by their father.

Forster, who made instruments for the private band of George III, produced particularly fine violas and cellos. His violas were usually barely over 15 in. (38.1 cm.) in body length, but had deep ribs. He copied the Stainer pattern for a while, but switched to Brothers-Amati and Nicolo Amati models for his later productions.

Until recently dealers sometimes found it difficult to dispose of instruments made by English makers. As a result many of the finest English violas were sold with Italian labels. Parker, Wamsley, Banks, and Forster are, finally in the 20th century, receiving the recognition they so justly deserve.

The demand for fine instruments in the late 18th century attracted several foreign born makers to open shops in London, most notably the Italian luthier, Vincenzo Panormo, who was born in 1734, in Monreal, near Palermo, and died in 1813, in London. He may have apprenticed with Carlo Bergonzi in Cremona. He opened a shop in Paris in 1760, and moved to London in 1772, where his instruments, which were patterned after those of Bergonzi and Stradivari, earned him an international reputation. The Panormo viola (1813), shown in Plate 29, is a small model—a size which was popular in London and Paris at that time—with the following dimensions:

> String length — 37.8 cm. (14 7/8 in.)
> Body length — 39.4 cm. (15 1/2 in.)
> Upper bout   — 18.5 cm. (7 1/4 in.)
> Middle bout — 12   cm. (4 3/4 in.)
> Lower bout   — 23.2 cm. (9 1/8 in.)

Vincenzo had two sons who were luthiers in England: Joseph Panormo (1773–1830), and George Louis Panormo (1774–1842). The latter turned to bowmaking, a craft in which he excelled. His viola bows are in great demand.

Plate 29. The James Panormo Viola, 1813.
Photographs furnished by Dr. Jan James, of Amsterdam, Netherlands.

England did not produce violists or viola music of the quality and quantity emanating from Germany during the 18th century; nor were the violas made there of the superlative standard of the Italians. There was, nevertheless, activity in the field of original composition; and in the craft of viola-making. English violists would not have their greatest period until the 20th century.

CHAPTER V

THE VIOLA IN GERMANY DURING THE 17TH CENTURY

Viola Material in German Treatises

Michael Praetorius (1571–1621) was a highly respected German organist, composer, and writer. During his illustrious life, he became director of music at both the chapel of the Duke of Braunschweig-Wolfenbüttel and at the Duke's court in Groningen. He was one of the most prolific composers of his time, producing over a thousand sacred and secular works. His most significant opus as a writer is the treatise *Syntagma Musicum* (1618–20). It contains a section entitled *De Organographia*,[1] which is devoted to the tunings, range, dimensions, tone-quality, and other aspects of all of the musical instruments of the early 17th century. Included is an Appendix of forty-two woodcuts depicting these instruments.

Praetorius named and furnished the tunings for all of the members of the *Viole de Braccio* or *Geigen* family, as they were known at that time (see Praetorius' Table 22).

---

[1]Michael Praetorius, *op. cit.* See Harold Blumenfeld's "Preface" to his English translation of Volume II, *De Organographia* (Kassel: Bärenreiter, 1962), p. 1.

Praetorius' Table 22—Tunings for Members of the *Viole de Braccio,* or *Geigen* (Violin) Family.

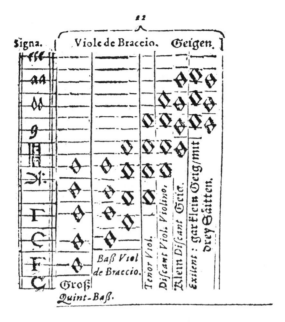

In the text, and in his illustrations, slightly different names and spellings appear (possibly engraver's errors). The following list furnishes the pitch relationships of the tunings of the instruments as shown in Praetorius' Table 22:

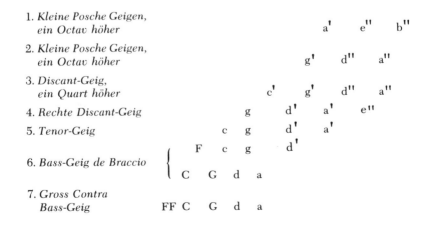

1. *Kleine Posche Geigen,*
   ein Octav höher   a^1 e^{11} b^{11}

2. *Kleine Posche Geigen,*
   ein Octav höher   g^1 d^{11} a^{11}

3. *Discant-Geig,*
   ein Quart höher   c^1 g^1 d^{11} a^{11}

4. *Rechte Discant-Geig*   g   d^1 a^1 e^{11}

5. *Tenor-Geig*   c   g   d^1 a^1

6. *Bass-Geig de Braccio*   { F   c   g   d^1
                               { C   G   d   a

7. *Gross Contra*
   Bass-Geig   FF C   G   d   a

Numbers 1, 2, and 3 of the above list are now obsolete. Number 4, *Rechte Discant-Geig,* is our present-day violin. Number 5, *Tenor-Geig,* is a small viola. Number 6, *Bass-Geig de Braccio,* has two tunings: the first, or high tuning, is a fifth lower than the *Tenor-Geig* and probably was a very large viola. The second, or low tuning, is an octave lower than Number 5 and corresponds to cello tuning. The term *Bass-Geig de Braccio* is somewhat confusing since some of these instruments may have been too large to be played "on the arm." The implication is that they belonged to the *Viole de Braccio,* or Geigen, family.[2]

The large tenor with the F c g d' tuning, although perhaps too large to be played "on the arm," may not have been played between the knees, "gamba style," either. From paintings and prints it appears that other positions were also used. Bernard Picart, in a print published in 1701, shows a musician playing a large tenor, or small cello, with the bottom of the instrument resting on a stool (see Plate 30). Paintings by Hans Mielich (1516–1573), of Munich, and Antonio Gabbiani (1652–1726), of Florence, also furnish pictorial evidence of how the large tenor violas were held and played. Sometime between 1565 and 1570, Mielich painted Orlando di Lasso[3] seated at the

Plate 30. Bernard Picart, 1701: Print of a Musician Playing a Large Tenor or Small Cello.

---

[2]*Loc. cit.*

[3]Orlande de Lassus (1530/32–1594), one of the greatest of the Netherlands composers, served in Sicily, Milano, Naples, Rome, Antwerp, and ultimately Munich (1556–94), where he became kapell-meister to Duke Albert V of Bavaria. He wrote more than 2,000 compositions.

harpsichord conducting the Bavarian Court Orchestra (Plate 31). Three performers of large tenors are depicted: the one in the right foreground is seated in front of the harpsichord; a second violist is standing on the left behind the gambist; and a third is standing immediately to the right and behind the harpsichord. The latter violist is shown holding his instrument crosswise to his body. His instrument is larger than the other two tenors, and probably corresponds with the instrument Praetorius identified as *Bass-Geig de Braccio* (high tuning). The other two musicians hold their tenors in a slanted downward position. Almost a century later Gabbiani, in a painting entitled "The Concert," included two performers of large tenors who also hold the instrument at a downward angle (Plate 32).

Violists could play the large tenors with body lengths up to 51 cm. (20 in.) comfortably with the scroll pointed downward. Their elbows rested on their chests, thus helping to avoid fatigue. The musical demands of the 16th and 17th centuries only occasionally took the tenor player out of the first position, and rarely beyond the third.

It is apparent from the tunings in Praetorius' treatise that the violin family at that time was an extensive aggregate of instruments. The various sizes suggest that the whole family was still modeled after the older chest of viols, whose contents varied from country to country and from household to household.

In addition to Praetorius, the following 17th century German writers also included some descriptive, didactic, and performance practice information in their publications on the playing of stringed instruments: Daniel Hizler (1575–1635),[4] Athanasius Kircher (1602–1680),[5] Johann Andreas Herbst (1588–1666),[6] Georg Falck (c.1630–1707),[7] Daniel Merck (?–?),[8] and Daniel Speer (1636–1707).[9]

With the exception of Speer, these writers furnished very little material on the viola, except to imply that it was played like the violin. They did, however, include explanations of clefs and tunings used for the alto and tenor. This information indicates that the tenor was not

---

[4]Daniel Hizler, *Extract Auss der Neuen Musica oder Singkunst*...(Nürnberg: A. Wagenmann, 1623).

[5]Anthanasius Kircher, *Musurgia universalis sive ars magna consoni et dissoni* (Rome: Corbelletti, 1650).

[6]Johann Andreas Herbst, *Musica Moderna Prattica*...(Franckfurt am Mayn: George Müller, 1658).

[7]Georg Falck, *Idea boni cantoris*...(Nürnberg: W. M. Endter, 1688).

[8]Daniel Merck, *Compendium Musicae Instrumentalis Chelicae*...(Augsburg: Johann Christoph Wagner, 1695).

[9]Daniel Speer, *Grund-richtiger kurtz liecht and nöthiger Unterricht der musicalischen Kunst*...(Ulm: G. W. Kühnen, 1697).

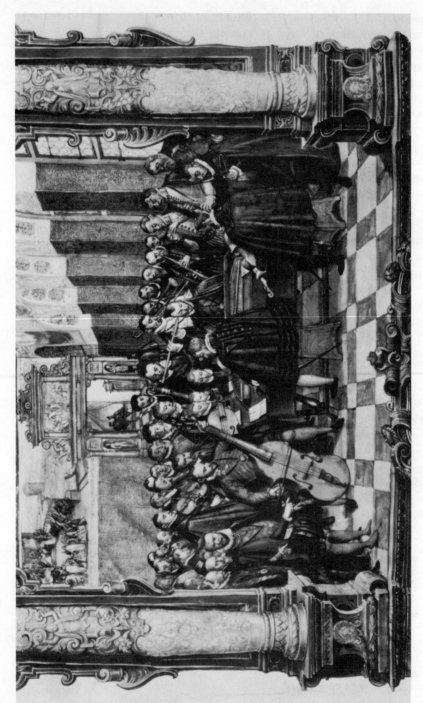

Plate 31. Hans Mielich: Painting of Orlando di Lasso and Orchestra.

Plate 32. Antonio Gabbiani (1652–1726): *The Concert.*

only responsible for a separate part in the ensemble, but also that at least some of the tenors were tuned to a lower pitch than the alto. Of particular interest is the multiplicity of names and spellings the German writers used for the viola (see Glossary I).

Hizler's treatise is primarily an instruction book for the singer. The "Appendix," however, contains brief instructions for playing the lute and members of the violin family. The instructional material for the violin family is limited to a wood-cut depicting a fingering chart of the violin.[10] The alto and tenor members of the violin family are mentioned only by their names, tunings, and clefs (Ex. 6).

Hizler's tenor was tuned a fifth lower than the viola, which would indicate that it was a very large viola—probably the same instrument listed as *Bass-Geig de Braccio* (high tuning) by Praetorius.

Ex. 6 Daniel Hizler: Viola tunings

Die Alt Geigen   Die Tenor-Geigen

---

[10]Hizler, *op. cit.*, p. 80.

Kircher's treatise is an elaborate work on the theory of music and instruments; it also contains canons and other compositions. Among the compositions is a *Symphonia pro chelybus* (Symphony of Violins) scored for *Duoi Violini, Alto e Basso di Viola* (Two Violins, Alto Viola, and Bass Viola).[11] The designation "Bass Viola" probably indicates a large tenor viola or a small tenor cello, since the part is written on the tenor clef. In the text, Kircher refers to this part as being for a *Basso Violone*. If he had intended it for the cello or the double bass, he would have probably scored it on the bass clef, as was customary at that time (see Ex. 7).

Ex. 7. Athanasius Kircher: Excerpt from *Symphonia pro chelybus*

Lib. VI. De Musica Instrumentali.   489

[Violin I]

[Violin II]

[Viola]

[Tenor ?]

Herbst's *Musica Moderna*, like the work by Hizler, is a singing manual. It contains material for accompanying instruments, including "many ornaments and variations to use especially for violins and cornets." His material for the viola is indeed brief:

> Viola di Braccio oder Brazzo—is eine Handgeige/die man auff den Armen halt.[12]

Falck's singing manual also contains some material for the accompanying instruments. His violin instructions are for the beginner or amateur, and not for the German virtuoso of that period (1688). Of special interest is Falck's recommendation of the French bow grip, in

---

[11]Kircher, *op. cit.*, pp. 487–8.
[12]Herbst, *op. cit.*, p. 76.

which the thumb is held under the hair. He also mentioned the occasional use of the sixth position, which would have taken the violinist
to the very end of the short fingerboard then in use. Falck's material
for the viola is conspicuous by its absence. His only direct reference
was by name, *Viola Braccio*, and by clef designations, using both alto
and tenor clefs.[13]

Merck's book is the first known German tutor published specifically for the violin family. The instructional material consists of
twenty-one pages. He made it clear that his *method* was not intended
for artists, but rather for students and beginners; "it does not include
instructions for *spiccato* and *harpeggiato*, techniques used by such
virtuosos as Herr von Biber, Herr Walther, and Herr Westhoff." Merck
discouraged the student from patronizing the teacher who charged the
lowest fees, since "it is far better to pay for a good teacher than to
employ a bungler *(stumpler)*."[14]

Merck's tutor illustrates the multiplicity of names for the viola in
Germany at that time (1695). It lists the usual tuning, c g d' a' and
explains that this tuning is for an instrument variously known as *Violetta*, *Viola vel Secunda*, *Soprano Viola*, *Cantus*, or *Französisch
Haute Contre*. Music for the *hohe Alt* and the *Französisch Taille*, the
book continues, is written on the mezzo-soprano clef, whereas the
ordinari Alt (regular viola) and the *Violas 1, 2*, and *3*, also known as
the *Französisch Quinte*, all use the alto clef. The list of names is
concluded with the statement that "the *Tenor*, also called *Viola*, plays
music written on the tenor clef."[15] Merck's reference to the *Viola 1, 2,
and 3*, "also known as the *Französisch Quinte*," is identical to Mersenne's three "instruments of the middle," and is obviously a reference to the French orchestral scoring for violas at that time.

Coming at the end of the century (1697), Speer's work from the
standpoint of the viola history, is second in importance only to
Praetorius' treatise. Speer gave the usual basic instructions on tuning
and clefs, and then presented two trio sonatas for two violas and continuo, *Sonata in F Major* and *Sonata in A Major*.[16] Both *Sonatas*
consist of two short movements, with the range of the higher part
remaining in the first position throughout. The Viola II player is required to read in both alto and tenor clefs, the latter one because, in
the low range, additional leger-lines would have been needed beneath the staff.

---

[13]Falck, *op cit.*, p. 189.

[14]Merck, *op. cit.*, sig. C2 (recto).

[15]Merck, *op. cit.*, sig C3 (verso).

[16]Speer, *op. cit.*, pp. 199–205.

Speer did not intend these *Sonatas* for professional violists, nor were they for beginners. Rather, they were for amateur violists, or for students who had mastered the basic techniques of bowing, fingering, and counting. The *Sonata in A Major* (Ex. 8) has only two sharps in the signatures of the viola parts. All three parts include *G♯*'s as accidentals. The continuo part *(Violon)* is not realized in *Example 8*, but is furnished just as it appears in Speer's treatise.

In the introductory material to the *Sonatas*, Speer stated that these works could also be played by viola da gambas. This mutual use of music by violas and viola da gambas was evidently commonplace by Speer's time, and perhaps earlier. This suggests that violists who wanted to play chamber music could choose from the abundant viola da gamba trio sonata literature.

Ex. 8. Daniel Speer: Excerpt from *Trio Sonata in A Major* for 2 Violas and Violon (Bass)

German Viola Music in the 17th Century

In the 17th century Germany consisted of many independent states, each with its own court vying to exceed the others in achieving political and intellectual prestige. The more affluent courts could afford the luxury of supporting a private group of professional musicians. The court of Saxony at Dresden imported the Italian violinist Carlo Farina of Mantua from 1625 to c.1632. His virtuoso pyrotechniques and his programmatic compositions, exploiting the violin's tonal and technical potential, influenced and inspired succeeding generations of native Germans in Dresden. Farina's best known composition, *Capriccio Stravagante*, printed in 1628, was scored for *Canto* (violin), *Alto* (small viola), *Tenor* (large viola), and *Basso* (cello).[17]

Johann Hermann Schein (1586–1630), who preceded J. S. Bach at the Thomasschule in Leipzig by an entire century, was one of the pioneers who introduced the new Italian monodic and instrumental styles into Germany.

His *Suite in G Major Canto, Quinta, Alto,* and *Tenore* is in five movements: *Padouana, Gagliarda, Courente, Allemande,* and *Tripla.* Hermann Beck included this composition in his book, *The Suite,*[18] but did not interpret the names of the instruments or the assignment of the parts in conformity with the standard practice of the early 17th century. His listing is: *Cantus* (violin I), *Quinta* (violin II), *Alto* (violin III), and *Tenore* (viola). He based his selection on the clefs used. The first three parts are written in the treble clef, and the *Tenore* is written in the alto clef. In spite of the clefs, Schein probably intended that this *Suite* be played by either one violin and three violas, or by two violins and two violas. Schein, himself a cantor as well as a composer of choral and organ works, would have justified the term *Cantus* as applying to the most important part. The terms *Quinta* and *Alto* were used in both Italian and French music to designate the viola. Only the *Tenore* part goes low enough to necessitate the alto clef.

Before the end of the 17th century, the courts of Saxony, Vienna, and Salzburg had native violin talent equal to the best Italian performers. In Saxony Johann Jacob Walther (1650–1717) and Johann Paul von Westhoff (1656–1705) were especially cited by their con-

---

[17]Gustav Beckmann, *Das Violonspiel in Deutschland vor 1700.* (Leipzig: N. Simrock, 1918), Appendix, No. 3.

[18]Hermann Beck, *The Suite* [from *Anthology of Music,* edited by K. G. Fellerer] (Cologne: Arno Volk, 1966), pp. 108–12.

temporary Daniel Merck for their artistry.[19] In Vienna, the chapel
violinist and composer, Johann Heinrich Schmelzer (c. 1623–80), established a school of violin playing which achieved international re-
nown. Schmelzer may have been the teacher of Heinrich J. F. von
Biber (1644–1704), who founded the German school of violin playing
in Salzburg, the school that later produced Leopold Mozart, father of
Wolfgang.

German music for the viola usually placed the instrument merely
in an accompanying role; several examples cited by Gustav Beckmann,[20] however, show that it sometimes enjoyed more than an
anonymous part in the continuo. He included a few bars of
Schmelzer's *Sonata Violino Solo cum Braccia*, a work in six parts, for
violin solo, four violas, and continuo. Another work by Schmelzer
which contains significant viola parts is his *Sacroprofanus concertus
musicus* (1662), a compilation consisting of sonatas for violin, viola,
and trombone.

Sheila M. Nelson discussed a work by Biber entitled *Sonatas tam
aris quam aulis* (1676) for two violins and four violas.[21] She pointed
out that the lowest viola part is written in the bass clef and goes below
the regular viola range, adding that this part may have been played on
a cello. But since the part is marked for viola, it seems much more
likely that it was played by the *Bass-Geig da Braccio* tuned to F c g d',
as described by Praetorius;[22] or on the *Tenor-Geigen*, with the same
tuning, mentioned by Hizler.[23]

Trio Sonatas

Wolfgang Sawodny, in "The Development of the Viola Sonata
from the Baroque until the early Romantic Period,"[24] pointed out that
trio sonatas including a part for viola, although rare, did exist in the
second half of the 17th century. He specifically cited works by Heinrich H. F. von Biber (1644–1704), Johann H. Schmelzer (1623–80),
Antonio Bestal (c.1605–69), D. Woja (?–1680), and six anonymous trio
sonatas. The Woja *Sonata*, Sawodny added, includes the interesting

---

[19]Merck, *op. cit.*, sig. C (recto).
[20]Gustav Beckmann, *op.cit.*, Appendix, No. 18.
[21]Sheila M. Nelson, *The Violin and Viola* (New York; W. W. Norton, 1972), p. 48.
[22]Praetorius, *op. cit.*, p. 26.
[23]Hizler, *op. cit.*, p. 85.
[24]Wolfgang Sawodny: a paper read at the 4th International Viola Congress held in Bad Godesburg, West Germany, 1976.

advice, "Zweyett Violin müss eine Brazzen gespielt werden, des Lieblichtert willen." (If the second violinist plays a viola, it will be delightful.)

Conclusion

By the end of the 17th century the viola was receiving more attention and prestige in Germany than in any other country. This interest and prestige laid the foundation that produced the earliest important solo music for the instrument in Hamburg, Cöthen, Berlin, and other German cities in the 18th century.

CHAPTER VI

THE VIOLA IN GERMANY AND AUSTRIA DURING THE 18TH CENTURY

The role of the viola in German orchestral music of the early 18th century is briefly described in treatises by Johann Mattheson (1681–1764), Johann Eisel (1698–175?), Johann Gottfried Walther (1684–1748), and Joseph F. B. C. Majer (1689–1768). Mattheson, a Hamburg cantor, composer, and writer of books about music, in his *Das Neu-eröffnete Orchester* of 1713, described and evaluated the role of the viola:

> The instrument filling in the middle parts [*die füllende*], the Viola, Violetta, Viola da braccio or Brazzo, is of larger structure and proportion than the violin, otherwise of the same family, except that it is tuned to c, g, d', a'. It serves for all the middle parts, . . . and is one of the most necessary constituents of a harmonious concert. For where the middle parts are missing the harmony will be wanting, and where they are indifferently filled all will be dissonant.[1]

Mattheson defined the terminology used in orchestral scores for the division of the *füllende* parts.

> The *viola prima* is responsible for the high and real alto range, and the *viola secunda* is like the French *taille* or tenor part.

Mattheson's reference to "the high and real alto range" indicates that the *viola prima* combined the two upper viola parts found in French writing of the Lullian period, resulting in a total of two viola parts as compared to three used by Lully.

The use of the viola as a solo and accompanying instrument was also commented upon by Mattheson:

> Sometimes a virtuoso will play the Braccio solo, and now and again whole arias are composed with the Violetta in unison, which, because of the low compass of accompaniment, sounds very unique and pleasant.

---

[1]Johann Mattheson, *Das neu-eröffnete Orchester oder gründliche Anleitung* (Hamburg, 1713), p. 283.

J. G. Walther, renowned composer and musicologist, offered a similar definition in his *Lexicon* (1732), describing the viola tersely as: "eine Geige zu Mittel-Partei," adding as an alternative that all middle parts could be played 'auf Braccien oder kleine Viole da Gamba."[2]

J. P. Eisel, a jurist, composer, and cellist, in a book entitled *Musicus Autodidaktos*, wrote that the viola not only was used for filling in the middle harmonies, but also served as a solo instrument in the concertos of "the famous Kapellmeister Telemann."[3]

Joseph F. B. C. Majer, a musician and author from Schwäbisch Hall, wrote a book entitled, *Neu-eröffneter theoretisch- und pracktischer Music-Saal* (1741).[4] Like the other writers he described the viola as a *füllende* instrument (see Plate 33).

Music for the Viola

In Germany, both the Italian trio sonata and the gradual change from five- to four-part harmonization had an adverse effect on the development of the viola as a solo instrument, just as it had in Italy and in other countries. It did, however, have a greater development in Germany in the 18th century than in any other country; although, even here, its rise was sporadic and limited geographically to several German cities, as was its music to a few composers.

In the historical development of viola music in Germany, the most prominent cities were Hamburg, with its flowering German opera; Berlin, with its court of Frederick the Great, which fostered excellence in music generally; Mannheim, with its fine orchestra; and Vienna, with its cultural and intellectual influence on the arts.

Composers who aided the cause of the viola were Reinhard Keiser, of the Hamburg Opera; Georg Philipp Telemann, one of the most prolific of German composers; Johann Sebastian Bach, who, besides all else, was also a violist; Johann Stamitz and sons, Karl and Anton, of Mannheim, all of whom played the instrument and wrote for it; Haydn, Mozart, and many others of Vienna, where the environment was conducive to creating all kinds of music, including solo music for the viola.

---

[2] Johann Gottfried Walther, *Musikalisches Lexikon oder Musikalische Bibliothek* (Leipzig, 1732), p. 637.

[3] Joseph P. Eisel, *Musicus Autodidaktos* (Erfurt, 1738), pp. 37–39.

[4] Joseph F. B. C. Majer, *Neu eröffneter theoretisch- und pracktischer Music-Saal* (Nürnberg, 1741), p. 78.

Plate 33. Joseph F. B. C. Majer's Description of the Viola.

The Viola in Hamburg Operas

Although late in the 17th century, Italian style opera was supported in Dresden, Munich, and other German cities; the real flowering of German opera took place in Hamburg. There, Reinhard Keiser (1674–1739) became the chief composer in 1695, and wrote over 100 operas in the ensuing years.

Two of the important functions of the opera orchestra are to set the mood for the scene and to give more intensity to the stage action. Keiser had a particular talent for orchestrating the accompaniments to arias in a manner that gave added dramatic emphasis to the libretto. He accomplished this through innovative uses of instruments and combinations of instruments. He was also doubtlessly familiar with the works in which composers of the Venetian school of opera had, earlier in the 17th century, occasionally utilized the viola as a solo or an obbligato instrument, thus elevating it out of the anonymity of its usual function as a member of the *füllende* or the continuo group.[5] Keiser's opera scores frequently demanded much more of the violist than playing the *füllende* parts, described by Eisel, Mattheson, Walther, and Majer in their treatises.

Andrew D. McCredie, of Sydney, Australia, while a graduate student at Hamburg University, investigated the development of orchestral writing among north German Baroque opera composers. He recorded his findings in a dissertation which has a separate section devoted to each instrument of the opera orchestra, as it was then constituted. The section on the viola is particularly pertinent, and much of the following material is drawn from McCredie's doctoral thesis.[6]

The viola parts in two of Reinhard Keiser's earliest surviving operas, *Adonis* (1697) and *Janus* (1698), are indicated by the term *Violette*. Dryante's aria in Act II of *Adonis* and Tiberius' aria in Act III of *Janus* are marked "Aria con Violette all'unisono." In *Nebucadnezar* (1704), Keiser scored three viola parts in a *Sinfonia affectuoso* occurring in the middle of Act I. He used soprano, alto, and tenor C clefs interchangeably in each of the three parts to avoid added leger-lines, a practice McCredie found to be in all of the Keiser scores.[7]

---

[5]See Chapter III, "The Viola in Early Opera."

[6]Andrew D. McCredie, *Instrumentarium and Instrumentation in the North German Baroque Opera*. Dissertation zur Erlangung der Doktorwürde der Philosophischen Fakultät der Universität (Hamburg, 1964), pp. 254–67. [Although this dissertation was completed in a German university, the language of the text is English.]

[7]*Ibid.*, pp. 258-59.

In *Octavia* (1705), Keiser used the viola's unique tone-color with dramatic effect in several solo accompaniments to Nero's arias. In *Orpheus* (1709) and *Arsinoe* (1710), a total of four arias are marked, "Aria con tutte les Violettes." In *Diana* (1712), Keiser extended the viola range upward to e'', which would have been near the end of the short fingerboards in use at that time. In Act I of *Cupido* (c.1724), the aria "Qual solings tortorella," an obbligato viola part includes a solo with a compass of c–e''.[8]

Other Hamburg composers who wrote operas containing significant solo or obbligato material for the viola were Christoph Graupner (1683–1760), Johann Mattheson (1681–1764), and George Frideric Handel (1685–1759). Their use of the viola in operatic scores reflects the influence Keiser had on all other Hamburg opera composers.

In 1703, Handel accepted a position as a violinist in the Hamburg Opera under Keiser, and later became a harpsichordist. As a member of the orchestra, Handel became familiar with Keiser's use of the viola to heighten the emotional content of his scores. It is not surprising that Handel, in his opera *Almira* (1705), used the viola for solo accompaniment in three arias, of which the most prominent is "Sprich vor mir ein süsses Wort," which exploits the tone-color of the C string in a way not previously heard in the Hamburg Opera. But in Osmin's aria in Act I and Tabarco's aria in Act II, the obbligato viola part does not employ the C string.[9] Later, when Handel had moved to London, he again gave the viola an important part in his opera, *Alexander's Feast* (1736), wherein the violas are used to paint a background of horror as Timotheus cries, "Revenge, these are Grecian Ghosts."

In Graupner's *Dido* (1707) and *Antiochus und Stratonica* (1708), a total of seven arias include parts for viola solo or duet obbligato. In the latter opera, Act II, Scene 1, Antiochus' aria, "Ja hochgekränkter Geist," includes a viola solo of almost virtuoso difficulty.[10]

Mattheson's opera *Henrico IV* (1711), Act II, Scene 2, has an aria by Alfonso, "Sanza offessa del tuo bello," that is accompanied by *Violino Solo e due Bracci*.[11]

Keiser left Hamburg in 1723 for Copenhagen, where he became Kapellmeister. In 1728 he returned to Hamburg as Cantor of the Katharienkirche. He had already turned away from composing secular opera music to writing music for the Church. Without Keiser's guiding genius, the Hamburg Opera declined rapidly into near oblivion.

---

[8]*Ibid.*, pp. 260–64.

[9]*Ibid.*, p. 260.

[10]*Ibid.*, pp. 263–4. McCredie furnished eight bars from the score of Antiochus' aria to illustrate the importance Graupner attached to the viola solo.

[11]*Ibid.*, pp. 264–5.

The viola as a solo or obbligato instrument in opera music was not exploited again until the end of the 18th century, when it was given recognition in Parisian operas.

Bach's Legacy to the Viola

Johann Sebastian Bach (1685–1750) was the first composer to understand completely the potential of the viola tonally and technically. Bach's musical training began at home under the direction of his father, Johann Ambrosius Bach, a versatile musician, who played the violin, viola, and trumpet. Johann Sebastian developed a love for the violin and viola at an early age, and there is evidence that he became quite proficient as a performer on both instruments. His first important professional position was at Weimar (1703), where he was appointed violinist and violist to Johann Ernst, younger brother of the Duke of Weimar.

Bach's career as a professional violist, however, was shortlived, because within a year he was offered a more prestigious post as organist at a church in Arnstadt. From that time on, Bach's reputation as an organist, choral conductor, and composer of works for the Church to some extent obscured his fame as a knowledgeable composer for stringed instruments. Still, he continued to write works that demonstrated his affection for the members of the violin family: notably the 6 *Violin Solo Sonatas*, 6 *Cello Suites*, 2 *Solo Concertos for the Violin*, 6 *Violin-Clavier Sonatas*, chamber music for strings and wind instruments, and of particular significance for violists, the 6 *Brandenburg Concertos.*

Carl Philipp Emanuel Bach, in a letter to Johann Forkel, described his father's continued activity as a violist and violinist:

> He heard the slightest wrong note even in the largest combinations. As the greatest expert and judge of harmony, he liked best to play the viola, with appropriate loudness and softness. In his youth and until the approach of old age, he played the violin cleanly and penetratingly, and thus kept the orchestra in better order than he could have done with the harpsichord. He understood to perfection the possibilities of all stringed instruments.[12]

Forkel, who wrote the first comprehensive biography of Bach, pointed out that in chamber music Bach preferred to play the viola:

> With this instrument he was, as it were, in the centre of the harmony, where he could hear and enjoy to the utmost what was going on on both sides of him.[13]

---

[12]Hans T. David & Arthur Mendel, *The Bach Reader* (New York: W. W. Norton: 1966), p. 277.

[13]Johann Nikolaus Forkel, *Über Johann Sebastian Bachs Leben, Kunst und Kunstwerke*, 1803 (English, 1820), p. 46.

Among Bach's many great compositions are the sacred choral works, of which over 300 are cantatas. The use of the viola in the accompaniment to some of the cantatas is tersely described by the Bach scholar, Philipp Spitta:

> It is well known that in the seventeenth century harmony in five parts was almost invariably preferred to four, and for this reason two violas were frequently added to the two violins. Bach himself had followed this custom in some of his earlier contatas, as in the Advent music, *Nun Komm der Heiden Heiland* (Come, O Saviour of the Nations) written in 1714, and the Easter cantata, *Der Himmel lacht* (The Heavens Laugh), in 1715. The cantata for Sexzgesima, which was written still earlier, *Gleichwie der Regen und Schnee vom Himmel fällt* (Like as the Rain and Snow from Heaven falleth) has four violas, the violins being altogether absent.[14]

Bach composed his six concerti grossi, known as the *Brandenburg Concertos,* in 1721 while living and working in Cöthen. The instrumentation of these works constituted quite a departure from the standard format set by Corelli and imitated by most Baroque composers. None of the six Concertos have the usual two violins and cello in the *concertino,* but instead the *soli* groups consist of unusual combinations of strings, or strings, harpsichord, and wind instruments.

Of particular interest to viola enthusiasts are the third and sixth Concertos. The *Brandenburg Concerto No. 3 in G Major* (BWV 1048) is scored for three violins, three violas, three cellos, and continuo (cembalo and double bass). Fuller-Maitland cautioned against using the full string section of the symphony orchestra for the *Brandenburg Concertos.* He explained that it is not a great mass of resonance that is desirable, but rather a clean and balanced sound.[15]

The *Brandenburg Concerto No. 6 in B♭ Major* (BWV 1051) has the most unique instrumentation of the entire set. No violins are employed. Two solo violas constitute the *concertino.* The *ripieno* includes two viola da gambas,[16] cello, and continuo. This composition can be performed with as few as six players. The solo parts should not be doubled if a true Baroque sound is desired, and there should not be more than three or four players on each of the *ripieno* parts.

Joseph Szigetti was impressed by the range used in the solo parts of the *Brandenburg VI:*

> Bach uses the upper register of the violas to such telling effect that it would not be difficult to consider these passages as sung by human voices and furnish them with an appropriate text.[17]

---

[14]Philipp Spitta, *J. S. Bach* (2 vols. 1873, '80). The quotation cited is taken from: Gerhard Herz, *Bach, Cantata No. 4, Christ lag in Todesbanden* (New York: W. W. Norton, 1967), pp. 117–18.

[15]J. A. Fuller-Maitland, *Bach's Brandenburg Concertos* (London. Oxford University Press, 1929), p. 23–4.

[16]Usually played by violas reading the tenor clef if viola da gambas are not available.

[17]Joseph Szigetti, *Szigetti on the Violin* (New York: Frederick A. Praeger, 1970), p. 107.

Frequently viola enthusiasts perform the *Brandenburg VI* in mass numbers—not in an attempt to be irreverent to Bach and the Baroque style, but rather to demonstrate their sheer joy and love for this music. Such a performance took place at the International Viola Congress held in Ypsilanti, Michigan, in 1975, when over a hundred violists gave an unrehearsed performance of the work on the stage of Pease Auditorium, Eastern Michigan University campus, with two successive readings. For the first reading the solo parts were performed by Ernst Wallfisch and Francis Bundra, violists, and Lauri Wallfisch, harpsichordist. The *ripieno* was performed by over one hundred violists, cellists, and double bass players. Dr. Edward Szabo conducted. For the second reading, the entire group of over a hundred violists played the two solo viola parts. For those in the audience, the over-all sound was thrilling and awe-inspiring (See Plate 34).

Violists, lacking original solo works by Bach, have, since early in the 19th century, turned to the unaccompanied *Six Solo Violin Sonatas and partitas* (BWV 1001–6) and the *Six Cello Suites* (BWV 1007–12). The general preference for the latter can be attributed to two factors: (1) the multiple-stops in the *Violin Sonatas* require an unusually large and strong hand to execute; and (2) it is not necessary to transpose the keys of the *Cello Suites* down a fifth, as it is in the *Violin Sonatas*.

The Six Cello Suites

The *Cello Suites*, composed in Cöthen, c.1720, were little known or appreciated until they were made popular and given their deserved recognition by the life-long dedication and promotion of Pablo Casals. The first printed edition appeared in 1825 by Kistner, followed in 1826 by the Breitkopf und Härtel edition. Editions for the viola appeared early in the 20th century, including one published in the United States in 1916 by G. Schirmer. Inasmuch as Bach left no dynamic markings, bowings, or tempo indications, these *Suites* have been a challenge to each successive editor to supply directions and fingerings that will aid the performer in achieving the Baroque style. As a result there are now many editions available to cellists and violists, often with conflicting bowings, fingerings, and dynamic markings. Artist performers and musicologists have written numerous articles on performance practices for these transcendent works. Here too, there is often disagreement, and the reader may be left more confused than informed.

In an attempt to clarify some of the problems inherent in the technical and stylistic performance of the *Suites*, the Utah Chapter of

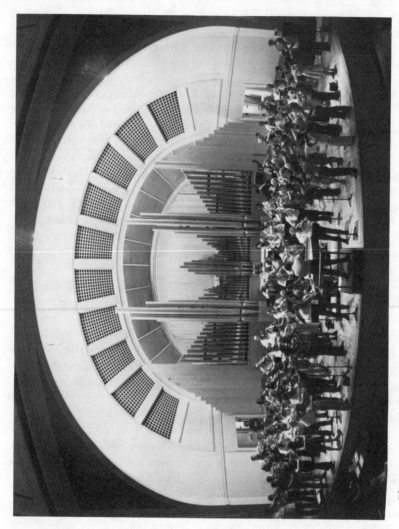

Plate 34. Mass Performance of Bach's *Brandenburg Concerto No. 6*, at the Third International Viola Congress held in Ypsilanti, Michigan, in 1975.

the American String Teachers Association sponsored a panel discussion entitled *Bach Symposium*, at the University of Utah in Salt Lake City, on July 15, 1979. The distinguished panel speakers included Dr. William Primrose and Milton Thomas, violists, and David B. Freed and Paul Olevsky, cellists. They discussed the various aspects of performing Bach's *Six Cello (Viola) Suites*.

Primrose's rich experience with these works as a performer and as a teacher was already known, but many in the audience were unaware of the meticulous scrutiny and scholarly research he has devoted to the *Suites*. Significantly, he does not consider the *Suite VI in D Major* suitable for the viola and has not included bowings and fingerings for it in his own edition. The panelists disagreed on several points of interpretation regarding the *Suites*, which made the discussion all the more interesting and stimulating. Each artist supported his views verbally and by performing portions of the *Suites* to demonstrate a particular bowing or interpretation.

Members of the audience frequently took part in the debatable issues raised concerning Baroque style. For example, Emanuel Vardi stated that he preferred to play the *Suites* as a 20th century violist, as he felt Bach would have done with present-day instruments and bows; and he emphasized that he did not want to be restricted by the type of instrument and bow used in Bach's time. Several members of the audience took issue with Vardi while others supported him, and a most rewarding discussion followed.

The conclusion drawn by many members of the audience, after hearing and participating in the enlightening discussion, was that the rich content of the *Suites* leaves ample latitude for each artist to perform and to interpret them according to the dictates of his own emotional and intellectual sensitivity. The performer can have this freedom and still play the *Suites* with good taste and in Baroque style.

Bach's Viola da Gamba Sonatas

Bach's *Three Sonatas for Viola da Gamba and Cembalo* (BWV 1027–29) in G Major, D Major, and G Minor were written at Cöthen between 1717 and 1723. Editions of them, entitled *Sonatas for Viola and Piano*, appeared before World War II, most notably o⸍ arranged by Ernst Naumann and published by Breitkopf & Härte⸍

Louise Rood, in an article written in 1952, recommen⸍ violists add these *Sonatas* to their repertoire. She then p⸍ write an analysis and a critique of the Ernst Naumanⁿ was critical of Naumann's license in altering notes and placing pitch gaps in the viola part by transcribing sections an octave higher.[18]

Following the war several newly arranged and transcribed editions were brought out by other publishers. Paul Doktor believed that all of these editions have a common fault: the editors used the original keys, which were intended for the viola da gamba, but which are not suitable for the viola.[19] He added that Bach frequently changed the key of his own compositions when transcribing a work for a different instrument. Doktor cited examples of Bach's using higher keys when rewriting recorder compositions for the flute, and vice versa. Bach's obvious intent was to select keys that would place the pitch in the best range of a particular instrument.

In an article published in 1976, Doktor elaborated on the problems of transcribing the gamba sonatas for the viola.[20] He explained that they are actually trio sonatas, with the gamba playing one part, and the right- and left-hand of the keyboard, the other two parts. If the original keys are used for the transcription, the viola part must frequently be transposed an octave higher, which results in a crossing of parts not intended by Bach, and interferes with the audibility of the voice leading in the contrapuntal texture of the music. To overcome this problem and to place the viola in a range of optimum sonority, Doktor transcribed the *G Major Sonata* to the key of B♭ Major; the *D Major Sonata* to F Major; and the *G Minor Sonata* to C Minor.[21]

Recently research scholars have discovered, edited, and prepared for publication an impressive number of Baroque works that were written originally for the viola by other composers. This expansion of the violist's literature is a most welcome trend which will in no way lessen the importance or popularity of the Bach transcriptions—music that will always constitute a significant part of the core of the violist's repertoire.

Telemann's Compositions for Viola

Georg Philipp Telemann (1681–1767), one of the most prolific composers of the Baroque Era, left a significant legacy of music for the

[18]Louise Rood, "Bach for Violists," *Repertoire* (January, 1952), pp. 169–171.

[19]From a Lecture-Recital given by Paul Doktor at the Fifth International Viola Congress held at the Eastman School of Music, June 3–5, 1977.

[20]Paul Doktor, "J. S. Bach's Three Viola da Gamba Sonatas: Their Adaptability for Viola," *Journal of the Violin Society of America*, II, No. 3 (Summer, 1976), pp. 6–10.

[21]The Paul Doktor transcriptions of the Bach *Viola da Gamba Sonatas* have been published by Vorldwide Music Publishers, 1966 Broadway, New York, N.Y. 10023.

viola. Many of his compositions feature the viola as a solo instrument or provide it with an important part in ensemble music, rather than the traditional *füllende* parts described by Telemann's contemporaries, Johann Mattheson and J.F.B. Majer. The fact that Telemann was a champion of the viola was well known to his contemporaries, as was substantiated by Johann Philipp Eisel, who pointed out in 1738 that the viola was not only used for filling in the middle harmonies, but also as a solo instrument in the "concertos and concert overtures of the famous Kapellmeister Telemann."[22]

Most of Telemann's viola compositions remain as undated manuscripts. Several, however, were printed during his lifetime and suggest that he was particularly active in viola composition during the first half of his career. His first dated viola composition, a *Trio Sonata in G Minor*, appeared in 1718, at a time when very few trio sonatas included a part for viola. His *Concerto for Viola in G Major* was published in 1731.[23] In 1734 Telemann published the *Scherzi Melodichi*, a collection of seven trio sonatas for violin, viola, and continuo, the largest single opus for viola up to that time.

Among the concertos written by Telemann for viola, in addition to the one in *G Major* are *Concerto in G Major for 2 Violas* (Violetten)[24] and *Concerto in A Major for 2 Violins, Viola, and Continuo*.[25] Franz Zeyringer lists *12 Sonatas for Viola and Keyboard* by Telemann, but indicates that most of them are modern editions borrowed from works for the viola da gamba.[26] These works, however, can all be rightfully considered as part of the violist's repertoire, because in Telemann's time, it was understood that compositions could and should be played by other suitable instruments.

The former paucity of Baroque trio sonatas that include a part or parts for viola is now being alleviated, thanks to scholarly research; and the works of Telemann have proven to be a treasure trove for this purpose. The following constitutes a partial list of his trio sonatas now available in modern editions: *7 Trios, Scherzi Melodichi*, from "Pyrmonter Kurwoche;" *Trio Sonata Polonese No. 1 in A Minor; Trio No. 5 in G Minor; Trio in B♭ Major;* and two *Trios in C Minor*. The *Scherzi Melodichi*, the *Polonese*, and the *G Minor Trios* are all scored

---

[22]Johann Philipp Eisel, *op. cit.*, p. 37–8.

[23]The *Concerto in G Major*, Telemann's best known work for the viola, was out of print for over two centuries until brought out in modern edition by Hellmuth Christian Wolff, pub. by Bärenreiter, 1941.

[24]Available in several modern editions.

[25]See *Breitkopf Thematic Catalogue*, 1962. Not yet available in modern edition.

[26]Publishers and dates of modern editions of listed *Sonatas* are given in F. Zeyringer, *Literatur für Viola.*

for violin, viola, and keyboard. The *B♭ Major* and one of the *C Minor Trios* are scored for flute (violin), viola, and keyboard. The other *C Minor Trio* is for oboe (violin), viola, and keyboard.

The *Scherzi Melodichi* includes seven pieces named for the days of the week, beginning with Thursday: *Lunedi* in A Major; *Martedi* in B♭ Major; *Sabbato* in G Minor; *Domenico* in D Major; *Mercordi* in G Major; *Gioverdi* in E♭ Major; and *Venerdi* in E Minor. Each piece consists of an introductory movement followed by six short movements in contrasting tempos.[27]

Telemann, more than any composer of his time, intentionally wrote music that could be used by violists. Many of Telemann's trio sonatas were titled for *Violino, Viola da Gamba, et Cembalo*, or for *Flauto traverso, Viola da Gamba, et Cembalo*. Since the gamba parts were written in the C (alto) clef, and rarely go below the viola range, the possibility of substituting the viola for the gamba was obviously intended by the composer, "especially since such a substitution was quite usual at that time, and Telemann expressly mentions this alternative in various compositions."[28] One of the many examples that can be cited for substituting instruments is illustrated in the title of the trio sonata, *Concerto à 3, Cornu (Viola), Flauto, con Cembalo et Fagotto*.[29] The title indicates that the work can be performed by either winds or strings or in combination. The horn part is interchangeable with the viola, the flute with the violin, and the bassoon with the cello.[30]

Telemann also composed ensemble works which contained parts for small and large violas. Such a work is his *Sonata in F Minor* à 2 Violini, alto Viola, Tenore Viola, Violoncello, e Cembalo.[31] In the original manuscript the *Tenore* part was written in the tenor clef, a common practice at the time.[32]

An appraisal of the total output of Telemann's compositions for viola leads to two conclusions: (1) very few of his works are masterpieces; (2) but all are quality works of considerable worth which have greatly enriched the Baroque literature available to violists.

---

[27]The recent modern edition, edited by Adolf Hoffmann, and published by Nagels, 1976, includes, in addition to the violin, and viola parts, a violin II part to substitute for the viola, a cello part for the continuo, and a keyboard part, realized by the editor.

[28]Karlheinz Schultz-Hauser, "Preface," G. P. *Telemann Trio Sonata in G* for Violin, Viola da Gamba (viola), and Piano (Peters Ed. #9145), 1970.

[29]Available in modern edition, G. P. Telemann, *Concerto à Tre in F*, Felix Schroeder (Wilhelmshausen: Netzel, 1962).

[30]For a listing of additional trio sonatas, see Richard Petzoldt, *Georg Philipp Telemann* (New York: Oxford University Press, 1974), p. 235.

[31]Available in modern edition, *Hortus Musicus*, No. 270 (Kassel: Bärenreiter, 1971).

[32]Mus. ms. 1042/21 in the Hessichen Landes-und-Hochschule-Bibliothek at Darmstadt.

The Viola in Mannheim

About the middle of the 18th century the city of Mannheim became the home of one of the earliest symphony orchestras. Karl Theodore (1743–99), Elector of Palzbayern, assembled the orchestra and was its patron. The Mannheim Orchestra, its conductors, and composers were among those in the forefront of the Classic movement. The ability of the Mannheim Orchestra to attain unusual dynamic nuances is well documented by such contemporary experts as the English music historian, Charles Burney, and the young Wolfgang Mozart.

Among the many fine composers, conductors, and performers in the Mannheim milieu, the Stamitz family is particularly noteworthy. Johann Stamitz (1717–57) and his sons, Karl (1746–1801) and Anton (1754–1809?), were virtuosos on the violin, viola, and the viola d'amore.

Johann joined the Mannheim Orchestra in 1745 as a violinist, but soon became the conductor. In addition to his conducting and the numerous symphonies and chamber music that he composed, he continued to perform as a soloist. On September 8, 1754, Johann made his debut in Paris at the *Concerts Spirituels*, where he played a violin concerto and a viola d'amore sonata; he also conducted one of his own symphonies.[33]

Karl and Anton received their musical training in Mannheim. They grew up in an environment rich in all forms of instrumental music. Both became members of the famed Mannheim Orchestra and frequently appeared as soloists in concertos or concertantes.

Karl's fame as a performer on the violin, viola, and viola d'amore soon became widespread, as evidenced by the accolade proffered by Gerber, the German lexicographer, who assessed Karl's playing as the standard for artistry:

> He who wished to succeed as a free artist in Germany must not have any less artistry than [Karl] Stamitz.[34]

Karl succeeded as a free artist. In 1770 he left the security of the Mannheim Orchestra to travel to Strasbourg, St. Petersburg, London, and Paris. In Paris he made his debut at the *Concerts Spirituels* in 1772. The success of his performances there is documented by the French violinist, composer, and musicologist Laborde, who wrote:

---

[33]Constant Pierre, *Histoire du Concert Spirituel 1725–1790* (Paris: Heugel, 1975), p. 268.

[34]Ernest Ludwig Gerber, *Neues Historisch-biographisches Lexikon der Tonkünstler* (Leipzig, 1812–14), III, p. 250.

The son of the celebrated Stamitz has written concertos for his instrument [viola], as agreeable to listen to as they are difficult to play, and they afford great pleasure when executed by him.[35]

Anton Stamitz, eight years younger than Karl, spent his early years somewhat in his brother's shadow, and did not receive the early recognition accorded to his brother. In 1770 he left Mannheim with Karl to seek his career in Strasbourg. In 1772 he joined Karl in Paris for a joint debut on March 25 at the *Concerts Spirituels*. The two performed a *Duo for Violin and Viola*, composed by Karl. They appeared again a month later at the *Concerts Spirituels* during the *Vacance des spectacles* (holiday performances).[36]

Paris audiences also had the opportunity of hearing Stamitz compositions performed by other artists. On February 2, 1774, Karl's *Symphonie Concertante in E♭ Major for 2 Violins, Viola, and Cello* was performed at the *Concerts Spirituels* by Capron and Guenin, violins; Monin, viola; and J. L. Duport, cello. The work was conducted by P. Leduc.[37]

Anton also became a member of the French royal orchestra, and his reputation as a performer brought him several talented students, including Rudolph Kreutzer (1766–1831). As a viola soloist, Anton appeared at the *Concerts Spirituels* on February 2, 1788, performing one of his own *Viola Concertos*. This was followed by a second *Viola Concerto* on concert number 985.[38]

The Stamitz family viola concertos and symphonie concertantes, which contain a solo part for viola, embody an invaluable part of the Classic literature available for the instrument. Not all of the compositions presently in print were originally written for the viola. Walter Lebermann has shown that the *Concerto in G Major*, by Johann Stamitz, published by Litoff/C. F. Peters in 1962, was adapted from an earlier concerto Johann had written for the flute.[39]

Karl Stamitz composed at least three concertos for viola:

No. 1 *Concerto in D Major for Viola and Orchestra*
No. 2 *Concerto in B♭ Major for Viola and Orchestra*
No. 3 *Concerto in A Major for Viola and Orchestra*.

---

[35]Jean-Benjamin de Laborde, *Essai sur la musique ancienne et moderne* (Paris, 1780), p. 304.
[36]Constant Pierre, *op. cit.*, p. 300.
[37]*Ibid.*, pp. 155 and 302.
[38]*Ibid.*, pp. 308–9. Constant Pierre assigned each of the *Concerts Spirituels* a chronological number.
[39]Walter Lebermann, "The Viola Concerti of the Stamitz Family," *Viola Research Society Newsletter*, 1974, p. 3.

No. 1 in D Major and *No. 2 in B♭ Major* were first published in Paris by Heine in 1774. *No. 1 in D Major*, again published in modern edition in 1900 by Rieter and Biedermann, has since gone through many editions.[40] No. 2, originally in B♭ Major, became available again in 1974, published by the Polish State. In the original version, the viola soloist tuned his instrument up one half-step and read from a part in the key of A Major. Jerzy Kosmala and Janusz Zathey, the editors, decided to transpose the orchestral parts to A Major, hence the present version of No. 2 is in this key. No. 3 was originally in the key of A Major, and has been available in that key since 1956 in an edition financed by the Cesky Hudebni Fund, and published by Bärenreiter. Several other viola concertos attributed to Karl are arrangements of pieces for other instruments, and one of the concertos contains movements composed by Jarnovic (Giornovichi).[41]

Anton Stamitz composed four known concertos for the viola, and all were published by Parisian publishers before 1785. Anton's four viola concertos are now available in modern publications, all expertly edited by Walter Lebermann:

No. 1 Concerto in B♭ Major for Viola and Orchestra, B. Schott, 1972
No. 2 Concerto in F Major for Viola and Orchestra, B. Schott, 1969
No. 3 Concerto in G Major for Viola and Orchestra, Br. & Hart., 1971
No. 4 Concerto in D Major for Viola and Orchestra, Br. & Hart., 1973.

Karl Stamitz composed over 80 symphonies, of which 26 are in the *sinfonia concertante* format. It was not uncommon to write symphonie concertantes for solo winds, and later adapt the same pieces for solo stringed instruments—or the other way around. It is believed that some of the following works of Karl's were also intended for either solo string or solo wind instruments:

Symphonie Concertante in D Major for Violin, Viola & Orchestra
Symphonie Concertante in E♭ Major for 2 Violins, Viola & Orchestra
Symphonie Concertante in D Major for 2 Violins, Viola & Orchestra
Symphonie Concertante in A Major for Violin, Viola, Cello & Orchestra.

As research scholars continue to bring more works to light, the above lists are almost certain to grow.[42]

---

[40]The *No. 1 Concerto in D Major* has appeared in many editions, usually erroneously designated as Op. 1, pub. in 1801.

[41]Lebermann, *op. cit.*, pp. 3–4.

[42]For more about Karl Stamitz' *Symphonie Concertantes*, see Friedrich Carl Kaiser, *Carl Stamitz, Biographische Beiträge. Das symphonische Werk* (Doctoral Dissertation), Phillips University of Marburg, 1962, in 2 Vols., contains themes, listings of Ms., and some biographical material.

Karl Stamitz' loyalty to the viola is further demonstrated by the large number of his works containing parts featuring the instrument: sonatas for viola and piano; duets for two violas; string quartets for violin, two violas, and cello; and other groupings of chamber music.

In the city of Mannheim, interest in the viola was not limited to the Stamitz family. The large number of compositions for it by Mannheim composers gives credence to the popularity of the viola in that city. Only a few examples of the many works written for viola are cited here; all of these are available in modern editions: Ignaz Holzbauer (1711–83),a Mannheim conductor and composer, wrote *Concerto in E♭ Major for Viola and Cello*, n.d.; Christian Cannabich (1731–98), one of Mannheim's most talented conductors, published *6 Duets for Violin (Flute) and Viola*, c.1775; Ludwig August Lebrun (1746–90), reputedly the greatest oboeist of the 18th century, wrote *6 Duos for Violin and Viola*, Op. 4, n.d.; Ernst Eichner (1740–77), eminent Mannheim bassoonist, published the first of three sets of *6 Duos for Violin and Viola* in 1776 (Plate 35); Franz Danzi (1763–1826), whose father was a Mannheim cellist, wrote *6 Duos for Viola and Cello*, Op. 9, before 1816; Joseph Martin Kraus (1756–92), who grew up in the Mannheim environment, composed *Sonata for Flute and Viola*, n.d.

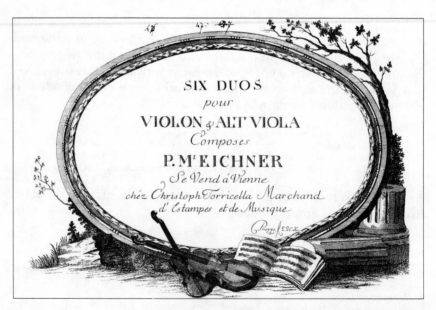

Plate 35. Ernst Eichner: Title Page of *Six Duos pour Violon & Alt Viola*. Courtesy of Die Musikabteilung der Stadtbücherei, Mannheim.

The Stamitz family and other members of the Mannheim school endowed future generations of violists with the lasting gifts of their creative works for the viola.

The Viola in Berlin and at the Court in Potsdam

Frederick II "The Great" (1712–86), in addition to being an able monarch, was a patron of music, an excellent flutist, and a composer. As Crown Prince, he assembled a chamber orchestra of the finest musicians available. When he ascended the throne of Prussia in 1740, he continued to invite to his court the best performers and composers obtainable. Some of them stayed only briefly, then continued their careers in other courts. Among those who were associated with Frederick's court music were C. P. E. Bach (1714–88), Franz Benda (1709–86), Georg Benda (1722–95), Karl Heinrich Graun (1701–59), Johann Gottlieb Graun (1702/3–71), and Johann Joachim Quantz (1697–1773). All wrote music for the viola.

The main function of the court orchestra was to entertain Frederick's guests and to accompany him on the numerous concertos the court composers wrote for him. The art of accompanying, accordingly, became an artistic endeavor. C. P. E. Bach and Quantz made exhaustive studies of the various styles, ornaments, and problems relating to accompanying, and later wrote authoritative treatises on the performance practices of the time. Bach incorporated his knowledge into a work for keyboard instruments, *Versuch über die wahre Art, das Clavier zu spielen* (two parts, 1753–62); and Quantz into a tutor for the flute, *Versuch einer Anweisung, die Flute zu spielen* (1752).[43] The latter work was the first to carry extensive descriptions of the violists of the time, and also to furnish instructions for playing Baroque viola music. This information is provided in Section III of Chapter XVII, entitled, "Of the Violist in Particular." Quantz first commented on the shortcomings of contemporary violists, and the qualifications he considered essential for adequate ensemble performers:

> The viola is commonly regarded as of little importance in the musical establishment. The reason may well be that it is often played by persons who are either still beginners in the ensemble or have no particular gifts with which to distinguish themselves on the violin, or that the instrument yields all too few advantages to its players, so that able people are not easily persuaded to take it up. I

---

[43]Now available in English translation by Edward Reilly, J. J. Quantz, *On Playing the Flute* (New York: Macmillan, 1966).

maintain, however, that if the entire accompaniment is to be without defect, the violist must be just as able as the second violinist.[44]

He suggested that violists should be more ambitious and develop an affirmative attitude toward their instrument, and added that more pleasure could be derived from playing accompaniments than by performing solo parts:

> ... So few violists devote as much industry to their work as they should. Many believe that if they only know a little about meter and the division of notes, nothing more can be demanded of them. This prejudice, however, is more than a little detrimental. If they applied the necessary industry, they could easily improve their lot in a large establishment, and gradually advance their position, instead of remaining chained to the viola to the end of their lives, as is usually the case. There are many examples of people who, after playing the viola in their youth, achieved great eminence in the musical world. And afterwards, when already qualified for something better, they were not ashamed to resume the instrument in case of need. One who accompanies actually experiences more pleasure from the music than one who plays a concertante part; and anyone who is a true musician takes an interest in the entire ensemble, without troubling himself about whether he plays the first or the last part.[45]

Quantz compared the sonority of the viola with other instruments in the orchestra, and furnished advice on when to play louder or softer in order to achieve ideal balance:

> Since one viola, if a good and strong instrument, is sufficient against four or even six violins, the violist must moderate the strength of his tone if only two or three violins play with him, so that he does not cover the others, especially if only one violoncello is present and no double bass. The middle parts, which, considered in themselves, provide the listener with the least pleasure, must never be heard as strongly as the principal parts. Hence the violist must decide whether the notes he is to play are melodic or simply harmonic. The former he must play with the same strength as the violins, the latter a little more softly.[46]

In trios or quartets Quantz cautioned the violist to

> carefully observe what kinds of instruments he has against him, so that he can adjust the strength and weakness of his tone accordingly. Against a violin he can play with almost the same strength, against a violoncello or a bassoon with equal strength, against an oboe a little more softly, since its tone is thin compared to that of the viola. Against a flute, however, he must play very softly, especially if it plays in a low register.[47]

---

[44]*Ibid.*, pp. 237–241. The reader who desires more information should read the entire Ch. XVII of Quantz' treatise, pp. 205–94.

[45]*Ibid.*, p. 237.

[46]*Ibid.*, p. 239.

[47]*Ibid.*, p. 240.

The great flutist covered the entire range of problems violists encountered in performing orchestral parts written specifically for their instruments, or as was often the case, of doubling the *continuo*. He concluded his material on the viola by suggesting that if the violist heeded all of the advice offered, and became a proficient performer, he would not always have to be relegated to the viola section:

> The remarks about the other aspects of bowing, about attacks and slurs, the expression of the notes, the staccato, loud and soft playing, tuning, etc., to be found in the preceding and in the last sections of this chapter may be turned to as much account by the violist as by the ripieno violinist, not only because he needs to know all of these things, but also because he does not, I presume, wish to remain always a violist.[48]

This final comment by Quantz was possibly directed at violists who were not in the court orchestra. The abundance of talent in Frederick's ensemble and the high standards of performance he demanded would seem to preclude participation by any but the most proficient of violists. Many of the court composers, including Quantz, wrote works for the viola that required more than ordinary skill to perform.[49] Some of these pieces were composed while at Frederick's court-in-residence in Berlin, others were completed after the composer had moved to a new location.

C. P. E. Bach, understandably, composed with the monarch in mind. Among his numerous compositions are no fewer than twelve ensemble pieces which include the viola. Of these, there are eight *Trios for Flute, Viola, and Piano*, and a *Duet for Flute and Viola*. Works which do not include the flute and which may have been written after Bach left the employ of Frederick are: *Trio in F Major for Viola, Cello, and Piano; Trio in C Minor for Violin, Viola, and Cello;* and, of particular significance because so few were written for the instrument itself, *Trio Sonata in F Major for 2 Violas and Piano*.

Franz Benda was the leader of Frederick's orchestra for forty years. In his autobiography he stated that he played the viola briefly before he joined the court orchestra. He had enough regard for the instrument to compose a *Sonata in C Minor for Viola and Continuo*.

Georg Benda, a younger brother of Franz, was in the court orchestra from 1742 to 1748. His works for viola were probably written after he left Berlin. They include two *Concertos in E♭ Major* and one *in F Major for Viola "mit grossem Orchester"*;[50] and two *Concertos in F*

---

[48]*Ibid.*, 241.

[49]*Breitkopf Thematic Catalogue*, 1766, p. 73, lists a *Sonata in A Minor for Viola and Continuo* by Quantz.

[50]According to Zeyringer, the Ms is in the Staats Bibliothek in East Berlin.

Major and *in E♭ Major for Viola, 2 Horns, and Strings.*[51] From the latter group the *Concerto in F Major* (c.1775) is available in a modern edition.[52]

Johann Gottlieb Graun was a violinist for Frederick's court from 1732 until 1741, when the king appointed him concertmaster of the new Royal Opera in Berlin. He either played the viola, or knew an exceptionally fine violist in Berlin, as is borne out by four of his works of considerable merit for the instrument. They are *Sonatas in B♭ Major, F Major, and C Minor for Viola and Cembalo with Cello ad lib;* and *Concerto in E♭ Major for Viola and Strings.* The titles of the *Sonatas* suggest an alternative of having a keyboard part played by harpsichord, supported by a cello playing the bass line, or by using the then-new piano, which had become popular in Frederick's court. All are available in a modern edition.[53]

Johann Gottleib Janitsch[54] (1708–63), one of the most neglected composers of the Berlin school, demonstrated considerable interest in the viola in both his solo compositions and in the chamber music he wrote. The *Breitkopf Thematic Catalogue* lists: a *Sonata in F Major for Viola, Cello, and Cembalo;* and four *Sonatas con altri Stromenti:* (1) *Sonata in E♭ Major for Viola, Cello, Flute, and Continuo;* (2) *Sonata in C Minor for Viola, Cello, Oboe, and Continuo;* (3) *Sonata in E♭ Major for 2 Violas, Oboe (or Flute), and Continuo;* (4) *Sonata in B Minor* [presumably for the same instrumentation as the third *Sonata*].[55] David Sills reports that he has obtained microfilm copies of string quartets by Janitsch from the Staatsbibliothek of East Berlin, and observes that these works give more prominence to the viola than compositions in this genre by Janitsch's contemporaries.[56] Violists will be richer when viola pieces by this composer are made available in modern editions.[57]

Karl Friedrich Zelter (1758–1832), prominent Berlin composer and conductor, was of a later generation than the musicians of

---

[51]See *Breitkopf Thematic Catalogue,* 1778.

[52]Ed. by Walter Lebermann, Pub. by B. Schott, 1968.

[53]The *B♭* and *F Major Sonatas,* Ed. by H. Christian Wolff, Pub. by Breitkopf & Härtel, 1937; the *C Minor Sonata,* Ed. by Gottfried Müller, Pub. by Sikorski, 1962. The *E♭ Major Concerto,* Ed. by Walter Lebermann, Pub. by Simrock, 1975.

[54]Also spelled Janitzsch.

[55]*The Breitkopf Thematic Catalogue,* Part II, 1762, pp. 72–3.

[56]David Sills, talented student of Lillian Fuchs, and semifinalist in the 1979 William Primrose International Viola Competition, is doing significant research in Janitsch compositions containing parts for viola.

[57]Zeyringer in his *Literatur für Viola* not only furnishes locations for most of these compositions, but also listed additional works by Janitsch.

Frederick the Great's court, and was well known as a composer of lieder and choral works. Among his instrumental compositions, however, is the particularly significant *Concerto for Viola in E♭ Major*, composed in 1779. The accompaniment is scored for strings and two horns. Although this composition is in the classic style of the time, it shows the influence of C. P. E. Bach and other composers of the earlier Berlin school.

The Viola in Vienna

In the second half of the 18th century, and extending on into the 19th, Vienna became one of the world centers of culture and the arts. Music flourished to the extent that talented composers and performers were attracted there from all other European countries, many of them taking up permanent residence. Vienna was the city of Haydn, Mozart, Beethoven, Schubert, and many other fine composers. Numerous musicians who did not live in Vienna were influenced by the developments in this Austrian capital, where the classic sonata, symphony, concerto, string quartet, and other chamber-music combinations were receiving particular emphasis, development, and refinement.

The viola prospered as never before from this flowering of Viennese music. Composers increasingly gave the viola more important parts in their symphonies and chamber music. Significant concertos and sonatas featuring the instrument were written by talented composers, whose reputations were overshadowed by the superior genius of Haydn and Mozart; and consequently, their works fell into neglect and were forgotten during the 19th century. In the 20th century, and especially since the end of World War II (1945), a renewed interest in these viola compositions has prompted scholars and editors to search libraries, museums, and private archives for these works. Many have already found their way to print in modern editions, disproving the old cliché that "the viola does not have a literature of original compositions from the Classic school."

Among the composers who lived in Vienna or were influenced by its music, the following wrote concertos for the viola:[58]

Karl Ditters von Dittersdorf (1739–1799), *Concerto in F Major;* and *Concerto in D Major for Viola and Doublebass.*

---

[58]For publishers and dates of publication consult Franz Zeyringer, *Literatur für Viola* (1976).

Georg Druschetzky (1745-d. after 1790), *Concerto in D Major.*
Roman Hoffstetter (1742–1815), *Concerto in E♭ Major; Concerto in C Major;* and *Concerto in D Major.*
Franz-Anton Hoffmeister (1754–1812), *Concerto in D Major.*
Wolfgang Mozart (1756–1791), *Symphonie Concertante in E♭ Major for Violin and Viola,* K. 364.
Johann B. Vanhal (1739–1813), *Concerto in C Major;* and *Concerto in F Major* (also for bassoon).
Anton Wranitzky (1761–1820), *Concerto in C Major for 2 Violas.*

Von Dittersdorf and Vanhal also wrote sonatas for viola and piano. These sonatas and the above concertos constitute only a partial listing of the viola compositions of the Viennese School. New editions are continually being added to those that were formerly available.

Franz Joseph Haydn

Franz Josef Haydn (1732–1809) did not write any known sonatas or concertos for the viola. His orchestral works and chamber music, however, included parts that lent dignity to the instrument and its players. His string quartets do not treat the viola as an equal with the first violin, but the parts are always of musical interest and occasionally, as in the "Kaiser" Quartet, the viola actually gets a featured solo.

In 1760 Haydn entered the employ of the Esterhazy family. In 1762, a year after the death of Prince Anton Esterhazy, the title passed to Prince Nikolaus, whose love of art and music was as great as his father's had been. Nikolaus' favorite instrument was the baryton (see Plate 36), on which he performed every day. Haydn was, therefore, required to compose a large number of pieces for the baryton. Many of these works were lost in a fire. Of those that are now extant, 126 are *Trios for Viola, Baryton, and Cello,*[59] written between 1761 and 1765. These works have been catalogued by Bela de Csuka.[60] Thus far very few of these works have found their way into modern editions. Those that are available are for the most part arrangements for violin, viola, and cello, or for two violins and cello.[61]

---

[59]Oliver Strunk. "Haydn's Divertimenti for Baryton, Viola, and Bass," *Musical Quarterly,* XVIII (1932), pp. 216–51.

[60]Bela de Csuka, *Haydn's Divertimenti for Baryton, Viola (Violin), and Bass,* MS in Library of Congress. A thematic listing of all movements in score. Present locations of the original MS are indicated for each work.

[61]See Peters and Bärenreiter catalogues for *Trios* available in modern edition.

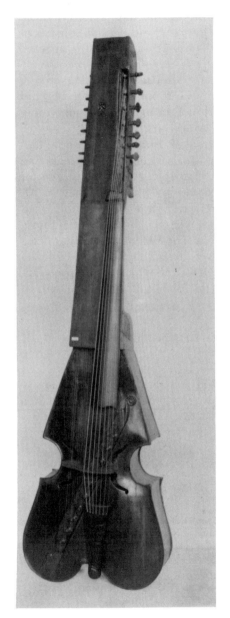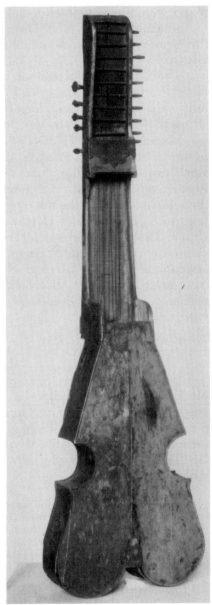

Plate 36. Baryton (Viola de Bordone)
The Metropolitan Museum of Art: The Crosby
Brown Collection of Musical Instruments, New York City.

De Csuka's catalogue of thematic scores shows that some of the works were probably intended for violin, baryton, and cello, and some for viola and two barytons. The usual format of these *Trios* consists of three movements: andante, allegro, minuet; or andante, minuet, allegro.

The baryton *Trios* cannot be considered as belonging among Haydn's most inspired works; but they do represent a large body of music that will serve an important function as material for young string players and for amateurs to play and to enjoy.[62]

Michael Haydn (1737–1806), younger brother of Joseph and friend of both Leopold and Wolfgang Mozart, composed at least one significant work for the viola, a *Concerto in C Major for Organ* (or Piano) *and Viola*, with a ripieno of 2 violins, viola, and bass.[63] Although composed in the town of Grosswardein, it was probably written to be performed for Haydn's employer, the Bishop of Salzburg, who had a special fondness for the viola. The Bishop on another occasion requested Michael to compose two duets for violin and viola, an assignment which he failed to accomplish, and which would probably have brought him into disfavor with the Bishop if the young Mozart had not come to his rescue.

Mozart

Wolfgang Amadeus Mozart (1756–91) was a child prodigy—pianist, violinist, and composer. As he grew older, physical demands and time requirements forced him to sacrifice the violin in favor of the piano and composition. In place of the violin, he more and more turned to the viola as his favorite stringed instrument. Otto Jahn (1813–69), in his biography of Mozart, affirms this inclination for the viola:

> ... after his stay in Vienna he never made proficiency on the violin his primary object, and it is well known that in later years, if he had to take part in a quartet or other concerted piece, he selected the viola in preference.[64]

When Mozart was 23 years of age, he composed one of the most noteworthy pieces in the violist's repertoire, *Symphonie Concertante for Violin, Viola, and Orchestra in E♭ Major*, K.364 (1779). Mozart

---

[62]*The Complete Edition of Haydn's Works*, Series XIV, in 4 Vols., pub. by the Joseph Haydn Institute in Cologne (1970), contain all of the known *Baryton Trios*.

[63]Available in a modern edition, Ed. by Paul Angerer, pub. by Doblinger, 1970.

[64]Otto Jahn, *Life of Mozart*, Trans. by Pauline D. Townsend (1891), Vol. I, p. 317.

may have played the viola part at the first performance. He played a small viola, and as was frequently the practice at that time, wrote the viola part in the key of D Major, necessitating tuning the viola a half-step higher than the regular accordatura. The purpose of this procedure was to make the viola more brilliant and more resonant, and thus to better balance it with the solo violin part.[65] For the orchestral accompaniment, Mozart included a second viola part in addition to the usual strings. This is one of the few works in which he wrote his own cadenzas. This *Concertante* has remained one of the most popular and most often performed of any work in the viola literature.

Another *Concertante for Violin, Viola, and Cello in A Major*, K. Anh. 104 (320d), composed in 1779, exists as a fragment of one hundred thirty-four bars. Alfred Einstein, the eminent Mozart scholar, suggested that another fragment of thirty-two bars, an orchestral rondo, "La Chasse," in A Major, K. Anh. 103 (320f), is part of the same unfinished *Concertante*.[66]

Mozart's string quartets furnish the violist with material that is full of technical challenge and rich in musical interest. In addition to the quartets, the chamber music he wrote between 1783 and 1791 demonstrates his very special interest in the viola. In this period of eight years, he composed the two *Duets for Violin and Viola in G and Bb Major*, K.423–24; the two *Piano Quartets in G Minor*, K.478, and *Eb Major*, K.493; the *Trio for Clarinet, Viola, and Piano in Eb Major*, K.498; the *Divertimento for Violin, Viola, and Cello in Eb Major*, K.563; and his four greatest *String Quintets for 2 Violins, 2 Violas, and Cello in C Major*, K.515; *G Minor*, K.516; *D Major*, K.593; and *Eb Major*, K.614.

Mozart's two excellent *Duets for Violin and Viola in G Major* and *Bb Major*, K.423–24 (1783), were written for Michael Haydn, who had been commissioned by the Bishop of Salzburg to compose them. Mozart had returned to Salzburg to try to settle some domestic problems caused by his marriage the previous year. His friend, Michael Haydn, was the concertmaster of the Biship's court and would have fallen into bad graces if he did not produce the duets. For some reason Haydn could not compose them. Mozart composed the duets and let his friend sign them as being the works of Michael Haydn. These duets are among the finest written for the violin and viola, and give

[65]Lionel Tertis used metal strings, tuned his viola up a half-step, and played the *Eb Major Concertante* in the key of D Major, as Mozart had prescribed.

[66]Alfred Einstein, *Mozart, His Character, His Work*, trans. A. Mendel and N. Broder (New York: Oxford University Press, 1945), p. 284.

the violist ample opportunity to exploit his skill as a performer of concerted music.

Mozart's *Trio for Clarinet, Viola, and Piano in E♭ Major*, K.498 (1786), was written for his former piano student, Franziska von Jacqum, but it is known as the "Kegelstatt-Trio," because of its use of the skittles-ground. In this work the composer wrote for his three favorite instruments: the clarinet, the viola, and the piano, and produced a work filled with Mozartian charm.

The Piano *Quartets for Violin, Viola, Cello, and Piano in G Minor*, K.478 (1785), and *E♭ Major*, K.493 (1786), both furnish the violist with ensemble parts of considerable merit. The *G Minor Piano Quartet* has a particularly gracious and rewarding part for the viola.

The *Divertimento for Violin, Viola, and Cello in E♭ Major*, K. 563 (1788), is one of the finest pieces in the literature for this combination of instruments, and requires players of great skill to produce an adequate performance.

Mozart wrote his first Quintet in B♭ Major, K.174, in 1773, when he was only 17 years old. It is not one of his greatest works. The *Quintet in C Minor*, K.406 (516b), was a hasty arrangement of an earlier *Serenade for Wind Instruments*, K.388 (1787), and is also not a Mozart masterpiece.

In 1787 he returned to the quintet as a means of creative expression with the *Quintet in C Major*, K.515, and the *Quintet in G Minor*, K.516, works which Charles Rosen described as two of Mozart's "greatest works of chamber music."[67] Rosen also commented that "the first movement of the *C Major Quintet* is the largest 'sonata allegro' before Beethoven, longer than any other that Mozart ever wrote or any that Haydn had written." Mozart's fondness for the string quintet instrumentation is further borne out by events toward the end of his life. Two more masterpieces in this form came from his pen at a time when his health was rapidly deteriorating, *Quintet in D Major*, K.593 (1790), and *Quintet in E♭ Major*, K.614 (1791). The latter was completed only a few months before Mozart's death.

Mozart's Violas

Mozart is believed to have owned at least two violas. One is presently on display in the "Mozart House" in Salzburg. It is labeled

---

[67]Charles Rosen, *The Classical Style: Haydn, Mozart, Beethoven* (New York: W. W. Norton, 1972), pp. 268–9.

as the work of Carlo Antonio Testore. It is kept in a glass case and we were not permitted to examine or measure it. It appears to be less than 40.6 cm. (16 in.) in body length.[68] The second Mozart viola, attributed to Gio: Paolo Maggini, contains a dubious label which reads, "Giouani Paulo Meggni Brescia 1615 [sic].[69] Otto Haas, a London antiquarian music dealer, announced in his Catalogue, c. 1937, that his shop would sell the "Meggni," and listed the former owners of the instrument: The "Meggni" was originally sold in 1791 by the Mozart heirs to a Dr. Zizius, a professor at the University of Vienna. A professor, Leopold Jansa (1795–1857), in turn acquired the viola from the Zizius estate in 1826. Jansa's widow sold the instrument to Lord Wentworth (1839–1906). Wentworth soon afterward became the Earl of Lovelace. The Dowager Countess of Lovelace sold the "Meggni" to the well-known collector, Edward Speyer in 1909. The Haas Catalogue describes the viola as being "a well preserved instrument of middle size, with a good tone," and lists the following dimensions:

Body length — 40   cm. (15 3/4 in.)
Upper bout — 17 1/4 cm. (6 7/8 in.)
Middle bout— 12   cm. (4 3/4 in.)
Lower bout — 22   cm. (8 5/8 in.).

The disposition of the "Meggni" viola following its listing in the Haas Catalogue, and the name of the present owner of the instrument are unknown to this author.

---

[68]In Mozart's time very few musicians played large violas. Most violists played instruments of 37.5 cm. (14 3/4 in.) to 40 cm. (15 3/4 in.).

[69]The spelling does not correspond with genuine Maggini labels; Maggini's name is always followed by "*in* Brescia," and Maggini did not date his instruments. The material on the "Meggni" viola was furnished to the author by Oscar Shapiro, antiquarian book dealer of Washington, D.C.

CHAPTER VII

THE VIOLA IN OPERA IN THE LATE 18TH AND EARLY 19TH CENTURIES

The Gluck Influence on the Use of the Viola

During the second half of the 18th century the very large violas (tenors) gradually fell into virtual obsolescence. Four-part harmonic writing for the string choir had replaced the five-part writing that many composers had still used in the early Baroque Era. This eliminated the need for the *haute-contre* and *taille* parts. The *taille* (tenor) had usually been associated with the continuo, or bass line. The *haute-contre* was usually a tenor part in the older system of harmonic writing. The *quinte*, or high viola part, remained in the scoring for the opera orchestra as an alto-tenor voice.

The gradual elimination of the large violas (tenors) in the late 17th century, because of their impractical size for a comfortable performance of the more intricate music then being written, resulted in the almost exclusive use of small violas (altos). These instruments did not produce a resonance as bright and penetrating as the violins and the cellos. Their characteristic tone color, somewhat muffled and nasal on the *C* string but somber and passionate on the three upper strings, was ideally suited to the dramatic demands of opera composers.

Writers of the early Venetian opera school, in the late 17th century, had explored the possible uses of the viola; and the Hamburg opera composers, in the early 18th century, had already demonstrated the possible uses of the viola for particular mood and emotional effects. But it remained for Christoph Willibald Gluck (1714–87) to really exploit the dramatic potential of the viola in the operatic orchestra music.

Gluck, after some degree of success in Vienna and an indifferent success in London, moved to Paris, where he exerted considerable influence on an entire generation of Italian opera composers who had moved to France to pursue their careers.[1] Gluck not only tried to rid Italian opera of some of its timeworn traditions, but he also experimented with orchestration in an attempt to make the music more effectively enhance the text and the stage action. Gluck's scoring for the string section was more harmonic than that of his predecessors. Double-stopping and divisi playing appeared in his violin and viola parts. He assigned a new importance to the viola, which Carse has described:

> To the viola, the Cinderella of the string orchestra, Gluck was the fairy-godmother who rescued the instrument from a mean position and made it not only independent and indispensable, but discovered in it an individuality which was quite its own, a peculiarity of tone-color with which no other member of the string family was endowed. Thus, although the viola part in Gluck's scores does sometimes run with the bass part, the normal function of the instrument is either to provide essential harmony notes in the tenor register, to balance or thicken the tone, to take part in the prevailing motion or figuration in company with first and second violins, or to create an effect by means of its own individual tone-color.[2]

In the Overture to *Iphigénie en Aulide* (1772), Gluck gave prominence to the lower harmony by having the violas give a soft accompaniment to the violins, thus preparing the listener, after a number of rests, for the attack from the bass section.[3]

In one of his greatest operas, *Iphigénie en Tauride* (1779), Gluck demonstrated the emotional power of the viola section in the scene where Orestes, pursued by the Furies, falls asleep with the words, "Le calme rentre dans mon coeur" (Peace returns to my heart). The violas' gloomy muttering by syncopation on the *D* string make it clear that Orestes' sleep does not result from peace of mind, but rather from exhaustion and remorse.[4]

Gluck's use of the viola exerted considerable influence on the orchestrations of Antonio Sacchini (1730–86), Luigi Cherubini (1760–1842), and Gasparo Spontini (1774–1851). Throughout the compositions of these men, the viola more and more assumed an individuality of its own; and although used sparingly as a solo instrument, it was finally recognized as having a unique tone color that could contribute beautifully to the dramatic action on the stage.

In Sacchini's masterpiece, *Oedipe à Colone* (1786), Act I, Scene 3, the *Violes* (Violas) enhance the merry-making (Ex. 9), while a young

---

[1]Donald J. Grout, *A Short History of Opera* (New York: Columbia University Press), p. 245 and p. 305.

[2]Carse, *op. cit.*, pp. 157–8.

[3]H. Berlioz-R. Strauss, *Treatise on Instrumentation*, Trans. by Theodore Front (New York: Edwin F. Kalmus, 1948), p. 63.

[4]*Ibid.*, pp. 61–2.

Ex. 9. Antonio Sacchini: Excerpt from *OEdipe à Colone*, Act I, Scene 3.

Ex. 9 Continued.

Ex. 9 Continued.

Athenian sings happily as he offers presents to Eriphil. In Act II, Scene 1, set in the desert near the Temple of Eumenides, during Antigone's aria *"Toutemon bonheur est de suivre vos pas,"* the *Violes* (Violas) are on equal terms with all the other strings for ten bars (Ex. 10); then they reinforce the cellos and basses *(col b)*. Cherubini, in one of his greatest works, *Les Deux Journées* (1800), wrote much of the orchestration with two viola parts. In the *"Marche con moto"* of Act III, for example, he used the instrument to particular advantage by heralding the pompous theme with the violas and cellos in unison (Ex. 11). Spontini, in *La Vestale* (1807), Act I, Scene 2, in the *"Hymne du Matin,"* has the *Altos* (Violas) set the meditative mood in a four-measure introduction; then in a two-part harmony with the bassoons, which are also *divisi*, they play *trés doux* to further enhance the religious scene (Ex. 12). In Act II, Scene 1, in *"Hymne du Soire,"* with all the string parts muted, the Violin II section plays the thematic material supported by the French horns, which are later joined by the bassoons; the *Altos*, meanwhile, are assigned an important obbligato melody (Ex. 13).

Gluck's interest in the viola also took root in the works of several native French opera composers, notably Etienne-Nicolas Méhul (1763–1817) and François-Adrien Boieldieu (1775–1834).

Méhul, acceding to the request of Napoleon, tried the experiment of entirely omitting the violins from the score of the opera *Uthal* (1806). He did this by using the viola tone-color to portray the melancholy of dreamy Ossianic poetry, and also giving most of the solo material to the violas. In the *Ouverture* (Ex. 14) and in the opening *"Air et Duo"* (Ex. 15), Méhul's two-part viola scoring sets the mood of the entire opera.[5] According to critics of the time, however, the orchestral tone-color became so monotonous that it impaired the success of the opera. André-Ernest-Modeste Grétry (1741–1813), after hearing *Uthal,* declared in a castigating critique:

> I should give a Louis d'or to hear a chanterelle [violin E string]. This [viola] quality which is so precious when judiciously used and cleverly contrasted with the tone of the violins and other instruments, will soon pall. It is too little varied and bears too much the character of sadness to do otherwise.
> The violas are nowadays often divided into firsts and seconds. In orchestras like that of our opera where they are approximately in a sufficient number this causes no inconvenience. In all other orchestras where they are only to the number of four or five this division can only be detrimental to a group of instruments which is in its entirety so weak that it is likely to be overbalanced by other groups.

---

[5]The orchestration includes *1re Quinte* (Viola I) and *2me Quinte* (Viola II) printed at the top of the orchestral score.

Ex. 10. Antonio Sacchini: Excerpt from *OEdipe à Colone*, Act II, Scene 1.

Ex. 11. Antonio Cherubini: Excerpt from *"Marche"* in *Les Deux Journées*, Act III.

Ex. 11 Continued.

Ex. 12. Gasparo Spontini: Excerpt from *"Hymne du Matin"* in *La Vestale*, Act I, Scene 2

Ex. 12 Continued.

Ex. 13. Gasparo Spontini: Excerpt from *"Hymne du Soire"* in *La Vestale*, Act II, Scene 1.

Ex. 13 Continued.

Ex. 13 Continued.

Ex. 14. Étienne-Nicolas Méhul: Excerpt from *"Ouverture"* to *Uthal.*

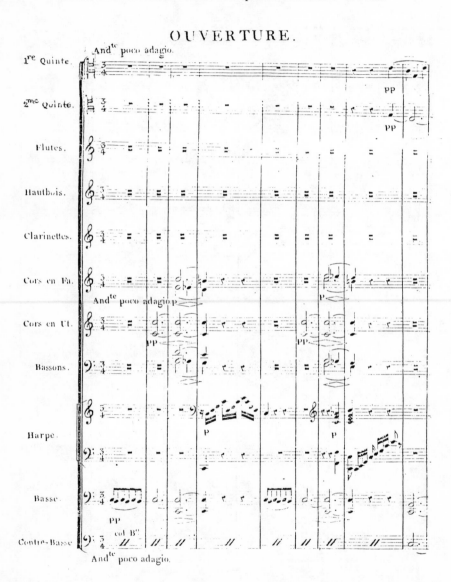

Ex. 14 Continued.

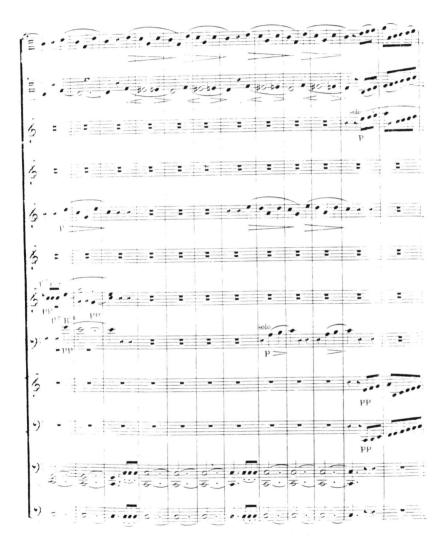

Ex. 15. Étienne-Nicolas Méhul: Excerpt from *"Air et Duo, No. 1"* in *Uthal*.

Ex. 15 Continued.

At this point Grétry makes a most important and revealing observation regarding the size and resultant lack of resonance of the violas in use at that time:

> Here it must still be said that most of the violas used at present in our French orchestras have not the necessary dimensions. They have neither the size, nor as a natural consequence the tone power of a real viola. They are mostly violins strung with viola strings. The musical directors should absolutely forbid the use of these bastard instruments whose tone deprives one of the most interesting parts in the orchestra of its proper colour, robbing it of all its power especially in the lower registers.[6]

François-Adrieu Boieldieu, in his opera *Le Petit Chaperon Rouge* (1818), gave the viola particularly fine parts in the *Trio in F*, No. 3 and in the "Dream Scene." Another French composer, Louis Maillart (1817–1871), recognized the peculiar tone color of the viola and used it effectively in *Les Dragons de Villars* (1856).[7] In the third act of this opera Maillart introduced a short but very expressive viola solo.

Giacomo Meyerbeer (1731–1864), German dramatic composer, after an up-and-down career in Gemany, Austria, and Italy, went to Paris in 1826, where he eventually became one of the leading composers of French opera. In his *Les Huguenots* (1836), he wrote effective solos for the viola and the viola d'amore which were performed with great success by the great artist Chrétien Urhan.[8]

Adolphe Adam (1803–56), in his ballet *Giselle* (1841), included the innovation of replacing the traditional violin with the viola for choreographic sequences—exploiting the sonority, which evokes a mysterious mood and which is profoundly romantic. This viola solo occurs in the second act as an accompaniment for the *pas de deux*.[9]

The Viola in German Opera

The preceding examples have been selected from operas performed in Paris, where composers were giving the tone quality of the viola an occasional prominence. In Berlin, far removed from the French influence, the viola was assigned its most important part in the early 19th century.

---

[6]Quoted and translated by Edmund van der Straeten, "The Viola," *The Strad*, Vol. XXIII, No. 268, p. 120.

[7]Also known under the title, "The Hermit's Bell," from the German version, "Das Glöckenen des Eremiten."

[8]See Chapter XI where *Les Huguenots* and Chrétien Urhan's participation are discussed in greater detail.

[9]"L'Alto," *Music Française*, Feb., 1968; 166: 43–44.

Carl Maria von Weber (1786–1826) is reputed to be the founder of romantic German opera. In *Der Freischütz* (1821), he gave the viola a solo part in which only one violist plays an obbligato throughout an entire aria. This occurs in the *"Romanze und Arie"* of Act III, Scene 3. The *"Romanze"* is announced by a cadenza played by the solo viola (Ex. 16), followed by Aennchen's solo, "Einst träumte meiner sel'gen Base." Thirty-seven bars later, at the conclusion of the *"Romanze,"* there are four brief *recitatives* sung by Aennchen, interspersed with coloratura passages by the obbligato viola. This section serves as an introduction to the *"Arie,"* a duet for Aennchen and the obbligato viola (Ex. 17).[10]

Ex. 16. "Romanze und Arie" from *Der Freischütz.*

Weber's duet part for the viola in *Der Freischütz* did not prompt other German composers to write similar obbligato parts for the instrument in their operas. Richard Wagner (1813–83), later in the century, however, made increasingly more technical demands on the violist in his music dramas. By the end of the 19th century, the opera viola section was no longer a place in which the incompetent violinist could hide.

---

[10]See Chapter X for more about Weber's interest in the viola.

Ex. 17. Carl Maria von Weber: Viola Obbligato in *"Romanze und Arie,"* in *Der Freischütz*

Recit. Viola Solo

Ex. 17 Continued.

Conclusion

Gluck was one of the first composers to understand the viola's potential tone colors in all registers. His successful use of the instrument to provide greater emotional impact on the audience made other Parisian composers aware of the viola's resources; and as a result, music assigned to it gradually assumed more importance in opera orchestral scores. Von Weber was the first 19th century composer to use the viola prominently in German opera.

CHAPTER VIII
VIOLA BOWS

The viola in its present form had evolved mostly before 1600, but outstanding luthiers continued to perfect the instrument during the 17th century. During this period, most makers also constructed bows and cases for the instruments they sold. The bow was not considered as important as the instrument itself, but it was continuously re-designed to keep pace with the music to be performed at the time the instrument was made. As music became more technical, bows had to be fashioned to meet the new demands. Usually this resulted in longer and lighter bows. With the increasing emphasis on *staccato* and *spiccato* bowing in the late 18th century, a more resilient wood was needed for the bow-stick.[1]

French bowmakers, after considerable experimentation in an attempt to meet the needs of such fine visiting Italian violinists as G. B. Viotti (1755–1824), as well as the many native virtuosi in the Paris milieu, ultimately achieved the ideal shape, length, and weight of the bow-stick. Pernambuco wood, being used at the time in dye making, was found best to meet the requirements for strength, weight, and resiliency.

The great demand for better bows toward the end of the 18th century influenced many French craftsmen to specialize exclusively in bowmaking. Since competition among the makers was inevitable under such incentives, the result was the production of many superlative products, especially in the Mirecourt and Paris shops. French bowmakers soon achieved the same type of world-wide reputation that had long been enjoyed by the Italian luthiers.

The sudden rise to success of French bowmaking can be largely attributed to the genius and artistry of François Xavier Tourte (1750–1835), whose bows actually became models of excellence that have never been surpassed. Tourte bows set standards for all later craftsmen to emulate.

---

[1]For an account of the development of the bow prior to Tourte, see 'Symposium: The Baroque Bow—Past and Present," (Moderator: Sonya Monosoff; Panel: David Boyden, Sergiu Luca, and Judith Davidoff), *Journal of the Violin Society of America* Vol. III, No. 4, (Fall, 1977), pp. 35–67. This article includes a fascinating illustrated lecture by David Boyden on the transitional bows of the 18th century.

William Salchow, the eminent contemporary New York bow-maker and expert in the history of bowmaking, furnished important information concerning viola bows. He stated that there is no standard length for viola bows, nor are they longer than violin bows. They are heavier than violin bows by about 10 grams (1/3 ounce), the average weight ranging from 64 to 74 grams (about 2 1/4 to 2 5/8 ounces). Tourte, he said, did not establish the dimensions of the modern viola bow; in fact, no one has. He maintained that present-day violists want heavier, but not necessarily larger, bows than those made in the early 19th century. A viola bow, he continued, requires about 10% more of the same strong unbleached hair than a violin bow. Viola bows of comparable quality cost more than violin bows because they are scarcer. Mr. Salchow says he presently makes about the same number of viola as violin bows.[2]

Mr. Salchow graciously furnished photographs of selected viola bows that have passed through his shop, along with measurements and other pertinent information. With the exception of Tourte, the makers and their products follow alphabetically in the text.

François Xavier Tourte, of Paris, is recognized as being the finest bowmaker of all time and was largely responsible in determining the length and shape of the bow in its present form. Etienne Vatelot, in his definitive book, *Les Archets Français*, observed:

> His fantastic skill allowed him to realize some incomparable work and has given rise to his nickname of the "Stradivari of Bowmakers."[3]

Salchow furnished the following information for the Tourte viola bow, c.1815, shown in Plate 37:

> Length of bow (wood only) is 72.8 cm. (28 5/8 in.), which is the standard length of a French bow, violin or viola. Some viola bows are up to 1.3 cm. (1/2 in.) shorter; very rarely, slightly longer. The Tourte has an unusually high head: 26 mm. (1 in.). The distance from the stick to the hair at the frog is 20.5 mm. (13/16 in.). This is high; most viola bows are about 19.5 mm. (3/4 in.). The Tourte bow, with whalebone winding, weighs 69 grams (2 7/16 ounces).[4]

Mr. Salchow stated that he has no idea how many Tourte bows are extant.

John "Kew" Dodd (1752–1839), born in Stirling, Scotland, into the family of Edward Dodd (1705–1810), made both violins and bows, but specialized in the latter. John "Kew" was known as the "English Tourte." According to Roda:

---

[2]William Salchow's responses to questions sent him in a letter of October 10, 1978.
[3]Etienne Vatelot, *Les Archets Français* (Nancy: Sernor-M. Dufour, 1977), Vol. II, pp. 918–9.
[4]William Salchow, letter to author, July 24, 1979.

His best bows, particularly those for viola and cello, are very fine . . . Most of his sticks were cut to the desired sweep, not shaped by heat.[5]

But the expert bowmaker, William Salchow, disputes Roda's statement regarding Dodd's method of placing the camber in bows:

Speaking of Dodd's bows, there is one canard about the curve which I would like to lay to rest . . . Some people maintain that Dodd sawed or cut the curve into the stick, rather than by bending it in with heat. This is undesirable from a technical viewpoint, because if you cut across the grain of the wood, you will severely weaken the bow and it is liable to snap at the head . . . Generally speaking, the idea that the curve was cut into the wood has no basis in fact.[6]

A beautiful example of a Dodd viola bow, c.1810, is shown in Plate 38.

Joseph Henry (1823–1870), born in Mirecourt, went to Paris in 1837 to work in Georges Chanot's shop, and later in Dominique Peccatte's. His bows were greatly influenced by the latter maker. In 1848, Henry joined Paul Simon, with whom he remained until 1851, when he set up his own atelier.[7]

Salchow stated that the head of the Henry gold tortoise viola bow (Plate 39) is 24.5 mm. (31/32 in.) high, which he said, "is about average." The distance from the stick to the hair at the frog of the gold Henry (Plate 40) is 20.3 mm. (13/16 in.), which "is higher than average." The weight of the gold Henry is 67 grams (2 3/8 ounces). Both of the Henry bows were made c.1860.

Joseph René Lafleur (1812–1879) was born in Paris, where he studied music with the intention of becoming a professional violinist. As a result, he did not apprentice as a bowmaker with his father, Jacques Lafleur (1757–1833). When his career as a performer failed of fruition, he turned to bowmaking as a profession. After several years of experimentation, Joseph René became an outstanding bowmaker in his own right.[8] A beautiful example of Lafleur's workmanship is shown in the viola bow, c.1840 (Plate 41).

Dominique Peccatte (1810–1874), born in Mirecourt, began work briefly as a violin maker. In 1826, he went to Paris and worked for Jean Baptiste Vuillaume, where he learned the art of bowmaking. In 1837, he took over the shop of François Lupot. In 1848, he returned to

---

[5]Joseph Roda, *Bows for Musical Instruments* (Chicago: William Lewis & Son, 1959), pp. 152–3.

[6]Panel Discussion (Moderator: William Salchow, Panel: Joseph Kuhn and Joseph Siegelman), "National Schools and Styles of Bowmaking," *Journal of the Violin Society of America*, Vol. III, No. 4, (Fall, 1977), pp. 103–4.

[7]Vatelot, *op. cit.*, Vol. I, p. 420.

[8]*Ibid.*, Vol. I., p. 480.

Mirecourt, where he worked until his death. He is recognized as one of the greatest craftsmen in the art of bowmaking.[9]

The bow, c.1850, shown in Plate 42, according to Salchow, is unusual in that the distance from the stick to the hair at the frog is only 18.6 mm., whereas the average for French bows is about 19.5 mm. The Tourte viola bow, shown in Plate 37 is 20.5 mm. The weight of this Peccatte bow is 67 grams, as compared to the 69 grams of the Tourte.

Eugène Sartory (1871–1946) was also born in Mirecourt. He was apprenticed in Paris with Charles Peccatte, and then with Alfred Lamy. He opened his own shop in 1889, and became one of the great master bowmakers.[10] The Sartory bow shown in Plate 43 was made c.1930, and is a fine example of his late period.

Mr. Salchow concluded his descriptions of viola bows with the following observations:

> The average weight range [of viola bows] is from 64 to 74 grams (2 1/4 ounces to 2 5/8 ounces). The older French bows often have high frogs. The modern makers, Sartory and later, tend to make lower frogs. Old French viola bows are quite rare; probably reflecting a lesser demand. But the modern viola bow appeared about the same time as the violin bow, i.e., c.1780.[11]

Salchow recommended that a violist selecting a bow should choose one which is found to be comfortable, which does what is wanted, and which produces the sound desired.

To mention all of the many fine French *archetiers* whose viola bows are not shown in this chapter goes beyond the space limitations of this book.[12] A very short representative list follows: Three generations of the Adam family: Jean (w.1790–1820), Jean Dominique (1795–1865), and Adam, known as "Grand-Adam" (1823–1869); members of the Lamy family: particularly Alfred Joseph (1850–1919), and his son Alfred, known as "Lamy Fils" (w.1919–1944); the Millant brothers: Roger (b.1901) and Max (b.1903), who opened their business in 1923 and closed it in 1969; members of the Ouchard family: Emile François, known as "Pere" (1872–1951), his son Emile A., called "Ouchard Fils" (1900–1969), Bernard Ouchard (b.1925), since 1971 professor of bowmaking at the violinmaking school in Mirecourt, and Jean-Claude Ouchard (b.1935); Pajeot (1791–1849); François Nicolas Voirin (1833–1885), "the most important bowmaker of the second half of the 19th

---

[9]*Ibid.*, Vol. II, p. 738.

[10]*Ibid.*, Vol. II, p. 816.

[11]William Salchow Letter, *op. cit.*

[12]For a complete listing of French bowmakers, see Vatelot, *op. cit.*, Vols. I and II. The "w." in dates is used to indicate "worked."

century"[13]; and Jean Baptiste Vuillaume (1798–1875), in whose shop many of the finest bowmakers of the 19th century were trained and employed.

Although French craftsmen certainly excelled in bowmaking during the 19th century, many makers in neighboring countries were also producing fine viola bows. In England, for example, there was the Dodd family: John "Kew" Dodd and his two brothers, James I (first half of the 18th century) and Thomas (c. 1760–1823). A son of James I, named James II after his father, also made good bows, but they scarcely equalled in quality those of his uncle, John "Kew" Dodd. Besides this family, there were also James Tubbs (1835–1921), called "The Modern English Tourte," and George Louis Panormo (1774–1842). Tubbs, as a young man, worked with Reitfort and other fine craftsmen for W. E. Hill & Sons, making bows that bore the "Hill" label. In 1860 Tubbs opened his own shop, and with the assistance of his son Alfred (d. 1912), is reputed to have made over 5,000 bows for violin, viola, and cello.[14]

In the second half of the 19th century families of German makers, mostly from Markneukirchen, made good viola bows patterned after the great French makers. As Markneukirchen became overcrowded with fine bowmakers, second and third generations of the established families sometimes migrated to other cities. Outstanding among the Germans were: Franz Albert Nürnberger II (1854–1931); Ludwig Christian August Bausch (1835–1871), known as the "German Tourte"; Heinrich Knopf (1835–1875), of Berlin, and Richard Knopf (1860–1939), who came to the United States in 1879 to work in Philadelphia, and later in New York City; Hermann Richard Pfretzschner (1856–1921); and Nicolaus Kittel (1839–1870), who migrated to St. Petersburg, Russia, where he became known as the "Russian Tourte."[15]

Conclusion

During the 19th century, there was not as great a demand for viola bows as for violin and cello bows because so many violists used very

[13]*Ibid.*, II, p. 984.

[14]Joseph Roda, *op. cit*, pp. 295–6.

[15]For more on bows, see the entire issue of "Proceedings of the Fifth Annual Convention, November 12–13, 1977," *Journal of the Violin Society of America* Vol. III, No. 4; (Fall, 1977), also see the same *Journal* Vol. IV, No. 3, (1978), which includes significant lectures on bows given by Andrew Hill, of the English firm of W. E. Hill & Sons, and by Etienne Vatelot, author of the definitive *Les Archets Français*. These latter lectures were given at the Convention of the Violin Society held at La Jolla, California, November 9–12, 1978.

small violas, or even violins strung as violas, which they played with violin bows. As a result, most of the fine bowmakers did not produce many viola bows. Ultimately, by around 1900, most violists had become cognizant of the desirability of playing their instruments with bows designed for their instrument. Today a fine 19th century viola bow is in such demand that it usually costs more than a comparable violin or cello bow. Because of the scarcity of 19th century bows, 20th century violists are turning increasingly to the products of contemporary bowmakers.

All of the photographs of viola bows, Plates 37–43, were furnished by William Salchow, of New York City.

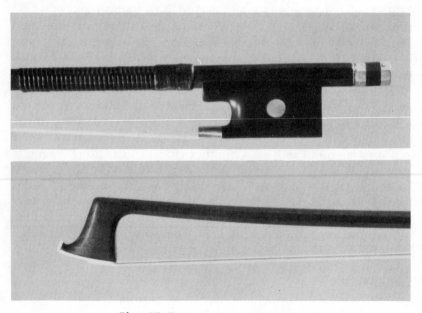

Plate 37. François. Tourte Viola Bow.

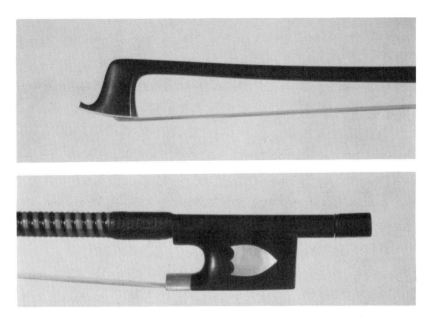

Plate 38. John "Kew" Dodd Viola Bow.

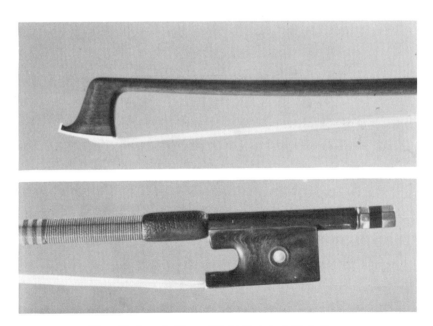

Plate 39. Joseph Henry "Gold-Tortoise" Viola Bow.

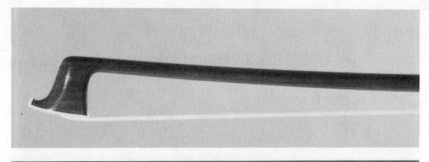

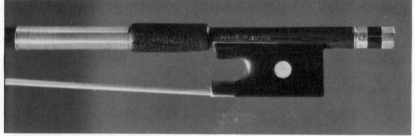

Plate 40. Joseph Henry "Gold" Viola Bow.

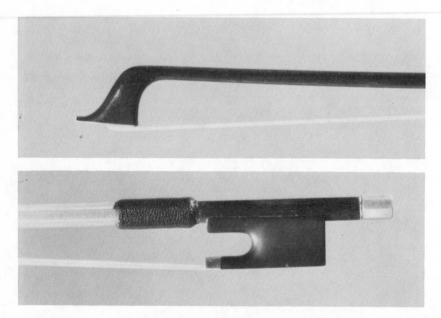

Plate 41. Joseph René LeFleur Viola Bow.

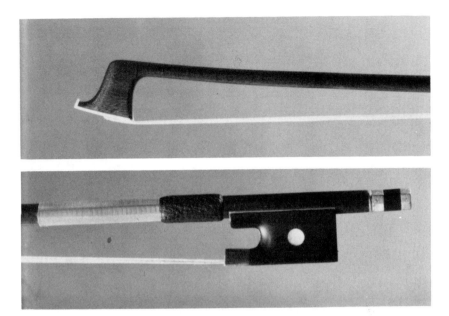

Plate 42. Dominique Peccate Viola Bow.

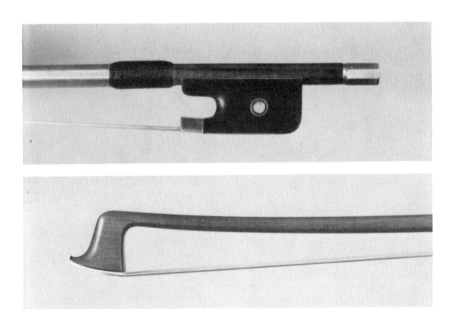

Plate 43. Eugène Sartory Viola Bow.

CHAPTER IX
INSTRUCTION FOR THE VIOLA

Early *Méthodes d'Alto*

The publication of an instruction book for an instrument results from a need, and the existence of a potential market for the sale of the book. In Germany several publications in the late 17th and early 18th centuries had furnished meager details for performing on the viola.[1] The German books usually gave the tunings for the *alto* and the *tenor*, and implied that they were played like the violin. These treatises were general works which also furnished information on such varied subjects as performance practices for other instruments, how to play a continuo part, how to learn solfege, etc. They were not in any sense actual instruction books for the viola.[2]

The earliest printed method books for the viola appeared in France over a half-century after similar publications for the violin and cello had been brought out in Paris, London, and Germany.

Late in the 18th century Karl and Anton Stamitz apeared in Paris as viola soloists at the *Concerts Spirituels*. Composers of operas in Paris, particularly Gluck, Sacchini, Cherubini, Spontini, Méhul, and Boieldieu were giving more and more recognition in their scores to the viola as an expressive instrument.[3] Indicative of the increasing importance of the viola in Parisian music in the late 18th century was the emergence of the following printed tutors for the instrument:

Michel Corrette, *Méthode d'Alto*, 1782 (perhaps as early as 1760)
Jean B. Cupis, *Méthode d'Alto*, c.1788.
Michel Woldemar, *Méthode d'Alto*, c.1795.

---

[1]See Chapters V and VI.

[2]For a much more detailed commentary on this subject see, Maurice W. Riley, *The Teaching of Bowed Instruments from 1511 to 1756* (Doctoral Dissertation, University of Michigan, Ann Arbor, 1954).

[3]See Chapter VII for more on the use of the viola in the Paris opera.

167

Among these works, Corette's Méthode is not only the earliest known, but it is also the most important, both musically and historically.

Meanwhile in London, an anonymous tutor had appeared, c.1795, entitled, *Complete Instructions for the Tenor*. The similarity of this work to the early French *Méthodes* might suggest that the English book was copied from, or at least influenced by, the French versions.

Shortly thereafter, three new *Méthodes* were published in Paris to meet the demand for more sophisticated tutors than the earlier works:

Bartolomeo Bruni, *Méthode d'Alto*, 1805.
M. J. Gebauer, *Méthode d'Alto*, 2nd edition, 1816; 1st edition perhaps as early as 1800.
Jacob Martinn, *Méthode d'Alto*, c.1815, perhaps as early as 1810.

Martinn's *Méthode* is still used today. Theodore Laforge, Professor of Viola at the Paris Conservatoire in the early 20th century, thought enough of this work to bring out an *urtext* edition. It was his hope that this publication would discourage the use of the "arranged" and mutilated editions on the market.

Of these last three tutors, by far the most important was the Bruni, which contained a set of 25 études. Although published in Paris, the work was written by an Italian violinist and composer, whose études reflected both the French influence of the classic studies written by Baillot, Rode, and Kreutzer,[4] and also Bruni's own early training in the Italian school of violin playing.

Two books of viola studies appeared in Austria and Germany after the turn of the century:

Franz Anton Hoffmeister, *12 Viola-Etuden*, c.1800.
Bartolomeo Campagnoli, *41 Capricen*, c.1805.

Hoffmeister, a composer and publisher, lived in the city of Vienna, where violists were performing solo works by Mozart, von Dittersdorf, Hoffstetter, Vanhal, Wranitzky, and others. He saw the need for a set of advanced studies for the viola; and being a pragmatic publisher, he wrote them himself.

Campagnoli, a highly gifted Italian violinist, spent part of his career in Leipzig, where he was concertmaster of the Gewandhaus orchestra and taught violin and viola at the Hochschule. It was to meet the technical needs of his advanced viola students that he composed

---

[4]*Méthode de Violon par les Cens. Baillot, Rode et Kreutzer . . . , Adoptée par le Conservatoire*, Paris, 1773.

the famous *Capricen,* which have aptly been called "the Kreutzer-Fiorillo of the viola."

All of the tutors mentioned above have either made a pedagogical contribution to the performance techniques of the instrument, or, at the very least, have achieved historical significance by their very existence. Each of these books will be examined to determine how its contents might be related to *The History of the Viola.*

Corrette's *Méthode*

Michel Corrette (1709–95) was a musician who, in addition to composing and performing music, wrote tutors for the clavecin, flute, vielle, and cello. He also wrote beginning and advanced method books for the violin. Besides, he authored the first known printed instructions for double bass and viola, entitled *Méthodes pour apprendre à jouer de la contre-basse . . . de la quinte ou alto.*[5] This book also includes a description of an instrument, *la viole d'Orphée,* which Corrette apparently had invented. A frontispiece (Plate 44) depicts the string bass and viola, but not the *viole d'Orphée.* The bass has C holes, and its lowest string is over-spun with wire. An iron key *(clef de fer),* pictured at the bottom of the plate, was to be used to facilitate turning the pegs. The viola has *f* holes and the shorter fingerboard typical of that time. Bow sticks for both instruments are straight.

Corrette began his didactic material with a discussion of the string bass, which is followed in turn by sections on the viola and the viole d'Orphée. In the preface to his tutor, he pointed out that the "alto, for which I also give principles of playing, is a very ancient instrument." He continued that in Lully's time the operas included three parts entitled: *haute-contre, taille,* and *quinte,* all written on a C clef, with C located on the first, second, and third lines respectively. Corrette explained that *quinte* was another name for the *alto.*[6] Later, the book states that scarcely any of the Italians composed concertos without using the viola. It suggests that students look at the "concertos by Corelli, Vivaldi, and Geminiani or the *Stabat [Mater]* by Pergolesi," and "*L'estro harmonico* by Vivaldi, [in which] there are two parts for viola." Corrette pointed especially to the "*Concerto,* Op.

---

[5]Michel Corrette, *Méthodes pour apprendre à jouer de la contre-basse à 3. à 4. et à 5. cordes, de la quinte ou alto et de la viole d'Orphée nouvel instrument ajusté sur l'ancienne viole . . .* (Paris: chez l'Auteur, n.d. [pub. c.1782 or earlier]. This work is now available in reprint edition, pub. by Minkoff, 1977.)

[6]*Ibid.,* p. 2.

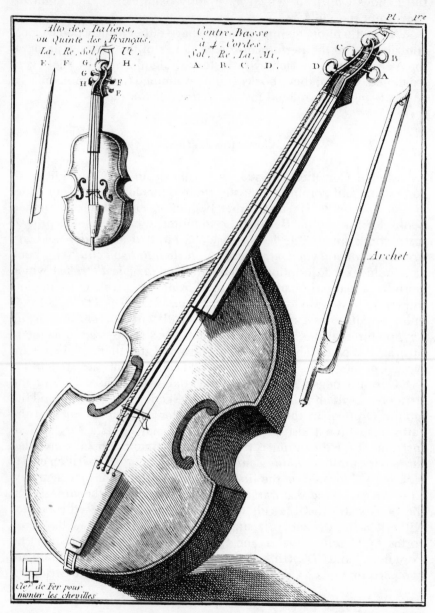

Plate 44. Michel Corrette: Frontispiece to *Méthodes pour apprendre à jouer... de la quinte au alto.*

1, No. 8, by Locatelli, [where] there are four parts for viola, of which two are in the concertino."[7]

Corrette's instructions for the viola begin with the statement that "Viola music is always notated on the clef which has C on the third line"; and then he furnished diatonic and chromatic fingerings (Ex's 18 and 19). In Corrette's fingering for the chromatic scale, the first finger is responsible for three pitches on each of the three lower strings. A printer's error occurs on the A string where $c\sharp$ wrongly precedes a $c\natural$ in the ascending scale.

Ex. 18. Michel Corrette: Diatonic fingerings for the viola

Ex. 19. Michel Corrette: Chromatic fingerings for the viola

Concerning ornaments, the book states that while *cadences*, *martellemens*, *port de voix*, and *coulés* are rarely played on the viola, the former two embellishments sound very satisfactory on the high string.

For bowing instructions, Corrette explained that the viola is bowed like the violin and the cello, and referred the student to the

[7]*Ibid.*, p. 18.

eighth page of his violin method and to the second chapter of his cello tutor for rules and examples on bowing.[8]

The exercises furnished for the student cover a wide range of difficulty. A viola duet follows the études, entitled "Marche des Ostrogots, Visigots, et Allobroges," which consists of a *Marche* and two *Minuets*. This duet is followed by a *Sonata for Two Violas*, and then in turn by a *Sonata for Viola and Bass*. The latter composition includes three movements: *Allegro, Aria,* and *Minuetto*. These two *Sonatas* are not elementary pieces, but represent the typical Baroque music played by mature performers of that time.[9]

Accompaniment, Corrette asserted, is more difficult to play with the viola than with the string bass, since the viola rarely played the root, but instead the third or fifth of the harmony. The performer, he added, must be particularly on the alert for flats and sharps and also for the mode of the composition.[10]

Some violinists, the book explains, prefer the viola to the cello for the accompaniment of their sonatas. In such an accompaniment, the viola sometimes has to play the bass an octave higher. Corrette did not consider a viola sufficient to carry a whole accompaniment, for he contended that the cello and clavecin should be added when the viola was used. He concluded the *Méthode d'alto* by citing illustrations where the viola was not used: "Some time ago in Paris I heard the famous Somis[11] and Guignon[12] play violin sonatas. They were accompanied not only by the cello and clavecin but also by the bass"; and he advised that in some of Leclair's sonatas only the cello and clavecin should be used.[13]

Cupis' *Méthode*

Jean Baptiste Cupis was born in 1741 into a Parisian musical family. He first studied music with his father, François Cupis, and then at an early age studied cello with the distinguished Martin

---

[8]*Ibid.*, p. 19.

[9]The *Sonata for Two Violas* and the *Sonata for Viola and Bass* are available in a modern edition, edited by Erich Doflein, published by B. Schott, 1972. For the latter piece Doflein provided a realization of the figured bass for keyboard, and a cello part to reinforce the continuo when performed with harpsichord.

[10]Corette, *op. cit.*, p. 30.

[11]Giovanni Battista Somis (1686–1763), student of Corelli and teacher of Leclair.

[12]Giovanni Guignon (1702–1774) played in the *Concerts Spirituels* as early as 1725, and was a rival of Leclair.

[13]Corrette, *op. cit.*, p. 31.

Berteau. When he was twenty, he was considered to be one of the finest cellists in France. He joined the Opéra Orchestra in Paris and was placed in the concertino section, which accompanied the soloists in arias. In 1771 he left this position in order to undertake a concert career. He went to Germany and Italy, and then returned to Paris. In the meantime he had married the singer, Julie Gasperini. They went to Milan in 1794. His life from this point is mostly a matter of conjecture, for the facts are unknown.

Cupis wrote a *Méthode de Violoncelle*, two *Concertos*, and several works with theme and variations for cello. He also wrote a *Méthode d'Alto*, which is now very rare.[14]

The title page of the *Méthode d'Alto* has no date indicated (see Plate 45). According to Wilhelm Altmann, however, separate editions of it were published before 1788 by both Decombe and Janet.[15]

The title page is followed by nine pages of introductory theoretical material that does not apply specifically to the viola. Directions for playing the viola begin on page ten: "De la maniere de tenir l'alto" (The way to hold the viola). Cupis' book directs the player to

> Press it [the viola] directly against the chest, tilted slightly toward the A string side. The chin is placed on the side of the fourth [C] string.
> Try to always hold the scroll of the viola at the same height as your mouth.
> Bring the left arm as far as possible toward the inside of the viola to give the fingers more facility when playing on the low strings.
> The fingers should strike the strings with force to make it possible for the viola to produce a maximum sound; [and] so that the fingers will not go to sleep.

For holding the bow the student is directed to "grasp it as near to the end as possible." This differs from the grip advised by Corrette in which the bow was held more toward the middle. Cupis' *Méthode* adds:

> Place the little finger an inch *(pouce)* from the screw. Place the thumb of the right hand between the hair and the stick.

This is unlike the "French bow grip," advocated by Corrette, in which the thumb is placed under the hair. Cupis' directions continue:

> Place the four fingers on the stick 3 or 4 lines from each other, and the thumb in the middle; the bow always leaning toward the fingerboard.

---

[14]Copies survive in the Bibliotheque der Gesellschaft der Musik-Freunde des Öesterrichischen Staates in Vienna and in the Kongelige Bibliothek in Copenhagen. A Xerox copy from the latter library was used for this investigation.

[15]Wilhelm Altmann and Vadim Borissovsky, *Literaturverzeichnis für Bratsche und Viola d'Amore* (Wolfenbüttel: Musikalische Kultur und Wissenschaft, 1937), p. 7.

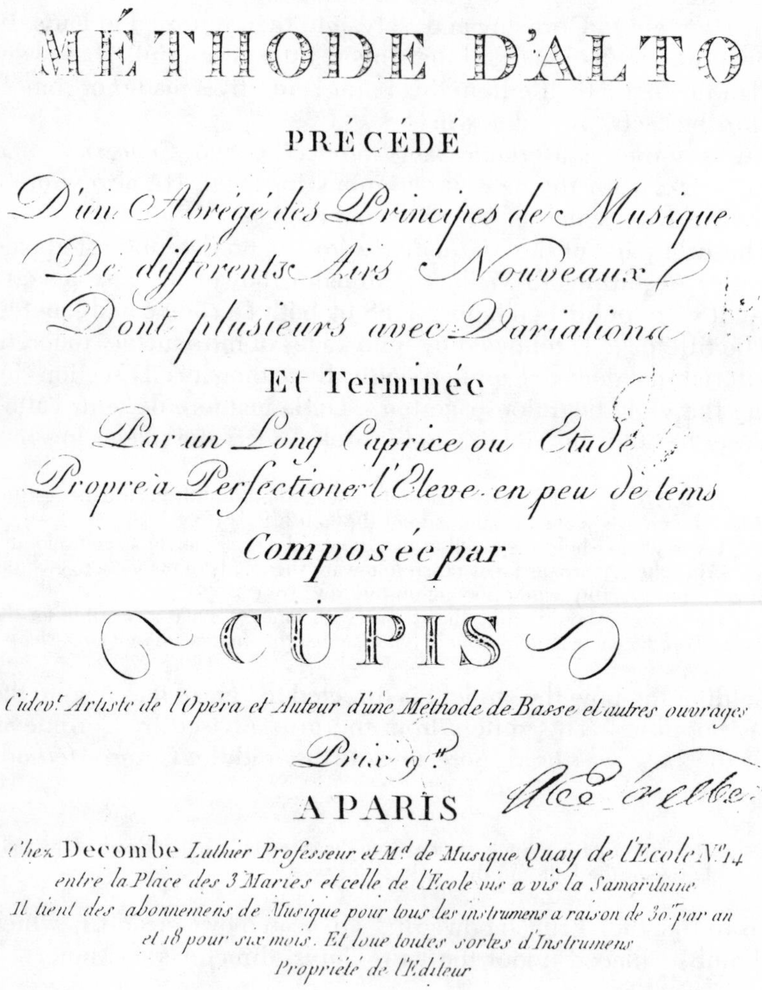

MÉTHODE D'ALTO

PRÉCÉDÉ

D'un Abrégé des Principes de Musique
De différents Airs Nouveaux
Dont plusieurs avec Variations

Et Terminée

Par un Long Caprice ou Etudé
Propre à Perfectioner l'Eleve en peu de tems

Composée par

CUPIS

Cidev.t Artiste de l'Opéra et Auteur d'une Méthode de Basse et autres ouvrages

Prix 9.es

A PARIS

Chez Decombe Luthier Professeur et M.d de Musique Quay de l'Ecole N.o 14
entre la Place des 3 Maries et celle de l'Ecole vis a vis la Samaritaine
Il tient des abonnemens de Musique pour tous les instrumens a raison de 30.f par an
et 18 pour six mois. Et loue toutes sortes d'Instrumens
Propriété de l'Editeur

Plate 45. Jean Baptiste Cupis: Title Page to *Méthode d'Alto*.

For bowing the viola, always endeavor to keep the bow one inch from the bridge.

In taking down and up bows, you should raise the arm to acquire lighter and faster bowing.

Some musical examples of fingerings for first, second, and third positions are next discussed and illustrated. Cupis explained that there are higher positions, but that the teacher should not use them with young students because they are too difficult. He added, however, that it is necessary to discuss the problem of half-position (*position près le sillet, ou demi position*) and furnished the following example (Ex. 20):

Ex. 20. Jean Baptiste Cupis: Half-position fingerings

The remainder of the *Méthode* contains fourteen duets for two violas (pp. 14–27), and concludes with a "Caprice or Etude," which, according to the title page, is "good for perfecting the student in a short time." This last piece is scored for viola and bass (pp. 28–31), and contains examples of difficult technical material from both the Baroque and the Classic eras, including passages of *bariolage, arpeggiando*, double stops, and string-crossing in the third position.

Complete Instructions for the Tenor

The earliest known viola tutor printed in England, *Complete Instructions for the Tenor . . .*,[16] appeared around 1790. The fact that

---

[16]*Complete Instructions for the Tenor Containing such Rules and Examples as are necessary for Learners with a selection of Favorite Song-Tunes, Minuets, Marches, Etc., Judiciously adapted for that Instrument by an Eminent Master* (London: Longman and Broderip, [n. d.]). Copies of this rare method book are in the British Museum Library and in the New York City Public Library.

it was published suggests that there was a growing interest in the
tenor[17] among beginners, and also amateur violinists, who wanted to
learn how to read viola music. The title-page promises to do just that:
"Containing such Rules and Examples as are necessary for Learners,
with a selection of Favorite Song-Tunes, Minuets, Marches, Etc." The
author of this book is unknown but the title page assures the reader
that it is by "an Eminent Master."

This instruction book is of oblong format and consists of twenty-
four pages of instructive material and music. The first three pages
cover basic note reading, contain a fingerboard chart with positions
indicated for finger placement, and inform the student that "The
tenor has four strings, two covered with silver wire and two of
catgut . . ." *Graces* (ornaments) according to the illustrations are to
be performed in the Baroque style. The viola student is informed that
his music will be written on the "tenor cliff" [sic], which is illustrated
as our alto clef. This illustration is followed by a fingering chart on
shifting (pp. 4–5); "If you put your first finger on this place [c or c♯ on
the A string] then it is called the *Half Shift* [present day second
position]." Third position is called *Whole Shift*, and sixth position is
called the *Double Shift*.[18]

The introductory section, consisting of 6 pages, is followed by 17
pages of music, which was probably intended for amateur violinists
who wanted to learn to play the *tenor*. The first piece is "God Save the
King," followed by minuets, hornpipes, marches, jiggs, Handel's
Gavotte, and popular songs of the time, such as "Blow, Blow, Thou
Winter Wind." It concludes with "Arno's Vale."

This tutor was published a short time after William Flackton
(1709–1793) published his *Sonatas for Viola and Piano;* Flackton,
therefore, has been suggested as a possible author of it. A more logical
conjecture is that the publisher reworked some of the English violin
instruction books of the time and also derived material from the
French *Méthodes d'Alto*.

Gebauer's *Méthode*

Michael Joseph Gebauer (1763–1812), according to Fétis,[19] was a
prodigy on the violin, viola, and oboe. At the age of fourteen, when he

---

[17]The word *tenor* was more commonly used than *viola* in England and referred to small- as well
as large-sized models.

[18]Peter Prelleur, in *The Art of playing on the Violin*, one of several tutors in a collection entitled
The Modern Music Master (London, 1731), used the same terminology for naming the positions.

[19]François-Joseph Fétis, *Biographie Universelle des Musiciens*, 2nd Ed. (Paris, 1878, III), p.
433.

was already an oboeist in the king's Suisse Garde, he lost his father. This made him head of the family and gave him the responsibility of tutoring his talented brothers.[20]

According to Fétis, Gebauer was appointed violist in the Chapell at Versailles at the age of twenty. It was believed at the time that, in addition to being able to play several wind instruments, he would become a violinist and violist of the first rank. Unfortunately, a tragic accident caused him to lose a joint of the little finger of his left hand, and he had to give up the viola and violin. He was able to fix a mechanical extension to his little finger, however, and returned to playing the oboe.

In 1794 he became professor of oboe at the Paris Conservatoire, a position he held until 1802, when he was appointed Chef de Musique of the Guarde Imperiale. During the following years, he wrote over a hundred marches. His military duties forced him to follow Napoleon's army in the campaigns of 1805, 1806, 1809, and 1812. He succumbed from fatigue in the Retreat from Moscow in 1812.

Although forced by events beyond his control to channel most of his talent into the field of woodwind instruments and military band music, Gebauer had already left his *Méthode d'Alto* as a legacy to the viola. No exact date of the publication is now known, but the title page of the second edition states that he is a member of the Guarde Imperiale, a position which he attained in 1802. The first edition was, in all probability, published before 1800 and possibly before he was forced to give up the viola in 1793.

Among his earlier works Fétis listed two sets of duets:

6 *Duos for Violin and Viola*, Op. 1 (Paris: Sieber, n.d.).
6 *Duos for Violin and Viola*, Op. 5 (Paris: Janet, n.d.).

The title page of Gebauer's tutor describes the format of the work as follows:

Method for the Viola, containing the principles of music, with accompanied scales in all keys, followed by little duet pieces taken from the most celebrated composers, such as Haydn, Mozart, and Boccherini. Composed and dedicated to the amateur, Monsieur Biancour, by M. J. Gebauer, member of the Legion of Honor and director of music of the Imperial Guard.

In addition to the composers mentioned in the title, the *Méthode* includes compositions by Rasetti and Wranitzky. None of these com-

---

[20]One of Gabauer's brothers, François-René, became Professor of Bassoon at the Paris Conservatoire at the age of 23. His compositions include 3 *Trios for Clarinet, Viola, and Cello* (Paris: Naderman, n.d.).

positions were originally written for the viola, but are transcriptions by Gebauer. The actual music for the viola begins on page 14, following the "principles of music." Gebauer's tutor presents an interesting and logical system of introducing the student to the various keys. Each page consists of a "*Gamme duo.*" The top part, for the student, is a scale; and the lower part, for the teacher, is an accompanying ornamentation of the scale. Each scale is followed by a composition in the same key for two violas. Page 14, for example, begins with the scale of C major, followed by an *Allegro* by Mozart. The scale of A minor, with an *Allegretto* by Rasetti appears on page 15; and the key of F major and a *Rondo* by Mozart on page 16. A *Vivace* by Haydn and the appropriate scale in D minor are presented on page 17. In all, there are twenty-six compositions, concluding with an *Air Polonaise* by Gebauer in the ridiculously difficult key of $D\sharp$ minor, which is on the last page of the tutor. The compositions do not contain technical problems, but progress from easy to more difficult keys.

Gebauer's *Méthode* must have met with some degree of success, since other editions appeared in 1816 and in 1820, published by Sieber; and there were still later printings by Lemoine, n.d., and Margueritat, n.d.

Martinn's *Méthode*

Jacob Joses Balthazar Martinn[21] was born in Antwerp in 1775 and died in Paris in 1836. As a young man he moved to Paris, where he played violin in the Opéra Orchestra and taught violin and viola at the Lycée de Charlemagne. Later he played the viola in the l'Opéra Buffa. He wrote numerous works, including tutors for both the violin and viola, and Solo Sonatas for the viola.

Martinn's *Méthode d'Alto* was published before 1816, perhaps as early as 1810, and is in two parts. The first section

> Contains scales and études in all keys; twelve Lessons [written as] Duets; and three easy Sonatas.

The second section, sometimes published separately, contains *24* [advanced] *Études.*[22] The Duet Lessons of the first section are for two violas, and are all in the key of C major, but become progressively

---

[21]French spelling: Jaques Joseph Balthazar Martinn.

[22]Modern reprint, containing excerpts from both sections and fingered by Théophile Laforge, then Professor of Viola at the Paris Conservatoire. Laforge used the *24 Études* in his teaching. *Nouvelle Edition*, published by Costallat, c. 1900.

more difficult with each succeeding piece. Lessons 10, 11, and 12 include material in the third position.

The 3 *Sonatas* are also written for two violas, and are more technically advanced than the *Lessons*. The first *Sonata* is in the key of C major, the second in D major, and the third in G major.

The 24 *Études* range from easy to difficult, and might be compared with the Mazas *Violin Études*, Op. 36, Bk. I. The second section of the Martinn tutor includes two études which are suitable to use as solos: No. 10, an *Andante in E♭ Major* is a tonal study of medium difficulty; No. 22, an *Adagio in E Major* is more difficult, requiring long sustained bowings, double stops, and a passage in third position on the C string.

Etudes 23 and 24 introduce the student to the treble clef and the fifth position. It is apparent from a perusal of the Martinn *Méthode* that he understood the problems in bowings and fingerings, in which students needed special examples for practice. The Martinn book, particularly the second section, is still used by many teachers with students who are not yet ready to play the more difficult Bruni or Campagnoli studies.

Woldemar's *Méthode*

Michel Woldemar was born in Orleans in 1750, and died in Clermont Ferrand in 1816. He was a violinist, violist, composer, and author of theoretical works. He studied the violin with the Italian maestro, Antonio Lolli. At an early age he developed an interest in the viola. In Paris there was a scarcity of good violists. In an attempt to obviate this problem, he "invented" the *violin-alto*. This was not actually an invention, as Woldemar claimed; it simply consisted of adding a C string to the violin, making it a five-stringed instrument. It was Woldemar's theory that fine violinists could play either violin or viola parts on the same instrument, and he believed that his "invention" would alleviate the paucity of fine violists.

Chrétien Urhan, the finest violist in Paris at that time, gave concerts on the instrument at the Conservatoire, including a *Concerto in C Major* composed by Woldemar and dedicated to Urhan. The *violin-alto*, however, was not accepted by Urhan, or any other musician in Paris, as a substitute for the viola. Grétry, Berlioz, and other composers and conductors were already dissatisfied with the small-sized violas played by most violists, and they were not about to accept a violin-sized instrument with its non-resonant C string.

Woldemar's *Méthode d'Alto,* which was for the four-stringed viola, met with better acceptance than his *violin-alto.* According to the title page, his *Méthode*

> Contains the first elements of music, the position fingerings, and the old and modern bow strokes, followed by [duet] Variations for viola and violin.

The gamut for the viola is illustrated with a *C Major* scale of three octaves, plus an extension to *g* in third position on the *A* string. The section on positions also includes fingerings for second position, with fourth finger extensions.

Seven pages of theoretical material and scales are followed on page 8 by viola and violin duets. The viola part, for the student, is printed on a staff above the teacher's violin part, which is printed on the lower staff. The music section of the book comprises only three pages, beginning with the theme entitled, *Polacca, Tempo de Minuetto,* which is followed by eight *Variations.* In *Variation I* the viola part is intended to develop good bow control through the use of long bows. In *Variation II* the violin plays the theme while the viola plays an ornamented part. In *III* the violist again plays the theme. In *IV* the violin plays the theme "guimbarde supres de chevalet"[23] (near the bridge [sounding like a] jew's harp). This is followed later in the *Variation* with the direction "sons ordinaire" (regular sounds). Each succeeding *Variation* gives the violist a more difficult part, and the *Méthode* concludes with the violin playing a new melody while the viola plays arpeggiated material based on the original theme.

Bruni's *Méthode*

Antonio Bartolomeo Bruni was born in Coni, Piedmont, Italy, in 1751 and died there in 1821.[24] He studied violin with Pugnani at Turin. He spent most of his adult career in Paris where he appeared in the *Concerts Spirituels* in 1780. In 1781 he joined the *Comedie Italienne* as a violinist, and after 1789, composed and conducted operas in Paris. During his stay in Paris, he also taught violin and viola. It was in the latter capacity that he discovered the need for literature for the advanced violist or for a violinist who wanted to learn the viola clef. Among the works he wrote for the instrument are *3 Solo Viola Sonatas,* Op. 27; more than 20 *Violin-Viola Duets,* including the

---

[23]*Sul ponticello.*

[24]Bruni's dates still appear in some music lexicons as 1759–1823. The corrected dates were verified in his biography: *Antonio Bartolomeo Bruni, Musicista Cuneese (1751–1821),* Collezione Luigi Burgo, Vol. I (Torino: S. Lattes & C. Editori, 1931).

available sets in Op. 12, 25, and 35; and his *Méthode d'Alto*, which is now better known as the *25 Études for Viola*

The earliest known edition of Bruni's *Méthode* was published by Janet and Cotelle in Paris in 1805. The title, *Méthode pour l'Alto, contenant les principes de cet instrument suivis de Vingt-cinq Études*, indicates that the book is in two parts, characteristic of most tutors. The first section contains an explanation of the elements of music, and a second section, the *25 Etudes*.

The Preface of Bruni's viola tutor tells the student that Bruni is dispensing with the usual elementary directions that are included in other *Méthodes*, and instead, is furnishing appropriate études "for the purpose of familiarizing the reader with the viola clef." Bruni assumed that the "reader" would be an advanced violinist. This is apparent from the technical demands of the *25 Études*.

Following the *Preface* Bruni's tutor discusses the timbre of the viola, and warns the student not to use the open strings too often because the instrument by itself is a little nasal, especially on the A string, or *chanterelle*. Today most violists would disagree with Bruni's advice regarding playing on open strings; it should be remembered, however, that Bruni's comments were probably influenced by the small-sized violas in general use at that time.

The eventual wide acceptance, universal popularity, and continued use to the present day of Bruni's *25 Etudes* is best illustrated by a partial list of the publishers who brought out subsequent editions of the work: Cocks of London, c.1810; Breitkopf & Härtel of Leipzig, 1819; Schott of Mainz, 1821; André of Paris, 1867; Litolff of Berlin, 1890; Desire Ikelmer of Paris, 1894; Schott of Mainz (augmented by H. Dessauer), 1897; Jurgenson, Moscow, c.1900; A. Noel of Paris, 1901; Augener of London, 1907; Carl Fischer of New York, 1910; Ricordi of Rome, 1919; Russian State Publishers, 1922; Paxton of London, 1928; and Russian State Publishers, 1935. This list does not include second and third editions of the same publisher, or the various "arranged editions," which have plagued most of the popular method books. Today almost all of the major music publishers have printed an edition of the Bruni *Méthode*. It continues to be one of the most used instruction books for the viola, constituting one of the standard sets of *Études* for the instrument.

Campagnoli's *41 Capricen*

Bartolomeo Campagnoli was born the same year as Bruni, in 1751, in Cento near Bologna; he died at Neustrelitz, Mecklenburg,

Germany, in 1827. His instruction on the violin was in the very best Italian tradition. His early training was in Bologna with Dall'Ocha, a pupil of Lolli. When he was twelve years old, he began to study in Modena with Paolo Gaustarobba, a pupil of Tartini. His most important studies were in Florence under the guidance of Nardini.

Campagnoli had a very successful career as performer, conductor, and teacher in Italy, Germany, Poland, and Sweden. His most prestigious positions were as concertmaster and conductor of the Gewandhaus Orchestra in Leipzig (1797–1818), and as court Kapellmeister at Neustrelitz (1818–27). His reputation as a teacher of the Nardini school of violin playing brought him many talented students on both the violin and viola. He wrote a method book for the violin and a collection of advanced études for the viola entitled *41 Capricen* (41 Caprices), Op. 22. The first printing of the *41 Capricen* was in Leipzig c.1805.

Of all Campagnoli's compositions, the *41 Capricen* have best withstood the ravages of time. They embody one of the didactic pillars for the development of left-hand and right-hand technique on the viola. Techniques required for playing solo, ensemble, and orchestral music of the Classic and early Romantic periods are adequately covered: scales and arpeggios (Nos. 19 and 20);[25] crossing strings and arpeggiando (Nos. 16, 17, 37); staccato (No. 7); and intervals, including octaves (No. 13). Several of the *Caprices* (Nos. 1, 2, 24, 34) begin with a slow introduction which includes melodic material and double stops, followed by a faster technical section; the introductions can be used as legato bowing studies; and in the more rapid part, the teacher can assign various bowings to meet the needs of the student. These latter studies, along with the slow tempo *Caprices* (Nos. 6, 23, 32, 39), are of sufficient merit to be used as recital pieces. The *Theme and Variations in F Minor* (No. 17) is definitely a work of recital dimensions.[26] Because of the almost unlimited potential of technical material available to the teacher in the *Caprices*, they are frequently called the "Kreutzer-Fiorillo" of the viola.

Hoffmeister's *12 Viola-Etuden*

Franz Anton Hoffmeister was born in Rottenburg-on-the-Neckar in 1754, and died in Vienna in 1812. In addition to writing a prodigi-

---

[25]Because of the diversification of numbering in various editions of the Campagnoli *Caprices*, the numbers used in this chapter are from the I.M.C. set, pub., 1958 (ed. by William Primrose).

[26]Piano accompanyment to the *Caprices* by Karl Albert Tottman, pub. by H. Litolff before 1900, is now out of print but worthy of republication. Piano accompaniment to *Theme and Variations* (No. 17) by Grazyna Bacewicz, pub. by Moeck, is available.

ous number of compositions, he was also active in the music publishing business. He was a co-founder of the Bureau de Music, which later became the famed C. F. Peters Publishing Company. He composed and published significant works for the viola: the *Concertos in D Major* and in B♭ *Major*, and the *12 Viola-Étuden*. The latter was probably published around 1800 or earlier. The *12 Études* contain problems in fingering and bowing that are challenging to advanced students, and are of comparable technical difficulty to the easier *Caprices* for violin written by Pierre Rode. The fifth Hoffmeister *Etude, Theme and Variations in G Major*, is of sufficient musical merit to be suitable for performance as an unaccompanied viola solo. The first section, an *Andante*, presents the theme in double stops. *Variations 1* and *2*, in *Allegro* tempo, contain material that is of technical interest to both the performer and the listener. The third *Variation* is written as a two-voice contrapuntal study with the melodic theme alternating from the upper to the lower part, embellished by a counterpoint of eighth and sixteenth notes. *Variation 4* is cast in the parallel key of *G* minor, followed by *Variation 5* in the original key, and concludes with a *Da Capo* of the *Theme*.

Viola Instruction in the 19th Century

In the 19th century the *Études* by Bruni, Martinn, Campagnoli, and Hoffmeister were not well known or generally available, and as a result they had limited use. In Europe, England, and the United States, most of the viola teaching was done by violinists who used transposed versions of the violin studies by Kayser, Mazas, Kreutzer, and Fiorillo for their students. There were two factors which led to this situation: first, most violinists were unfamiliar with the collections that had been written specifically for the viola; and second, there was a widely-believed, mistaken idea which held that the viola was played exactly like the violin—hence the classical violin études were considered adequate as basic study material for the viola. Violinists, who had not analyzed special fingering or bowing problems as related to the viola, used identical teaching procedures for the two instruments. Furthermore, they felt more comfortable using études and techniques with which they were familiar.

Fortunately this was not a universal practice. Several violists did subscribe to the use of studies written for the viola, and others composed new collections for the instrument, including those by Alessandro Rolla, c.1820; Alexis de Garaudé, 1823; Casimir-Ney, c.1850;

Léon Firket, 1873;[27] Hilaire Lütgen, 1874; Hermann Ritter, c.1890; Friedrich Hermann, 1899, and Emil Kreuz, c.1900.

Berlioz, in a letter written around the middle of the 19th century, to his friend, Humbert Ferrand, expressed his disapproval of the curriculum in instrumental music at the Paris Conservatoire:

> If a Conservatoire is an institution intended for the maintenance of all departments of musical art and the instruction directly pertaining to them, it is strange that not even in Paris should they have yet succeeded in carrying out such a programme. For a long time our instrumental school had no classes for the study of the most indispensable instruments, such as the double-bass, trombone, trumpet, and harp. True, these gaps have been filled up of late years, but, unhappily, there are many others, which I shall now point out.[28]

Berlioz was especially critical of the Conservatoire regarding the lack of instruction for the viola:

> It is to be regretted that there is no special class for the Viola. This instrument, notwithstanding its relation to the violin, needs individual study and constant practice if it is to be properly played. It is an antique, absurd, and deplorable prejudice that has hitherto handed over the performance of the tenor part to second- or third-rate violinists. Whenever a violinist is mediocre, it is said, "He will make a capital tenor." From the stand-point of modern music this is false reasoning, for trashy parts are no longer written for the orchestra (at least by the great masters), but each has an interest proportionate to the effect to be reproduced, and a condition of inferiority in any one part with regard to any other is not recognised.[29]

In 1894, the Conservatoire finally announced a curriculum which made it possible for a student to select the viola as a major instrument. To implement this new course of study, the Conservatoire appointed Théophile Laforge (c.1860–1918) *le Professeur d'Alto.* Louis Bailly (1882–1974), who graduated in 1900 with first prize in viola, was one of the first students to complete the new curriculum. Later he became one of the pioneers in bringing recognition to the viola in the United States, as an instrument worthy of study. Bailly joined the faculty of the Curtis Institute of Music in 1925, as Professor of Viola. Samuel Belov (1884–1954) had already been appointed to a similar position in 1922, at the newly founded Eastman School of Music.

Most of the American conservatories of music and university music departments were too cautious to follow the Eastman and Curtis

---

[27]*Firket's Conservatory Method for the Viola* (based on Leon Firket's *Méthode pratique*, pub. by Schott, 1873) was published in Boston by Jean White in 1879. This was one of the earliest publications in the United States of a method originally written for the viola.

[28]Hector Berlioz, *Memoirs from 1803 to 1865* (Trans. by Rachel and Eleanor Holmes). Annotated and revised by Ernest Newman. New York: Alfred A. Knopf, 1932, p. 404.

[29]*Ibid.*, p. 405.

innovation; they continued to treat the viola as a secondary instrument, unworthy of specialization. Viola instruction, if offered at all, was usually assigned to one of the school's violin teachers.

After the end of World War II (1945), there was a trend in many American Universities to add to the faculty a string quartet-in-residence, and to name the quartet's violist *Professor of Viola*. This inevitably led to the adoption of new curricula, which made it possible for students to select the viola as their major instrument.

Meanwhile, many of the leading European music schools had likewise elevated the viola to a status of equality with the violin and cello, and they had employed teachers who were conversant with the performance problems peculiar to the instrument.

Viola Instruction in the 20th Century

In the 20th century many new scale books and étude collections appeared in Europe, England, and the Americas; and most of the standard works for the violin have been re-edited with fingerings and bowings characteristic of viola technique. Among those who have written original studies or have re-edited older works are Watson Forbes, Lillian Fuchs, Leonard Mogill, Johannes Palaschko, Enrico Polo, William Primrose, Lionel Tertis, and Maurice Vieux.

Many violinists continue to teach the viola, but are more and more recognizing that there are differences in fingering and bowing techniques, as well as separate postures for holding the instrument and for drawing the bow. Some of these differences are subtle, but nevertheless crucial to producing the characteristic viola sound and to performing with a facile technique. Large violas frequently require the use of half-position, extensions, substitution of the fourth finger for the third to accommodate small hands in excessive reaches, and substitution of the second finger for the third in arpeggiated passages to obviate an awkward stretch that would otherwise occur between the third and fourth fingers. To obtain maximum resonance and response on many violas, it is necessary to bow with the hair flat on the string rather than at the angle characteristic of the violin. These are only a few differences between violin and viola technique, of which teachers are now increasingly cognizant.[30]

Teaching the viola is now recognized as a separate entity from teaching the violin. This does not preclude a fine violin teacher from

---

[30]See Maurice W. Riley, "From Violin to Viola," *Educational Music Magazine* (Jan.-Feb., 1957), for a more complete coverage of this subject.

givng adequate instruction to a violist, provided the teacher is aware of
the special problems that are inherent in playing the viola.

The teacher should carefully peruse solo, ensemble, and orchestral music to determine if the printed fingerings and bowings are
indigenous to the viola. The choice of fingerings should also be
determined by the size of the student's hand and finger length. It is
particularly relevant that the scales and études which are assigned
bring an awareness to the student of the performance techniques that
are peculiar to the viola. It is paramount to the student's growth that
the teacher select études that contain the musical challenge and technical demands which will contribute to developing the full potential
of the violist's talent.

CHAPTER X
19TH CENTURY LITERATURE FOR THE VIOLA

There is a common assumption that composers of the Romantic School composed almost no solo literature for the viola. It is true that four of the major works that are frequently performed by violists were not written especially for that instrument: Beethoven's *Notturno*, Op. 42. (arranged from the *Trio for Violin, Viola, and Cello*, Op. 8); Schubert's *Arpeggione* (written for an instrument called the "Arpeggione"); and Brahms' *Sonatas in F Minor* and *E♭ Major*, Op. 120, Nos. 1 and 2 (written for the clarinet). These works, notwithstanding their original intention, are still favorites in the repertoire of most violists, and their inclusion can be justified historically, esthetically, and musically.

It is, of course, not true that Romantic composers wrote almost no original viola solo literature. Among the better known 19th century composers who wrote for it were Hector Berlioz, Michail Glinka, Johann Nepomuk Hummel, Franz Liszt, Felix Mendelssohn, Anton Rubinstein, Robert Schumann, and Carl Maria von Weber. Also there were several composers whose creative period overlapped into the 20th century, but who wrote in the Romantic idiom, such as Max Bruch, Max Reger, Joseph Jongen, and Richard Strauss. Among the Romanticists who are less well known today, but who were, nevertheless, composers of great skill, Charles-Valentin Alkan, Robert Fuchs, Heinrich v. Herzogenberg, Friedrich Kiel, Georges Onslow, and Carl Reinecke should be included.

To these lists should be added the names of the virtuoso violinists, who also played viola, and who wrote significant works for it, including Joseph Joachim, Johann Kalliwoda, L. Casimir-Ney, Niccolò Paganini, Alessandro Rolla, Ludwig Spohr, and Henri Vieuxtemps.

Compositions Borrowed for the Viola

The term "borrowed" is used by Franz Zeyringer to classify works that were originally designated for other instruments, or for combinations of other instruments. For example, he included the Beethoven *Notturno*, the Schubert *Arpeggione Sonata*, and the two Brahms *Viola Sonatas* in this classification.[1]

Ludwig van Beethoven (1770–1827) was himself a teen-age violist in the Bonn Court Orchestra, in which Antonin Reicha (1770–1836) played flute, and Joseph Reicha (1752–95) was the director. Joseph, the uncle of the better known Antonin, wrote a *Viola Concerto in E♭ Major*, which Michael Goldstein suggests might have been written for the young Beethoven.[2] Beethoven's experience in Bonn must certainly have made him aware of the potential of the viola, and probably influenced the many choice parts he later gave the instrument in his orchestral works and in his chamber music.

Beethoven's *Notturno in D Major for Viola and Piano*, Op. 42, is an arrangement of an earlier work, namely the *Serenade in D Major*, Op. 8. Musicologists still debate whether the arrangement is by Beethoven or by some one else. Sidney Beck furnished the historical background and cited various theories concerning its genesis in the prefatory "Note" to his excellent edition of this work.[3] Beethoven was certainly aware of this arrangement and made no attempt to disown it. It is a good piece and a standard part of the violist's repertoire.

Of the many examples of Beethoven's fine writing for the viola, several typical ones are worthy of note. The two *Quintets in C Major*, Op. 29 (1801) and the *Fugue in D Major*, Op. 137 (1817) contain more thematic material for the Viola I than for the Violin II part. The *Septet in E♭ Major*, Op. 20 (1800) foreshadowed the type of parts he gave the viola in his later chamber music in that he assigned the melody to the viola in the first variation.

The viola presents the "Theme Russe" in the *Maggiore* of the *Allegretto* of the *Quartet in E Minor*, Op. 59, No. 2, and introduces the main theme in the *Allegro molto* of the *Quartet in C Major*, Op. 59, No. 3. In the *Allegretto con Variazioni* of the "Harp" *Quartet*, Op. 74, the viola has a leading part. Its solo part in the second variation is one of the most inspired sections in the entire composition.

Less significant than Beethoven's other chamber music is the *Sonata in E♭ Major*, "Duett mit zwei obligaten Augenläsern," for viola and cello. This duet was probably written for amateurs, and in great haste. Only two movements were completed: I *Allegro* and III

---

[1]Franz Zeyringer, *Literatur für Viola.*

[2]See the Preface to Joseph Reicha, *Concerto for Viola and Orchestra in E♭ Major*, ed. Michael Goldstein (Hamburg: N. Simrock, 1978).

[3]L. van Beethoven, *Notturno for Viola and Piano*, Revised and Edited by Sydney Beck (New York: G. Schirmer, 1949).

Minuetto. The second movement exists only as a manuscript fragment. [4]

Beethoven also wrote five *Trios for Violin, Viola, and Cello;* each has a particularly interesting part for the violist. Of these works, the *Serenade in D Major,* Op. 8, contains a greater independence in the viola part than the earlier *Trio in E♭ Major,* Op. 3. In the *Serenade* the instrument is treated as an equal with the violin and the cello. Op. 9 consists of three *Trios: G Major, D Major,* and *C Minor.* Here the viola parts approach the style of virtuoso importance that appeared later in the Op. 18 *Quartets.*

Franz Weiss (1778–1831) was Beethoven's favorite violist. Weiss was a member of the Rasoumowsky Quartet and also of the Schuppanzig Quartet. These groups played most of Beethoven's chamber music from manuscript, with the composer present. Weiss' artistry perhaps influenced Beethoven to write viola parts that were the musical and technical equals of the violin and the cello.

Franz Schubert (1797–1828) studied the violin as early as the age of eight, and occasionally played the viola in chamber groups during his adult years. He wrote the *Arpeggione Sonata* in 1824, for G. Staufer, a friend, who had invented a bowed instrument in 1823, which he called the *Arpeggione.* It was almost as large as a cello, but was shaped more like a guitar, and was tuned E,A,d,g,b,e'. Only two or three of the instruments were ever built. Cellists gradually appropriated this composition as one of their own; violists, however, certainly have just as much claim to its use. A beautiful work, it is now well entrenched as a standard part of the viola repertoire.

Schubert's use of the viola in his chamber music and orchestral works shows a strong Beethoven influence, and goes far beyond the technical demands of most of his contemporary composers.

Johannes Brahms (1833–1897) composed two *Sonatas for Clarinet and Piano: in F Minor* and *in E♭ Major,* Op. 120, No's. 1 and 2, in 1894. These *Sonatas,* although inspired by, and written for, the virtuoso clarinetist Richard Mühlfeld (1856–1907), have long become staple parts of the violist's repertoire. Brahms, himself, made alterations in the original clarinet parts for the viola editions, including the addition of double stops and the changing of registers by an octave in several places to better accommodate the range and sonority of the viola. Violists need not apologize for "borrowing" these *Sonatas* for

---

[4]In the British Museum, London. See Wilhelm Websky, *Versuch eines möglichst vollständigen thematisches Katalogs der Duo-Literatur für Bratsche und Violoncello* (Kassel: Viola-Forschungsgesellschaft, n.d.).

their own use, since Brahms certainly abetted the intention. It is unfortunate that viola editions of these works continue to have only the
clarinet parts printed on the piano score.

As early as 1863 Brahms began work on *Zwei Lieder für Alt,
Bratsche, und Piano: Gestillte Sehnsucht, und Geistliches Wiegenlied*
(Two Songs for Contralto, Viola, and Piano: Appeased Desire [Long-
ing], and Sacred Lullaby), Op. 91. Brahms was an admirer of Joseph
Joachim's wife, Amalie, who had been an operatic singer. It was his
intention to dedicate the songs to Amalie, who would sing them, with
Joachim playing the viola parts. Brahms was not aware at the time that
the Joachims were having unreconcilable marital problems. When the
news of their divorce reached him in 1881, he was so shocked that he
refused to communicate with Joachim for several months and delayed
publication of the *Two Songs* until 1884.[5] Printed editions include an
alternate cello part, but there can be no doubt that Brahms preferred
that the viola share in the ensemble with voice and piano. Karl
Geiringer, the astute Brahms scholar, commented:

> . . . In Op. 91—perhaps inspired by Bach—Brahms adds the viola, his favorite
> string instrument, to the pianoforte and contralto voice parts. In *Geistliches
> Wiegenlied* (Cradle Song of the Virgin), the second of these two songs, the won-
> derful old German cradle song, *Joseph, lieber Joseph mein* (Blessed Joseph,
> Joseph Dear), is given to the viola, while the voice contributes gentle, floating
> melodies. This song is especially significant, not only for its peculiar color effects,
> but even more for the profound emotional content and the imaginative use of the
> *canto firmo* technique. The first song, *Gestillte Sehnsucht* (When I Yearn No
> More), once more expresses Brahms's deep love of Nature. How delicately is the
> soughing of the wind portrayed by the broken chords gliding across the strings of
> the viola! In fact, Brahms's love of Nature is an inexhaustible theme.[6]

Brahms's chamber music demonstrates his high regard for the
viola by the many choice parts to be found in the two *Quintets*, Op. 88
and Op. 111; the *Sextets*, Op. 18 and Op. 36; and the *Quartets*, Op. 51,
No. 1 and 2; and especially the *Quartet in B♭ Major*, Op. 67. Although
all movements of the latter contain interesting and challenging material for the viola, the third movement, *Agitato (Allegretto non
troppo)*, is a particular favorite of violists. In this movement the main
theme, in 3/4 measure, is introduced immediately by the unmuted
viola, and Brahms made it clear that the viola is to predominate by
directing the violins and cello to play *con sordino* throughout the
entire movement.

---

[5]For a complete account of Brahms's relationship with Amalie and Joseph Joachim see Karl
Geiringer, *Brahms, His Life and Work* (New York: Oxford University Press, 1947).
    [6]*Ibid.*, p. 285.

19th Century Composers Who Wrote for the Viola

Hector Berlioz (1803–1869) composed *Harold en Italie*, in 1834, one of the most famous works ever written for the viola. This piece has probably been performed more times with orchestra than any other composition written for this medium. The background that led to its creation and its subsequent performances constitutes a series of events that have been chronicled many times, but in *The History of the Viola* the facts are worthy of repetition.

The actual conception of *Harold en Italie* took place a year before its first performance. The great violinist Niccolò Paganini was in the audience at the premier of another Berlioz work, namely *King Lear*. Paganini was so impressed by Berlioz' creative talents that he called on him a few weeks later. "I have acquired a marvelous Stradivarius viola, and I want to play it in public," Paganini stated. He then informed the surprised Berlioz, "You are the only one I would trust with such a commission."

Berlioz considered it for a moment and replied that his knowledge of the viola was not suitable for composing a work equal to the vituosity of such an artist. Paganini was adamant, "No, no, I insist, you will manage. I can't possibly do it, I am too ill to compose."[7]

Berlioz set to work. His original plan was for the work to be in the style of the *Symphonie Fantastique*. It would be a dramatic fantasy for orchestra, chorus, and viola solo, with the title, "Des Derriers Instans de Marie Stuart" (The Last Moments of Mary Stuart).[8] Berlioz turned instead, however, to the then popular autobiographical poem by Lord Byron, *Childe Harold's Pilgrimage*.[9] A typical verse from this work describes the glories of Venice:

CANTO THE FOURTH

I

I stood in Venice, on the Bridge of Sighs;
A palace and a prison on each hand;
I saw from out the wave her structures rise
As from the stroke of the enchanter's wand:
A thousand years their cloudy wings expand
Around me, and a dying Glory smiles
O'er the far times, when many a subject land
Looked to the winged Lion's marble piles,
Where Venice sate in state, throned on her hundred isles![10]

---

[7]*The Memoirs of Hector Berlioz*, trans. David Cairns, (London: V. Gollancz, Ltd., 1969) p. 224.

[8]*Hector Berlioz, Memoirs*, trans. E. Newman (New York: Alfred A. Knopf & Co., 1932), p. 201.

[9]Book I and II were published in 1812, Book III, in 1816; and Book IV, in 1818.

[10]George Gordon, Lord Byron, *Childe Harold's Pilgrimage* (Chicago: Geo. M. Hill Company), p. 185.

These beautiful lines are a fragment of the long narrative poem which Lord Bryon wrote as a journal of his own travels. Inspired by Byron's saga, Berlioz composed his masterpiece, *Harold en Italie.*

Berlioz was excited by the opportunity to write a work of new concepts. In fact, the piece in its final form is not a traditional concerto, but a symphonic poem with occasional colorful solo passages for the viola. When the first movement was completed, Paganini requested to see it. To his dismay, he found that there were many long rests in the solo part, and he told Berlioz of his displeasure: "There is not enough for me to do here. I should be playing all the time."[11] Berlioz agreed and told him that such a concerto could only be written by Paganini. Disappointed and very ill, Paganini left for Nice. It was three years before Berlioz saw him again.

No longer under the pressure to write specifically to please Paganini's ego, Berlioz expanded his new concept. He composed orchestral scenes in which the viola would take part, much as an actual person would in the varied scenes of life. He combined experiences from his own travels with impressions taken from Byron's poem. The title, *Harold en Italie,* is a designation of the Italian section only of *Childe Harold's Pilgrimage.* Berlioz selected four sub-titles around which to build the four movements of the composition: (1) "Harold in the Mountains, Scenes of Melancholy, Happiness, and Joy"; (2) "March of the Pilgrims Singing an Evening Prayer"; (3) "Serenade of an Abruzzi Mountaineer to his Mistress"; and (4) "Orgy of the Brigands [with] Recollections [of themes] from the Preceding Movements."

Berlioz also incorporated in the final version an idea he had used in his *Symphonie Fantastique,* wherein a principal theme is established and then repeated throughout the entire composition.[12] He had considered the theme of the *Symphonie Fantastique* to be somewhat obsessive and overpowering, and so in *Harold* he sought to superimpose the theme so that it would not alter the complex orchestral development.

Finally, on November 23, 1834, at the Paris Conservatoire, the work was premiered. The viola soloist was Chrétien Urhan. There were problems caused by the conductor, Narcisse Girard, who misunderstood the score. Nevertheless, the audience was enthralled, and the second movement had to be repeated as an encore. During the next four years *Harold* was performed often, with continued success.

---

[11]*The Memoirs of Hector Berlioz,* Cairns, *op. cit.,* p. 225.
[12]Berlioz called the principal theme an *Idée fixe.*

Paganini had never heard a performance nor seen the score of *Harold en Italie*, since he had returned to Nice some years before. But on December 16, 1838, he was again in Paris when Berlioz conducted a concert at the Conservatoire which featured both the *Fantastique* and *Harold*. Berlioz, in poor health with bronchitis, was very exhausted after the performance, when Paganini, accompanied by his son Achille, appeared backstage to praise him. Unable to speak loud enough because of his throat disease, Paganini whispered into his son's ear, who then relayed the message. The son told Berlioz that his father had never before been so deeply affected by a musical piece as he was by *Harold*, and it was all that his father could do to keep from kneeling in praise. Paganini then knelt and kissed Berlioz' hand in appreciation. Berlioz was flustered to the point that he was unable to speak.

Two days later, Achille went to visit Berlioz, who was sick in bed. He delivered the following letter from his father:

My dear friend:

Beethoven being dead, only Berlioz can make him live again; and I who have heard your divine compositions, so worthy of the genius you are, humbly beg you to accept, as token of my homage, 20,000 francs, which Baron de Rothschilde will remit to you on your presenting the enclosed (letter).
Believe me ever your affectionate friend.

Niccolò Paganini.

For Berlioz, this gift of 20,000 francs could not have arrived at a more opportune moment, because, strangely enough, Berlioz' compositions had never made him a great deal of money. Now he was able to satisfy his creditors and still retain a handsome sum on which to live. Soon, news of the gift was published, and it insured that Berlioz would finally be acclaimed as a leading composer. *Harold en Italie*, recognized as the masterpiece that it is, immediately joined the ranks of the truly outstanding compositions in the orchestral and soloistic repertoire.

Michail Glinka (1804–57), pioneer Russian national composer, played both the viola and the piano. He wrote an unfinished *Sonata in D Minor for Viola and Piano* between 1825 and 1828. It is now available in an edition prepared by the great Soviet violist, Vadim Borissovsky.

Johann Nepomuk Hummel (1778–1837) was a real champion of the viola. Although not a composer of the first magnitude, many of his compositions, nevertheless, demonstrate a fine creative talent. Such a work is the *Sonata in E♭ Major for Viola and Piano*. Also important in the violist's repertoire are his *Fantasie for Viola, 2 Clarinets and Strings*, and *Potpourri for Viola and Orchestra*, Op. 94.

Hummel's chamber music likewise contains many ingratiating parts for the viola, particularly his string *Trios in G Major* and *in E♭ Major*, and his celebrated *Septet in D Minor*, in which the viola is assigned a major share of the thematic material.

Franz Liszt (1811–1886) wrote two works that are important to the violist: the piano accompaniment for *Harold en Italie*, and *Romance Oubliée* for Viola and Piano. According to Humphrey Searle, Liszt transcribed the supporting orchestral score of Berlioz' *Harold en Italie* for piano in 1836.[13] Thus there is a piano accompaniment available for performers who wish to play *Harold en Italie* with piano.[14] The *Romance Oubliée* (1880) was dedicated to Hermann Ritter, the German virtuoso violist, who played so brilliantly in Wagner's orchestra at the opening of the Bayreuth theater.[15]

Felix Mendelssohn (1809–1847), in addition to being a pianist prodigy, played the viola with enough skill to perform chamber music with Niels Gade, Paganini, Ferdinand David, and other noted instrumentalists. Mendelssohn's *Sonata in C Minor for Viola and Piano* was composed in 1823–24, when he was only 15 years old. His chamber music includes many interesting parts for the viola, particularly the *Quintets in A Major*, Op. 18, and the *B♭ Major*, Op. 87. Mendelssohn wrote many interesting parts for violists in his orchestral works, of which the thematic material in the second movement of the *"Italian" Symphony*, assigned to the viola section, is a pertinent example.

Anton Rubinstein (1829–94) wrote two works for the viola. Since 1954, when a modern edition appeared, violists have become increasingly interested in the *Sonata in F Minor for Viola and Piano*, Op. 49, which was composed in 1855 and published in 1857. This sonata was dedicated to Alexander Drobisch (1818–79), an excellent ensemble musician, who played equally well on both the viola and the cello. Less well known are the *Three Pieces for Viola and Piano*, Op. 11.

Robert Schumann (1810–1856) composed the *Märchenbilder* (Fairyland Pictures) *for Viola and Piano*, Op. 131, in 1851. It consists of a set of four pieces, which were dedicated to Joseph W. von

---

[13]Humphrey Searle, *The Music of Franz Liszt* (London: Williams & Norgate, Ltd., 1954. Dover Reprint, 1966), p. 8.

[14]Hector Berlioz, *Harold in Italy for Viola and Piano*, Trans. by Franz Liszt, Ed. by Maurice W. Riley (Ann Arbor: University Music Press, 1959.).

[15]See "Herman Ritter," in Chapter XI. The *Romance Oubliée* was based on an earlier vocal work Liszt had composed for Mme. Pavloff in 1848, entitled "Oh pourquoi donc." Liszt also made a transcription of the song for two pianos.

Wasielewaski, concertmaster, and later conductor of the Düsseldorf Orchestra. The first performance of this work was given by Wasiele- waski and Clara Schumann. Schumann's chamber music also contains much fine writing for the viola. From the violist's point of view the most interesting part is in the *Märchenerzählungen* (Fairy Stories) *for Clarinet, Viola, and Piano,* Op. 132, written in 1853, only four months before his mental breakdown.

Carl Maria von Weber (1786–1826) received his early musical instruction from his older stepbrother, Fritz von Weber (1761–183?), a professional violist. In 1809, Carl Maria composed the *Andante und Rondo Ungarese for Viola and Piano* for his brother, who apparently kept the work for his own use. But Carl Maria had the same work published in 1813 for bassoon and piano. It is now available for the viola in several excellent editions. Fritz' competence on the viola may have influenced Carl Maria to write the famous viola obbligato to Aennchen's "Romance und Arie," in the third act of *Der Freichütz.*[16]

Composers Whose Creative Period Overlapped
into the 20th Century

Max Bruch (1838–1920) lived during a period of many changes in musical idiom, but he remained a Romanticist. Between 1910–13, he composed ten pieces that are of particular importance to the viola. The first was a collection of 8 *Pieces for Clarinet, Viola, and Piano,* Op. 83 (1910), all single movement works, with optional parts for violin and cello. Seven of the eight pieces are cast in minor keys. The other two works by Bruch are *Romance in F Major for Viola and Orchestra,* Op. 85, (1911) and *Concerto in E Minor for Clarinet, Viola, and Orches- tra,* Op. 88 (1913).

Max Reger (1873–1916) composed four works that are of impor- tance to the viola repertoire: *Sonata in B♭ Major for Viola and Piano,* written c.1900 and published in 1909 (the composer included an al- ternate solo part for the clarinet); and *Drei Suiten für Bratsche allein,* Op. 131 (1916). The three solo suites are of moderate difficulty; they contain many double stops, and the range occasionally goes beyond the alto clef.

Richard Strauss (1864–1940) composed the symphonic poem *Don Quixote* in 1897. The *Don Quixote* theme is assigned to the cello, and it is the cellist who gets top billing on the program, usually featured in

---

[16]Aennchen's aria and the viola obbligato are discussed in Chapter VII.

the same manner as a cellist who performs a concerto. Less important, but quite essential to the performance, is the *Sancho Panza* theme, assigned to the solo violist. This theme, featured in the third variation, portrays Sancho's wishes and his peculiarities of speech. A scordatura tuning is necessary for the viola solo: the *C* string must be tuned down a half step to *B*. In the early part of the 20th century Pablo Casals and Lionel Tertis were frequently featured with orchestras when this work was performed.

Less Well Known Romantic Composers Who Wrote for the Viola

Charles-Valentin Alkan (1813–88), French pianist and composer, wrote *Sonate de Concert for Cello (Viola) and Piano*, Op. 47, in 1857. The separate viola edition was edited by L. Casimir-Ney.

Robert Fuchs (1847–1927), Austrian composer, was highly regarded by Brahms. He wrote an impressive amount of chamber music that always has good parts for the viola. His best of several solo pieces for the instrument is *Sonata in D Minor for Viola and Piano*, Op. 86 (c. 1909).

Heinrich v. Herzogenberg (1843–1900), Austrian composer, was a friend of Brahms and Joachim. To the latter he dedicated *Legenden for Viola and Piano*, Op. 62. This is a set of three pieces which can be played separately or as a suite.

Friedrich Kiel (1821–85), German composer, wrote *Sonata in G Minor for Viola and Piano*, Op. 67 (c.1870); and *Three Romances for Viola and Piano*, Op. 69. Referring to the latter, Harold Truscott, British musicologist, in a lecture at the Sixth Viola Congress in London (1978), stated, "The writing is superb for both instruments, separately and as a team, and the whole is a work worthy of any violist's while to master."

Georges Onslow (1784–1853) was a French cellist and composer, and a prolific writer of chamber music, including 36 string quartets. His *Sonata for Viola and Piano in C Minor*, Op. 16, No. 2, has an alternate solo part for the cello. The Sonata was composed c.1820 or earlier.

Carl Reinecke (1834–1910), German pianist, composer, and writer, was very fond of the viola. He wrote *Sonata in A Minor*, Op. 42, and *Fantasiestücke for Viola and Piano*, Op. 43, (c.1857). The latter is a particularly important work for the viola.

Virtuoso Violinists Who Wrote for the Viola

Joseph Joachim (1831–1907) was a German violinist, composer, and friend of Brahms. As a violinist he was certainly one of the greatest of all time. As a composer, unfortunately, he is less well known, perhaps because he was always in the shadow of Brahms. Two of his compositions for viola are particularly significant: *Hebrew Melodies for Viola and Piano*, Op. 9 (c.1851); and *Variations for Viola and Piano*, Op. 10 (c.1852). The Op. 9 consists of a set of three pieces based on "Impressions of Byron's Poems." The Op. 10 contains ten variations and an extended coda based on the composer's original theme.

Johann Wenzel Kalliwoda (1801–1866), Czechoslovakian violinist and prolific composer, included among his works the well-known *6 Nocturnes for Viola and Piano*, Op. 186.

Niccolò Paganini (1782–1840), generally considered to be one of the greatest violin virtuosos of all time, also played the viola, and became particularly interested in the instrument from 1833 to 1834.[17] In 1834, he composed *Sonata per la Grand' Viola e Orchestra en E Minor*, Op. 35, which he premiered in London the same year. In addition to this *Sonata*, Paganini wrote two other works which are significant in viola literature: *Trio for Viola, Guitar, and Cello*, Op. 68, and *Serenade for Viola, Guitar, and Cello*, Op. 69.[18]

Alessandro Rolla (1757–1841) was an Italian violinist, violist, composer, conductor, and teacher. As a virtuoso performer on the violin and viola, he needed music that would demonstrate his skill; as a composer, he fulfilled this need by turning out an amazing number of works. From a total output of over 400 compositions, 60 are violin-viola duets, 33 are trios for 2 violins and viola; and 20 are trios for violin, viola, and cello. Rolla also wrote no fewer than twelve works for viola and orchestra; of this number, nine are concertos.[19] The other three are titled *Adagio e Tema con Variazioni*, *Rondo*, and *Divertimento*. These three and his *Concerto in E♭ Major*, Op. 3, *Concerto No. 6 in F Major*, and *Concerto No. 9 in E♭ Major*, are available in modern editions.[20] More publications of Rolla's viola compositions are presently in preparation.[21]

---

[17]For more about Paganini and the viola see Chapter XI.

[18]The opus numbers for Paganini compositions are not the composer's, but were selected by Arturo Codignola, a Paganini scholar, and published by the Municipality of Genoa in 1935. Codignola's numbering was done arbitrarily by classification, and does not represent a chronological order.

[19]Franco Sciannameo, "Alessandro Rolla and his Viola Concertos," *The Viol*, 1, No. 1, pp. 16–18.

[20]*Ibid.*, The concerto numbers are from the Sciannameo catalogue.

[21]For more on Rolla see Chapter XI, "19th Century Virtuoso Violists."

As a Professor of Violin and Viola at the Milano Conservatory, he wrote a considerable amount of music for his students: method books, études, caprices, etc. From the many works he wrote in this category, three artist-level"*Esercizios*" are now available in a set entitled *Tre Pezzi per viola sola;* they are pieces suitable for a teacher to use as advanced assignments, or for a performer to use on a recital program.[22]

Ludwig Spohr (1784–1859) was a prominent German violinist, conductor, and composer. His major work for violists is the "Grand" *Duo in E Minor for Violin and Viola,* Op. 13, a work that must be included with the Mozart duets as being among the finest for the violin-viola combination.

Henri Vieuxtemps (1820–1881), born in Belgium, became one of the greatest violinists of his time. He also liked to play the viola in string quartets, and owned a Gasparo da Saló viola, which was used by his son-in-law in the Vieuxtemps Quartet. Three of his compositions were for the viola: *Capriccio in C Minor for Viola Alone,* Op. Post.; *Elegie for Viola and Piano,* Op. 30 (1854); and the consequential *Sonata in B♭ Major for Viola and Piano,* Op. 36 (1863).

The full development of the technical and musical requirements of the viola in orchestral and chamber music in the 19th century goes far beyond the scope of this chapter. Furthermore, Hans Kunitz has already done significant research regarding the role of the viola in orchestral music, which is chronicled in his book *Violine/Bratsche, Die Instrumentation.*[23] Although his book is one in a series intended primarily as textbooks for students of orchestration, it is also a treasure trove of information for the curious violist. Also the viola as used in chamber music has been expertly discussed by Rebecca Clarke in her article on "The Viola," in Cobbett's *Cyclopedic Survey of Chamber Music.*[24]

Conclusion

A perusal of Zeyringer's *Literatur für Viola* will show that the compositions listed in this chapter constitute only a small fraction of the total output of works for viola by Romantic composers. Besides the

---

[22]Alessandro Rolla, *Tre Pezzi,* ed. by Luigi Alberto Bianchi (Milano: Suvini Zerboni, 1974).

[23]Hanz Kunitz, *Violine/Bratsche, Die Instrumentation,* Teil 12 (Leipzig: Breitkopf & Härtel, 1960), pp. 1338–1393.

[24]W. W. Cobbett, *Cyclopedic Survey of Chamber Music* (London, 1929); also see Rebecca Clarke, "The History of the Viola in Quartet Writing," *Music and Letters,* IV, No. 1, pp. 6–17.

additional solo pieces, Zeyringer also catalogues many different clas-
sifications of works for the viola in various ensemble groupings.

Not all of the compositions listed in this chapter, or in the Zeyringer catalogue, are masterpieces, but they are of sufficient merit to
be worthy of study and performance; and they represent a much larger
repertoire of Romantic works for violists than is generally believed to
exist.

CHAPTER XI

19TH CENTURY VIOLISTS

There was a significant advance in the performance technique of bowed instruments during the last quarter of the 18th century, and extending into the 19th. Among those in the forefront of this movement were Giovanni Battista Viotti (1753–1824), violinist; Jean-Louis Duport (1741–1818), cellist; and Alessandro Rolla (1757–1841), violist. Of the many great Italian violinists, including Corelli, Torelli, Vivaldi, Tartini, and Viotti, Rolla was the first to choose the viola as the instrument of his preference. He made a life-long career of playing, composing for, and teaching the viola.

Just as Karl and Anton Stamitz had been attracted to Paris because of the prestige of playing in the *Concerts Spirituels,* so was the Italian Viotti. Duport was a native of Paris. The artistry of these four musicians was equalled or sometimes surpassed by the native wave of talented violinists who appeared in Paris at the same time or shortly after. This group included such virtuosi as Pierre Gavinés (1726–1800), Rudolph Kreutzer (1766–1831), Pierre Baillot (1771–1842), and Pierre Rode (1774–1830). It was in this Paris environment of great string talent that Chrétien Urhan (1790–1845), the brilliant violist, lived and flourished.

Niccolò Paganini (1782–1840), the most acclaimed virtuoso of the 19th century, was also attracted to Paris, where he enjoyed some of his greatest triumphs. There he made the decision to become a violist also, and commissioned Berlioz to write a concerto that he could perform on his newly acquired Stradivari viola.

Following Urhan and Paganini, there was a dearth of fine violists until almost the end of the 19th century. Violists in string quartets were, with few exceptions, violinists who played the part because of their love for chamber music, but who rarely pursued a career as a soloist on the larger instrument. Composers, including Richard Wagner, often bemoaned the paucity of competent violists in contemporary symphony and opera orchestras. Ironically, two of the best violists of the second half of the 19th century were the famous violinists, Henry Vieuxtemps (1820–1881) and Joseph Joachim (1831–1907). Both played the viola and wrote significant works for it.

Many of the orchestral violists of the 19th century were not only incompetent performers and musicians, but they also played on small violas, which lacked an even sonority in all registers, instruments that rarely had a good C string resonance. Hermann Ritter (1849–1926), a German artist violist and a dedicated teacher of the instrument, did much to improve this situation. He promoted the use of a large viola and designed a new model, which he called the *Viola-alta*.

Allessandro Rolla

Alessandro Rolla was born in Pavia in 1757 and died in Milan in 1841. He lived a long and fruitful life as a violinist, violist, composer, conductor, and teacher. His principal violin teacher was Gianandrea Fioroni, Maestro di Capella of the Duomo in Milan. Rolla was concertmaster for several years at the Venice Opera. In 1784 he was called to Parma as court solo violist. A short time later he was appointed conductor of the Ducale Orchestra, a position he held until the death of the Duke in 1802. Then he became conductor of the La Scala Opera in Milan until 1833. In 1805 he was appointed solo violinist to the Viceroy of Italy, Eugène Beauharnais, stepson of Napoleon I. In 1807, at the founding of the Milan Conservatory of Music, he became its first Professor of Violin and Viola. In this last capacity, he spent a great share of his time and devotion for the remainder of his life.

In addition to all his other activities, Rolla found time to expand his principal interest, the viola. Sydney Beck points out that "the most striking aspect of Rolla's career was his early predilection and enthusiasm for the viola, which led to a special study of its technique and eventually influenced the course of his artistic life."[1] He performed extensively as a violist, both as soloist and as a member of chamber music groups. As a soloist he usually included one of his own works. He wrote, in fact, over 400 compositions, many of them for his own performance, and many also for his students. Rolla's compositions must have had wide acceptance in his time, since most of them were published during his lifetime. But after his death, his music was gradually forgotten. This was particularly unfortunate for violists, because Rolla composed at least ten viola concertos, and great quantities of duets, trios, and other chamber music which included viola parts.[2]

---

[1]Sydney Beck, Ed., "Foreword," Allessandro Rolla, *Concerto for Viola and Orchestra in E♭*, Op. 3 (New York: Ricordi, 1953).

[2]For more about Rolla's viola compositions, see Chapter X.

As a teacher, he has been credited with founding the Lombardy school of violin playing. The account of the young Paganini's studying with Rolla has never been verified, nor has it been disproven. More reliable, however, is the long list of fine violinists and violists who benefited from his commitment and dedication as a teacher, including Eugenio Cavalini, Angelo Maria Bonincori, Andrea Restori, Giuseppe Anzoletti, Achile Simonetti, Cesare Pugni, Luigi Arditti, and Girolamo Biaggi. Following the example of their teacher, most of these students also composed works for the violin and the viola.[3]

Chrétien Urhan

Chrétien Urhan was born on February 16, 1790, at Montjoie, near Aix-la-Chapelle (Aachen), and died on November 2, 1845, in Paris.[4] As a child Urhan demonstrated such musical talent that there could be no question as to his future vocation. His father gave him his first lessons on the violin. At the age of five he appeared in concerts. Without adult assistance, he taught himself how to play the horn, trumpet, flute, guitar, and piano. Also he demonstrated a precocity for composition by writing a *Theme and Variations* and *Valses* for the piano before he was ten years old.

When he was sixteen, he was presented to the Empress Josephine, wife of Napoleon, who was so impressed by his youthful talent that she decided to sponsor his musical education, introducing him to Jean-François Le Sueur, music director of the Emperor's Royal Chapelle. Urhan lived for five years in Le Sueur's home, where he was treated like a son. Le Sueur believed that Urhan's chief talent was composition, and planned to enter one of his works in the composition contest for the *Prix de Rome*.[5]

Meanwhile Urhan was having excellent rapport with F. A. Habeneck, Rudolph Kreutzer, and Pierre Baillot, professors of violin at the Paris Conservatoire. Whether he studied with these masters or simply patterned his playing after them is not known. But Le Sueur's determination to make Urhan a composer limited his activities as a violinist.

---

[3]For more about Rolla as a teacher, see Franco Sciannameo, "Alessandro Rolla and his Viola Concertos," *The Viol*, I, No. 1 (Nov., 1975), pp. 16–18.

[4]According to Jean-Baptiste Weckerlin (1821–1910) in his *Denier Musiciana*, p. 321, Chrétien Urhan was not his real name but a pseudonym chosen by his father. Weckerlin claimed he knew Chrétien's real name; however, if he did, he took it with him to his grave. The mystery of his true name has led to speculation that he might have been the person who used the name L. E. Casimir-Ney.

[5]Paul Garnault, "Chrétien Urhan (1790–1845)," *Revue de Musicologie*, IX (1930), pp. 98–99.

Plate 46. Chrétien Urhan. By Permission of Bibliothèque Nationale de Paris.

Napoleon's defeat and the entry of the Allies into Paris in 1814 made far-reaching changes in Urhan's musical career. As a Prussian citizen, he was declared ineligible to compete for the *Prix de Rome*, to Le Sueur's great disappointment; and as a result, thereafter he spent less time on composition, and increasingly gave more effort to performance. At the same time, the young Chrétien became a devoted religious mystic.

In 1814 Baillot organized his string quartet and string quintet, asking Urhan to play viola in both groups. Thus Urhan began a long association with the finest string players in Paris. Several times each month Urhan participated as a violist in the *Baillot Matinées Musicales*.

In addition to playing with the Baillot groups, Urhan formed his own string ensemble; he also played the organ at Saint-Vincent-de Paul Church; and he was cembalist at the Capranico Theatre. He joined the Paris Opéra Orchestra in 1816, playing at the first desk of the violin section, and succeeded Baillot as concertmaster in 1825. In this connection, there is an interesting reminder of his deep religious devotion; he joined the Opéra Orchestra on the condition that he be permitted to sit with his back toward the stage so that he could not see the "wicked" and "non-Christian" action of the singers and dancers.

Urhan's ability to play many instruments exceedingly well was recognized by several contemporary composers, who wrote special parts in their operas for Urhan to perform. Schneitzhoffer wrote a brilliant solo for the viola d'amore in the ballet to the opera *Zemire et Azor* (1821); likewise, Rudolph Kreutzer composed a special solo for the viola d'amore in the opera *Le Paradis de Mahomet* (1822); and Meyerbeer in *Les Huguenots* (1836) featured Urhan's artistry on both the viola d'amore and the viola in special solos. In *Les Huguenots* the prelude includes a solo for the viola d'amore; and later, in one of Raoul's arias, the solo viola is given the accompaniment. Berlioz, in his *Traité*, voiced his admiration for Urhan, and stated that he was the only artist in all of Paris who could play the viola d'amore.[6]

Urhan's concertizing was not limited to opera solos. On April 3, 1825, he performed at the Royal Academy of Music in Paris as part of a concert conducted by Habeneck that included orchestral works, as well as vocal and instrumental solos. Chrétien played "*Variations pour l'Alto*, composé et executé par M. Urhan."[7] Habeneck, conductor

---

[6]H. Berlioz-R. Strauss, *Treatise on Orchestration* (New York: Edwin Kalmus, 1948), p. 75.

[7]From a poster exhibited in the William E. Hill & Sons Store when it was located at 140 New Bond Street. The "Royal Academy of Music," was the official name of the Grand Opéra of Paris at that time.

at the Conservatoire, in recognition of Urhan's artistry, appointed him concertmaster of the *Société des Concerts du Conservatoire* in 1828, with the understanding that he would also serve as soloist on the viola and viola d'amore when the need occurred. In this capacity he played solos in 1829, 1830, 1835, and 1839 on these two instruments. He also played on the *violon-alto*, an instrument invented earlier by Michel Woldemar (1750–1816), a violinist and composer from Orléans, who had added a low *C* string as the fifth string of a violin. Woldemar had written a *Concerto in C Major* for his instrument, which Urhan played with great success.

Berlioz, after having his *Harold en Italie* rejected by Paganini, turned without hesitation to Urhan to perform the solo part. Following the premier of *Harold* on November 13, 1834, the Paris press extolled Urhan's performance by calling him the "Paganini of the Viola," the "Byron of the Orchestra," and the "Salvatore Rosa of the Symphony." Berlioz also wrote, "You performed a great impersonation of him [Paganini] at this occasion."[8] Urhan performed this work many times during the remainder of his life. Paganini, on the other hand, never performed *Harold*.

In addition to the very busy life led by Urhan as a performer, he continued to compose. Several of his works were published during his lifetime, including: *Variations on a Theme by Mayseder for Flute, Clarinet, and Viola; Quintet for 3 Violas, Cello, and Double Bass;* and *2 Quintets Romantiques for 2 Violins, 2 Violas, and Cello.*

Urhan continued to play in the Opéra Orchestra until he suffered a stroke during a performance. Tulou, the flutist, saw Urhan faint during the *Entr'acte* and carried him to the foyer where he might breathe better air. After Urhan had received the first rites from the Friars of Saint-Jean-le-Dieu, he was carried to the home of his barber, R. François Nicolle, where he died on November 2, 1845. The funeral was held at Notre Dame Cathedral, a special tribute to a man who had always been faithful to his God and to his music.[9]

Paganini and the Large Viola

Niccolò Paganini (1782–1840) is one of the most interesting individuals in the history of music, and certainly he was one of the greatest violinists of all time. In 1828, at the age of forty-six years, he left

---

[8]Garnault, *op. cit.*, p. 107.
[9]*Ibid.*, pp. 108–9.

Italy for the first time, on a concert tour of Europe and England. His performances were sensational. In the brief period between 1828 and 1835, he appeared in most of the leading music centers of Europe and England. In their writings Berlioz, Liszt, Chopin, Spohr, and others attest to the success of his performances, and to the lasting impression Paganini made on everyone who heard him play the violin.

In considering this extraordinary talent, it is most interesting to note that for a period of two years (1833–34) he contemplated giving up the violin and turning to the viola for concertizing. His physical stature, with his long arms and long strong fingers, was ideally suited for the viola.

Paganini is believed to have been largely self-taught. He did have a six-month association, however, with Alessandro Rolla (1757–1841), beginning in the autumn of 1795, which may have contributed to his early interest in the viola; for Rolla indoctrinated all of his students with a love for the instrument.[10]

Paganini's fascination for large violas might have stemmed from his frequent visits, when he was in Paris, to the atelier of Jean Baptiste Vuillaume (1798–1875). Vuillaume repaired several of Paganini's instruments, including the famous "Cannon" Guarneri del Gesù (1742) violin. In Vuillaume's shop, Paganini was probably made aware of the luthier's long series of experiments with violas in an attempt to design an instrument with a bigger and more even sound throughout its registers.[11]

Paganini, it is true, had developed an interest in large violas previous to 1833, but it was in that year that an overwhelming desire impelled him to perform on such an instrument. This fact is confirmed by letters to his best friend, Luigi Gugliemo Germi:[12]

February 28, 1833

Germi:

It's now four months since I've looked at, or played the violin; but today I want to pluck it a little. If I should need your big viola to play in London, would you send it to me? I shall call this instrument the contra-alto.[13]

---

[10]Franco Sciannameo, *op. cit.*, questioned the often repeated statement in music dictionaries and encyclopedias that Paganini studied with Rolla. Sciannameo, however, did not furnish any proof for his contention.

[11]For a description of Vuillaume's *Contralto* and its dimensions, see Chapter XII, "Experiments to Improve the Viola."

[12]Germi was a lawyer and an amateur violinist from Genoa, who was a lifelong friend of Paganini's. A voluminous correspondence between these two men furnishes one of the best insights into Paganini's interests and ambitions.

[13]Geraldine I. C. de Courcy, *Paganini, the Genoese* (Norman, Oklahoma: University of Oklahoma Press, 1957), p. 127.

Later the same year Paganini again wrote to his friend, indicating that he had received the large viola and intended to concertize on it:

October 29, 1833

Germi:
    I'm just back from a rapid tour of England during which I went to Scotland also and gave fifty-two concerts in two months and one week . . . I must return to London in April to play the large viola.[14]

As for Germi's large viola, neither the maker nor the dimensions are known; a letter,[15] however, written forty years later by the English violinist, Charles Severn, indicates that the instrument was exceptionally large:

July 15, 1874

W. Edge, Sr.
My Dear Sir;
    . . . Had I been aware that you were writing of this great man, I could have furnished you with a good many anecdotes of Paganini, at whose last Concerts in London I played, and quite close to him! I played from the same double desk with him, when he played his variations for the Tenor, so large an instrument that his arm was stretched out quite straight. What has become of this Tenor Solo? . . .

Severn's description of Paganini's arm being stretched out quite straight suggests a 45.7 cm. (18 in.) or larger viola.

    In January and February of 1834, Paganini had composed a new work *Sonate per la Grand Viola e Orchestra in c*, Op. 35. This *Sonata* has four movements: *Introduzione, Recitative, Cantabile, e Tema con variazone*.[16] It may be the last movement of this composition that Severn refers to in the above letter.

    Geraldine de Courcy quoted from an article that corroborates the largeness of the Germi viola.

    . . . He has long played with the idea of developing an instrument with the tones of the human voice. He has succeeded and need fear no competitor, for it will be impossible to play it because man's arms are not long enough.[17]

In referring to the instrument, the article also named Paganini as the inventor [sic] of the instrument.

---

[14]*Ibid.*, p. 134.

[15]The author is indebted to Oscar Shapiro, the antiquarian music book dealer in Washington, D.C., for permission to quote from this letter.

[16]Paganini's *Sonata for Large Viola* is now available for viola and piano, Ed. U. Drüner (Mainz: B. Schott, 1975).

[17]G. de Courcy, *op. cit.*, II, p. 127 n. The article is in *Journal des Artistes*, June 29, 1834.

Paganini's debut as a violist occurred in London on April 28, 1834, in the Hanover Square Rooms. Perhaps it was this concert to which Charles Severn referred in his letter. *The London Times* carried an article which pointed out that

> ... Some of the passages on the lower strings had an exceedingly rich and mellow effect ... but the upper notes were not so clear and flexible, nor were the very rapid divisions [variations], through the greater extension of fingers, so completely under his command as on the violin.[18]

The Times commented further that Paganini should stay with the violin and not deviate to the viola. Perhaps the author was personally prejudiced in expecting something violinistic, because the article did conclude:

> ... The audience was a musical one and we never heard the Signor play better or receive more applause than he did last night.

Evidently Paganini was the victim of a group of critics who were not ready to accept the viola as a solo instrument. He gave two more concerts outside of London, but did not find the critics any more favorable than those in that city.

In 1833, during an earlier concert tour of England, Paganini had purchased from the dealer John Corsby, a Stradivari viola made in 1731.[19] Later Paganini heard a performance of Berlioz' *Symphonie Fantastique* on December 9, 1833. After the concert he expressed his deep admiration to the composer. Several weeks later he visited Berlioz, who gave the following account of their conversation, begun by Paganini:

> "I have a wonderful viola, an admirable Stradivari, and would greatly like to play it in public. But I have no music for it. Would you write me a solo? I have no confidence in anyone but you for such a work."[20]

The resultant composition, *Harold en Italie*, which Paganini refused to play, was premiered by Chrétien Urhan.[21] Henry Hill (1808–1856), English violist, gave the London premier performance of *Harold en Italie* in 1848, with Berlioz conducting the orchestra (See Plate 47).

---

[18]G. de Courcy, *op. cit.*, II, p. 158.

[19]The 1731 Strad viola was purchased in the 18th century by the English violin maker, John Betts (1755–1823), who sold it to E. Stephenson, a banker. In 1831 George Corsby purchased the instrument from the Stephenson estate. Herbert K. Goodkind, in *Violin Iconography of Stradivari* (1644–1737), has photographs of this viola on pp. 651–53. At the present time it is owned by the Corcoran Gallery, Washington, D.C., and is part of the Paganini quartet of Strad instruments, (*ibid.*, p. 767). For additional information about this viola see Henri Temianka, "Wood, Glue, and Genius," *Hi Fi/Stereo*, Vol. V (Sept., 1960), pp. 35–40.

[20]Hector Berlioz, *Memoirs*, Revised English translation by Ernest Newman, (New York: Alfred A. Knopf, Inc, 1932), pp. 201–2.

[21]See Chapter X, "19th Century Literature for the Viola," under *Berlioz* and *Paganini*.

Plate 47. Portrait of Henry Hill. Photograph by Desmond Hill.

Paganini accumulated much wealth from his concertizing. It was inevitable that he would invest some of his earnings in the purchase of instruments, including violas. In 1828, when he departed for Vienna to give a concert, Paganini left seven of his instruments with Carlo Carli, his banker in Milan, for safekeeping. Included in the inventory list is "1 Antonio and Girolamo Amati viola, with leather case. Label 1612."[22] According to Herbert K. Goodkind, Paganini owned three Stradivari violas at various times: instruments made in 1721, 1723, and the previously mentioned one of 1731.[23]

Shortly before his death, Paganini drafted a letter to Germi in which he mentioned his instruments. He stated that he still owned eleven violins, one viola, and four cellos.[24] As for the identification of the very large viola loaned to Paganini by his friend Germi, there is presently no satisfactory answer. The deteriorating state of Paganini's health precluded his continuing a concert career as a violist, and there is no further record of the large Germi viola.

Hermann Ritter

Hermann Ritter was born in Wismar, September 16, 1849, and died in Würzburg, January 25, 1926. He studied the violin, music theory, and music history in Berlin at the Neue Akademie für Musik. His first important position was as a violinist in the Schertin Court Orchestra. His outstanding talent was soon recognized by his appointment as municipal Musikdirektor in Heidelberg, where he also continued his education at the University in philosophy, history of art, and archaeology. In the meantime his performance interest had shifted from the violin to the viola. He believed that his future calling lay in improving the status of the violist, mainly by raising the standard of performance. Also he believed that the instrument itself needed to be redesigned.[25]

The voluminous literary writings of Richard Wagner constituted a significant influence on Ritter, just as they did on many other young

---

[22]G. de Courcy, *Nicolo Paganini: Chronology of his Life* (Wiesbaden: Rud Erdmann, 1961), p. 78.

[23]Herbert K. Goodkind, *op. cit.*, p. 723.

[24]Harold Spivacke, "Paganiniana," *The Library of Congress Quarterly Journal of Current Acquisitions*, II, No. 2 (February, 1945), p. 12.

[25]See Chapter XII, "Experiments to Improve the Viola," where a much more detailed assessment of Ritter's contribution can be found.

German musicians. Wagner's views on German violists was particularly pertinent. In his monograph *Ueber das Dirigiren (On Conducting)*, 1869, Wagner was explicitly critical of the violists in German orchestras:

> The viola is commonly (with rare exceptions indeed) played by infirm violinists, or by decrepit players of wind instruments who happen to have been acquainted with a stringed instrument once upon a time; at best a competent viola player occupies a first desk, so that he may play the occasional solos for that instrument; but I have seen this function performed by the leader of the first violins. It was pointed out to me that in a large orchestra which contained eight violas, there was only one player who could deal with the rather difficult passages in one of my later scores!
>
> ... it arose from the older methods of instrumentation, where the role of the viola consisted for the most part in filling up the accompaniments; and it has since found some sort of justification in the meagre method of instrumentation adopted by the composers of Italian operas, whose works constitute an important element in the repertoire of the German opera theatres.[26]

Ritter believed that the first step in correcting the viola problems in German orchestras would be to use larger instruments, which would have more sonority. Based on his acoustical studies, Ritter designed a viola with a body length of 48 cm. (18.9 in.).

In Würzburg, Ritter commissioned Karl Hörlein, a luthier, to build an instrument according to his specifications. His first instrument, which Ritter named the *Viola alta*, was so completely satisfying to Ritter that he took it as soon as possible to Munich to demonstrate for Richard Wagner. Wagner was so impressed by the instrument and by Ritter's playing that he engaged Ritter to play principal viola at the opening of the new Wagner Theater in Bayreuth in 1876.

The first complete performance of the entire *Der Ring des Nibelungen* was presented at the opening of the new Wagner Theater in Bayreuth, August 13–17, 1876. Wagner supervised all the performances; Hans Richter conducted the orchestra; August Wilhelmj led the violins; Hermann Ritter led the violas, playing his new *Viola alta*. Ritter's appearance at Bayreuth was an unqualified success. He met Liszt, Rubinstein, von Bülow, and many other famous musicians. Liszt was so impressed with the new instrument that he later composed a piece entitled *Romance Oubliée* for viola and piano, dedicating it to Ritter.[27]

---

[26]Richard Wagner, *On Conducting, a Treatise on Style in the Execution of Classical Music* (London: William Reeves, modern reprint 1940), pp. 3–4.

[27]For the genesis of the *Romance Oubliée*, see under Liszt, Chapter X, "19th Century Viola Literature."

Ritter not only played his instrument as principal viola in orchestras conducted by Richard Wagner, but also those of many other famous conductors, including Hans von Bülow and Richard Strauss. He also played it in his own string quartet. Furthermore, he soon discovered that he was in demand as a concert artist. For three years he toured Germany, Switzerland, Holland, and Russia. His concerts were an unqualified success. In many of the cities on his tours, however, he was disappointed by the poor taste demonstrated by his audiences. Consequently, he determined that he could best serve the cause of music by dedicating his life to teaching. He returned to Würzburg, where he was appointed Professor of Viola and Music History at the University.

As a teacher he discovered that there was an astounding lack of viola literature that he considered worthy of his students. To fill this void he composed, edited, and transcribed an impressive number of works for the instrument. This included didactic works, solo pieces, and ensemble music, most of which were published by Kistner & Siegel of Lippstadt between 1883 and 1907; also, he persisted in editing works for the *Viola alta* until almost to the time of his death in 1926. Two works representative of his creative contributions are *Im Träume for Viola Alta and Piano* (Ex. 21), and *Konzert-Fantasie for Viola Alta and Orchestra* (Ex. 22, an extract from the second movement). Today, most of his compositions have become obsolete or forgotten, possibly because he was too busy to perfect them or had stretched his talents too thin. Still he laid a good foundation for his students. One of them, Clemens Meyer (1868–1958), was particularly productive in editing and transcribing for the viola. In fact, all of Ritter's students were indoctrinated with the importance of playing large violas.

In addition to his many and varied contributions to the viola, Ritter became a noted German musicologist, writing and publishing numerous works dealing with various aspects of music history. He continued, however, to promote the use of the *Viola alta*, with the result that Hörlein was selling his instruments as fast as he could produce them. But the new-found popularity of this instrument was short-lived with most violists; it was simply too large for the average performer to manage. Notable exceptions were Michael Balling, Clemens Meyer, and Paul-Luis Neuberth.[28] In 1898, Ritter added a fifth string (the violin *e*) to the *Viola alta* to eliminate the necessity of playing above the third position over the wide upper bout.[29]

---

[28]For more about Balling, Meyer, and Neuberth, see Appendix I.
[29]For more about the five-string *Viola alta*, see Chapter XII.

Ex. 21.

IM TRÄUME

Viola Alta und Klavier

Viola Alta

Hermann Ritter, Op. 32, No. 2 (1886)

Ex. 21 Continued.

Ex. 22. Extracted from the "*Andante.*"

KONZERT-FANTASIE

c-moll
Für Viola Alta mit Orchester

Viola Alta

Hermann Ritter, Op. 35 (1886)

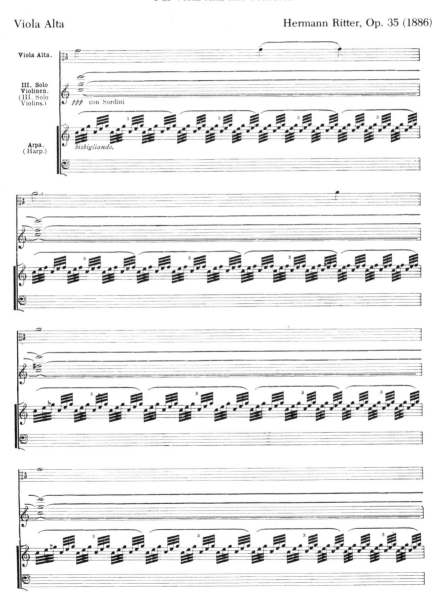

Ex. 22 Continued.

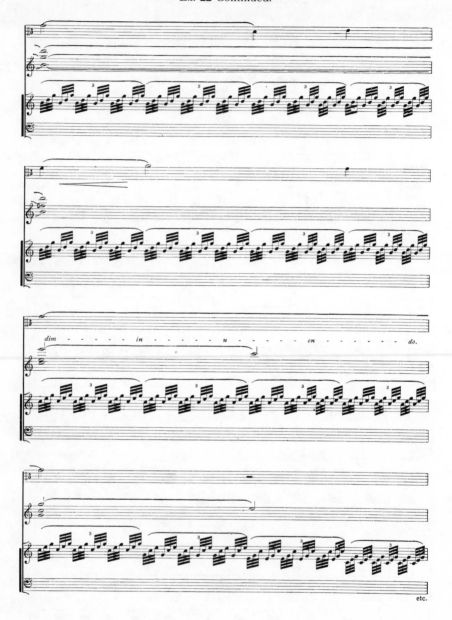

In 1905 Ritter founded the Ritter Quartet, in which the first violin part was played on a traditional instrument and the other three parts were played on instruments he himself had designed. The members of the Ritter Quartet, their parts, and their instruments were: W. Schulze-Prisca, first violin; Ritter played the second violin parts on his five-stringed *Viola alta*; E. Cahnbley played the viola parts on the *Viola tenore*; and H. Knöchel played the cello parts on the *Viola bassa*.[30] With these instruments, it was Ritter's intention to enlarge the registers and to increase the sonority of the three larger ones in order to match the brilliance of the violin. He believed that in string quintets the ideal instrumentation would consist of two violins, *Viola alta*, *Viola tenore*, and *Viola bassa*. Felix Weingartner (1863–1942), the famous German conductor, was sufficiently impressed with the sound of the new instruments and the performances of the quartet to write two complimentary articles.[31]

Ritter's dedication to, and love for, the viola was but one of the several facets of his busy and productive life. He was a pioneer in the use of larger violas and in his emphasis on excellence of performance among violists. His influence was principally on German players. Many present-day German players have studied with one or another of Ritter's students.

---

[30]For tunings and a description of these instruments, see Chapter XII, "Experiments to improve the Viola."

[31]Weingartner's articles are discussed and quoted in Ch. XII.

CHAPTER XII

PROBLEMS IN CONSTRUCTION AND RENOVATION OF VIOLAS AND EXPERIMENTS TO "IMPROVE" THE INSTRUMENT

The viola has produced more problems for luthiers during the last three centuries than have the other members of the violin family. Two problems were common to the violin, viola, and cello: (1) the need to splice the top and back when the available quality acoustical wood was of insufficient width; and (2) the need to lengthen the neck and fingerboard of instruments made before c.1780 in response to the new demands of performers toward the end of the 18th century. A third problem for violas consisted of making the old *tenors* short enough to be playable. This was solved by cutting them down. The fourth problem is related to the shape and dimensions of the viola. Many small violas lack a desired resonance, and many tenor-size violas are too large to play comfortably. As a consequence, for over three centuries there have been numerous "experiments to improve the viola" by altering its shape, or by changing its dimensions or tuning.

Splicing

Luthiers sometimes acquired wood of fine acoustical quality, but of insufficient width for the top or back of the instrument they planned to make. The problem was solved by adding extensions, sometimes called *wings,* on the sides to obtain the desired width (Plate 48). The Primrose Andrea Guarneri viola, shown in Plate 23, was constructed in this manner.

Lengthening the Neck and Fingerboard

The fine instruments made in the 16th, 17th, and 18th centuries had shorter necks and fingerboards than most of those made after

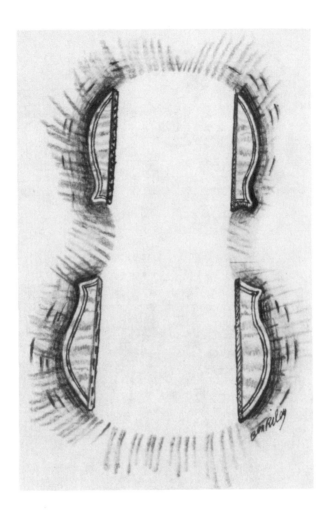

Plate 48. Splicing Sides to Utilize Fine Acoustical Wood.

c.1780. The greater technical facility demanded by the music, along with the extension of the pitch range of the instruments of the violin family during the 18th century, brought an accompanying need for longer necks and fingerboards. For the older instruments, luthiers replaced the original neck and fingerboard with longer ones (see Plate 49). When possible, the original peg-box and scroll were retained because they represent a part of each maker's individual artistry, and are often one of the means of identification of the instrument. This required an ingenious grafting operation. In addition, the extension of

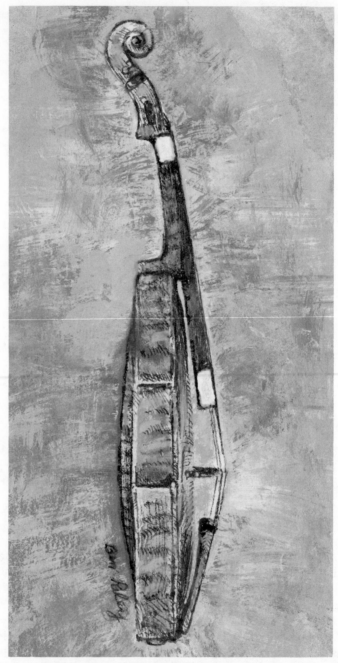

Plate 49. Lengthening Neck and Fingerboard.

the fingerboard necessitated a higher bridge, and the bass bar was usually replaced with a longer or thicker one.

Cutting-down the Large Tenor Violas

In the 16th and 17th centuries, the *alto* (small viola) and the *tenors* (large violas) were assigned to the three parts of the middle harmony in the five-voice music of the time. With the gradual change to four-part writing, performers chose the smaller *alto* viola because it was easier to play, and the *tenor* viola was not needed.

From c.1780 to c.1825, composers and conductors were insisting on obtaining a more resonant sound from the orchestra viola sections. As a result, violists gradually began to demand larger instruments. Before c.1780 a viola that had a body length of more than 40.6 cm. (16 in.) was identified as large; and a viola that was over 43.2 cm. (17 in.) was considered too large to be playable. The large *tenors* of the 16th and 17th centuries were made with body lengths ranging from 43.2 cm. (17 in.) to over 50.8 cm. (20 in.). In an attempt to meet the demands for instruments with more sonority, particularly on the C string, many of the old masterpieces were reduced in size to lengths varying from 39.4 cm. (15 1/2 in.) to 43.2 cm. (17 in.).

The most frequently used method for cutting-down violas was to cut a crescent off each end as shown by the shaded areas in Plate 50. This, of course, required an appropriate shortening of the ribs, resetting of the end blocks, and refitting the neck and fingerboard.

Shortening in the central section was occasionally used as a way to cut down violas (Plate 51). This was a formidable operation, leaving scars that were difficult to conceal. A photograph of a Brothers-Amati viola, which received this type of mutilation, is shown in Ernest N. Doring's book entitled *The Amati Family*, page 22.

Many of the great violas described in Chapter III of this book were reduced in body length. When the operation was done by an accomplished luthier, the results usually were completely satisfactory, and the resonant qualities of the original instrument were retained. Unfortunately many of the former masterpieces were permanently ruined for future use by unskilled makers in their attempt to make the large *tenors* salable.

Experiments to Improve the Viola

The dimensions of the violin have been standardized for over 300 years. The large-pattern violin is approximately 36 cm. (13.9 in.) in

Plate 50. Shortening Ends to Cut Down a Viola's Size.

body length. On the other hand, there has never been a standard body length for the viola. It has varied from 38 cm. (15 in.) to over 50.8 cm. (20 in.). The smaller violas often suffer from a lack of sonority, particularly on the C string, and many of the old tenors were too large to play comfortably. The average viola is about 1/5 larger than the violin. This size does not compensate for its range, which extends 1/5 lower in pitch. As a result many violas have a somewhat nasal or veiled tone as compared with the violin and cello.

Through the years there has been a steady stream of acousticians, performers, and luthiers who have attempted to design and build an instrument that would produce a sound comparable to a violin or

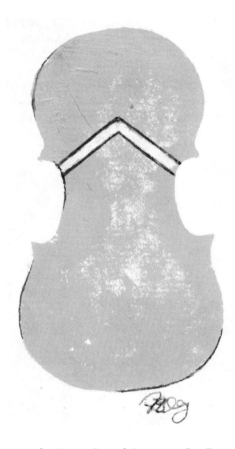

Plate 51. Shortening the Upper Central Section to Cut Down a Viola's Size.

cello, and at the same time give it dimensions that would make it comfortable to play.

Johann Sebastian Bach is erroneously believed to have suggested the specifications for Johann Christian Hoffman (1683–1750), who built several instruments known as the *Viola pomposa*.[1] It was a large-size viola with a violin *e* string added, resulting in a five-string accordatura of c, g, d', a', e".

Several of Hoffman's instruments are extant. One made in 1732 has a total length of 76 cm. (29.9 in.) and ribs, which have been cut down to 3.8 cm. (1.15 in.). With this width of ribs, it can be played with

---

[1]Heinrich Husmann, "Die Viola pomposa," *Bach-Jarbuch*, 1936, p. 90.

the instrument held under the chin.[2] Another example, made in 1742, (Plate 52), has a total length of 78 cm. (30.7 in.) and ribs of 8 cm. (3.15 in.). The ribs are original, and with this width the instrument could not be held comfortably under the chin, but would have to be held against the chest.[3]

By the beginning of the 19th century, music for the viola was covering a greater pitch range and also was assuming a more important role in the total ensemble, be it orchestral or chamber music.

Plate 52. Johann Christian Hoffmann: Viola Pomposa, 1741.

---

[2]Now in the possession of Leipzig luthier, Albin Wilfer. Husmann, *Ibid.*, believes the ribs of the 1732 instrument were lowered by 4 cm. (1 9/16 in.).

[3]Now in Heyer Museum, *Kinsky Catalogue*, p. 555.

Composers and conductors became critical of many viola sections, where the players were not only using small violas, but were even playing violins strung with viola strings. The tone quality of these viola sections caused Grétry, Berlioz, Wagner, and others to write scathing commentaries on the inadequacy and lack of artistic standards among violists in the nineteenth century orchestras.

Many instruments were designed and produced in the 19th century in an attempt to solve the problems of facility and of the small muffled sound of the violas then in use. One of the first was an instrument "invented" by Michael Woldemar (1750–1816), violinist, violist, composer, and teacher in Paris around 1800. Actually Woldemar's idea was to add a *C* string to a violin, making it a five-stringed instrument. According to Grétry many of the violists were already playing violins strung as violas, so that Woldemar's invention was not revolutionary, nor did it solve the acoustical problem. It was tried briefly by the finest violist in Paris at the time, Chrétian Urhan, who even performed on it in a concert at the Conservatoire, playing a *Viola Concerto* written both for him and the instrument by its inventor, Woldemar.

There was a particular concern in Paris in the early 19th century regarding the problem of viola sonority. Felix Savart (1791–1841), French scientist and Professor of Acoustics at the College de France, in his treatise, *Memorie sur la construction des instruments à chordes et à archet* (1819), commented that the body of the viola was much too small in relation to its intended tonal range (See Plate 53 for one of his experiments).[4]

B. Dubois, a French luthier, built an instrument he called the *Violon-tenor* in 1833, which had a body length of 43.5 cm. (17 1/8 in.) and an overall length of 71 cm. (27.0 in.). It was tuned an octave lower than the violin: G, d, a, e'. It was intended that the instrument be held between the knees and played cello-fashion.

Charles Henry (1803–59) constructed a *Baryton* in 1847, tuned like Dubois' *Violon-tenor*, an octave lower than the violin.

The most famous of all French luthiers, Jean Baptiste Vuillaume (1798–1875), built a *Contralto* in 1855 (Plate 54). The total length is 67.5 cm. (26 1/2 in.); the body length is 41.3 cm. (16 1/4 in.); and the ribs are 5 cm. (2 in.). These measurements are within standard bounds; however, the upper bout of 29.2 cm. (11 1/2 in.), and the

---

[4]Savart did some experiments with new violin shapes, most notably a trapezoid shaped violin without middle bouts (Plate 53). François Chanot (1783–1823), formerly a student at l'Ecole Polytechnique, and a naval officer, showed one of his inventions at the Paris Exposition of 1819, a guitar-shaped violin with *c* holes and the strings fastened to a glued-on bridge. The scroll was slanted backward in an attempt to facilitate easier fastening of the strings to the pegs.

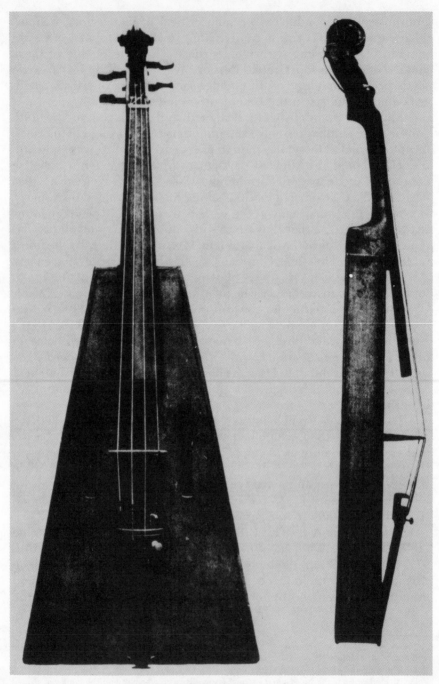

Plate 53. Felix Savart: Trapezoid Violin.

Plate 54. Jean-Baptiste Vuillaume: Contralto, 1855.

lower bout of 36 cm. (14 3/16 in.) make the instrument virtually un-playable above the third position.[5]

The increasing number of luthiers and musicians seeking to "improve" the viola alarmed some devotees of the instrument. Wecker von Gonterhausen warned these "zealots of progress" of the probable outcome of their experiments:

> Its [the viola's] tone has a gentle somberness to which a peculiar nasal quality imparts a distinctive charm . . . The resonance of our violas is weak in comparison with that of the violin and of a different tone color. By raising the ribs the power of its sound might easily be increased, but thereby the characteristic gentleness combined with a homely nasal quality of its tone would be sacrificed, which is of the greatest advantage to our orchestras.[6]

[5]Robert Millant, *J. B. Vuillaume, His Life and Work* (London: W. E. Hill & Sons, 1972), p. 117.

[6]H. Welker von Gonterhausen, *Über den Bau der Saiteninstrumente und deren Akustik . . .* (Frankfurt: M. C. Winter, 1870).

Von Gonterhausen's advice apparently fell mostly on deaf ears. For example, Hermann Ritter, a virtuoso violist, had an obsession to design a new instrument that would "correct" the qualities which von Gonterhausen had described as the ideal and admirable characteristics of viola sound.

Herman Ritter

Hermann Ritter (1849–1926), a virtuoso German violist, with inspiration and support from Richard Wagner, "invented" the *Viola alta*.[7] The *Viola alta* with its companion instruments, the *Viola tenore* and the *Viola bassa*, were among the most significant experiments conducted with new models and new dimensions for members of the violin family during the 19th century.[8]

It was common practice in most German orchestras to use small violas, many of them little larger than violins. The resultant muffled tone and lack of resonance became Ritter's chief concern. The general attitude of conductors and composers throughout the 19th century regarding the viola was illustrated in the satirical poem by Schnyder von Wartensee, which Ritter was later to quote in the book that recorded his research on the historical and accoustical background of the viola. Von Wartensee's poem and a translation follow:

Die Bratsche
Man nennt mich Frau Base,
  Denn etwas sprech' ich durch die Nase,
Doch ehrlich mein' ich es und treu.
Altmodisch bin ich, meine Sitte
Ist stets zu bleiben in der Mitte
  Und nie mach' ich ein gross' Geschrei.

(They call me Frau Gossip.
  As you might suppose.
I'm honest and friendly,
  But talk through my nose.
I shun the big noise,
  And I'm old-fashioned, too;
And I stick to the middle
  Whatever I do.)[9]

---

[7] See Chapter XI, "19th Century Violists," for more about Ritter as a performer.

[8] Ritter wrote a series of monographs covering his research and the resultant *Viola alta*, beginning with *Die Viola alta*, Heidelberg, 1876; followed by *Die Geschichte der Viola alta und die Grundsätze ihres Baues*, Leipzig, 1877; and a third edition, *Die Viola alta oder Altgeige*, Leipzig, 1885. The second edition is available in a reprint, Wiesbaden: Dr. Martin Sändig, 1969.

[9] Schnyder von Wartensee, a composer and the publisher of Paganini's "Method of Violin Playing" *(24 Eutdes)*, included the above humorous birthday poem in a letter addressed to his friend, C.M.F. Guhr, Kappelmeister of Frankfort am Main, 1830. This poem was quoted by Hermann Ritter in his book *Die Geschichte der Viola-Alta und die Grundsätze ihres Baues*, 1876. The English version of the poem is by Dr. Fred G. Walcott, Professor Emeritus, University of Michigan.

Ritter's acoustical research, conducted between 1872 and 1875, included study of the pamphlet by Antonio Bagatella, *Regole per la Construzione dei violini, viole, violoncelli e violoni* . . . , which was written in 1782 and published in 1786. Bagatella's conclusions were adopted by Ritter as the solution for the problems related to the resonance of the viola. He wanted an instrument that would have the same carrying power, sonority, and beautiful tone in all registers as the violin and the cello. He concluded that the violin and viola had the relationship of tonic to sub-dominant. He determined that the dimensions of the "box," or air chamber, should be constructed with a mathematical relationship to the violin of 2:3, or 1:3/2.

The assignment of making the viola to Ritter's specifications was given to the luthier Karl Adam Hörlein (1829–1902) of Würzburg, who had apprenticed with Jean Vauchel (1782–1856).[10] Ritter's relationship with Hörlein was so mutually satisfying that the violist later settled in Würzburg. Hörlein, using Ritter's drawings and dimensions, constructed the first *Viola alta* (the name selected by Ritter) in 1875. This instrument had a body length of 48 cm. (18.9 in.), and ribs of 4.3 cm. (1.7 in.). Ritter's desired proportion of 2:3 would have required a viola length of 54 cm. (21 1/4 in.). He was compelled to compromise and accept the 48 cm. instrument, the maximum length he believed would be possible to play (see Plate 55).

Knowing Richard Wagner's attitude about violas, he made haste to visit the composer in Munich.[11] There he played the new instrument for the great master. Wagner was in the final stages of planning the performances of the tetralogy *Der Ring des Nibelungen*, to be premiered at Bayreuth in 1876. He was so impressed by Ritter's *Viola alta* that he engaged Ritter to play in the orchestra at the historical opening of the new Theatre in Bayreuth.

Wagner sent a letter to the "inventor," on March 28, 1875, which stated:

> . . . I feel certain that the universal introduction of the Viola Alta into our orchestras would serve not only to throw a proper light on the intention of those composers who had to content themselves with the ordinary Bratsche while they required for their melody the true *Alto-violin* tone, but that it might also bring about an advantageous change in the treatment of the string quartet.
> The free A string of this no longer thin and nasal, but now free and brilliant, sounding instrument will be able to take over many an energetic melody from the

---

[10]Hörlein had built a *tenor viola* for E. Hermann in 1848, when he worked in Vienna with Anton Hoffman and Lemböck.

[11]See Chapter XI, "19th Century Violists," where Wagner's opinions on violas and violists are quoted.

Plate 55. Karl A. Hörlein: Ritter Model Viola Alta, 1875.

hemmed in A string of the violin which hitherto was so impeded in its energetic expression of tone, that, for instance, Weber was already obliged to add a wind instrument (clarinet or oboe) in such cases to strengthen the violin part.

The Viola Alta will obviate all this, and will therefore no longer compel the composer to use mixed colors where the pure string character was originally intended. It is desirable that the improved and vastly ennobled instrument should be given to the best orchestras, and that its cultivation should be urgently recommended to all the best viola players. We shall have to be prepared to meet with great opposition in this, as in the majority of our orchestras the viola players do not constitute the flower of bow-instrumentalists.

A courageous beginning will, however, draw followers and finally conductors and directors will have to encourage the good example . . . Please let me know how the excellent court-musician Thoms, in Munich, has received your instrument; friend Fleischhauer (Concertmaster in Meiningen) has already declared his willingness to recommend the Viola Alta for use at the forthcoming Festival performances at Bayreuth. If that lets me hope to see at least two of these instruments used in my orchestra, I regret only not to have six already to assist in the same way. Perhaps it would have been impossible.

Ritter was a large man and could play the *Viola alta* with apparent ease. Most violists, however, found the instrument to be too large. Those that could barely reach first position complained that the upper bout was so wide that they could not play in the higher positions. In 1898 an attempt to solve this problem was made by Ritter by adding a fifth string, the violin *e*, in order to extend the needed range in the first three positions. He described his new "invention" in a monograph printed in 1899.[12]

In 1905 Ritter presented an entirely new string quartet. The first violin was of standard size. The second violin part was played on his five-stringed *Viola alta*. The third part was played on a new instrument, the *Viola tenore*, which had a body length of 72 cm. (28 1/3 in.), and was constructed with dimensions in a ratio of 2:1 to the violin. The *Viola tenore* was played cello style, held between the knees. Its tuning was an octave lower than the violin, or G, d, a, e'. He named the fourth member of the quartet the *Viola bassa*. It had dimensions in a proportion of 2:1 to the *Viola alta*, or 96 cm. (37.8 in.), making it larger than a cello. The tuning, however, was the same as the cello, an octave lower than the *Viola alta*. Ritter's quartet had the mathematical proportions of 2 (violin) to 3 (*Viola alta*) to 4 (*Viola tenore*) to 6 (*Viola bassa*). Ritter was assisted in the planning and production of the instruments of his new quartet by Philipp Keller (1868–1948), formerly a solo cellist, who took over Hörlein's shop, when the latter died in 1902.[13]

---

[12]Hermann Ritter, *Die fünfsaitige Altgeige Viola alta*, Bamberg, 1899.

[13]Heinrich Bessler, *Zum Problem der Tenorgeige* (Heidelberg: Müller-Thiergarten, 1949), p. 13.

The most frequent criticism of the Ritter *Viola alta* was that it lacked the nasal, somber tone quality characteristic of the viola, and that it sounded more like a cello.

There was, however, a very positive reaction to the *Viola alta* by one of the greatest conductors of the early 20th century, Felix Weingartner (1863–1942), who wrote favorably of the Ritter Quartet and the *Viola alta* in 1904.[14] In 1912 he recommended that the *Viola tenore* should be used in string quintets and also in symphony orchestras:

> If a tenor violin is added to the normal [string] quartet as a fifth instrument, a quintet of well-balanced and many-colored tone would result. I believe not to be wrong if I predict a rich future for the string quintet of such instrumentation . . . Also, the tenor violin should be taken into serious consideration for the orchestra.[15]

Thirty years later, in the 1940's, the world famous conductor Leopold Stokowski proposed a similar idea of using *tenors* in the New York Philharmonic Orchestra to give the string section a richer sound. He went so far as to contract Frederic E. Haenel, who worked in Toronto and New York City, to produce the instruments. Many musicians considered this just one more attempt by Stokowski to obtain publicity, and the proposal of using *tenors* in the New York Philharmonic died from lack of support.

Many of the Ritter model violas are still in use, and several are in collections and museums. In the United States the Vitali Import Company of Los Angeles, California, has in its collection a five-string *Alt-geige*, made by Karl Niedt (1872–1950) of Würzburg, in 1902; Hans Weisshauer, the eminent Los Angeles luthier, has in his collection a *Viola alta* made by Phillip Keller, of Würzburg, in 1882. The Berlin Instrument Museum catalogue describes two of these instruments in their collection: a 4-string A.K.A. Hörlein Ritter-Model Viola, Würzburg, 1893, 46.9 cm, (18 1/2 in.); and a 5-string *Viola alta*, Phillip Keller, Würzburg, n.d., 45.5 cm. (17 7/8 in.).[16]

In addition to Hermann Ritter, other Germans were designing large violas, most notably Heinrich Dessauer (1863–1917) of Linz and Johann Reiter (1879–?) of Mittenwald. Dessauer built a viola with a conservative body length of 42 cm. (16 1/2 in.), but with a fingerboard

[14]Felix Weingartner, "Das Ritter Quartet," *Die Musik 4*, 1904/5, No. 9, p. 169.

[15]Felix Weingartner, *Akkorde*. Leipzig, 1912, p. 262. Quoted from an excellent article by Hans Bender, "The Tenor Violin—Past, Present, and Future," *American String Teacher*, XIX, No. 4, 1969, p. 28 (English translation by John Christie).

[16]Irmgard Otto and Olga Adelmann, *Katalog der Streichinstrumente, Musikinstrumenten-Museum Berlin* (Berlin: H. Heenemann 1975), pp. 242–3.

and string length identical to that of the violin. The intention was to make it easier for a violinist to double on the viola, and vice versa. The tuning remained c, g, d', a'. Reiter's instrument, an *Octave violin*, was the same length as Dessauer's, but was tuned an octave lower than the violin: G, d, a, e'.

Dr. Alfred Stelzner (1852–1906), of Wiesbaden and later Dresden, made an instrument for Mehr Erfolg in 1891, a *Violetta*, with a body length of 41 cm. (16 1/8 in.) and a total length of 71.5 cm. (27.9 in.). Stelzner was both composer and luthier, and his *Violetta* evoked more interest than any other viola invention in the 19th century, with the exception of the one made by Hörlein for Ritter. It resembled the instruments made by the Frenchmen Dubois and Henry. Special compositions were written for the instrument by Max Schillings, Felix Draeseke, Arnold Krug, and the inventor, Stelzner.

Eugen Sprenger (1882–1953), of Frankfurt am Main, made one of the most successful experiments, a viola with a comfortable body length of 40 cm. (15 3/4 in.), and an overall length of 66 cm. (26 in.). By widening the bouts, and at the same time raising the ribs, he was able to increase the air-chamber by one-third. His instrument preserved the dark viola tone, but had a much greater penetrating sound than other violas of a similar body length. Paul Hindemith was particularly enthusiastic about the instrument and played it and other Sprenger models in the 1920's. Sprenger patented his instrument in 1930. He also built a *Tenorgeige* in 1922 (Plate 56), in which he doubled the total violin length to 116 cm. (46 in.).

There was also experimentation in Italy, most notably in Florence, where the luthier Valentino de Zorsi (1837–1916) made a *Contraviolino* in 1908. The tuning was G, d, a, e'.

The viola experiments were also carried on in Russia, where Eugen Vitachek, a Moscow luthier, built a large tenor viola in 1912. Vitachek's tenor was greatly admired by the composer Serge Taneyev (1856–1915), who wrote a *Trio in E♭*, Op. 31, specifically to include the new tenor, with an instrumentation of violin, viola, and tenor viola.

Many violists have had physical problems attributed to playing large violas. Included in these ailments have been severe soreness of the chin and neck, tendonitis, bursitis, and fibrositis of the arms and shoulders. Lionel Tertis (1876–1975), in his younger years, played a large 43.5 cm. (17 1/8 in.) Montagnana viola. He was not a large man, and the strain finally brought about his first retirement from concert performance in 1937. Prior to his retirement he had spent much time planning and designing a viola of smaller dimensions that would produce as fine a sound as his Montagnana. Ultimately he took his

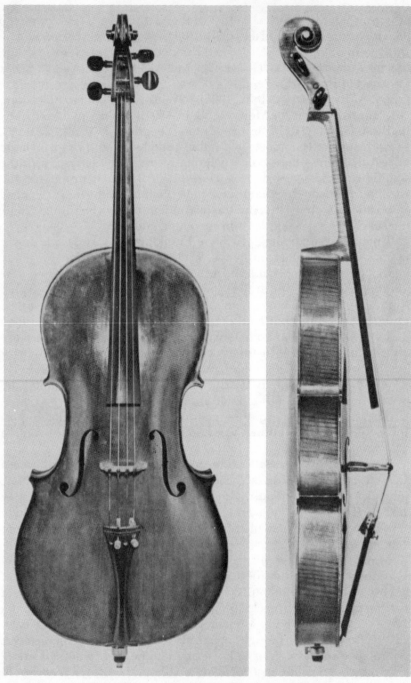

Plate 56. Eugen Sprenger: Tenorgeige, 1922.

drawings and measurements to Arthur Richardson, a luthier whose shop was in Crediton, Devon, England. Richardson made the first *Tertis Model Viola* in 1937. The instrument had a body length of 42.5 cm. (16 3/4 in.). Complete specifications for the *Tertis Model Viola* are given in the two autobiographies by Tertis: *Cinderella No More*, 1953; and *My Viola and I*, 1974. Subsequently, Richardson made over a hundred *Tertis Model Violas*. Other makers of *Tertis Model Violas* listed in *Cinderella No More* include Lawrence Cocker; William H. Moennig, Jr., Philadelphia; Emilio Petraglia, Argentina; George Schlieps, New York City; A. E. Smith, Australia; M. Vatelot and Son, Paris; Karel Vavra, Czechoslovakia; Pierre Vidoudez, Switzerland; and E. & P. Voight, London. Many violists, particularly students of Tertis, recommend and play a *Tertis Model Viola*.

On December 4, 1950, the *Tertis Model Viola* was demonstrated at an exciting concert, which featured performances by Primrose, Copperwheat, Hambourg, Lush, Danks, Townshend, Wooton, and Harding. All but Primrose had been pupils of Tertis. The coming-out party for the 16 3/4 in. (42.5 cm.) viola was highly successful and a great satisfaction to Tertis.

In February of 1959 the Associazone Nazionale Liuteria Artistica Italiana announced that they would sponsor an exhibition of modern violas in Ascoli Piceno the following September 20–27. Also the society sent out a questionnaire to performers, luthiers, conductors, dealers, teachers, and composers to determine their preferred dimensions for a viola. There were 200 responses (126 Italian, 74 foreign); 93 were luthiers (48 Italian, 45 foreign); 107 were from the other categories mentioned above (78 Italian, 29 foreign). Of the total responses, 186 were in favor of a viola having a minimum body length of 42 cm. (16 1/2 in.). Of the 186, 13 preferred a minimum of 42.5 cm. (16 3/4 in.); four preferred 43 cm. (16 15/16 in.); two preferred 44 to 46 cm. (17 5/16 to 18 1/8 in.); a Professor of Viola named Neuberth preferred 48 cm. (18 7/8 in.).

The questionnaire indicated that six performers preferred two different viola body lengths: a 40 cm. (15 3/4 in.) to 42 cm. (16 1/2 in.) for chamber music, and a 42 cm. or larger for symphonic music. All of the composers and conductors favored the minimum 42 cm. body length.

Dr. Professor Gioacchino Pasqualini, Professor of Viola at Saint-Cecilia Academy in Rome and also the President of the Associazone Nazionale Liuteria Artistica Italiana, drew up the following minimum dimension recommendations based on the questionnaire:

Body length — 42 cm. (16 1/2 in.)
Neck length — 15 cm. (5 29/32 in.).

His report concluded that luthiers could build even larger violas, but recommended that the maximum length be limited to 43 cm. (16 15/16 in.).[17]

When the announced exhibit took place, it comprised over 150 violas, most of large dimensions, made by craftsmen from sixteen countries. Among the foreign visitors at the exhibit was Lionel Tertis, who had brought his own viola model, made by Wilfred Saunders. Tertis' instrument elicited considerable interest from those attending the exhibition. The spirit of the meeting and the recommendations of the Associazone Nazionale Liuteria Artistica Italiana prompted Tertis to write, "For me, to my great satisfaction, the Exhibition portends a further eradication of the under-sized so-called viola. Orchestral conductors please note, and eschew small violas."[18]

Carleen M. Hutchins, American luthier and scientist, of Montclair, N.J., has spent over twenty years doing acoustical research and constructing instruments in an attempt to develop the "missing links" in the violin family. She has been assisted by two Fellowship Grants from the John Simon Guggenheim Memorial Foundation, and by the request of Henry Brant, composer in residence at Bennington College, for a "balanced series of eight violin-type instruments tuned in fifths (fourths for the two basses), covering the approximate range of the piano keyboard." The outcome was the production of a complete family of instruments: the *treble,* tuned an octave above the violin; the *soprano,* tuned an octave above the viola; the *violin;* the *viola;* the *tenor,* tuned an octave lower than the violin; the *cello;* the *small bass,* tuned A, D, G, C; and the *large bass,* with the traditional tuning. Her extensive research is described in numerous articles in scientific and music journals.[19]

William Berman, formerly principal violist of the Oklahoma Symphony (1941) and of the National Symphony of Washington, D.C. (1946), and Professor of Viola at Oberlin College (1957–77), had the end-pin removed from a 20 inch vertical tenor made by Ms. Hutchins,

---

[17]From two articles by Dr. Prof. Gioacchino Pasqualini, "Referendum internationale sulla viola moderna," *Saint Cecilia,* April, 1959, 8 pp. 81–83; "Risultati sul referendum internationale, A.N.L.A.I. sulla viola moderna," *Saint Cecilia,* 1960, pp. 73–4.

[18]Lionel Tertis, *My Viola and I* (London: Elek Books, Ltd., 1974), p. 117.

[19]See Carleen M. Hutchins, "The Physics of Violins," *Scientific American,* Nov. 1962, pp. 78–93; "Founding a Family of Fiddles," *Physics Today,* Feb. 1967, pp. 23–37; "The New Violin Family," *American String Teacher,* Spring, 1965, pp. 42–44. Articles in the *Catgut Acoustical Society Newsletter,* 1963–.

and for five years played it "viola fashion" under the chin without a chin-rest.

On August 4, 1968, there was a performance on a *Violino grande* made by the Swedish luthier, Hans Olaf Hanson. The concert occurred at Dartmouth College, Hanover, New Hampshire. The composition, *Concerto for Violino Grande and Orchestra*, was composed by Krzysztof Penderecki in 1967. The *Concerto*, commissioned by the Swedish government, was performed by Bronislaw Eichenholz. The *Violino grande* is a five-stringed viola tuned c, g, d', a', e".

Hans Weisshaar, of Los Angeles, California, has built a *Tenor violin*, using specifications of tenors built in 1905 by Phillip Keller, and in 1922 by Sprenger. The instrument, held between the knees, is played by the cellist Alberta Hurst, who has made recordings with the tenor both as a soloist and in ensemble for Crystal Records.

Franz Zeyringer, of Pöllau, Austria, and the founder-president of the Viola Forschungsgesellschaft, has determined after many years of research that the ideal body length for a viola is 41.2 cm. (16.22 in.); length from inner *f*-hole notch to nut is 37.5 cm. (14.76 in.); length from level of inner *f*-hole notch to the beginning of the neck is 22.5 cm. (8.86 in.); and the neck length is 15 cm. (5.9 in.). Zeyringer also carefully computed all of the other dimensions of the "ideal viola." Leo Mayr, of Bayerisch-Gmain, a village near Salzburg, constructed a viola made to Zeyringer's specifications in 1977. This instrument was shown and demonstrated at the International Viola Congress held in London in 1978. Zeyringer's research and dimensions for "the ideal viola" are contained in a monograph published in 1979.[20]

One of the greatest problems for many violists when they play large violas is the difficulty of reaching across the upper bout to play in higher positions, particularly on the second, third, and fourth strings. Otto Erdesz, of Toronto, Canada, a fine viola maker, has solved this problem by designing the right side of the upper bout with a concave shape instead of the traditional convex curve. The indented upper bout thus permits a violist with a small hand an accommodation to the upper positions without undue strain or fatigue (see Plate 57). Erdesz has made an additional change in constructing his violas. He uses the bass-bar as the center of graduation of the top of the instrument.

Professor Lowell M. Creitz,[21] cellist of the Pro Arts Quartet (in Residence at the University of Wisconsin-Madison), has done exten-

---

[20]Franz Zeyringer, *The Problem of Viola Size* (New York: The American Viola Society, 1979).

[21]Material is taken from letters Creitz sent the author dated October 29, and November 8, 1978, and January 8, 1979.

Plate 57. Otto Erdesz: Viola Model to Facilitate Playing in Higher Positions.

sive research on the subject of the small cello of the period from
c.1550 to c.1830. According to Creitz, these instruments had various
tunings: G,d,a,e', or C,G,d,a,e', and later C,G,d,a. The small cello
came in at least three different body lengths of 71, 76, and 81 cm.
Creitz points out that the cellos made by J. B. Guadaganini were
usually of smaller dimension than those made by most of his contemporaries, and that other luthiers, including Giovanni Grancino,
also made small cellos.[22]

---

[22]Creitz prefers the term "small cello" rather than "tenor."

After a search of twenty years Creitz acquired a mint condition Grancino *tenor violin*, which according to his research, has the dimensions of "the true solo cello of the 18th century." The dimensions of this Grancino are:

Body length — 69   cm. (27 5/32 in.)
Upper bout — 32   cm. (12 5/8 in)
Middle bout — 22.3 cm. (8 3/4 in.)
Lower bout — 40   cm. (15 3/4 in.)
Upper ribs — 9.8 cm. (3 7/8 in.)
Lower ribs — 10.2 cm. (3 15/16 in.)

Creitz plays this instrument in The Rogeri String Trio, a concert ensemble which consists of violin, viola, and tenor violin. This group has re-discovered a large repertoire of compositions by Haydn, Boccherini, and Schubert which are ideal for their instrumentation.[23]

Bruce Carlson, an American luthier living in Cremona, Italy, made a five-string tenor for Creitz in 1979, using patterns by Stradivari he found in the Cremona Library. The four lower strings are tuned like a cello, the highest string is tuned a fifth higher, resulting in an accordatura of C, G, d, a, e'.

One of the latest in the succession of experiments appeared in 1978. It is the *Neola*, a tenor instrument made from plastics and aluminum, invented and sold by Goronwy Davies, of Cwmllynfrll Swansea, England. This instrument has an end-pin and is played cello fashion.[24]

Conclusion

None of the experimental instruments described in this chapter have thus far been given any general acceptance, but each has made at least a small contribution to the development of interest in the problems of the viola. The various experiments have brought about an awareness that perhaps there is a need for a real *tenor*. Whether the *tenor* should be tuned like the viola, or an octave lower than the violin, or to some other accordatura will require the combined agreement of performers, composers, and conductors. Whether the *tenor*

---

[23]For more concerning Lowell Creitz' research into the tenor violin see his article, "The New and the Old Violin Families," *The Catgut Acoustical Society Newsletter*, No. 30 (November, 1978).

[24]*The Strad*, July, 1978. p. 289.

should be made with the right dimensions to be played with a viola-style or with a cello-style is an even greater issue.

Also, there is a question as to who would play the *tenor*? Can cellists be convinced that they should double on the *tenor*, as many violinists double on the viola? Or should violists play the *tenor*, since the *tenor* is historically related to the viola?

If there is ever a strong enough incentive and a sufficient demand for performers on the *tenor*, there doubtlessly will be musicians who will learn to play the instrument, and luthiers will respond by producing more instruments of the desired dimensions.

Many violists believe that there are fine violas both of the past and present which produce the true viola sound. The true viola sound, they contend, which leading composers have written for, is of a more mellow and broader color than the brilliant violin or the resonant cello. They reason that just as the English horn should not sound like an oboe, and the trombone should not sound like a trumpet, the viola should not sound like the violin. They conclude that the different shades within the same families of instruments are essential in the overall palette of colors of orchestral sound.

The most fundamental point is to determine what kind of sound the viola should produce: Should the sound be like the alto, the con-tralto, or the tenor timbre? Should the resonance be slightly nasal or completely clear?

With man's inherent curiosity and refusal to accept any problem as unsolvable, the search will continue. There doubtlessly will be more research and experiments in the future with different dimensions, tunings, and shapes, in an attempt to produce the "ideal" viola. However, many violists will always be satisfied with, and prefer, the old Italian models, whatever their shortcomings, believing that they produce the true viola sound.

CHAPTER XIII

LIONEL TERTIS AND
THE ENGLISH SCHOOL
OF VIOLA PLAYING

Hermann Ritter, German virtuoso violist in the late 19th century, impressed German conductors and composers by his artistry and dedication to the viola and pioneered the use of his large model *Viola alta*. Maurice Vieux was the teacher of an entire generation of excellent French violists. He inspired new works for the viola from the pens of several French composers as well as masterpieces by the Belgian composer, Joseph Jongen. Vladmir Bakaleinikoff laid the foundation at the Moscow Conservatory for the Russian school of viola playing, a groundwork upon which his brilliant student, Vadim Borissovsky, later built the modern Soviet school of viola playing.

Ritter, Vieux, and Bakaleinikoff each had far reaching influence on viola performance in his own country. This they achieved by the high standard of excellence they demonstrated in their own playing, and which they also demanded from their pupils. None of these three had long sustained careers as soloists. Ritter, although continuing to play and teach the viola throughout his life, became increasingly more interested in developing an acceptance of his large violas, in musicology, and in the writing of books on music history. Bakaleinikoff migrated to the United States when he was 42 years old to pursue a successful career as violist, conductor, and composer. Vieux, a superb artist and a gifted teacher, was little known outside the borders of France.

It remained for Lionel Tertis, more than any one else up to his time, to develop a favorable climate for the viola as a solo instrument in England. Through his unstinting efforts and artistry, the viola was gradually accepted by English composers and conductors as an instrument worthy of performance opportunities. The result was a blossoming of viola talent from 1910 until the second World War. Many of the fine English violists were students of Tertis, including Rebecca Clarke, Eric Coates, Winifred Copperwheat, Paul Cropper, Harry Danks, C. Sidney Errington, Watson Forbes, Max Gilbert, Hope

Plate 58. Lionel Tertis.

Hambourg, Raymond Jeremy, James Lockyer, Frederich Riddle, Ian Ritchie, Bernard Shore, Gilbert Shufflebotham, Jacqueline Townshend, Maurice Ward, and Lena Wood.

The English school of viola playing includes many other violists who had not been Tertis' students, but who were affected by his influence on their careers in that Tertis had broken down the barriers that had formerly relegated violists to a position of secondary importance. The successful careers of Cecil Aronowitz, Nannie Jamieson, John White, William Primrose, and others were made easier to achieve because of the interest and acceptance Tertis had engendered in viola performance. These violists appeared frequently in London recitals and with English orchestras, performing new works composed for them, or works that had originally been dedicated to Tertis.

After World War II, the London school of viola playing eventually cast an influence on violists in North America through William Primrose, who had migrated to the United States. Although Primrose was not a student of Tertis, he had benefited by the London environment which was so conducive to the fulfillment of the ambitions of young violists. It was from this milieu that Primrose, the greatest violist of the 20th century, emerged.

Thus the influence of Lionel Tertis, the "father" of the English school of viola playing, has probably touched all later violists in some degree. His high standards of performance have permeated solo, ensemble, and orchestral playing world-wide.

Lionel Tertis

Lionel Tertis, C.O.B.E., F.R.A.M.,[1] was born December 29, 1876, at West Harterpool, England; and died in February, 1975, in London. His life experiences and career are well documented in his two autobiographies, Cinderella No More (1953),[2] and My Viola and I (1974).[3]

Cinderella No More, as the title suggests, presents Tertis' conviction that the viola had arrived at its rightful place in the musical world. In order to substantiate his thesis, he reached into his own life experiences. This is fortunate for all violists, and for musical historians as well, because Tertis' musical life and achievements brought about the recognition and elevation of the viola to a place of prominence that it

---

[1]See p. 246.
[2]Lionel Tertis, Cinderella No More (London: Peter Neville, 1953).
[3]Lionel Tertis, My Viola and I (London: Elek Ltd., 1974).

had previously lacked. His virtuosity and artistry as a performer resulted in the production of a new literature for the instrument which was so sorely needed. Many composers wrote concertos, sonatas, and other works for viola, and dedicated them to Tertis. *Cinderella No More* is not just an autobiography of Tertis, but is also a history of the viola's coming into its own place in the early part of this century.

My Viola and I is an up-dated and expanded version of the earlier autobiography, containing additional material and earlier essays, including *Beauty of Tone in String Playing* (1938).[4]

The Early Years

Tertis' family moved to London when he was three months old. His father, a cantor in a London synagogue, was of Russian Jewish origin, and his mother was Polish. Tertis remembered his father's beautiful singing as being his first musical experience and believed that he inherited his own talent from his father's side of the family, although his mother was the one who saw that he practiced.[5]

Tertis' formal musical training began with piano lessons at the age of five. It was as a pianist that he had his first professional experience, and as a teenage pianist he was able to support himself and also to pay for his earliest lessons on the violin.

In 1892 he entered Trinity College of Music in London, where he studied piano with R. W. Lewis and violin with B. M. Carrodus. He had only enough money for two terms of schooling and was forced to return to playing piano in small bands until he had saved enough to return to Trinity the following year. This time he concentrated on the violin, an ambition he had nourished for several years.

He went to Leipzig in 1894 to study violin with Professor Bolland at the Conservatorium. This experience turned out to be a sad disillusionment for Tertis, who had been led to believe that he would receive better training in Germany than in England. Because of his disappointment, he remained in Leipzig only six months.

After returning to London, Tertis became an intermittent student at the Royal Academy of Music, where he studied violin with Hans Wessley until 1897. He received tuition assistance at first from Lionel de Rothschild. It was during this period that a fellow student suggested that he play viola in a string quartet. Tertis derived great satisfaction

---

[4]Lionel Tertis, *Beauty of Tone in String Playing* (London: Oxford University Press, 1938).
[5]See Tertis, *My Viola and I*, pp. 1–18 for a description of Tertis' childhood.

from playing in this quartet, an experience that soon led to a career dedicated to the viola.

During 1899–1900, he returned to the Royal Academy of Music as sub-professor. His chief duty was to play viola in the string orchestra conducted by the French violinist, Emile Sauret. In 1901, he was appointed full professor and invited to play viola in a quartet led by his former teacher, Hans Wessley. Also during this period, he met Ada Gawthrop, who became one of his viola students, and later his wife.

Tertis stated that the most significant event in his early musical training was the first time he heard Fritz Kreisler play in London in 1901. Kreisler's marvelous tone and phrasing was a revelation that was to influence the future style of Tertis' own playing.[6] Twenty years later he joined Kreisler in playing the Mozart *Concertante* in London, in New York, and in Boston.

In 1901, Tertis joined Henry Wood's Queen's Hall Orchestra, sitting at the end of the second violin section. Within a year he was promoted to principal of the viola section, a position he held until 1904, when he resigned to devote full time to becoming a viola soloist. He was given little encouragement by fellow violists:

> In 1906 it was the rarest thing to hear a viola solo, and even so the upper range of the instrument was unexplored. Players never went above the second leger-line in the treble clef. Once I played Mendelssohn's violin concerto on the viola at an Academy concert, and I remember Alfred Gibson's reproaches. He played viola in the Joachim Quartet. "The viola," he burst out, "is not meant to be played high up! This is the pig department! I suppose the next thing is you will be playing behind the bridge."[7]

As soloist with the Royal Philharmonic Society in 1908, Tertis introduced York Bowen's *Viola Concerto*. This was the first of many viola works written by English composers specifically for Tertis.

For one year, 1909, he played as principal violist in the Thomas Beecham Orchestra. Later, in 1916, he was featured, along with Ysaÿe, as soloist in the Mozart *Concertante* with Beecham conducting.

In 1911, Tertis played in recital Bach's *D Minor Chaconne* from the violin solo sonatas, in a *G Minor* version he had transcribed for viola. This was one of many transcriptions that Tertis made for his chosen instrument.

As recognition for entertaining Belgian troops near the front lines in 1915, King Albert bestowed on him the first of many honors that he received. During his career he was appointed "Fellow of the Royal

---

[6]Tertis, *Cinderella No More*, p. 26.
[7]*Ibid.*, p. 27.

Academy of Music," (F.R.A.M.); the Worshipful Company of Musicians awarded him the Cobbett Gold Medal for services to Chamber Music in 1946; King George VI appointed him "Commander of the Order of the British Empire" (C.O.B.E.), in 1950; the Musicians' Benevolent Fund gave him the "Kreisler Award of Merit" in 1950; and the Royal Philharmonic Society awarded him their Gold Medal in 1964.

After World War I Tertis became even more active as viola soloist, performer of chamber music, teacher of viola, and promoter of new literature for the viola.

On February 4, 1937, Tertis was invited to play *Harold in Italy* with the B.B.C. Orchestra, directed by Ernest Ansermet. Because of the acute fibrositis which had been afflicting his bow arm during the previous two years, he decided that this concert, celebrating his sixtieth birthday, would be his last public performance. On June 13, 1937, a banquet held in Tertis' honor was attended by over two hundred friends. Speeches of commendation were given by Eugene Goossens, Bernard Shore, Vaughn Williams, Sir Thomas Beecham, and William Murdoch. Telegrams expressing affectionate greetings and regrets at being unable to attend were sent by Fritz Kreisler, William Walton, Arthur Schnabel, John Barbirolli, and Joseph Szigeti. Among the congratulatory letters read at the banquet were those from Pablo Casals and the managers of both the London Philharmonic Orchestra and the Royal Philharmonic Society.

It was in this same year, 1937, that Tertis began experiments to develop specifications for an ideal model viola. He believed that most violas were too small to have a resonant tone and that the violas that did have a good sound were too large for most violists to play comfortably and with optimum skill. His experiments resulted in the choice of a viola 16 3/4 inches (42.55 cm.) long, "an instrument of practical size for playing under the chin, capable of producing what is one of the glories of the viola, namely, a grand C string sonority, which cannot be achieved on smaller (so called) violas."[8]

Tertis resumed playing again in 1939, to raise money for charities and to introduce his *Tertis Model* Viola. In 1950, at the age of 74, he gave a return recital at Wigmore Hall to introduce his *improved model*. He also gave a brief speech, explaining his reasons for developing the new model. Assisting him on the musical portion of the program, were violists William Primrose, Winifred Copperwheat, Hope Hambourg, Harry Danks, Jacqueline Townshend, Stanley

---

8"The 'Tertis Model' Viola," *The Strad*, April, 1956, p. 468.

Wooton, and Kenneth Harding. Primrose played the four movements of Brahms' *F Minor Sonata* on four different violas, "from all of which he evoked sonorous, full-bodied tone of fine quality." Also on the concert were two of Tertis' transcriptions: Mozart's *Andante for Two Violas* (from the *Duet for Violin and Viola in B♭*) and Beethoven's *Trio for Three Violas* (from *Trio for Two Oboes and English Horn*, Op. 87). Contemporary works on the program were Benjamin Dale's "expressive and unique *Short Pieces for Six Violas*" and a *Concertante and Divertimento for Four Violas* by Kenneth Harding.[9]

Tertis as a Performer

Tertis' chief asset in winning recognition for the viola was his own artistry as a performer. The impact of his playing on his students and friends has recently been chronicled in several sources. The British chapter of the Viola-Forschungsgesellschaft was appropriately founded in December, 1976, one hundred years after Tertis' birth. Their first *Newsletter* was dedicated to the memory of the late Lionel Tertis. Former students and friends penned eulogies and also commented on various aspects of their association with the great violist. Paul Cropper, one of Tertis' students, wrote about him as a teacher and performer. Concerning the latter, he stated in part:

> He produced a wonderful sound, impeccable intonation, and played with great conviction . . . Tertis was, in my opinion, the most successful at projecting his splendid tone above the whole orchestra. This was not just in the loud passages, for he also produced the most wonderful pianissimo playing, which again stood out from the orchestral accompaniment.
> The first time I remember hearing Tertis was one of the most impressive performances of the Bach *Chaconne* that I have ever heard, a notoriously difficult piece to bring off on the violin, but almost impossible on a very large viola.[10]

Other students wrote with equal praise, always describing his playing in glowing terms and superlatives.[11]

Tertis performed with some of the greatest virtuosi of the 20th century: Kreisler, Rachmaninoff, Melba, Ysaÿe, Solomon, and many others. Arthur Rubenstein, the renowned pianist, paid written tribute

---

[9]"Tertis Model Viola Concert," *Musical Opinion*, Feb., 1951, p. 195. For more about the "Tertis Model" viola see Chapter XII.

[10]Paul Cropper, "Two Views of Lionel Tertis," *English Branch of Viola Research Society Newsletter*, No. 1 (Dec., 1976), p. 8.

[11]Other students who wrote about his artistry were Harry Danks, C. Sydney Errington, Winifred Copperwheat, and Bernard Shore. Eric Fenby, Cecil Aronowitz, Gordon Jacob, and Harold Coletta also contributed articles to the *Newsletter* praising Tertis' viola playing.

to the great violist. Once when Rubenstein was at a friend's home, he heard Jacques Thibaud, Albert Sammons, Tertis, and Augustin Rubio play the Debussy Quartet in an informal session. Rubinstein recorded his impressions as follows:

> From the first bars on, I became aware of a new element in their ensemble, a sonority I had never heard before. The sound came to light by the powerful, singing, soulful tone of the viola as played by Lionel Tertis. Here was one of the greatest artists it was my good fortune to know and to hear . . . After the Debussy, I played with him, Thibaud, and Rubio the *C Minor Piano Quartet* by Brahms. The sound of his solo in the first movement still rings in my ears.[12]

On another occasion when Pablo Casals was present, Rubenstein describes the great cellist's reaction when hearing Tertis play:

> We were having supper while a quartet of Mozart was played in the studio. Pablo stood still at the front door and asked suddenly: "Who plays the viola?" He discerned Tertis' tone from that long distance. It was a happy meeting for these two great artists. A curious coincidence: both were born on the same day of the same year.[13]

Viola Music Written for Tertis

One of Tertis' most valuable contributions to the viola was the new repertoire written for him. A list of composers who wrote works for Tertis is impressive. It includes: Arnold Bax, Stanley Bate, W. H. Bell, Arthur Benjamin, Arthur Bliss, York Bowen, Benjamin Dale, T. F. Dunhill, H. Farjeon, Gustav Holst, John McEwen, Richard L. Malthew, William Reed, Cyril Scott, William Walton, Ralph Vaughn Williams, and Waldo Warner. Only a few of these were outstanding composers, and many of the works they wrote for Tertis were not masterpieces; but Tertis encouraged them to write, promising to perform their compositions. After playing them in public, he passed the manuscripts along to his students, who in turn played the new viola literature.

Many of the composers mentioned wrote more than one piece for Tertis. He performed them all publicly with one exception, the *Viola Concerto* by William Walton, which he said he did not understand. Later he studied the work, reversed his earlier appraisal, and thereafter recommended the Walton *Concerto* to his students. The composition of this excellent piece can be attributed, at least in part, to the composer's expectation that Tertis would give it the premier perform-

---

[12]Arthur Rubenstein, *My Young Years* (New York: Alfred A. Knopf, 1973), p. 416.
[13]*Ibid.*, p. 418.

ance. Many of the viola compositions written for Tertis eventually worked their way into print and have become available to all violists.

Music for Multiple Violas

In addition to the solo compositions Tertis transcribed for viola and the original compositions composed for Tertis, he also transcribed and did much to promote original music for, and performance of, works for multiple violas. Chamber music for violas, which excludes other instruments, exploits the full range and the various tone colors of the instrument. Ensembles of violists promote a sense of independence and pride beneficial to the performer's ego. Participation in a choir of violas results in a particular pleasure and satisfaction, together with a congenial association with other musicians who have mutual interests.

The idea of the viola ensemble was not original with Tertis; Anton Wranitzky (1761–1820) composed works for multiple violas before 1800. Tertis, however, exploited the performance of such music to a greater extent than any one before his time.

Dr. Thomas Tatton, of Whittier College in California, has done exhaustive research into the area of music for multiple violas. He gave a lecture and demonstration at the Fourth International Viola Congress held in Bad Godesburg (1976), entitled, "Lionel Tertis and English Viola Literature Written Prior to 1937;"[14] and again at the Sixth International Viola Congress in London (1978), entitled, "Works for Viola Ensemble." In the latter lecture, he was assisted by the Viola Section of the BBC Symphony Orchestra, directed by Harry Danks. In both of Tatton's lectures, music written for Tertis played a conspicious part. On the latter occasion, Dr. Tatton distributed to members of the London audience a list of 29 original works for multiple violas. The list was comprised of pieces written for 3 to 12 violas, and covered a time span from Wranitzky's works (1800) to the present. Most prominent on the list are compositions dedicated to Tertis himself.[15]

Tertis as a Teacher

In the *Newsletter* described in the section, "Tertis as a Performer," several of his students also wrote on the subject, "Tertis as a

---

[14]Based on Tatton's Doctoral Thesis, *English Viola Music* (Urbana: University of Illinois, 1976).

[15]Tatton also directed a concert of works for multiple violas at the Seventh International Viola Congress in Provo, Utah, 1979.

Teacher." A few pertinent statements follow. Harry Danks, Principal
Violist of the B.B.C. Symphony Orchestra, reminiscing on his student
days with Tertis, described his first lesson:

> . . . I had prepared his own arrangement of the Elgar *Cello Concerto* but before I
> was half way down the first page he attacked my poor intonation, in fact in the
> years that followed he never ceased to do this and on a number of occasions
> brought me to a point of despair.[16]

Danks, however, continued by stating that the rigorous discipline
of Tertis' lessons made him work to the utmost of his capacity in order
to achieve the goals set for him by his teacher. Danks added:

> My lessons always consisted of pieces for the repertoire, never scales or
> studies. In fact they were never mentioned. I believe he expected a pupil to attend
> to such things outside the lesson and leave the period spent with him completely
> free for interpretation.[17]
> He liked to spend at least one hour over a lesson, but many times this was
> exceeded for me if he could spare the time; and I never remember him discussing
> money or fees. He certainly did not make much profit out of me.[18]

C. Sydney Errington, another Tertis student, corroborated Danks'
statements in describing his first lesson with Tertis and explained that
students who were employed did pay for their lessons:

> . . . That concluded a most inspiring lesson. He took me for a brisk walk, and then
> dinner, after which he packed me off back to Leeds. Fee (as I was a young profes-
> sional), twenty five shillings![19]

Paul Cropper wrote of his teacher both as a person and an instruc-
tor:

> His kindness, utter sincerity, also, his supreme confidence in his convictions
> and yet, as with most truly great artists, his great humility, are the things I remem-
> ber most about him as a man.
> As a teacher, these great attributes were evident all the time along with infi-
> nite patience. Tertis was immensely thorough and would not let the slightest
> technical or musical fault pass, and any faulty intonation, no matter how slight,
> was anathema to him.[20]

In 1938 Tertis summarized the elements of artistic performance
which he stressed with his pupils in a publication entitled *Beauty of*

---

[16]Harry Danks, "Lionel Tertis," *Newsletter*, p. 4.

[17]Danks was an advanced student and very talented. Tertis did prescribe scales for other
students, as explained in the preface of his transcription of the Sevcik *Scale Studies*, Op. 1, No. 3
(Bosworth, 1953).

[18]Danks, *op. cit.*, p. 5.

[19]C. Sydney Errington, "My First Lesson with Lionel Tertis," *Newsletter*, p. 6.

[20]Paul Cropper, "Two Views of Lionel Tertis," *Newsletter*, p. 7.

Tone in String Playing.[21] Fritz Kreisler was so impressed after reading the manuscript that he wrote an unsolicited *Foreword*. The little book comprises only 22 pages, but contains Tertis' philosophy of tone production and much valuable advice for the performer, be he teacher, student, or artist.

The book discusses the importance of intonation, the necessity for a continuous vibrato to achieve a beautifully shaped phrase, and the judicious use of portamento to avoid gaps in melodic passages. It recommends for the right hand that the performer practice to develop equality of tone from all parts of the bow, and also work to make a smooth change from down- to up-bow without any perceptible sound of changing bow. It particularly emphasizes the importance of changing the bow cleanly from one string to the next, and recommends that the left hand assist the right by leaving the finger down and vibrating until the note on the next string is sounding.

Tertis' Recordings

Dr. François de Beaumont, the Swiss expert in viola discography, has prepared a separate listing of the recordings made by the great English violist, entitled *Lionel Tertis (1876–1975) Discographie*.[22] The title-page includes the following Tertis quotation: "... to sing the praises again and again of what has been the love and tyrant of my life—the viola." This *Discographie* contains an imposing number of recordings, considering that the period covered, c.1915 to c.1936, represents a time when there was a great paucity of such recordings by other violists. Most of the recordings consist of short encore pieces that had been arranged or transcribed by Tertis—much in the same manner as Fritz Kreisler, Mischa Elman, and other artists were making at that time. This was before the advent of long-playing records and tapes, at a time when very few sonatas or concertos were recorded. He did, however, record the Mozart *Symphonie Concertante*, with Albert Sammons, violin, and the London Philharmonic, conducted by Sir Hamilton Harty, and the Arnold Bax *Sonata for Viola and Piano*, with the composer at the piano.

Tertis' recordings gave the viola a highly favorable reputation which made the way easier for the younger virtuosos, like Paul Hindemith and William Primrose, to be accepted as recording artists.

---

[21]*Beauty of Tone in String Playing* is included as a special section in Tertis' recent book, *My Viola and I*.

[22]Published by Dr. François de Beaumont, 1975.

Tertis Contributions to Violists

Bernard Shore, one of Tertis' viola pupils, stated, "The viola was given its present position as a solo instrument by Tertis . . . It is impossible to overrate the influence of this great artist on the art of viola-playing throughout the world. . ." Shore cited four areas in which Tertis made lasting contributions to the viola: 1. Tertis' own artistry had inspired the composition of new literature for the viola, and he had extended the range almost an octave above b'', the accepted upper limit before 1876. 2. Tertis advocated the large viola, and to facilitate playing it, devised fingerings which eliminated awkward stretches. This he accomplished by using half, second, and fourth positions on an equal basis with the first, third, and fifth. 3. He used the vibrato as much as violinists and cellists, a new practice for his time. 4. Tertis freed the viola of its unfortunate reputation of having unequal strings, and exploited all of the tone colors of the instrument in ways that had not been previously thought possible.[23]

Tertis and Casals

Similarities, comparisons, and differences are often made concerning Tertis and Casals. They were both born on December 29, 1876. They both enjoyed century-long, fruitful lives in the service of music, Casals living to be 97, Tertis to 99. Both were protagonists for their respective instruments in a world that had not yet equated the viola and cello with the same high regard as the violin. They opened up new frontiers of technical potential for their instruments, much as Paganini had done for the violin early in the 19th century. Tertis and Casals were the first performers on their respective instruments to be compared favorably with the great virtuosos of the violin and piano.

Tertis' struggle for recognition was much more difficult than was Casals'. Occasionally a violist might perform Berlioz' *Harold in Italy* or Mozart's *Symphonie Concertante*, but for the most part they were limited to playing in orchestras and string quartets. There was little or no precedent for a violist to seek a career as a concert artist. On the other hand, there had been many cellists who had concertized successfully prior to Casals, although not in the grand manner of the great violin virtuosos, but nevertheless furnishing a precedent that made Casals' rise to fame much easier.

---

[23]Berthold Tours and Bernard Shore. *The Viola* (London: Novello, 1943), "Preface," p. iii.

Perhaps their chief difference was Casals' involvement and Tertis' lack of involvement in world affairs. Casals' name became associated with political and sociological struggles for freedom, when, in 1936, he went into voluntary exile, announcing that he would not return to his home in Spain as long as the dictator Franco was in power. He brought world attention to the cause and to himself, becoming an idol of many people who had never heard him play the cello.

In the same year, 1936, Tertis retired as an active concert artist, and in the following years—with the trauma of World War II—was all but forgotten by the musical world for whom he had done so much. He did retain, however, a coterie of loyal friends and students who benefited by their association with him and assisted in promoting his *Tertis Model* viola. As Tertis neared the century mark for longevity, his name was again in the public eye, and a new international veneration developed. Violists, in particular, read his book, *My Viola and I,* and realized the great contribution he had made to them and their instrument.

Both Tertis and Casals were giants of their time, and the world is in great debt to them for their lifelong dedication to the art of music.

CHAPTER XIV

THE VIOLA IN EUROPE IN THE 20TH CENTURY

At the close of the 19th century, the generally poor standard of viola performance, augmented by the increasing technical demands of the viola parts in orchestral music, began to cause concern in most of the leading European Conservatories. In answer to this need for better violists, the Paris Conservatoire in 1894 instituted a discipline for the study of the instrument that was comparable to that of the violin and the cello. Here, Théophile Laforge led the way for a group of gifted violists who together raised the standard of French viola playing to new high levels. In Belgium, Leon Van Hout at the Brussels Conservatoire taught many talented violists, and here also the French influence of Maurice Vieux was particularly felt. In Italy, Renzo Sabatini, the renowned performer, composer, and teacher, became a positive influence on many Italian violists. Oedoen Partos, a Hungarian viola virtuoso, likewise exerted tremendous influence as a performer, composer, and teacher on violists in Israel following World War II. In Russia, at the Moscow Conservatory, Bakaleinikoff's most talented student, Vadim Borissovsky, taught over 200 artist violists, who today hold most of the leading positions in Soviet orchestras and conservatories. In Austria and Germany, the students of Hermann Ritter continued to exert influence toward the raising of standards. There, the emergence of Paul Hindemith as a virtuoso violist and composer of many works for the instrument coincided with the contributions of Prof. Dr. Wilhelm Altmann in his attempts to better the performance and prestige of all violists.

Unfortunately, two World Wars, mostly localized in Europe, were deterrents to the greatest possible progress for the viola. After World War II, however, rising performance levels, new compositions, and the increasing availability of Baroque and Classic works for the instrument gave new impetus to improving the status of the viola.

The publication of the first edition of Franz Zeyringer's *Literatur für Viola* in 1963, and the founding of the Viola-Forschungsgesellschaft (Viola Research Society) in 1966 by a small group of dedicated central European viola enthusiasts helped initiate a new era for violists which became world-wide. The large number of entries in the Zeyringer book, and in its two subsequent editions in 1966 and 1975, has been a revelation to players who formerly believed that they had a very limited literature originally written for their instrument. The Viola-Forschungsgesellschaft has since become international in scope, and has become a positive influence for all violists.

The French Viola School

After the Conservatoire National de Musique de Paris gave recognition to the viola as an instrument worthy of a separate curriculum in 1894, and made it possible for students to graduate with the viola as their major instrument, an ever-increasing number of French violists developed notable stature in their own country and abroad. Among these viola virtuosi in the early 20th century were Théophile Laforge (c. 1860–1918), Pierre Monteux (1875–1964), Henri Casadesus (1879–1947), Paul-Luis Neuberth (1881–?), Louis Bailly (1882–1974), and Maurice Vieux (1870–1951).

Laforge was the Professor of Viola at the Conservatoire for many years. Monteux was the violist in the Geloso Quartet until 1911, when he resigned to give full time to his conducting career. Casadesus was the editor of two important works (actually he composed them), the G. F. Handel *Viola Concerto in B♭ Major* and the J. C. Bach *Viola Concerto in C Major*. He was the violist in the Capet Quartet until 1903, when he resigned to give his complete attention to the Viola d'amore and to his Société des Instruments Anciens. Neuberth was the Principal Violist in l'Orchestre Colonne for 20 years, where he promoted interest in the large *Viola alta* designed by Hermann Ritter.

Louis Bailly was one of the earliest viola graduates from the Paris Conservatoire (1898).[1] After playing for several years in the Paris Opéra Orchestra, he joined the Lucien Capet String Quartet (1903–1911); this was followed by membership in the Geloso Quartet (1911–1914). The latter group disbanded when all the members enlisted in the French Army at the outbreak of World War I. During the preceding years, he had enhanced his reputation as a soloist by frequent appearances as a recitalist; and in recognition of his artistry, Laforge invited him to serve on the annual Juries at the Conservatoire. Pierre Monteux, having observed Bailly's artistic growth, succeeded, with

---

[1]For a more detailed description of Bailly's early career, see, Maurice W. Riley, "Louis Bailly (1882–1974)," *Journal of the Violin Society of America*, III, 3 (1977), pp. 33–57.

Plate 59. Louis Bailly. Photograph furnished by Dr. Vladimir Sokoloff of Philadelphia.

the assistance of Alfred Cortot and the French Minister of Fine Arts, in obtaining his release from the French Army in 1917, in order that he might go to the United States to join the Flonzaley Quartet as violist.[2]

After an absence of twenty years, Bailly returned to Paris in 1938 and gave a concert which evoked glowing praise from the music critics. In the January 31, 1938, issue of *Excelsion*, Emile Veuillermoz wrote:

> Louis Bailly, returning from a concert tour of Warsaw, Budapest, and Vienna, stopped in Paris this week long enough to give a recital and then left for Amsterdam and London before returning to the United States. Louis Bailly, who is one of the most talented French virtuosi of the viola, left us some twenty years ago to settle in the United States where his exceptional talent was immediately recognized. During twenty years of methodical activity of intelligently sustained work, Mr. Bailly has been able to perfect his technique and so reach the summit of his art. The musicians who heard him last Monday will not forget two magnificent hours during which Mr. Bailly's extraordinary talent asserted itself. Mr. Bailly's presence on the stage is one of outstanding simplicity and authority. . . . He has to control a "Gasparo da Salò" of a large size, a marvelous example of the stringed instruments created at the end of the 16th century, possessing a magnificent tone that only a player with muscles of steel can really tame. The viola is a restive instrument, difficult to master because it possesses a dangerous lack of balance between its cold chanterelle and its three warm strings. Mr. Bailly plays it with the same graceful bearing and the same ease as if it were the small fiddle of a ballet master. The tonal quality and the sureness of his style are unequalled. We ought to hear again, before a large audience (this concert was given on invitations), this admirable virtuoso who, with bow and baton, has brilliantly acquainted foreign countries with all the repertoire of French music (in recognition of it he received "le ruban de la Legion d'honneur) and who serves so effectually the prestige of our school of instrumentalists.

M. Barraud, in *Le Journal*, January 26, 1938, also praised the concert in superlative terms:

> One cannot conceive a more human and a richer sonorousness, a more flowing virtuosity, and a more accurate musicianship. Louis Bailly is indeed a very great artist.

Florent Schmitt, writing for *Le Tempo*, February 5, 1938, commented:

> Mr. Bailly needs no introduction as he was, many years ago, the violist of the famous Capet Quartet; this statement contains all I could bestow in the way of praise for his marvelous technique, his bowing, the beauty of his tone, the nobleness of his style, the vigor, the color, and the expression of his playing.[3]

---

[2]For the continuation of Bailly's career, see "The Viola in America in the Early Twentieth Century," Chapter XVI.

[3]The clippings above from the Louis Bailly Memorabilia were translated and furnished by Thérèse Rochette.

Maurice Vieux, "the father of the modern French Viola School," studied with Laforge at the Paris Conservatoire, where he took first prize in viola in 1902. For many years he was the Principal Violist of the Paris Opéra Orchestra. In 1918, after the death of Laforge, Vieux was appointed head of the viola department at the Conservatoire, where he exerted a continuing influence for a high standard of viola performance. Many fine French violists were his students, including François Broos, Marie-Thérèse Chailley, Etienne Ginot, Colette Lequien, Alice Merkel, Leon Pascal, and Pierre Pasquier.

In a brief article written in 1928, Vieux emphasized the need for violists of the 20th century to develop a technique of the same dimensions as that required for contemporary violinists.[4] He served annually on the juries at the Paris Conservatoire, and frequently as a guest of the juries of the Brussels Conservatoire.

Plate 60. Maurice Vieux. Furnished by the Library of Congress.

[4]Maurice Vieux, "Consideration sur la technique de l'alto," *Courrier Musical et Théatrical*, XXX, No. 7 (1928), p. 216.

He was a frequent soloist in the *Société des Concerts du Conservatoire* and took part in the most important chamber-music performances. As a soloist he introduced viola compositions of contemporary French composers, and all of the viola solo literature composed and dedicated to him by the Belgian composer, Joseph Jongen (1873–1953).[5] Among the didactic works Vieux composed for the viola, the following are particularly significant: *20 Etudes* (dedicated to his best students) Edition Heugel; *10 Etudes sur des traits d'orchestre*, Edition Leduc, (1928).

Belgian Violists and Composers

The modern Belgian viola school's genesis can be credited to the brilliant violist, Leo Van Hout, who was born in Liège c. 1885, and died in Brussels in the 1940's. He was the Principal Violist of the Théatre Royal de la Monnaie in Brussels for many years, and violist in the Ysaÿe Quartet at the time Debussy wrote his *E Minor Quartet* for this group. At the Brussels Conservatoire, where he was Professor of Viola, he taught an entire generation of Belgian violists. The Van Hout tradition of excellence in viola performance was carried on by many of his students, among whom were Robert Courte, who succeeded Van Hout as Professor of Viola at the Brussels Conservatoire and later migrated to the United States to become violist in the Paganini Quartet; Charles Foidart, who taught at Northwestern University, and succeeded Courte in the Paganini Quartet when the latter accepted an appointment at the University of Michigan; and Gaston Jacobs, who followed van Hout as Principal Violist of the Théatre Royal de la Monnaie. Before World War II, Jacobs was in great demand as a chamber music player. He died a premature death after spending several years in a Nazi concentration camp.

Among the Belgian composers whom van Hout inspired to write important works for the viola, were François de Bourguignon (1890–?), *Suite for Viola and Orchestra*, Op. 67, (1940); Jan Abail (1893–?), *Concerto for Viola and Orchestra*, Op. 54; Albert Huybrechts (1899–1938), *Sonatine for Flute and Viola;* Raymond Chevreuille (1911–?), *Concerto for Viola and Piano in E♭ Major*, Op. 36, (1946).

Maurice Vieux, the great French violist, also influenced Belgian composers to write for the viola, particularly Joseph Jongen. Most of

---

[5]For a list of works Jongen wrote for Vieux, see the next section, "Belgian Violists and Composers."

Jongen's viola pieces were dedicated to, and premiered by, Vieux, among which the following have become a part of the violist's standard repertoire: *Trio for Violin, Viola, and Piano in F♯ Minor*, Op. 30, (1907); *Suite in D Major for Viola and Orchestra*, Op. 48, (1928); *Allegro Appassionato in D Minor for Viola and Piano*, Op. 79, (1926); and *Introduction and Danse for Viola and Piano*, Op. 102, (1935).

The Viola in Italy

The fine quality of viola playing in the leading Italian opera houses has now become legend. In chamber music groups and in ensembles specializing in 17th and 18th century works, Italian violists have increasingly demonstrated technical and musical excellence. In the area of solo performance, Renzo Sabatini (1905–73) established a competency of the highest level. He was outstanding on both the viola and the viola d'amore as a concert and as a recording artist. In 1941 he was appointed Professor of Viola at the Accademia di Santa Cecilia in Rome, where he became recognized as one of the great teachers of the 20th century.

Aurelio Arcidiacono (b. 1915) is representative of Italian violists who as performers and as teachers are still contributing to higher standards. In addition to a busy schedule of concertizing, recording, and teaching, he is Inspector for the Ministry of Public Instruction of Conservatories of Music. He has composed several excellent compositions for the instrument. He participates in the activities of the Internationale Viola-Forschungsgesellschaft. He has also published a brief history of the viola and its music, *Gli Instrumenti Musicali: La Viola*.[6]

Bruno Giuranna (b. 1933) has achieved a world-wide reputation as a viola soloist and as a teacher of the first rank. In addition to a busy concert schedule, he teaches regularly at the Conservatorio di Santa Cecilia in Rome, at the Accademia Chigiana in Siena, and at the Nordwestdeutsche Musikakademie in Detmold, West Germany. Giurana is in great demand as a teacher of master classes in all countries, and many of today's finest violists were his students.

The Russian Viola School

Vadim Borissovsky (1900–72) was born in Moscow. His study at the Moscow Conservatory included violin with Michael Press, and

---

[6]Aurelio Arcidiacono, *Gli Instrumenti: La Viola* (Milano: Berben, 1973).

later, viola with Vladmir R. Bakaleinikoff.[7] The latter exerted a lasting influence on Borissovsky's choosing a career as a violist. He graduated from the Conservatory in 1922 with first prize in the viola class. He became the violist in the Moscow Beethoven Quartet in 1923, and succeeded Bakaleinikoff[8] as Professor of Viola at the Conservatory in 1927, a post he retained until his retirement in 1970. He played and taught works by Hindemith, Bloch, Bax, Honegger, and contemporary Soviet composers. To fill gaps in the viola literature, he edited and transcribed 253 published works that he felt violists should have in their repertoire. He promoted the use of a large viola, playing a Gasparo da Salò (Plate 61) that has a body length of 46 cm. (18⅛ in.). He had T. F. Podgorny, one of Soviet Russia's finest luthiers, make copies of the da Salò for his students. Podgorny also made the viola d'amore that Borissovsky played (Plate 63).

In 1927 Borissovsky met Paul Hindemith in Berlin, where they began a lasting friendship. They both saw the need for some kind of society or organization for violists. They decided to call it "The Violist's World Union," and Hindemith insisted that Borissovsky be President of the new society. The success of their dream was aborted by the sudden rise to power of the Hitler government in Germany and the resulting catastrophic events.

While in Berlin he collaborated with the German musicologist, Wilhelm Altmann, in the preparation of a catalogue of all the known works for the viola and the viola d'amore. Borissovsky had begun his own research during his student days at the Moscow Conservatory, and after 17 years, the catalogue finally appeared in 1937.[9]

Borissovsky, an indefatigable worker, somehow found time to edit and transcribe 253 published works for the viola and the viola d'amore. Two of his last transcriptions for viola and piano were "Four Pieces" from music written by Shostakovich for the film *The Gadfly*, and "Seven Fragments" from Prokoffief's *Romeo and Juliet Ballet.*[10] Both are virtuoso works in the grand style. The composers not only approved these transcriptions, but encouraged them.

---

[7]For a more complete coverage of Borissovsky's contribution to the Russian Viola School, see Maurice W. Riley, "A Visit with Alexandra de Lazari-Borissovsky, Russia's Mother Viola," *Journal of the Violin Society of America*, Vol. IV, No. 2 (Spring, 1978), pp. 32–42.

[8]Bakaleinikoff, a virtuoso violist, conductor, and composer, migrated to the United States in 1927.

[9]Wilhelm Altmann and Vadim Borissovsky, *Literaturverzeichnis für Bratsche und Viola d'Amore* (Wolfenbuttel: Verlag für musikalische Kultur und Wissenschaft, 1937).

[10]Jun Takahira, 19-year-old Japanese student of William Primrose, gave a brilliant performance of the Prokoffiev composition at the Primrose International Viola Competition in Provo, Utah, 1979. Members of the audience were greatly impressed by the expert craftmanship displayed in Borissovsky's transcription.

Among his many outstanding viola students are Rudolph Barshai,
I. Boguslavsky, Fyodor Druzhinin, G. Metrossova, P. Shebalin, E.
Strachov, M. Tolpygo, and over 200 others.[11] In 1977 his biography
was published, appropriately entitled, V. *Borissovsky, the Founder of
the Soviet Viola School.*[12]

In Europe and America Rudolf Barshai, through his concert performances and recordings, is perhaps the best known living violist in
Soviet Russia. More and more, however, he has turned to conducting
in lieu of solo performance.

Madam Alexandra de Lazari-Borissovsky, his widow, furnished
the additional names and dates of a few of the Russian violists of
particular distinction:[13]

```
Vladimir Bakaleinikov, b. 1885 in Moscow, d. 1953 in Pittsburgh, Pa., U.S.A.
Vadim Borissovsky, b. 1900 in Moscow, d. 1972 in Moscow
Evgeny Strachov, b. 1909 in Moscow, d. 1978 in Moscow
Michail Teryan, b. 1905 in Moscow
Galli Metrossova, b. 1923 in Krasnodaz
Yury Kramarov, b. 1929 in Leningrad
Fyodor Druzhinin, b. 1932 in Moscow
I. Boguslavsky, b. 1940 in Moscow
Michail Tolpygo, b. 1943 in Cheliabinsk
Yury Bashmet, b. 1953 in Rostov na Donu.
```

Perhaps the most momentous event in recent Soviet musical history related to the viola was the completion by Dmitri Shostakovich of
his last composition, before his death in 1975, of his *Sonata for Viola
and Piano,* Op. 147. It was dedicated to, and premiered by, Fyodor
Druzhinin. Druzhinin had replaced his teacher Borissovsky as Professor of Viola at the Moscow Conservatory and as violist of the Moscow
Beethoven String Quartet c.1968. His recent recording of the Shostakovich *Viola Sonata* with the Soviet pianist Michail Muntian is particularly noteworthy.

The Israeli Viola School

Oedoen Partos (1907–77) was born in Budapest, Hungary, where
he studied violin with Hubay and composition with Kodaly. After a
brilliant career in Europe as a performer, conductor, and composer, he

---

[11]See Myron Rosenblum, "Vadim Borissovsky—Violist, Teacher, Scholar," *The American String
Teacher,* XXIV, 3 (1974), p. 46.

[12]Viktor Juzefovitsch, a student of Borissovsky, wrote the biography.

[13]Names and dates furnished by Madame Borissovsky in a letter to this author dated March 11,
1979.

Plate 61. Vadim Borissovsky and his Gasparo da Salò Viola.

Plate 62. The Moskow Beethoven String Quartet (1958) D. Tsyganov, and V. Shirinsky, violins, S. Shirinsky, cello and V. Borissovsky, viola.

Plate 63. V. Borissovsky and his Viola d'Amore made by the Soviet luthier T. F. Podgorny.

Plate 64. Fyodor Druzhinin, Michail Tolpygo, and I. Bogoslovsky, all Borissovsky alumni.

Plate 65 V. Borissovsky and 13 violists of the Bolshoi Orchestra, all former students (1969).

migrated to Israel in 1938. In Israel he exerted a profound influence as a violist, composer, and teacher. Most of the fine Israeli violists of the present day were his students. In recognition of his contributions to all music students, he was appointed Dean of the Academy of Music at Tel-Aviv in 1951. Among his many significant compositions for the viola are: *Yiskor (In Memorium) for Viola and Orchestra* (1947); *Song of Praise, Concerto No. 1* (1949); *Orienta Ballada for Viola and Orchestra* (1956); *Concerto No. 2* (1957); *Agada (A Legend) for Viola, Piano, and Percussion* (1960); *Sinfonia Concertante for Viola and Orchestra* (1962); *Fusiona (Shiluvim) for Viola and Chamber Orchestra* (1970).

Among Partos' many excellent students are Rivka Golani-Erdesz and Uri Mayer, both now active in Canada, and Ron Golan, eminent performing artist and teacher at the Conservatory of Music in Geneva, Switzerland.

Bulgarian Violists

Stephan Sugarev (1907–58) was a pioneer of solo viola playing in Bulgaria, and as Professor of Viola at the Academy of Music in Sofia from 1947 to 1958, he exerted a positive influence on many violists. One of his artist students, Zahari Tchavdarof, is now one of the leading violists in Sweden.

Hungarian Violists

Two of the most famous Hungarian violists are Gustav Szeredi-Saupe (b. 1909), eminent soloist and teacher; and Pál Lukács, recording-artist who teaches at the Franz Liszt Zenemuveszeti Foiskola, in Budapest. Both artists are in demand throughout Europe as soloists.

The Viola in Austria and Germany

The Viola situation in German and Austrian orchestras in the second half of the 19th century, as so disapprovingly described by Richard Wagner,[14] was later improved in some cities through the efforts of Hermann Ritter. In the early 20th century, however, many

---

[14]See Wagner's castigation of German violists in Chapters XI and XII.

German violists were still disparagingly referred to as players of the "Penzioninstruments." According to William Primrose, the term designated a violinist too old and too lacking in talent to play the violin professionally; hence, he was relegated to the viola.[15] This description, however, could hardly apply to such artists as Michael Balling, Clemens Meyer, Hubert Froehlich, Paul Hindemith, and others who did uphold the highest standards of performance.[16]

During this period, in the area of historical research, Prof. Dr. Wilhelm Altmann was laying the foundations for later German scholars who would discover and make available modern editions of viola works from the Baroque and Classic eras.

After World War II, a new generation of fine German and Austrian violists came into their own, including Albrecht Jacobs, Eberhard Klemmstein, Ulrich Koch, Ernst Morawec, Rudolf Nel, Max Rostal, Georg Schmid, Emil Seiler, Karl Trötzmüller, Berta Volmer, Franz Zeyringer, and many others. Three artist-violists, Paul Doktor, Walter Trampler, and the late Ernst Wallfisch, migrated to the United States, where they have taken leading roles as performers and teachers. Ulrich Drüner, with a private library of over 3,500 items, is one of the world's foremost scholars of the viola. Walter Lebermann has discovered and edited for publication over twenty significant 18th century works for the viola.

German and Austrian composers also wrote numerous compositions for the viola. Among the significant concertos, sonatas, and other works for the instrument are those by Paul Hindemith (1895–1963), Paul Angerer (b.1927), Boris Blacher (b.1903), Helmut Degen (b.1911), Wolfgang Fortner (b.1907), Harald Genzmer (b.1909), Ottmar Gerster (1897–1969), Hermann Grabner (1886–1969), Karl Haidmayer (b.1927), Karl Hartmann (1905–63), Hans Werner Henze (b. 1926), Walter Jesinghaus (b.1902), Arnold Matz (b.1904), Gunter Raphael (1903–60), and Otto Siegl (b.1896). Angerer, Matz, and Siegl, like the late Paul Hindemith, are excellent violists.

Wilhelm Altmann (1862–1951), an outstanding German musicologist and editor of classical music and music catalogues, was also an avid viola enthusiast.[17] A scholar and writer with many interests, he nevertheless found the time to do research into the history and literature of the viola. His article, "Zur Geschichte der Bratsche und der

---

[15]William Primrose, *Walk on the North Side: Memoirs of a Violist* (Provo, Utah: Brigham Young University Press, 1978), p. 19.

[16]For more about German and Austrian violists see Appendix I under their names.

[17]Altmann was Director of the Music Section of the State Prussian Library of Berlin from 1915 to 1927, and chief music reviewer of the *National-Zeitung* for many years beginning in 1904.

Bratschisten" (On the History of the Viola and Violists),[18] only two pages in length, illustrates the meager resources available to the scholars of the viola in the early 20th century. More significant were his efforts to found an international viola society, and his publication of a catalogue of viola literature.

Altmann believed that there was a need for the formation of *Bratschen-Bundes* (Viola Brotherhoods) to promote the cause of all violists. To achieve this goal he introduced a new journal on March 29, 1929, which had the title *Die Bratsche*.[19] In the first issue he proposed the objectives which he thought were essential for the success of the organization: 1. To promote respect for the viola in solo, chamber, and house-music (music played for pleasure). 2. To promote respect for, and an improved status for, the violas in orchestras. 3. To promote prize competitions for solo and chamber music compositions. 4. With the advice of an artist panel, to publish compositions and etudes of valuable old, out-of-print works, as soon as revisions could be made. 5. To reduce the cost of all these publications to *Bund* members through subscriptions. 6. To make *Die Bratsche* the official publication of the *Bund*. 7. To promote and supervise possible improvements and proposed alterations in the viola. 8. To promote recognition of the viola d'amore. 9. To encourage historical studies and other research on the instrument.

The first issue of *Die Bratsche* contained only sixteen pages. Of these, pages 1–10 included short articles and listings of new publications for the viola; and pages 11–16 were devoted to advertising. Each succeeding issue contained less advertising, until the fifth, and last, issue contained only two pages. The loss of this financial support, and perhaps other reasons, forced Altman to cease publication. Thus came to a temporary end his ambition to organize a society of violists.

Altmann's interest in the viola surfaced again in 1937, when, in collaboration with the Soviet virtuoso-violist Vadim Borissovsky, he published what was then the definitive catalogue of works for the viola and the viola d'amore, *Literatur-verzeichnis für Bratsche und Viola d'amore*.[20] By the time the catalogue was available, Europe was embroiled in political strife that soon erupted as World War II, and Altmann's ambition of founding *Bratschen-Bundes* was again dealt a

---

[18]Wilhelm Altmann, "Zur Geschichte der Bratsche und der Bratschisten," *Allgemeine Musikzeitung*, Vol. 56, (1929), pp. 971–2.

[19]*Die Bratsche*, No. 1–5 (1929–30), published in Leipzig by Carl Mersenburger.

[20]Wilhelm Altmann und Vadim Borissovsky, *Literaturverzeichnis für Bratsche und Viola d'amore* (Wolfenbüttel: Verlag für musikalische Kultur und Wissenschaft, 1937).

disastrous blow.[21] Nevertheless, it was Altmann's pioneering activities that presaged the founding in 1966 of the Viola-Forschungs-
gessellschaft by a group of German and Austrian enthusiasts.

Paul Hindemith

Paul Hindmith (1895–1963) was a performer, composer, conductor, and teacher. His greatest contributions to the viola are his compositions, of which over twenty were written for this instrument. Among
his first works for the viola are No. 4 and No. 5 in the Op. 11 set of
pieces published in 1919: *Sonata for Viola and Piano* and *Sonata for
Solo Viola*. These works furnished a most promising foretaste of the
future viola music that was to come from his pen.

Hindemith performed his *Sonata for Viola and Piano*, Op. 11, No.
4, in 1919 in Frankfurt, with pianist Emma Lubecke-Job. With this
performance, he began his career as a concert violist and as a highly
significant composer of music for the instrument. This initial opus for
the viola was written in a much more conservative idiom than the
works that were to follow. Many violists hear in the Op. 11, No. 4
Sonata the French influences of César Frank, Gabriel Fauré, and
even Claude Debussy. Such influences were not uncommon to young
composers of that time.

In the Opus 25 series of compositions written in 1921, however,
Hindemith's viola works show an advanced individuality of style and
idiom, characterized by dissonance and even extremes of tempo. The
latter characteristic is best illustrated in the fourth movement of the
Solo Viola Sonata, Op. 25, No. 1, which has the descriptive title,
"Rasendes Zeitmass. Wild. Tonschönheit ist Nebensache" (Tearing
tempo. Wild. Tonequality is irrelevant); and it has the almost in-
credible metronome marking for the quarter note of 600 to 640.

Hindemith began his performance career as Concertmaster of the
Frankfurt Orchestra (1916–23). A preference for the viola surfaced
when he joined the Amar Quartet as violist (1922–29). His love for
chamber music also found its fruition later, when he formed a trio as
violist with Symon Goldberg, violinist, and Emanuel Feuermann,
cellist.

As a viola soloist he did not limit his repertoire to his own works.
On October 3, 1929, he premiered William Walton's *Concerto for*

---

[21]See in the material on Vadim Borissovsky in this Chapter the account of another attempt by
the Soviet violist and Paul Hindemith to form a society called "The Violist's World Union." This
plan was also thwarted by World War II.

Viola and Orchestra at a Promenade Concert in London.[22] On December 15, 1929, Hindemith played the premier performance of Darius Milhaud's *Viola Concerto*, Op. 108, with the Concertgebouw Orchestra in Amsterdam, conducted by Pierre Monteux. The composition, of course, was dedicated to Hindemith, who returned the compliment a year later when he dedicated his *Konzertmusik for Viola and Large Orchestra* (1930) to Darius and Madeline Milhaud.

By 1930 Hindemith was recognized as one of the world's leading viola virtuosos. He was an excellent pianist also, and a master of the viola d'amore, but it was as a composer that he was best known. In 1927 he had been appointed Professor of Composition at the Hochschule für Musik in Berlin.

Hindemith's ability to write music at great speed is well authenticated. The events in which three of his viola works were composed demonstrate this talent. In 1934 he was recording his *Sonata for Solo Viola*, Op. 25, No. 1. At the end of the recording session the technical engineer informed Hindemith that there was still four minutes left on one side of one of the records. Hindemith describes the events of the following day: "At five in the morning I started to compose the piece. At 8:20 it was finished and at 9:00 I recorded it with Feuermann." The result was his *Duet for Viola and Cello*, published by B. Schott in 1934. On April 19, 1937, while riding the train to Chicago to give a concert, he composed his third *Sonata for Solo Viola*, and performed it that same evening. The other viola work alluded to above was his well known and popular *Music of Mourning for Viola and String Orchestra*. The interesting succession of events which prompted the writing of this work will be described below.

Hindemith premiered *Der Schwanendreher* (Concerto after Old Folksongs), one of his most ambitious works for the viola, on October 14, 1935, in Amsterdam, with the Concertgebouw directed by Willem Mengelberg. In January of 1936, he went to London to introduce the same work. On the eve of the concert King George V died. The concert was postponed a day and then shifted from Queen's Hall to the BBC studios. It was soon decided that *Der Schwanendreher* would be unsuitable for the program, which would be a memorial to the deceased King. Hindemith was asked if he could write something appropriate. He thus described the events of the following day:

---

[22]Walton had intended to dedicate the *Concerto* to Lionel Tertis, but Tertis refused to play it, saying that he did not understand the work. Tertis recommended Hindemith for the performance. Donald Tovey, in his *Essays in Musical Analysis*, wrote favorably, "This seems to me one of the most important modern concertos for any instrument and I can see no limit to what may be expected of the tone-poet who could create it." Tertis later changed his opinion of the Walton Concerto, and recommended it to his students for study and performance.

... a studio was cleared for me, copyists were gradually stoked up, and from 11 to 5, I did some fairly hefty mourning. I turned out a nice piece, in the style of *Mathis* and *Schwanendreher* with a Bach chorale at the end *(Vor deinen Thron tret' ich hiermit*—very suitable for kings) ... We rehearsed it well all yesterday, and in the evening the orchestra played [it] with great devoutness and feeling.[23]

This composition, entitled *Trauermusick* (English title: *Music of Mourning*), was broadcast on January 20, 1936. It was conducted by Sir Adrian Boult, with Hindemith playing the solo viola part.

In 1937 Hindemith came to the United States to perform and to conduct his works. In Washington, Boston, New York, Chicago, and Buffalo he performed *Der Schwanendreher*. The Washington performance was conducted by Carlos Chavez; the Boston by Arthur Fiedler; the New York Philharmonic by Artur Rodzinski; and the Chicago by Frederick Stock.

Although not of Jewish birth, Hindemith became the object of an ever-increasing Nazi harassment, both because of his own resolute opposition to Hitler's policies and because of his wife's Jewish ancestry. They therefore left Germany and lived briefly in Switzerland and in England.

Hindemith came to the United States in 1940 and was appointed to the faculty of Yale University from 1941 to 1945. In 1947, he returned to Europe and was honored by having his compositions performed again. His teaching, conducting, composing, and writing had long since precluded his continued career as a viola soloist. Perhaps it is best that he be remembered as the composer of works for the viola rather than as a performer. Tertis, for example, did not think Hindemith was a great artist, although he conceded that he played with consummate technique.[24] Primrose also found Hindemith's viola playing somewhat cold and in the unemotional German tradition.[25]

In addition to the compositions already cited, the following important pieces should be noted: *Sonata in C for Viola and Piano* (1939); *Kammermusik No. 5 (Viola Concerto) for Viola and Large Chamber Orchestra* (1927); and *Sonata for Viola and Piano*, Op. 25, No. 4 (1922), which has until recently been available only in manuscript.

Consistent with Hindemith's philosophy of *Gebrauchsmusik* (utility music), many of his solo works were intended for use by several different instruments. The *Meditation* was scored for viola, or

[23]Geoffrey Skelton, *Paul Hindemith, the Man Behind the Music* (London: Victor Gollancz, 1975), p. 130.

[24]Lionel Tertis, *Cinderella No More*, p. 38.

[25]William Primrose, *Walk on the North Side: Memoirs of a Violist*, pp. 167–8.

violin, or cello.[26] The title of his *Sonata for Trumpet (or Viola)* is indicative of Hindemith's attempt to make his compositions more generally useful. In the Preface to his *Sonata for Clarinet and Piano* (1939), he explains that the clarinet part "can be played on a viola, transposed a whole tone downwards (the clarinet being a B♭ instrument), although the effect will be different from that originally intended."

Marna Street, violist in the Pittsburgh Symphony, has been doing research in conjunction with the Hindemith Institute of Frankfort, regarding the composer's unpublished works for viola. These works will probably be published posthumously in the near future.

Hindemith's Violas

In the 1920's, when Hindemith was playing the viola regularly, he frequently performed on one made for, and loaned to, him by Eugen Sprenger of Frankfort, an instrument with a body length of 40 cm. (15¾ in.).[27] This instrument with its big tone was particularly suitable for playing the many viola concertos he performed. The Sprenger viola is now owned and played by Hans Bender, of Monrovia, California.

Hindemith's favorite viola, however, was an anonymous instrument of the Milano School, according to a Hamma Certificate (Plate 66), with a body length of 42.2 cm. (16⅝ in.). It was Hindemith's intention that this instrument be passed on to his friend, artist-violist Karl Trötzmüller. Trötzmüller had played the Hindemith works as early as 1930, when he performed the *Little Sonata for Viola d'Amore and Piano*, Op. 25, No. 2 (1923). In a letter to this author dated May 19, 1978, Trötzmüller commented on the Hindemith viola:

> Its story was acknowledged by Hindemith by signing the certificate himself as well as having the viola sign it 'in trembling handwriting, the viola being so very old.' (Hindemith was always ready for a joke!) Hindemith told me he had purchased the viola in 1931 from a musician in Prague because he did not want to go on playing only on loaned instruments. I heard him play the *Schwanendreher* in Vienna in 1937. On the enclosed photograph, which was taken at a rehearsal for this concert, one can see clearly that it is really this (the Milanese) viola.

At their last meeting, following the Vienna Concert, when Trötzmüller obtained the viola, "Hindemith smiled and said, 'I am going to

---

[26]The *Meditation* is Hindemith's arrangement of a melody from his "Nobilissima Visione" (1938), a ballet based on the life of St. Francis of Assisi.

[27]The Sprenger viola is described in Chapter XII.

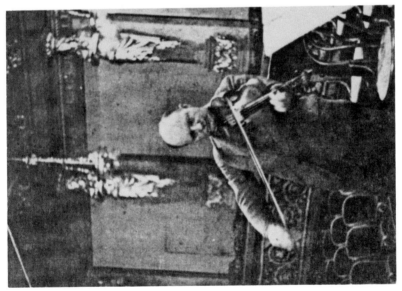

Plate 66. a) Paul Hindemith; b) Hindemith's Viola (Early Milano School). Photographs furnished by Karl Trötzmüller.

Plate 67. Franz Zeyringer, Viola, President of the Viola-Forschungsgesellschaft, and Mryon Rosenblum, Viola d'Amore, President of The American Viola Society, after a concert given at the Third International Viola Congress, Ypsilanti, Michigan, 1975.

live on for another little while.' Alas, in another month he died unexpectedly."

The Viola-Forschungsgesellschaft

A far reaching event, having its genesis in Austria and Germany in 1966, was the founding of the Viola-Forschungsgesellschaft (Viola Research Society). A small group of viola enthusiasts, headed by Prof. Franz Zeyringer, of Pöllau, Austria, laid the foundation for what has become a world-wide organization, one which now sponsors and holds annual International Viola Congresses. Among the founding group, besides Zeyringer, were Prof. Dietrich Bauer of Kassel, Walter Lebermann of Bad Homburg, Wilhelm Websky of West Berlin, Dr. Prof. Wolfgang Sawodny of Oberelchingen-Ulm, Dr. François de Beaumont of Neuchatel, Switzerland, and Prof. Uta Lenkewitz von Zahn of West Berlin. In addition to their fondness for the viola, several of this illustrious group have other vocations: Sawodny is a Professor of Chemistry, de Beaumont is a medical doctor, and Lenkewitz von Zahn is a Professor of Languages.

The initial project of the society was the establishment of the Viola Archives at the Murhard Library in Kassel, Germany. The Archives were to contain the entire literature related to the viola, its music, its makers, its players, and its memorabilia. De Beaumont, volunteered to bring out a *Discography* for the viola, a work which is now in its third edition (1976). Zeyringer would continue his monumental research of cataloguing the music written for the instrument, *Litertur für Viola*, now in a third edition (1976). Websky would prepare a thematic catalogue of known duets for viola and cello. It was completed and published c.1970, with the title *Versuch eines möglichst vollständigen thematischen Katalogs der Duo-Literatur für Bratsche und Violoncello*. Bauer would oversee the Viola Archives in Kassel. The other founding members would carry on research in the fields in which they specialized: Lebermann in 18th century viola music; Sawodny in quartets for two violas and early sonata literature for the viola; and Websky in the cataloguing of duets for viola and cello.

After a few years it became apparent that the accommodations at Kassel would be too small for the collected material of the Viola Archives. In 1978, therefore, the Archival materials were moved to the Mozarteum Library in Salzburg, Austria, where they are supervised and administered by Dr. Heinz Kraschi. There the full resources of the Mozarteum are available for cataloguing and housing the Viola

Archives. Materials in the Archives are available to all violists, viola enthusiasts, and research scholars.

The Viola-Forschungsgesellschaft has already begun to achieve many of its initial goals. One of its objectives was to inform violists and other musicians that there is now available a rich literature, originally written for the viola. This literature comprises compositions of the Baroque, Classic, Romantic, and Contemporary eras. Violists no longer need to be limited to the use of transcriptions and arrangements for teaching and for performance. Many transcriptions have been, and will continue to be, an indispensable part of the violist's repertoire; it is now possible, however, also to choose from a multitude of works written specifically for the viola, works that are personally rewarding and worthy of performance. The preparation of 18th century compositions for 20th century performance requires the painstaking efforts of a dedicated and talented musicologist, such as Walter Lebermann.

Walter Lebermann (b.1910) typifies the many German scholars who have found and edited for publication previously unavailable Baroque and Classic compositions. He has produced over eighty such works, of which more than twenty are for his chosen instrument, the viola. He was recognized by the *Frankfurter Allgemeine Zeitung*, February 21, 1975 (p. 42), in an article honoring his 65th birthday, entitled "Music Detective Lebermann":

> ... The title "Music Detective," which a well known musicologist used, seems to be perfectly suitable, considering the conditions under which his discoveries occur ... Lebermann has arranged his vacation trips for many years to research collections and libraries. Many of these archives had not yet been listed, so that the "Detective," himself, had to establish numerous reference catalogues. Besides systematic work, however, knowledge of historical details, a good memory, and an accurate instinct are sometimes the only help for a solution. ... Special fields of research, with regard to geography, include the composers of Lebermann's native area, the Mannheim School; and with regard to instruments, he has enlarged the often neglected literature for the viola by over twenty editions ... which also includes the composition of cadenzas and the realization of a continuo for the keyboard.

Lebermann's editions have greatly enriched the violist's literature, and represent a fulfillment of one of the objectives of the Viola-forschungsgesellschaft.[28] The following partial list[29] is presented chronologically according to Lebermann's publication dates:

---

[28]For more about Lebermann's editions for the viola see Maurice W. Riley, "The Contributions of Walter Lebermann to Viola Literature," *American String Teacher*, XXVII, No. 2, (Spring 1977), p. 19.

[29]A "partial list" because the indefatigable Lebermann is presently editing additional works that soon will be ready for publication.

Plate 68. Walter Lebermann. Portrait by Erla Lebermann.

Carl Stamitz, *Six Duets for 2 Violas.* Mainz: B. Schott, 1955.

K. D. von Dittersdorf, *Concerto in F Major for Viola and Piano,* Krebs T. V. 168. Mainz: B. Schott, 1959.

Georg Benda, *Concerto in F Major for Viola and Piano.* Mainz: B. Schott, 1968.

K. D. von Dittersdorf, *Duo in E♭ Major for Viola and Cello,* Krebs T. V. 218. Mainz: B. Schott, 1969.

K. D. von Dittersdorf, *Divertimento in D Major for Violin, Viola, and Cello,* Krebs T. V. 131. Mainz: B. Schott, 1969.

P. Nardini, *Six Duets for 2 Violas.* Mainz, B. Schott, 1969.

Carl Stamitz, *Duo in C Major for Violin and Viola.* Mainz: B. Schott, 1969.

J. F. K. Sterkel, *Six Duets for Violin and Viola,* Op. 8. Mainz: B. Schott, 1969.

J. N. Hummel, *Sonata in E♭ Major for Viola and Piano,* Op. 5, No. 3. Mainz: B. Schott, 1969.

Anton Stamitz, *Concerto No. 2 in F Major for Viola and Piano.* Mainz: B. Schott, 1969.

Carl Stamitz, *Sonata in B♭ Major for Viola and Piano.* Mainz: B. Schott, 1969.

Joseph Haydn, *Six Sonatas for Violin and Viola.* Mainz: B. Schott, 1970.

F. X. Brixi, *Concerto in C Major for Viola and Piano.* Mainz: B. Schott, 1970.

Georg Ph. Telemann, *Concerto in G Major for 2 Violas and Piano.* Mainz: B. Schott, 1970.

Jean-Marie Leclair, *Six Sonatas for 2 Violas.* Mainz: B. Schott, 1971.

R. Hoffstetter, *Concerto in C Major for Viola and Piano.* Mainz: B. Schott, 1971.

Anton Stamitz, *Concerto No. 3 in G Major for Viola and Piano.* Wiesbaden: Breitkopf & Härtel, 1971.

Anton Stamitz, *Concerto in B♭ Major for Viola and Piano.* Mainz: B. Schott, 1972.

Anton Stamitz, *Concerto No. 4 in D Major for Viola and Piano.* Wiesbaden: Breitkopf & Härtel, 1973.

Francesco Geminiani, *Adagio and Fugue in E♭ Major for Solo Viola.* New York: C. F. Peters, 1974.

Heinrich Biber, *Passacaglia in C Minor for Solo Viola* (Transposition of the violin version). New York: C. F. Peters, 1976.

Johann G. Graun, *Concerto in E♭ Major for Viola and Piano.* Hamburg: Simrock, 1976.

The objectives of the Viola-Forschungsgesellschaft are also being promulgated through the establishment of Chapters in other countries. Presently Chapters exist in Australia, Austria, Canada, England,

Plate 69. Members of the Viola Forschungsgesellschaft with William Primrose, after he had been conferred an Honorary Doctor of Music Degree by Eastern Michigan University, 1975: (left to right) Dietrich Bauer, Myron Rosenblum, Dr. William Primrose, Maurice W. Riley, Franz Zeyringer, and Wolfgang Sawodny.

the Federal Republic of Germany, the German Democratic Republic, Japan, New Zealand, and the United States. A related feature of the Viola-Forschungsgesellschaft is its annual convention, which since 1973 has become the International Viola Congress:

> 1972—Radstadt, Austria
> 1973—Ulm, West Germany, First International Viola Congress
> 1974—Bad Homburg, West Germany, Second I.V.C.
> 1975—Ypsilanti, Michigan, U.S.A., Third I.V.C.
> 1976—Bad Godesburg, West Germany, Fourth I.V.C.
> 1977—Rochester, New York, U.S.A., Fifth I.V.C.
> 1978—London, England, Sixth I.V.C.
> 1979—Provo, Utah, U.S.A., Seventh I.V.C.

Future meetings are planned at:

> 1980—Graz, Austria, Eighth I.V.C.
> 1981—Toronto, Canada, Ninth I.V.C.
> 1982—Stuttgart, West Germany, Tenth I.V.C.

The achievement of the objectives of the Viola-Forschungs-gesellschaft can be attributed to the world-wide contributions of many violists, but principally to the unstinting efforts of Professor Franz Zeyringer, President of the International Society. His inspired leadership, devotion, and dedication have furnished other members of the organization with the stimulus so essential to the development and growth of a successful organization.

CHAPTER XV

WILLIAM PRIMROSE

D<small>r.</small> William Primrose, C.B.E., F.G.S.M., is recognized throughout the world as the outstanding violist of our time. He was born in Glasgow, Scotland, in 1904, into a musical environment. His father was a violinist in the Scottish Orchestra of Glasgow, and also played viola in the Ritter Quartet. Camillo Ritter (a pupil of Joachim and Ševčik), leader of the quartet, was entrusted with William's early violin training. As a child prodigy, Primrose gave concerts in Glasgow. In 1919 he was taken to London by his parents to study violin with Max Mossel at the Guildhall School of Music. In 1923 the young Primrose gave a debut concert at Queen's Hall, performing Lalo's *Symphonie Espagñole* and Elgar's *Violin Concerto*. He graduated from Guildhall in 1924, winning the gold medal.

Sensing the need for study with an artist of international reputation, he enrolled for private study with Eugène Ysaÿe in 1926. For the three following years Primrose studied with the great Ysaÿe, while at the same time continuing his professional career as a performer. While at Ysaÿe's home, he frequently played the viola in string quartets and ensembles. Recognizing his unique aptitude for the instrument, Ysaÿe encouraged Primrose to pursue a career as a violist. Actually this had been his ambition from an early age when he played his father's Brothers-Amati viola.

In 1930 Primrose was selected to fill the vacancy of violist in the London String Quartet, and for five years he toured Europe, North America, and South America with this world-famous ensemble. His desire to be a violist had reached fruition. During this 1930–35 period he also appeared frequently as viola soloist with symphony orchestras in Europe.

Primrose's reputation as an artist violist of the first magnitude brought him an appointment in 1938 to join the new NBC Symphony, which was being formed for Arturo Toscanini. For four years Primrose played the viola solo parts for the great maestro.

Determined to pursue a career as a concert violist, an undertaking for which he was admirably suited, Primrose resigned from his post in the NBC Symphony in 1941. The following year he joined Richard Crooks, the very popular American tenor, in a tour of over forty con-

Plate 70. William Primrose.

certs. Crooks, the established artist, insisted on giving Primrose equal billing, which helped to launch the gifted violist into the career he so rightly merited. For several subsequent years this duo relationship with Crooks continued, adding to Primrose's prestige as a unique viola soloist.

It is little wonder that Primrose, in recognition of the assistance given to him by Crooks, entitled his autobiography, *Walk on the North Side, Memoirs of a Violist.* As Primrose explains, "Walk on the North Side" was chosen because it relates to his chance meeting with Richard Crooks one day in 1941 in front of the Steinway Building. On that particular day instead of walking along the south side of 57th Street to his club, where he usually had lunch, he crossed to the north side of the street to get a better view of a portrait of Rachmaninoff, which was in the Steinway window. There he encountered Crooks, and in the ensuing conversation it was agreed that the violist and the tenor would tour together the following year.

By the conclusion of World War II in 1945, the name Primrose had become a household word in music circles. Just as the names Kreisler and Heifetz had become synonymous with the word *violin,* so the name Primrose became synonymous with the word *viola.* Primrose was recognized as the dean of all living violists.

In addition to his career as a soloist, Primrose played chamber music with most of the great string players of the 20th century, including appearances with Pablo Casals at Prades; the Primrose String Quartet, which he formed in 1939 with Oscar Shumsky and Josef Gingold, violins, and Harvey Shapiro, cello; and the Festival Piano Quartet with Victor Babin, piano, Symon Goldberg, violin, and Nikolai Graudan, cello. In 1961 he joined Heifetz and Piatigorsky in California, where the trio gave numerous concerts, made recordings, and taught at the University of Southern California.

Music for Primrose's Performances

Primrose was in great demand to perform the solo part of Berlioz' *Harold in Italy* and Mozart's *Symphonie Concertante,* K.364. To provide additional solo material for his recitals with piano, and for his engagements with symphony orchestras, he wanted to expand the literature available to violists. As a result Primrose arranged, transcribed, and edited many works both for himself and for all aspiring violists. In these works he furnished bowings and fingerings that were often different from the traditional violin markings that had previously permeated viola literature. Primrose did not consider the viola as a large-size violin, but rather as a separate, autonomous instrument, with its own individual bowing and fingering problems.

In addition to the wealth of music Primrose added to viola literature through his arrangements, transcriptions, and editions, he inspired and commissioned original compositions by leading contemporary composers. Primrose was asked to comment on these compositions. In a letter to the author dated October 20, 1978, Primrose wrote:

> As to works, commissioned and otherwise. The Milhaud,[1] the second concerto that is, I found the most outrageously difficult work I ever tackled, and for all the immense labor I devoted to it, never appealed to the public. He delivered the ms. to me at a recital I gave at the San Francisco Opera House, and being an expert reader, I told him I would come to Mills College, where he was teaching, and go through it the following morning. One glance at it before retiring that night convinced me that this was even beyond my powers. I called him and told him how difficult it was. "Mon cher," he replied on the 'phone, "all concertos should be difficult!" Nuff said.
>
> Peter Fricker, who is now on the faculty of University of California Santa Barbara, was greatly admired in his young days by the late Arthur Benjamin, and at

Plate 71. Former Students honor their teacher, Dr. Primrose, at the Seventh International Viola Congress by performing works he edited or transcribed: Jun Takahira, Donald McInnes, Karen Tuttle, Dr. Primrose, Alan deVeritch, and Yizhak Schotten.

---

[1]Darius Milhaud, *Concerto for Viola and Orchestra*, No. 2, Op. 340, 1954/5.

Arthur's behest I asked Fricker for a work. It duly arrived and I was entranced with it.[2] It had a vast success at the Edinburgh Festival with Boult in 1953, and later in London with Sargent. Its subsequent career is mentioned in my book.

Edmund Rubbra wrote a work for me about this time.[3] Highly original in that it entails little of the transcendental virtuoso challenges, but sings, and sings, and sings. So eminently suited to our instrument, don't you think?

For some reason which I cannot quite explain I gave few performances of dear Quincy Porter's engaging *Concerto*.[4] Largely, I believe, because of the difficulties I encountered in obtaining appearances with American orchestras, and which I describe in my book.

These are the most important works written for me, other than the Benjamin *Sonata*[5] which I played on many occasions, as I did Britten's *Lachrymae*[6] composed for me for the Aldeburgh Festival in the early fifties.

This list should also include William Bergsma's *Fantastic Variations on a Theme from Tristan for Viola and Piano*. It was commissioned in Primrose's behalf by the Harvard Music Association. He gave the first performance of this composition at one of their Club meetings in 1962. Primrose described the work as follows:

> The theme is taken from the Helmsman's unaccompanied off-stage song which opens Act I of Wagner's *Tristan und Isolde*. It appears first in the viola after a stormy introduction. Six variations follow. The work ends quietly, with a simplified version of the theme and two shifting chords in the piano. Its publisher is Galaxy Music Corporation.

Those in attendance at the Seventh International Viola Congress, held in Provo, Utah, July 12–14, 1979, had the privilege of hearing premier performances of three new compositions which were dedicated to Dr. Primrose and brilliantly performed by three of his former students. These new pieces included: *Sonata for Viola and Piano* by George Rochberg (b. 1918), performed by Joseph de Pasquale, violist, and Vladimir Sokoloff, pianist; *Rhapsody for Viola and Orchestra*, by Maurice Gardner (b. 1909), performed by Jerzy Kosmala; and *Homages for Viola and Orchestra*, by Merrill Bradshaw (b. 1929), performed by Jun Takahira. Both the Gardiner and Bradshaw pieces were performed with the United States Air Force Symphony Orchestra, Captain Lowell E. Graham, conductor, and Dr. David Dalton, guest conductor. Those in the audiences at the Congress were unanimous in the opinion that they had heard three excellent works—works that will constitute significant additions to the viola repertoire.

---

[2]Peter Fricker, *Concerto for Viola and Orchestra*, Op. 20, 1952.

[3]Edmund Rubbra, *Concertino in A*, Op. 75, 1952.

[4]Quincy Porter, *Concerto for Viola and Orchestra*, 1948.

[5]Arthur Benjamin, *Sonata in C Minor for Viola and Piano*, 1947.

[6]Benjamin Britten, *Lachrymae (Reflections on a Song of Dowland) for Viola and Piano*, Op. 48, 1950.

Of all the compositions associated with Primrose, none elicited more general interest than the *Concerto for Viola and Orchestra* by Béla Bartók, a work that Primrose described as "a sensitive and inspired work and a real contribution to the literature for the viola."[7]

When first approached by Primrose in 1945, Bartók was reluctant to accept the assignment, saying that he did not know enough about the potential of the viola to write a concerto for the instrument. Primrose suggested that he attend a concert in which he was to play the William Walton *Concerto* with the NBC Orchestra, conducted by Sir Malcom Sargent. The composer was unable to attend, due to illness, but he did hear the broadcast. He was so impressed with the manner in which Walton used the viola, and by Primrose's superb performance, that he accepted the commission to write the *Concerto*. Primrose paid Bartók $1,000 in advance, a handsome fee at that time, and left on a concert tour to South America. When he returned, a letter was awaiting him from Bartók which read in part:

> I am very glad to be able to tell you that your Viola Concerto is ready in draft, so that only the score has to be written . . . If nothing happens I can be through in 5 or 6 weeks, that is, I can send you a copy of the orchestral score in the second half of October.[8]

Alas, on September 25, 1945, Bartók died. Owing to his failing health, the piece was still uncompleted. It was not in a state of legible notation suitable for a performer to read, or for a publisher to publish. It was generally agreed by the heirs to the Bartók estate that Tibor Serly was the only one close enough to the composer to unravel the seemingly impossible enigma of reconstructing the composition.

After the piece was ultimately performed and published, Halsey Stevens, Bartók's biographer, cast a shadow of doubt on the authenticity of the *Viola Concerto*, when in assessing Bartók's concertos he wrote:

> At this point the *Viola Concerto* cannot be properly evaluated, since it was completed by another hand. No matter how skillful the reconstruction, it must be admitted that no one but the composer himself could have decided exactly how it was to be done; and for that reason there will always be reluctance to accept the *Viola Concerto* as an authentic work of Bartók.[9]

---

[7]Halsey Stevens, *The Life and Music of Béla Bartók*, (New York, 1953, rev. 1964), p. 253.

[8]Quoted from the preface to the piano part in the printed viola and piano reduction made by Tibor Serly and printed by Boosey & Hawkes, 1949

[9]Halsey Stevens, *op. cit.*, p. 228.

As a result of Stevens' statement, it was generally accepted at that time that the *Viola Concerto* was really the conception of Tibor Serly, based on unfinished thematic material by Bartók.

Two important testaments, however, came to light in the 1970's which should forever silence any doubt as to the authenticity of the Bartók *Viola Concerto*. The first is the doctoral dissertation of David Dalton, *Genesis and Synthesis of the Bartók Viola Concerto*, which was completed at Indiana University in 1970.[10] The second was an article by Tibor Serly, "A Belated Account of the Reconstruction of a 20th Century Masterpiece," which appeared in *The College Music Symposium* in 1975.[11] The Dalton dissertation represented exhaustive research, including iterviews with Serly and Primrose. Serly's article described in detail the problems and how he solved them, measure by measure, in reconstructing and putting the *Viola Concerto* into its present form. It was certainly a labor of love for Serly, and he is sincere in his desire to give full credit to Bartók for the composition. The problems are described in Serly's own words:

> First, there was the problem of deciphering the manuscript itself. Bartók wrote his sketches on odd, loose sheets of music paper that happened to be on hand at the moment, some of which had parts of other sketches already on them. Bits of material that came to his mind were jotted down without regard for their sequence. The pages were not numbered nor the separation of movements indicated. The greatest difficulty encountered was deciphering his corrections of notes, for Bartók, instead of erasing, grafted his improvements on to the original notes.
>
> The next problem involved the matter of completing harmonies and other adornments which he had reduced to a form of shorthand.[12]

Primrose gave the world premier performance of the Bartók *Viola Concerto* on December 2, 1949, with the Minneapolis Symphony, conducted by Anatal Dorati. This was followed in January, 1950, by the radio premier with Primrose and the NBC Symphony, conducted by Ernest Ansermet. The first recording was made in October, 1950, with Tibor Serly conducting; the recording engineer was Peter Bartók, son of the composer. The recording was issued under the label of Bartók Records.

The Bartók *Viola Concerto* suddenly became one of the most important and most popular works in the literature for the instrument. Primrose himself performed this work over one hundred times. By

---

[10]Highlights of Dalton's dissertation were reprinted in *Music and Letters* (April, 1976), pp. 117–129.

[11]*The College Music Symposium*, Vol. XV (Spring, 1975), pp. 7–25.

[12]Quoted from Tibor Serly's preface to the Béla Bartók *Viola Concerto*. This preface appears in the orchestral score and in the piano part to the "Reduction for Viola and Piano" edition.

1969 Boosey & Hawkes, publisher of the *Concerto,* stated that the annual number of live performances had increased to over 100, with no indication that there would be a decrease.[13]

Violists who would like to be cognizant of Primrose's thoughts regarding interpretation, tempos, and other stylistic matters related to the Bartók *Concerto* may find them in Dalton's interview with the great virtuoso.[14]

Primrose the Teacher

Dr. Primrose began his distinguished teaching career at the Curtis Institute of Music in 1942. Later he taught in numerous institutions, including Juilliard, the Eastman Summer School of Music, the Aspen Festival, the University of Southern California, Indiana University, Tokyo University of Fine Arts, and Banff Centre of Fine Arts. His artistry and humanity constitute an immeasurable influence on his many outstanding students.

The high regard and veneration of students for him as a teacher are well known. One of them, Karin Pugh, who studied with Primrose at Indiana University, wrote an informative article which describes his principles of viola performance as shared with his students.[15] Ms. Pugh listed six of Primrose's admonitions to his students:

1. Keep the elbow of the bow arm fairly low.
2. The vibrato motion of the left hand is constant during finger changes [other than when the aesthetic demands of the music so dictate].
3. Experiment with using another finger to help the fourth finger hold down the string [in octave playing].
4. Play détaché passages in the upper third of the bow, turning the bow so that the stick is closer to the face than the hair.
5. In technically difficult passages, create exercises which isolate the problem.
6. Scales are always practiced with vibrato.

Ms. Pugh added that Primrose likes to coach the student and his accompanist simultaneously, and explained,

> He knows both parts by memory, and has a wealth of ideas about interpretation. He takes great liberty in changing notes for technical ease or musical effect. He is unique among my teachers in urging his students to use open strings and harmonics whenever possible for the sake of heightening the timbre of the instrument.

---

[13]Dalton, *op. cit.,* p. 125.

[14]Dalton, *op. cit.,* pp. 128–9.

[15]Karin Pugh, "A Student's View of William Primrose, ASTA's 1970 Teacher of the Year," *American String Teacher,* XXI, No. 1 (Winter, 1971), pp. 16–17. Material in brackets added by Primrose in letter to author, May, 1979.

For building technique Primrose had Ms. Pugh work in two books, which he had edited: *The Art and Practice of Scale Playing on the Viola*, and Campagnoli's *Forty-one Caprices*. She commented:

> He had written a number of difficult fingerings into fast passages of the *Caprices*, and he taught me to play these with a spirit of prideful virtuosity.

In his *Memoirs* Primrose explained his rationale for using extensions to facilitate fingering problems. He divulged that his teacher, Ysaÿe, thought of the entire fingerboard as one position, and that he shares this concept.[16]

Two works that explicate Primrose's concepts on teaching and learning how to play the viola are his *Technique is Memory*,[17] a method for violin and viola players based on finger patterns; and the book written jointly with Yehudi Menuhin, *Violin and Viola*,[18] which includes photographs of Primrose demonstrating proper positions for holding and bowing the instrument.

Another important pedagogical work is now in preparation, a book which will comprise Primrose's methodology of teaching and his principles of performance practice. Teachers and students of the viola await this book with great expectations.

Dr. Primrose's inspirational teaching has influenced the artistry and musicianship of many violists. To name all of his outstanding students would be difficult. David Dalton, Nathan Gordon, Oscar Hoogland, Martha Strongin Katz, Jerzy Kosmala, Donald McInnes, Joseph de Pasquale, Myron Rosenblum, Yizhak Schotten, Jun Takahira, Andras von Töszeghi, Karen Tuttle, and Alan de Veritch represent only a few of the many talented violists who have studied with him.

Primrose's Recordings

A Primrose Discography is included as an Appendix to his *Walk on the North Side, Memoirs of a Violist*. Primrose received his greatest acclaim as a recording artist in 1954, when his recording of Berlioz' *Harold in Italy* became the best selling non-jazz record of the year.

It is most unfortunate that very few of his recordings are now available, a particularly sad loss to the generation of violists who have

---

[16]William Primrose, *Walk on the North Side*, p. 55.

[17]William Primrose, *Technique is Memory* (London: Oxford University Press, 1960).

[18]Yehudi Menuhin and William Primrose, *Violin and Viola* (London: Macdonald and Jane's, 1976).

matured since 1965. It would be a valuable legacy to all violists if some of the master recordings could be reissued.

Primrose's Violas

Primrose has performed on different violas during his career, including his father's Brothers-Amati viola of C.1600,[19] the famous Andrea Guarneri of 1697,[20] the Macdonald Stradivarius of 1701,[21] as well as several instruments made by 20th century makers. His own comments on the violas he has used follow:

> Now, as to my violas: After the Bros. Amati (It belonged to my good father, and was the apple of his eye. He bought it from the then well known dealer, Andrew Smillie, in Glasgow, years and years ago, and I don't know who owned it before him.), I played for a number of years on a magnificent instrument made for me by Bill Moennig. Dimensions? Ask him.[22] I am never aware or take much interest in dimensions. I am only concerned with sound. I am not sure, but I believe it was ultimately purchased by Carlton Cooley. Following that one, of course, I had the Guarneri. And you know all about that.
>
> During the early years of my residence in Japan I met a number of very excellent young Japanese craftsmen, most of whom had studied in Europe, and one of them, Yu Iida, made an exact copy of the Guarneri which I have used with immense satisfaction until this day. Of course, the Japanese are wondrous craftsmen in anything they undertake. He recently made a copy of the Macdonald Strad for Peter Schidlof of the Amadeus group. The Macdonald (then owned by Gerald Warburg) was the instrument I used in my early performances, and later recording, of 'Harold' with Koussevitzky in 1943 (?).
>
> While I prefer the mezzo quality violas, I found it, the Macdonald, too much so, as I have found all Strads, and weak on the 'C' string. The Gasparos while very great instruments, have too much contralto quality for me. They are the ideal of many players, and who am I to disagree with their choice?
>
> I also had a Vidoudez for a while, which Pierre made for me . . . I used it at all my Swiss appearances at the time; the middle forties and early fifties.[23]

Honors and Recognition

There can be no question that Primrose has become a legend in his own time. As a result of his life dedicated to music and to the viola, he has been the recipient of many honors and accolades of recogni-

---

[19]For photographs and a description of the Brothers-Amati viola, see Chapter II.

[20]For photographs and a description of the Andrea Guarneri viola, see Chapter III.

[21]For more about the Macdonald Stradivarius viola see Chapter III.

[22]See "A Viola by William Moennig, Jr.," The Strad (March, 1947), pp. 326–7, for pictures and specifications. The article describes a viola made for William Primrose in 1945, with a body length of 41 cm. (16 1/8 in.). Moennig blended measurements of Stradivarius and Amati to get Amati's mellow roundness and Stradivarius' greater brilliance of tone.

[23]Quoted from Primrose's letter to the author, October 20, 1978.

tion. In addition to his already-mentioned appointments as Professor of Viola in several of the most prestigious schools of music, and his selection to perform with many of the finest artists and greatest orchestras of the 20th century, he has received additional noteworthy recognition.

His name is followed by the letters C.B.E., which designate that he has been honored with the title, "Commander of the British Empire," by order of Queen Elizabeth in 1951, bestowed in 1953; and by F.G.S.M., bestowed by his alma mater, designating the honorary title of "Fellow of the Guildhall School of Music."

In 1970 Primrose was named "Artist Teacher of the Year" by the American String Teachers Association.

The title of Dr. preceding his name indicates that he was granted an honorary Doctor of Music degree by Eastern Michigan University during the Third International Viola Congress held on the E.M.U. campus, Ypsilanti, Michigan, in 1975 (Plate 69). An entire day of the Congress was devoted to recognition of Primrose's many contributions to the viola. He was honored separately by the officers of the Viola Forschungsgesselschaft, by the American Viola Research Society, and by thirteen of Primrose's distinguished alumni, who were present at the Congress. Each of these three groups presented him with a plaque, denoting their praise and appreciation for his contributions to the viola.

Plate 72. Judges and Winners of the International William Primrose Viola Competition held in Snowbird, Utah, 1979: Ralph Aldrich, Judge; Jun Takahira; Dr. Primrose; Geraldine Walther, Patrica McCarty; and Joseph de Pasquale, Judge.

In 1976 Franz Zeyringer's definitive tome, *Literatur für Viola*, was published with a title page which reads: "Herrn Prof. Dr. h. c. William Primrose gewidmet" (dedicated to the Honorable Professor Doctor William Primrose).

Just preceding the Seventh International Viola Congress of 1979, an event of importance to all violists, particularly those of the ages 18–30, took place at Snowbird, Utah, on July 8–11. This was appropriately entitled, *The William Primrose International Viola Competition*.

In 1978 Brigham Young University at Provo, Utah, established an archives, *The William Primrose Viola Library and Memorabilia*, which contains many of the original manuscripts of works commissioned by Primrose, photographs, programs, and other items related to his brilliant career. The Primrose Archives will constitute permanent source material for violists and research scholars to peruse and utilize.

Dr. William Primrose, his wife Hiroko (an accomplished Suzuki teacher), and family moved from Australia back to the United States in the summer of 1979. They have taken up permanent residence in Provo, Utah, where he is now affiliated with Brigham Young University.

CHAPTER XVI

THE VIOLA IN NORTH AMERICA IN THE 20TH CENTURY

At the turn of the 20th century, the United States of America was importing most of its musical artists, composers, and teachers from Europe; and young precocious American musicians were being sent to Europe to receive their advanced training. But even in Europe, students who aspired to become violists were usually forced to limit their study to the violin.

Antonin Dvořák (1841–1904), eminent Bohemian composer and violist, came to the United States briefly (1892–95). Although he did not compose any known solos for the viola, his *String Quartet in F Major* ("The American Quartet") opens with the viola introducing the main theme, and the instrument maintains a prominent part throughout the entire composition. Ernest Bloch (1880–1950), from Switzerland, wrote all of his viola works while living in the United States, works which have become a part of the standard repertoire.

Following World War I, two new Schools of Music which included instruction on the viola in their curriculums, were founded in the United States: The Eastman School of Music, in Rochester, New York; and The Curtis Institute of Music, in Philadelphia, Pennsylvania. At Eastman, Samuel Belov, an emigrant from Russia, was employed in 1921 to teach viola and to direct the school orchestra; and at Curtis, Louis Bailly joined the faculty in 1925 to teach viola and chamber music. Thus, both schools had fully recognized the study of the viola as a major field of endeavor. No other American schools followed the lead of Eastman and Curtis immediately, but the precedent had been established.

During the time between the two World Wars, many of the world's most competent violists played in the major symphony orchestras of the United States. Among the many excellent European violists who migrated to the United States then was Ferenc Molnar (b.1896) from Hungary, who can be singled out as a man of multiple talents. In addition to serving for twenty years as Principal Violist of the San Francisco Symphony, having over twenty works composed for him, and being an eminent teacher in the San Francisco area, he is a mechanical engineer and inventor of international reputation.

In 1937 the National Broadcasting Company formed a special orchestra for Arturo Toscanini to conduct. The finest talent available was assembled for this great orchestra, including the viola section. William Primrose was among those employed to play for the great maestro. Primrose and the other violists in the NBC Symphony Orchestra later took leading roles as performers and teachers of the viola throughout the United States.

Following World War II, several Universities in the United States appointed string quartets-in-residence, the members of which became a part of the teaching faculty. This development set in motion several trends that were important to advanced viola students.

In the 1970's two new organizations were formed which have been extremely beneficial to violists: The Viola Research Society (now The American Viola Society) and The American Society for the Advancement of Violin Making (now The Violin Society of America). The former group gave violists an organization with which they could especially identify—an organization dedicated to the promotion of the instrument, both in its performance, and in the publicizing of its literature. The Violin Society of America has as its principal goal the promotion of the making of bowed instruments by contemporary luthiers. The response to this Society's activities has been the increased production of many excellent instruments sold for reasonable prices to meet the needs for an ever-burgeoning number of string players.

The Eastman School of Music

In 1921 the new Eastman School of Music in Rochester, New York, invited Samuel Belov to join the faculty as Professor of Viola and Conductor of the Eastman Student Orchestra. Belov was born in Yekaterinoslav, Russia, in 1884, and died in Rochester, New York, in 1954. He migrated to the United States in 1905, and continued his study of the violin with Professor Heimandahl in Baltimore, Maryland. He gradually shifted to the viola, both as a performer and as a teacher. He joined the Philadelphia Orchestra as violist in 1908 and remained with this illustrious organization until 1920, serving as principal of the section from 1919 to 1920. During all of this time he was also on the faculty of the Philadelphia Conservatory of Music. As Professor of Viola at the Eastman School of Music, he gradually built up the viola department until it became one of the most prestigious schools for violists in the world. In 1949 he was succeeded by one of his former pupils, Francis Tursi. In addition to performing as a soloist, conducting, and teaching, Belov also served at various times as violist with distinction in the Russian, the Rich, the Kindler, and the Kilbourn String Quartets.

The Curtis Institute of Music

In 1925 the Curtis Institute of Music appointed Louis Bailly Professor of Viola and Chamber Music. He served on the faculty until 1940. Bailly, an outstanding violist of the French School,[1] came to the United States in 1919 to join the Flonzaley Quartet. He became a protagonist of the viola in both the United States and Canada, as a quartet performer, as a soloist, and as a teacher. In addition to his performances in the quartet, Bailly appeared at the Berkshire Music Festival, where with Harold Bauer, pianist, he gave the premier performance of Ernest Bloch's *Suite for Viola and Piano (Orchestra).*

Bailly gave what was probably the first full recital by an artist-violist in New York City. It took place at Town Hall, March 28, 1925. *The Musical Digest* of April 7, 1925, ran Bailly's photograph with the caption, "Louis Bailly, violist, won remarkable commendations in his recital. He was formerly a member of the Flonzaley Quartet." The article lists a program consisting of works by Strube, Jongen, Schumann, and Hindemith. *The Digest* quoted from an article by Olin Downes, music critic of *The New York Times:*

> Mr. Bailly's instrument is one of the finest Gasparo da Salòs the writer has had the privilege of hearing. Mr. Bailly, for that matter, would doubtless draw from another viola a tone of exceptional fineness and richness of color. . . . [His playing] was that of an exceptionally accomplished musician who unites the most substantial knowledge with unusual feeling and control of tonal nuance.

The Digest continued with the glowing report published in the *New York Herald Tribune,* which described Bailly's tone quality and technique:

> His lower tones had the characteristic rich mellowness . . . his higher notes were violinistic, with the slightly cloudy timbre of the larger instrument. Mr. Bailly's technical skill was beyond exception.

The Digest concluded the report of the concert with quotes from *The New York Sun,* which commented that "Schumann's *Märchenbilder*

---

[1]For Bailly's connection with the French School, see Chapter XIV.

served Bailly for a display of the rich tonal beauty afforded by the viola."

Bailly gave a concert at the Curtis Institute of Music on March 5, 1926, of works written originally for viola, including Bloch's *Suite for Viola and Piano*. Other composers represented on the program were Hindemith, Jongen, Schumann, and Strube. Bailly's artistry inspired his students at the Curtis Institute to the attainment of the highest standards of achievement. Among his many artist-students were: Max Aronoff (b.1906), who remained at the school as a teacher of viola and member of the Curtis String Quartet; Albert Falkove, who joined the Los Angeles Philharmonic Orchestra; Paul Ferguson, who played in the Philadelphia Orchestra and the Baltimore Symphony; Sheppard Lehnhoff (1902–78), who joined the Chicago Symphony; Stephen Kondaks (b.1919), who became Professor of Viola at McGill University; Leonard Mogill (b.1911), who joined the Philadelphia Orchestra; Virginia Majewski, who made a career as violist in the Hollywood motion picture studios and also as a chamber music artist; and Joseph de Pasquale (b.1919), who was Principal Violist of the Boston Symphony, and is now Principal Violist of the Philadelphia Orchestra.[2]

Dr. Bailly sent a note of introduction for one of his students who was to meet Pablo Casals at Prades in 1950. Casals responded:

> I have never forgotten your art. Never has a violist made such an impression on me. Will we meet again? Let us be happy and thankful that we could, at our age, enjoy music and serve it.[3]

After Bailly left the Curtis Institute in 1940, the school has had a succession of eminent viola teachers, including William Primrose, Joseph de Pasquale, and Max Aronoff. The latter has taught there since 1926. Among those who have studied with Aronoff are Toby Appel, William Berman, Joseph de Pasquale, David Schwartz, and Francis Tursi.

Ernest Bloch and His Works for Viola

Ernest Bloch was born in Geneva, Switzerland, in 1880, and died in Portland, Oregon, in 1950. His parents sent their precocious son, at

---

[2]For a much more detailed description of Louis Bailly's contributions to American music, see Maurice W. Riley, "Louis Bailly (1882–1974)," *Journal of the Violin Society of America*, Vol. III, No. 3, (Summer, 1977), pp. 33–49.

[3]The quotation from Casals' letter and the newspaper clippings concerning Bailly's New York concert were furnished to this author by Thérèse Rochette, formerly head of the CBC Music Library (Radio Canada) in Montreal.

the age of 16, to Brussels to study violin with Eugène Ysaÿe. Although he was a conscientious violin student, he also spent considerable time composing. When Ysaÿe saw some of Bloch's compositions, he urged the young man to develop his career as a composer. Bloch followed Ysaÿe's advice, and the world of music is the richer as a result. Violists are particularly fortunate that Bloch chose composition and not violin performance as his life's calling.

In 1916 he migrated to the United States, and it was in America that he composed his works for the viola, beginning with the *Suite for Viola and Piano (Orchestra)*, which won first prize in the 1919 Elizabeth Sprague Coolidge Chamber Music Competition, held at the Berkshire Music Festival. Louis Bailly, violist, and Harold Bauer, pianist, gave the premier performance at the Festival.[4]

Several years later, after Bloch had become the Director of the Cleveland Institute of Music, Bailly gave a recital in Cleveland. The following letter expressed Bloch's thoughts regarding Bailly's performance, and also regarding the viola in general:[5]

Cleveland, Ohio
March 25, 1924

Dear Louis:

The viola has always been one of my favorite instruments and it happens that, without my knowledge, in my symphonic works and in "Macbeth" the viola part is the longest and often the most important. But in my youth, this instrument was neglected and forsaken; and only mediocre violinists were finding in it a kind of refuge. The saddest part was that they were trying to play violin on the viola without understanding that the technique of these two instruments was different. *Again today the viola is unrecognized.*

So apart from an immense joy for me to meet an artist and accomplished musician like yourself who has understood the technique and soul of this magnificent instrument to which he has devoted all his life, your interpretation of my *Suite* puts in value all the musical and poetical intentions contained in this work proving that the viola could express all the scale of feelings and passions with an intensity and color that very few were suspecting.

I don't think that it would be possible to surpass nor even to equalize the poignant emotion with which you have interpreted the "Nocturne" of this *Suite*, as much as for the pure beauty of sounds as for the style and intensity of expression. It is an unforgettable souvenir.

Consequently I wish that not only you could play this work but that your inevitable success in this country reveals to all what the viola can do when it is played by a great artist and stimulates the composers to write for this instrument.

I would be too happy if this very insufficient appreciation of your great talent could help in giving you the place that you deserve.

Affectionately yours,
Ernest Bloch

---

[4]The second prize for chamber music was awarded to Rebecca Clarke for her *Sonata for Viola and Piano*. This was a significant breakthrough for the viola. Very few pieces of consequence had been written for the viola in the United States up to that time.

[5]Letter furnished by Thérèse Rochette.

Bloch's fondness for the viola is further substantiated in a letter to this author by Lucienne Bloch Dimitroff, dated December 21, 1976, in which she writes, "The viola was Bloch's favorite instrument."

Other significant works for viola from Bloch's pen did not appear until the *Concertino for Flute, Viola, and String Orchestra* was commissioned by the Juilliard School of Music in 1948 and premiered there in 1950. This work does not have the Jewish thematic material common to many of Bloch's works. David Kushner aptly described the piece as a "light divertissement. The writing is intentionally simple, and there is no attempt at profundity. Wit and taste are the work's principal attributes."[6]

Bloch's best known and most frequently performed work for the viola is the *Suite Hébraïque for Viola (or Violin) and Piano (Orchestra)*. It was composed for, and dedicated to, the Chicago Covenant Club. In December, 1950, the Covenant Club sponsored a week-long festival of Bloch's works to commemorate the composer's 70th birthday. The work was originally intended for viola and orchestra, and was first performed by the Chicago Symphony, conducted by Jan Kubelik, with Milton Preves, Principal Violist, playing the solo part. Bloch was so touched by this magnificent performance that he wrote the *Meditation and Processional* especially for Preves. The *Hébraïque Suite* and the *Meditation and Processional* were published in 1951.

In 1950, the year of his death, Bloch composed *Suite for Viola Solo,* one of his last works. Bloch's daughter, Suzanne, has written concerning this composition: "Work on his *Suite for Viola* was interrupted by major surgery and was never finished. Thus the fourth (last) movement ends suddenly with an unfinished phrase. Though I brought this manuscript to him often, urging him to go on with it, he would smile and say, 'Later.' After his death in the hospital, I returned to his bedroom in Agate Beach and found the manuscript on his night table."[7]

One of several features of the Seventh International Viola Congress, held in Provo, Utah, 1979, was the performance of all the works written by Bloch for the viola. The Congress opened appropriately with a lecture by the composer's daughter, Suzanne Bloch, entitled "Ernest Bloch and the Viola." The composer's viola compositions were performed by the following distinguished violists: Yizhak

---

[6]David Kushner, "A Commentary on Ernest Bloch's Symphonic Works," *The Redford Review,* XXI, 3 (1967), p. 119.

[7]Suzanne Bloch in collaboration with Irene Heskes, *Ernest Bloch, Creative Spirit* (New York: Jewish Council, 1976), p. 103.

Schotten, *Suite Hébraïque;* Raphael Hillyer, *Suite for Viola Solo;*
Karen Tuttle, *Meditation and Processional;* Joseph de Pasquale, *Suite
for Viola and Piano;* Milton Thomas, *Concertino for Flute, Viola, and
String Orchestra.* In the latter work, the flute part was played by
Theodore Wight, with the United States Air Force String Orchestra,
conducted by Captain Lowell E. Graham. These excellent performances were a fitting tribute to Bloch, who gave so much to the viola.

The Viola in the Public Schools

Following World War I, the public schools in the United States
initiated instruction in band and orchestra performance as a part of
free public education. Unfortunately, viola players were not usually
available in sufficient numbers in these orchestras to give the string
choir proper balance. When Joseph Maddy (1891–1967) founded the
National Music Camp at Interlochen, Michigan, in 1928, he discovered that there was a great scarcity of high school violists. In order
to maintain a balanced string section in the National High School
Orchestra, he required all violinists enrolled at the Camp to play the
viola in several concerts. Following World War II, the viola balance at
the National Music Camp gradually improved until, by 1960, there
was a sufficient enrollment of high school violists to meet the demands of a balanced section. This situation was accompanied by a
vastly improved recruitment of violists for the high school orchestras
throughout the United States. Joseph Maddy, who was himself a violist and an avid chamber music enthusiast, can be credited for much of
the attention placed on developing interest in the viola in the public
schools of the United States.

The National Broadcasting Company Symphony

As formerly mentioned, in 1937 the National Broadcasting Company formed an orchestra specifically for the great conductor Arturo
Toscanini. Many of the world's finest instrumentalists were engaged
to play under the great maestro, resulting in the inclusion of perhaps
the greatest aggregate of talent ever before assembled in one orchestra. The viola section was no exception, since it included such artists
as Harold Coletta, Carlton Cooley, Nathan Gordon, Milton Katims,
Louis Kievman, Rolf Persinger, Tibor Serly, David Schwartz, and
Emanuel Vardi, with the incomparable William Primrose performing
the solo parts. After the break-up of this great orchestra, all of these
violists continued to be protagonists for the instrument: Harold

Coletta became Professor of Viola at Yale University; Carlton Cooley became Principal Violist of the Philadelphia Orchestra; Nathan Gordon became Principal Violist of the Detroit Symphony; Milton Katims became conductor of the Seattle Symphony; Louis Kievman became a leading performer and teacher in Los Angeles; Rolf Persinger became Principal Violist of the Minnesota Symphony and later the San Francisco Symphony; the late Tibor Serly composed significant works for the viola, and was responsible for making the Bartók *Viola Concerto* available for performance and publication; Emanuel Vardi pursued a successful career as soloist, recording artist, and conductor.[8]

After World War II

In the United States after 1945, following World War II, there was a great general renaissance of the arts, which had been in a decline owing to the War. Orchestras gradually took on longer seasons and paid higher salaries. Colleges and universities broadened their curricula to include advanced training and the granting of degrees in all areas of musical performance. Many major universities engaged a permanent string quartet-in-residence, as was evidenced by:

the University of Indiana—The Berkshire String Quartet;
the University of Illinois—The Walden String Quartet;
the University of Michigan—The Stanley String Quartet; and
the University of Wisconsin—The Fine Arts String Quartet.

The violists in these quartets were appointed to the position of Professor of Viola, and a curriculum was structured which made it possible for students to major on the viola and receive a degree in the field of their choice. Now, almost every major university has a string quartet-in-residence. This recognition by universities of string music was a major breakthrough which had a far-reaching effect on improving the prestige of violists.

Among the many prominent violists who migrated to the United States following World War II were: from Belgium, Robert Courte (1910–1979), as Violist of the Paganini and Stanley Quartets and teacher at the University of Michigan; from Germany, Paul Doktor (b.1919), as internationally famous concert artist and teacher at the Mannes College of Music and the Juilliard School of Music; Walter

---

[8]For more about the violists of the NBC Symphony, see under their names in Appendix I.

Trampler (b.1915), as world-renowned soloist and recording artist, and teacher at Juilliard and at Boston University; and Ernst Wallfisch (1920–1979), as one of the 20th century's finest violists, and as teacher at Smith College; and, from Cuba, Guillermo Perich (b.1924), as violist of the Walden Quartet, teacher and research scholar in Latin-American-Spanish viola music at the University of Illinois. They and many other foreign-born violists became American citizens and made significant contributions as performers, teachers, and recording artists.

Among the native talented violists are many artists who have played in string quartets and other chamber music groups; there is an even larger number who have made careers in symphony orchestras; and there are those who have taught. To mention all of the performers and teachers who have served the cause of the viola would be impossible and go far beyond the space limitations of this book. Many of them are mentioned, however, elsewhere herein, or are listed in *Appendix I.* A few of those who have been outstanding in advancing the cause of the viola as performers and teachers are: Max Aronoff (b.1906), at the Curtis Institute of Music and Head of the New School of Music in Philadelphia; Lyman Bodman (b.1915), of the Beaumont Quartet, at Michigan State University; Francis Bundra (b.1927), at the University of Michigan and at the National Music Camp in Interlochen, Michigan; David Dawson (1913–75), of the Berkshire Quartet, at Indiana University; Lillian Fuchs (b.1910), at Juilliard, the Manhattan School of Music, and other New York schools, and at Aspen, Colorado; Raphael Hillyer (b.1914), for many years of the Juilliard String Quartet, and now at Yale University; Milton Katims (b.1910), conductor of major symphony orchestras, editor of numerous solos for the viola, now at Houston University; Louis Kievman (b.1910), teacher in the Los Angeles area, editor of "Viola Forum," in *The American String Teacher,* 1972–78, and author of several string methods; William Lincer (b.1907), Principal Violist of the New York Philharmonic Orchestra for 31 years, and now a teacher and editor of works for student violists; Leonard Mogill, (b.1911), in the Philadelphia Orchestra for over forty years, also teaching at Philadelphia College for the Performing Arts and at Temple University, editor of important works for the viola; Joseph de Pasquale (b.1919), Principal Violist of two of the world's greatest orchestras: the Boston Symphony and the Philadelphia Orchestra, and teacher at the Curtis Institute of Music; Milton Preves (b.1909), Principal Violist of the Chicago Symphony Orchestra; Virginia Majewski, one of the first women violists to achieve success as a soloist and chamber music artist in the Hollywood film milieu; David Schwartz, Principal Violist of the Cleveland

and Detroit Orchestras, now teacher in Los Angeles, California; Stanley Solomon (b.1916), Principal Violist of the Toronto Symphony since 1946; Milton Thomas (b.1920), recording artist, now at the University of Southern California; Francis Tursi (b.1917), at the Eastman School of Music; and Karen Tuttle, soloist, chamber music player, and teacher at the Curtis Institute and the Peabody Conservatory.

Among the younger generation of violists, a few of the multitude of names must suffice to illustrate the growing involvement in the American musical scene: Ralph Aldrich (b.1933), at the University of Western Ontario and at the Banff Music Centre in summers, a guiding light in the development of interest in the viola in Canada; Toby Appel (b.1952), formerly violist in the Lenox String Quartet, now an established concert artist; Richard Blum (b.1929), of the Pro Arte Quartet, and at the University of Wisconsin, Madison; David Dalton (b.1934), at Brigham Young University, also research scholar, and host chairman of the Seventh International Viola Congress, and active in the International Viola-Vorschungsgesellschaft; Burton Fine (b.1930), Principal Violist of the Boston Symphony and teacher at the New England Conservatory of Music; Rivka Golani-Erdesz (b.1946), at the University of Toronto, student of Oedoen Partos, and authority on the performance of his compositions; Jacob Glick (b.1926), credited with over 200 first performances as soloist and ensemble player of new works—many with tape;Rosemary Glyde (b.1926), of the Manhattan String Quartet and research scholar; Jerry Horner (b.1935), formerly Principal Violist of the Dallas and the Pittsburgh Symphonies, now at Indiana and Illinois Universities; Martha Strongin Katz (b.1943), of the Cleveland String Quartet; A. Baird Knetchel, one of Canada's leading music educators; Jerzy Kosmala, a native of and with an early career in Poland, now at Akron University, Ohio; Patricia McCarty (b.1954), Assistant Principal Violist of the Boston Symphony and Principal Violist of the Boston Pops; Donald McInnes (b.1939), at the University of Washington and Cincinnati College-Conservatory of Music, premier performances of many works written for him; William Preucil (b.1931), at the University of Iowa; Samuel Rhodes (b. 1941), of the Juilliard String Quartet, and teacher at the Juilliard School of Music; Myron Rosenblum (b.1923), at Queensborough Community College, New York City, founder and president of The American Viola Society and the Viola d'Amore Society; Yizhak Schotten (b.1943), formerly Principal Violist of the Cincinnati Symphony, now Visiting Violist at the University of Washington; Thomas Tatton (b.1943), at Whittier College, California, expert on, and editor of, works for multiple violas; Marcus Thompson (b. 1946), at the Massachusetts

Institute of Technology, inspirer and performer of many contemporary works for viola; Michael Tree (b.1934), of the Guarnerius String Quartet, and teacher at the Curtis Institute of Music; Geraldine Walther, winner of the William Primrose International Viola Competition 1979, Principal Violist of the San Francisco Symphony; Ann Woodward (b.1940), at North Carolina University; Bernard Zaslav (b.1926), of the Fine Arts String Quartet, and teacher at the University of Wisconsin, Milwaukee.

The above list could very well contain twenty or thirty more names because there is so much progressive activity by violists in America, and throughout the world, as we approach the 1980's.[9]

The Primrose Influence

Unquestionably Dr. William Primrose has been the greatest single influence that brought about the present high standard of viola performance in America. Every violist in the United States and Canada has been touched directly or indirectly by his concert work, his recordings, and his teaching, as well as by his writing and by his generous contributions as a clinician and lecturer. American violists who have studied with him have been particularly fortunate; as have those of Japan, since his teaching has recently extended there.[10] Many violists who were not fortunate enough to study with him have been, nevertheless, the recipients of the rich legacy he has given to music and to the viola, which has ramified outward from his exemplary career.

The American Viola Society

The American Viola Society (formerly the Viola Research Society) is a Chapter of the International Viola-Forschungsgesellschaft (IVFG). Article II of the Society's Constitution states the purpose of the organization: "The object of the Society shall be to promote, study, and further the research and performance of the viola and its repertory." Dr. Myron Rosenblum, of a suburb of New York City, is the founder and president of the organization, and is also the editor of

---

[9]See Appendix I for other names than those listed.
[10]For the names of a few of the artist-violists who have studied with Primrose, see Chapter XV.

its *Newsletter,* which is published twice a year.[11] The *Newsletter* has become an important medium for members, informing them of new publications and recordings, concerts of particular interest to violists, historical lore, and viola activities in other countries.

The American Viola Society has sponsored three International Viola Congresses, the first being held at Eastern Michigan University, Ypsilanti, Michigan, in 1975, Dr. Maurice W. Riley, host chairman; followed by the Eastman School of Music, Rochester, New York, in 1977, Dr. Louise Goldberg, host chairman; and Brigham Young University, Provo, Utah, in 1979, Dr. David Dalton, host chairman. The Congresses provide an opportunity for the participants to hear performances of seldom heard viola works played by some of the world's finest violists, to exchange ideas in panel discussions, to encourage the composition of new works, to discuss pedagogical problems, to hear papers read on historical aspects of the instrument, and to participate in the general exchange of ideas that concern the viola. The American Viola Society spends most of its modest budget in assisting the host schools to advertise and to finance the Congresses.

The Society has also contributed to the commissioning of several significant works for the viola, including *Concerto for Viola and Orchestra,* by Clark Eastham, which was premiered at the Third International Viola Congress by Nathan Gordon, accompanied by the United States Air Force Orchestra, Major Albert A. Bader conducting; and the *Sonata for Viola and Piano,* by George Rochberg (b.1918), premiered by Joseph de Pasquale, violist, and Vladimir Sokoloff, pianist, at the Seventh International Viola Congress.

The Violin Society of America

The Violin Society of America (formerly The American Society for the Advancement of Violin Making), founded in 1973 by a small group dedicated to promoting the art of stringed instrument and bow making, which included Dr. Albert J. Kaplan, Eric Chapman, Dr. Ray Abrams, Albert Mell, Herbert K. Goodkind, Milton M. Koskoff, Anthony Piccirillo, and Herbert G. Schick. Dr. Kaplan, an eminent psychiatrist, became the first president of the Society. Eric Chapman,

---

[11]Other officers of the American Viola Society are Dr. Louise Goldberg, Music Librarian at the Eastman School of Music, Vice President, 1976–77; Dr. Maurice W. Riley, Emeritus Professor of Viola, Eastern Michigan University, Vice President, 1978– ; Dr. Ann Woodward, concert artist and Professor of Viola at North Carolina University, Treasurer, 1976– ; Marna Street, violist in the Pittsburgh Symphony, Secretary, 1976–.

a former teacher, violist, and now a dealer in stringed instruments, is now president of the Society. Dr. Ray Abrams, Emeritus Professor of Music at the University of Pennsylvania in Philadelphia, is the treasurer. Albert Mell, Professor of Music at Queen's College in New York City, is editor of the Society's excellent quarterly publication, *The Journal of the Violin Society of America*. Herbert K. Goodkind, realtor, specialist in the history of stringed instruments, and author of the monumental *Violin Iconography of Antonio Stradivari*, serves as vice-president, and is in charge of advertising for the *Society Journal*. Milton M. Koskoff, distinguished lawyer and violist from Plainsville, Connecticut, serves as legal advisor to the board of directors of the Society.

None of the founding members were luthiers, but they had a common bond: a desire to promote through all possible means the making of bowed-instruments. Luthiers and dealers immediately gave their support to the new organization and its worthy objectives.

The Violin Society has worked closely in conjunction with two of the Viola Congresses. They sponsored their first makers' competition at the Third International Viola Congress at Ypsilanti in 1975, a competition limited to violas. Forty-three violas were entered by luthiers from all over the world. The excellent quality of the entries was a revelation to everyone attending. Gold medals for craftsmanship and tonal quality were awarded to David Wiebe, Otto Schenk, and David Burgess, three young American luthiers. Eric Chapman, an avid violist, collaborated with this author in organizing the event.

The Violin Society also held an exhibition of violas in conjunction with the Seventh International Viola Congress held at Brigham Young University, in Provo, Utah, in 1979, to the mutual benefit of both the violists and the luthiers. Other exhibits and competitions are sponsored annually by the Violin Society. The exposure and publicity aroused by these events has vitalized the craftsmanship of bowed-instrument making and has given luthiers an opportunity to receive constructive criticism from expert judges, to compare their work with other makers, and also to find buyers for their products.

With the present shortage of fine stringed instruments and the scarcity and inflated astronomical prices of the old Italian masterpieces, the availability of fine instruments from contemporary makers is essential to fostering the perpetuity of bowed-instrument performance. Many violists give their support to the Violin Society of America because they appreciate and commend its objectives and accomplishments.

CHAPTER XVII

THE FUTURE FOR THE VIOLA

There is a great deal of information still to be learned about the history of the viola. Who were the violists for whom the 18th century composers wrote their music? This is one of the most intriguing questions, as yet unanswered, and wide open for research scholars. What was Chrétien Urhan's real name? Who was the mystery violist and composer, L. E. Casimir-Ney, and why did he choose to disguise his identity? There will always be a search for the old instruments and verification of their makers. Much is happening in Europe, North America, and Argentina, as is evidenced by the vitality of the Viola Forschungsgesellschaft and its national chapters. But what is happening in Brazil and the other Latin American countries regarding the viola? We are a little more fortunate in our knowledge of the status of the viola in Korea and in Japan, but additional information is still needed to describe fully the progress being made by violists in these countries. The Suzuki Method of string teaching is accomplishing much with young string players. How is this affecting young viola players? And what about China?

The College of Music, Seoul National University, Korea, invited Paul Doktor, in 1978, to play concerts, conduct seminars, and teach master classes for outstanding young violists. He wrote in glowing terms of the sincerity and artistry of the young violists in Korea.[1] He also stated that the success of the Korean viola students is due in large part to the expert teaching and inspiration furnished by Professor of Viola, Dong-Ok Shin (Mrs. Clara Whang, M.M.). The fine facilities in the School of Music, including the excellent accoustics of their concert hall, impressed him favorably. According to Doktor, Korea seems to have great promise.

In recent years, Dr. William Primrose has gone to Japan to give Master Classes at the Tokyo University of Fine Arts and Music—an assignment which he describes as one of the most rewarding of his many teaching experiences.[2] In response to a request for information regarding Japanese violists, Primrose replied:

---

[1]Letter to this author, September 18, 1978.
[2]William Primrose, *op. cit.*, p. 209.

Japanese violists? They are legion. Young Jun Takahira, who is continuing his studies with me, you will encounter at the next Viola Congress. He is the greatest viola talent to come my way. There are, too, Yoshinao Higashi (another student) and Mrs. Tahaka (who is married to the concertmaster of the NHK Symphony); a Miss Shinohara, and Nobuko Imai. To extend the list would take a vastly long time, and I can't remember all the names! To leave out the others is somewhat invidious, but we have to draw the line somewhere.[3]

Jun Takahira, a 19-year-old prodigy, and Makiko Kawahito, a student of Yoshiaki Nakatsuka at Tokyo University, demonstrated the superlative quality of viola playing in Japan at the William Primrose International Viola Competition, in which Takahira won second place, and Kawahito was a semi-finalist. Three days later Takahira played the premier performance of *Homages for Viola and Orchestra,* by Merrill Bradshaw (b.1929), at the Seventh International Viola Congress in Provo, Utah. Takahira was accompanied by the United States Air Force Orchestra, directed by Guest Conductor David Dalton.

Until recently there have been no international contests for the viola with sufficient prestige to launch a violist into a concert career. Violinists and cellists have had the Tschaikowsky Competition in Moscow, and the Queen Elizabeth Concours in Belgium, both of which bring world-wide publicity and an assured concert career to the winners. Other contests, such as the Wieniawski in Warsaw and the Paganini in Genoa, have been of value to violinists, but these contests also are not open to violists. At the present time violists are included in the competitions in Geneva, Switzerland, and in Munich, Germany, both of which are of the highest level, but do not receive the publicity or the international recognition they so justly deserve.

The violists' outlook in this field has already taken a decided turn for the better, as illustrated by The William Primrose International Viola Competition held in Snowbird, Utah, in July of 1979. Another event that promises to be of great benefit to violists is the Lionel Tertis International Viola Competition and Workshop to be held in Port Erin, Isle of Man, August 23–29, 1980. The competition will be open to violists of all nationalities born on or before March 2, 1951. Besides monetary awards, the winner will be invited to London to give the first performance of the *Concerto No. 2 for Viola and String Orchestra* by Gordon Jacob (who celebrates his 85th birthday in

---

[3]Quoted from a letter to this author, dated October 20, 1978.

1980). The Workshop, open to all, will include recitals and lectures.[4] These competitions presage a new era in which virtuoso violists can receive the recognition and publicity necessary to set in motion a successful concert career.[5]

Many fine violinists have had more than a passing interest in the viola. Niccolò Paganini, Joseph Joachim, and Henri Vieuxtemps had a particular fondness for the instrument; they frequently played it and composed important works for it. Fritz Kreisler and Eugène Ysaÿe played chamber music together whenever possible. On such occasions they vied with each other for the opportunity to play the viola parts. Following World War I, Jascha Heifetz played Bach's *Chaconne* for unaccompanied violin on the viola.[6] Since World War II, many violinists, including Yehudi Menuhin, the late David Oistrakh, Max Rostal, Oscar Shumsky, Henri Temianka, and Pinchas Zukerman have turned to the viola for occasional performances. It may be that benefit for the popularity of the viola will be derived from the involvement of artist-violinists who perform on this noble instrument because of its beautiful richness of tone. When this does not deprive an artist-violist, who has devoted his life to the instrument, from opportunities for performance, then such helpful interest in the promotion of the viola and its music is to be commended and welcomed.[7]

The repertoire for the viola is being steadily enlarged by the composition of new additions and by the recovery of significant 18th century works that have long been out of print, or have existed only in archives in manuscript form. The future prestige of violists and the opportunities that are becoming increasingly available to viola players are a promising reality. The possibility of seeking a career as a concert artist has been enhanced by recent developments such as the exposure and publicity attached to several new viola compositions. The

---

[4]Jury for the Lionel Tertis Viola Competition will include Harry Danks, United Kingdom; Paul Doktor, United States; Csaba Erdelyi, Hungary; Piero Farulli, Italy; Milan Skampa, Czechoslavakia; and Gerald McDonald, Chairman. Invited to participate in the Workshop were: The Smetana Quartet, Donald McInnes, Bruno Giuranna, Andros von Toszeghi, Nobuko Imai, Dr. Gordon Jacob, Thomas Tatton, Wilfred Saunders, Tully Potter, Bernard Shore, Peter Schidlof, Lady Barbirolli, Mrs. Lionel Tertis, Richard Rodney Bennett, John White and members of the jury.

[5]Also important for violists was the Scottish Viola International Workshop held in Glasgow, August 17–21, 1979, under the direction of Michael Beeston, in association with the Royal Scottish Academy of Music. Master Classes were conducted by Beeston, Csaba Erdelyi, and James Durrant. Included in the offerings were: 1. Soloists Concerto Class; 2. Sonata Class; 3. Teaching Workshop; and 4. Chamber and Modern Music Workshops.

[6]Gilbert Ross, "The Auer Mystique," *Michigan Quarterly Review*, XIV, 3 (Summer, 1975), p. 315.

[7]William Primrose, in a lecture at the Seventh International Viola Congress, voiced his disapproval of violinists crossing over into the violist's domain.

world's greatest composers are writing more solos for the viola. Recording companies are giving more and more attention to the instrument and are producing records and tapes in ever greater numbers.

Music scholars continue to make 18th century works available that were composed originally for the viola, as illustrated by the recently published *Concerto for Viola in B♭ Major* by Franz Anton Hoffmeister (1754–1812).[8] Another significant addition to the violist's repertoire has been edited by Rosemary Glyde, and is soon to be published: the *Concerto pour l'Alto Principal* [in G Major], Op. 10, by Johann Andreas Amon (1763–1825).[9] There are other important works for the viola that will eventually find their way into print by Friedrich Wilhelm Rust (1739–96), Johann Gottlieb Janitsch (1708–63),[10] and Wilhelm Gottlieb Hauff (1755–1817). The latter wrote no fewer than seven concertos for the viola.[11] Wenzel Pichl (1741–1803) was a Bohemian musician who was active in the Viennese scene for much of his life. He composed over 700 works, many of them for the viola. It is quite possible that after scholars have had an opportunity thoroughly to assemble, catalogue, and study his compositions, some of his works for the viola may be found worthy of publication.

The resources at hand to contemporary research scholars now are making manuscripts and out-of-print viola compositions available for study. Scholars are no longer limited to Robert Eitner's *Quellen-Lexicon*[12] for the locations of such music, but now have the continuing resources of the *Repertoire International des Sources Musicales*,[13] as well as recent editions of catalogues of the complete works of heretofore lesser known composers, and catalogues of the holdings of most

---

[8]F. A. Hoffmeister, *Concerto for Viola and Piano in B♭ Major*, Ed. by Alison A. Copland (Mainz: B. Schott, 1975).

[9]The Amon *Concerto* was brilliantly performed for the Fifth International Viola Congress at Eastman School of Music by Walter Trampler, accompanied by the United States Air Force Symphony Orchestra conducted by Capt. Lowell Graham.

[10]Works for viola by Janitsch are discussed in Chapter VI.

[11]Walter Lebermann, in a letter to this author, dated March 25, 1978, stated that Hauff's *Viola Concertos* are accompanied by strings, 2 flutes, and 2 horns. Four of them are numbered and three are unnumbered as follows: E♭ *Major*, No. 1; *G Major; D Major; C Major; G Major*, No. 5; *D Major*, No. 6, composed in 1796; and *G Major*, No. 10. Lebermann explains that of the unnumbered *Viola Concertos*, the one in *D Major* is identical to Hauff's *Violin Concerto*, No. 6; and the one in *C Major* is identical to the *Violin Concerto*, No. 4.

[12]Robert Eitner, *Biographisch-Bibliographisches Quellen-Lexicon der Musiker und Musikgelehrten christlicher Zeitrechnung bis Mitte des neuzehnten Jahrhunderts*. 10 Vols. (Leipzig: Breitkopf & Härtel, 1899–1904).

[13]*Repertoire International des Sources Musicales*. (Publie par la Société Internationale de Musicologie et l'Association Internationale des Bibliothèques Musicales).

of the world's greatest libraries and music archives.[14] The recent reprint of *The Breitkopf Thematic Catalogue* has also provided scholars with a rich source of 18th century works for the viola.

Availability and location of fine playable instruments have been increased immensely by the existence and efforts of the Violin Society of America. Their close connections with the American Viola Society have called the attention of luthiers to the growing needs of violists.

The Future Status of Violists

The status of violists has improved rapidly since 1900. The future portends a continued improvement in their prestige. The far-reaching achievements of the International Viola-Forschungsgesellschaft and its growing national chapters are gradually becoming a positive influence for bettering the advancing recognition of the instrument and its players.

Violists, however, still must face the difficult struggle to launch a concert career, and therefore, most must depend for financial security on an orchestral position, or on membership in a chamber music group, or on a teaching career. Fortunately the vast majority of violists do not have aspirations for a concert career, but play the viola because they love the sound of the instrument and the music written for it. These are the musicians who assure the success of the many orchestras, string quartets, and other chamber music groups that contribute so much to the artistic culture of the world. Many of these violists have an aptitude for teaching and so assure the continued success of the instrument by giving instruction to the budding musicians of the future. For all of these violists, the future holds great promise.

The world needs to be made increasingly aware of the remarkably beautiful sound of the viola. With a good supply of fine modern instruments available and the rich resources of music, both old and new, dedicated to the special role of this noble instrument, we may confidently expect an immense increase in the number of devotees of its glorious voice, in ensemble, in orchestral, and in solo-playing. Tertis and Primrose succeeded as concert artists because of their dedication to the instrument, their love of it, their ability to convince others of the viola's potential, and, above all, their great artistry. Others, lacking

---

[14]See Vincent Duckles, *Music Reference and Research Materials* (London: Collier-MacMillan, 1964). Also see François Lesure, "Archival Research: Necessity and Opportunity," *Perspectives in Musicology*, Ed. by Barry S. Brook, Edward O. D. Downes, and Sherman Van Solkema (New York: W. W. Norton, 1972), pp. 56–79.

their artistry and charisma, can do, and are doing, much for the instrument and for themselves by developing and spreading a faith in its unique qualities, and by constantly promoting, publicizing, and propagandizing the salient virtues of this magnificent voice.

The future of the viola depends upon the violists themselves!

But here is the finger of God, a flash of the will that can,
Existent behind all laws, that made them and, lo, they are!
And I know not if, save in this, such gift be allowed to man,
That out of three sounds he frame, not a fourth sound, but a star.

Consider it well: each tone of our scale in itself is naught;
It is everywhere in the world—loud, soft, and all is said:
Give it to me to use! I mix it with two in my thought:
And, there! Ye have heard and seen: consider and bow the head!

from *Abt Vogler,*
by Robert Browning

APPENDIX I
BRIEF BIOGRAPHIES OF VIOLISTS

The following alphabetical listings of persons who have contributed to the performance history of the viola are necessarily too brief to cover all of each one's meritorious activities and accomplishments. Regrettably certain biographical information was not available for some listings, including important dates. Mistakes and omissions are inevitable in a venture of this type and scope, which has had no precedent. The most unfortunate omissions are those names of violists that rightfully deserve inclusion in this Appendix. It is presently planned to bring out an expanded and corrected version of Appendix I within the next three or four years.

Readers are requested to correspond with the author at the address below to supply missing information, corrections, and the names of significant violists who are not included in this Appendix.

Franz Zeyringer, President of the *Internationale Viola-Forschungsgesellschaft* (IVFG), has recently appointed this author to be the official biographer of all violists, worldwide, for the Archives of the IVFG at the Mozarteum in Salzburg. All biographical information, programs, and other relevant materials sent to the author will be placed permanently in the Archives in Salzburg, where it will be available to viola enthusiasts and research scholars.

—Dr. Maurice W. Riley
512 Roosevelt Blvd.
Ypsilanti, Michigan 48197

ABBREVIATIONS

—	to present	Arr	Arrange, Arrangement
Acad	Academy	Assoc	Associate, Association
Amer	America, American	Asst	Assistant, Assist

ASTA	American String Teachers Association	Edu	Education
		Ens	Ensemble
AVS	American Viola Society, formerly Viola Research Society	Fac	Faculty
		Fest	Festival
b	Born	Fl	Flourished
B.A.	Bachelor of Arts	Found	Founding, Founder
B.M.	Bachelor of Music	Grad	Graduate
B.S.	Bachelor of Science	Incl	Include, including
Chm	Chairman	Insti	Institute
Chmb	Chamber Music	Int'l	International
Coll	College	Instru	Instrument
Compt	Competition	IVFG	Internationale Viola-Forschungsgesellschaft
Comp	Compose, Composition, Composer		
		Mbr	Member
Conc	Concerto	M.M.	Master of Music
Cond	Conduct, Conductor	Ms	Manuscript
Cons	Conservatory	Nat'l	National
d	Died	Orch	Orchestra
Ded	Dedicated	Pf	Performance
Dir	Direct, director	Phila	Philadelphia
DMA	Doctor of Musical Arts	Philh	Philharmonic
Ed	Edit, Editor, Edition	Ph.D.	Philosophy, Doctor of

Pre Pf	Premier Performance	St	State
Prep	Preparation	Str	String
Prof	Professor	Stud	Student at, Studied with
Pr Va	Principal or Solo Viola		
Prz	Prize	Symp	Symphony, Symphonic
Pt	Part	Tch	Taught, Teach, Teacher of
Pub	Publish, Publication	Trans	Transcribe, Transcription
Q	Quartet	U	University
RAM	Royal Academy of Music, London	Unacc	Unaccompanied
RCM	Royal College of Music, London	Va	Viola, Violist
Record	Record, Recording	VFG	Viola-Forschungs-gesellschaft
Rcd	Received	VRS	Viola Research Society, became AVS, 1978
Rctl	Recital	Vn	Violin
Sch	School		

ABBAS, ALFONS, 1894–? Va in Meiningen Q.

ALDRICH, RALPH, b 1933 New Zealand. Stud Victoria U, N.Z.; Guildhall Sch of Mus and Drama, London, Eng., Prof Nannie Jamieson; Vienna State Acad, Austria, Prof Franz Samohyl; Cologne, Ger. & Berne, Swit., Prof Max Rostal. Rosner Q, N.Z, 1957; U of Western Ontario Q., 1967–; Pr Va Vienna Haydn Orch, 1960; Va Bath Fest Orch (Menuhin), London Mozart Players, 1961; Trio Chelys, Luxembourg. Head of Str Program, Cambridge Coll of Arts (UK), 1964–66; Assoc Prof U of West. Ont., London, Ont., Can., Dr Va Insti Banff Sch of Fine Arts, Banff, Alberta, Can., 1967–. Examiner, Adjudicator, Clinician, Jury mbr William Primrose Int'l Va Compt 1979, panel mbr 7th Int'l Va Congress, Provo, Utah 1979.

ALLEKOTTE, WILLIAM, b1850. Stud Cologne Cons. Succeeded F. Karges as Va in Heckman Q.

APPEL, TOBY, b 1952 Elmer, N. J. Stud New School of Music, Philadelphia, Pa. 1961–65, Max Aronoff; Curtis Institute of Music, 1965–69, Max Aronoff and Joseph de Pasquale. Mbr 16 Concerto Soloists, Phila Pa., 1967–69. Asst Pr Va St. Louis Symp 1970–71. Lenox Q 1972–77. Asst Prof S.U.N.Y., Binghampton, N.Y. 1972–. Member Tokyo Chamb Soloists 1974. Marlboro Music Festival 1970, 1976, 1977. Int'l Musicians Seminar, Cornwall, Eng. 1977–78. Bach Brandenburg No. VI with Walter Trampler and the Chamber Series Orch 1978. Solo recitals in Alice Tully Hall, England, Holland, and numerous American cities. Lincoln Center Chamb Society Guest Artist. Soloist: Amer Symp, "Wall to Wall Bach", 1978; St. Paul Chamb Orch, Denis Russel Jones, cond. Pre Pf World, Ezra Laderman *Viola Concerto* 1978, *Elegy* 1976, *Other Voices-3 Violas* 1977 (all "3 violas" played by one violist), all on C.B.S. T.V. Record with Lenox Q for Desto and Columbia; solos for B.B.C.: Bloch *Suite*, Rebecca Clarke *Sonata*. Plays 17 3/4 in. Hieronymus II Amati Viola (1705) "in mint condition."

ARA, UGO, b 1876 Venice; d 1936 Lausanne, Swit. Stud Cons Benedetto Marcello, Venice, P. A. Tirindelli; Cons in Liége, Cezar Thompson. Flonzaley Q 1903–17.

ARAD, ATAR, b 1945 Tel Aviv, Israel. Stud Acad of Mus, Israel, Andre Gertler Vn. Switched to Va 1972. Prof Va Chapelle Musicale de la Reine Elizabeth 1973–5. Tch Royal Northern Coll of Mus, Manchester, Eng. 1975–. 2nd Prize Carl Flesch Compt 1972; 1st Prize Geneva Compt 1972. Raphael D'Haen comp for him *Four Intermezzi for Solo Va*. Rctls: Hindemith's Op. 25, No. 4 at Berlin Festival; Int'l Va Congress, London 1978. Many record for Telefunken-Decca.

ARCIDIACONO, AURELIO, b 1915 Palermo, Italy. Stud Cons di Musica di Palermo, G. Ferrari, L. Liviabella. Pr Va, Va d'amore Orch sinfonica RAI Torino 1941–60. Trio da Camera 1947–50; Trio d'archi di Radio Torino 1950–52. Prof of Va and Va d'amore, Cons Torina, Bari, Palermo, Rome 1956–77. Appointed Inspector for the Ministry of Public Instruction for Conservatories of Music, 1978–. Pre Pf in Italy works by Frank Martin, *Sonata da Chiesa* (Torino), 1953; his own *Due*

Movimento for Va and Va d'amore, with Rudolf Nel (Bayerischer Rundfunk), 1956; Vivaldi, *Concertos* for Va d'amore (Milano, Palermo), 1960. Also composed *Variazioni per Iuna manolova* for Va and 8 Instruments. Author of *La Viola, Gli Instrumenti Musicali*, 1973.

ARONOFF, MAX, b 1906 New York City, Stud Henry Such. Curtis Insti of Mus; one of first Va students; on Fac before graduation, 1928–; stud with Carl Flesch, Louis Bailly. Curtis Q 1927–. Philadelphia Orch 1944–45. Found Pres., and Dir New School of Music, 1944–. Among outstanding pupils are: Joseph de Pasquale, Pr Va Philadelphia Orch; Francis Tursi, head of Va Dept Eastman Sch of Mus; William Berman, head Va Dept Oberlin; Toby Appel, formerly Lenox Q; David Schwartz, formerly Yale U Fac, Paganini Q, now Hollywood. Tours throughout major cities of U.S. and Europe. One of America's most eminent viola teachers.

ARONOWITZ, CECIL, b 1916 King William's Town, So Africa, d 1978 Snape, Eng. Stud Royal Coll of Mus, London, Achille Rivarde. Pr Va Eng Chmb Orch 1948–76, London Mozart Players, Boyd Neel Orch, Philharmonia of London. Found mbr of Melos Ens; Pro Arte Ens; Duo with wife, Nicola Grunberg, piano. 2nd Va with Amadeus Q for Quintets. Va with all London Symph Orchs. Prof Va and Chmb Mus Royal Coll of Mus, Manchester 1973–77; Dir of Strings Britten/ Pears Sch for Advanced Musical Studies, Aldeburgh, Suffolk 1977–; Musical Advisor to Purcell Sch for Specialised Young Musicians, London 1977–. Cobbett Chmb Mus Medal for Services to Chmb Mus 1977. Many Pre Pf; over 100 record; Member of Int'l juries; Va master classes. Rectl at 1978 Int'l Va Congress, London.

BACH, JOHANN SEBASTIAN, b 1685 Eisenach, Thuringia, E Ger, d 1750 Leipzig, E Ger. One of the greatest composers of all time, was also a violist. Left a legacy of compositions that constitutes a bulwark for the violist's repertoire. See Chapter VI.

BACHRICH, SIGISMUND, b 1841 Zsambokreth, Hungary; d 1913 Vienna. Stud Vienna Cons 1851–57. Elder Hellmesberger Q c.1865–77, Rosé Q. Pr Va in Vienna Philh and Opera. Prof of Va and Vn Vienna Cons.

BAILLY, LOUIS, b 1882 Valenciennes, Fr; d 1974 Cowansville, Quebec, Can. Va soloist and the most sought after Q violist of the early 20th century. See Chapters XIV and XVI.

BAKALEINIKOV, VLADMIR, b 1885 Moscow, d 1953 Pittsburgh, Pa. USA. Stud Imperial Cons, Michael Press. Grand Duke Mecklenburg-Strelitz Q 1913–20. Prof of Va and Cond Petrograd Cons 1913–20; Moscow Cons 1920–24. As Prof of Va was a pioneer in promoting artistic standards for the instrument; among students was Vadim Borissovsky. Moved to USA 1927. Pr Va and Assoc Cond Cincinnati Symp 1927–37. Cond Pre Pf in USA Milhaud *Viola Concerto*, Op. 108 (Rosen soloist). Tch and Cond summers Nat'l Mus Camp, Interlochen, Mich. Comp numerous works for Va incl *Viola Concerto*. Wrote *Complete Course for Viola*, 1938.

BALLING, MICHAEL, b 1866 in Heidingsfield, Eng., d 1925 Darmstadt, Ger. Early convert to Hermann Ritter *Viola-alta*, played it with great success in Wagner festivals, Bayreuth, later cond there. Promoted *Viola-alta* in England. Cond Hallé Orch, Manchester, Eng 1912–14.

BANDINI, BRUNO, b 1889 Faenza, Italy; d Buenos Aires, Argentina. See Appendix II.

BARSHAI, RUDOLF, b 1924, Labinskaya, Russia. Stud Moscow Cons, Vn Lev Zeitlin, Va Vadim Borissovsky, graduated 1948. Great Soviet violist. Cond Moscow Chamber Orch 1955–; Fac Moscow Cons.

BARRETT, HENRY, b 1923, Birmingham, Ala., d 1978. Stud U of Alabama, B.S. and M.A.; Columbia U.; Aspen, Colo. Prof of Va Alabama U, 1950–. Cadek Q 1950–. Author, *The Viola, Complete Guide for Teachers and Students* (U of Alabama Press, 1972. Revision, 1978).

BAUER, DIETRICH, b 1936, Schneidermühl, Pommern. Stud Musikhochschule, Berlin, Prof Emil Seiler. Rias Youth Orch, Berlin, 1957–61; Teach Mus Kassel, 1963–; Founding mbr VFG; curator VFG Archives in Kassel 1965–76. Ed of: *Viola-Discographie* by Dr. François de Beaumont (Bärenreiter: Kassel, 1973).

deBEAUMONT, FRANÇOIS, b 1932 in Switzerland. M.D. who practices medicine in Switzerland. Not a professional musician but a lover of the viola. Pub very important *Viola-Discographie*, Bärenreiter, 1973; 2nd Ed, self-published for Ypsilanti Int'l Va Congress 1975; *Lionel Tertis (1876–1975) Discographie*, self-pub 1975; *The Viola and Its Interpreters, Discographie 1920–1976*, 3rd Ed 1976, self pub.

BECK, SYDNEY, Va and librarian, b 1906, New York City. Stud Inst of Musical Art (NYC); Mannes Sch; N Y U; Amer Orchestral Society, William Kroll, Joseph Fuchs, Louis Svecenski. Fac Mannes Coll of Mus, 1953–68; New England Cons, 1968–70. Head, Rare Book and Ms Collections. Ed Mus Pub, Mus Div, N Y Public Library, 1931–68; Found, Curator Toscanini Memorial Archives, Lincoln Center, 1963–68. Dir Libraries, New England Cons, 1968–76. Dir Consort Players, 1953–63 which Pf Library of Congress and Command Pf White House, Apr 1963. Tch Samuel Rhodes of Juilliard Q. Numerous pub; scholarly ed of Beethoven's *Notturno*, Op. 42 (1949), Aless. Rolla's *Concerto in E♭ Major*, Op. 3 (1953).

BECKER, IRVING, b 1920 NYC. Stud Juilliard Sch of Mus; Manhattan Sch of Mus, B.M. 1957; Duquesne U, M.M. 1959; Vn Raphael Bronstein, Louis Persinger, Robert Gerle; Va Nathan Gordon. Brilliant career as Vn, solo, orch, chmb mus. Cond of many groups. Prof of Vn-Va, U of Southern Mississippi 1962–68. Pr Va Syracuse Symp 1968–. Cazenovia Coll Q 1968–73, Onondaga Q 1974–.

BELOV, SAMUEL, b 1884 in Yekaterinoslav, Russia; d 1954 in Rochester, New York. See Chapter XVI.

BENDA, FRANZ (1709–1786). Longtime concertmaster to Frederich The Great, stated in his Autobiography that he played the viola c.1720. His equally talented brother, Georg Benda (1722–1795), wrote an important *Concerto in D Major for Va* c.1775.

BENDER, HANS, 1st Vn of the Heidelberg Bach Q, which did important experimentation with instruments made by Eugen Sprenger. See Chapter XII, "Experiments to Improve the Va."

BERMAN, WILLIAM, b 1916 Cleveland, Ohio. Stud with brother, Louis Berman; Juilliard, Harold Berkley; New Sch of Mus, Max Aronoff; privately Lillian Fuchs; Va d'Amore with Karl Stumpf in Vienna. Pr Va Oklahoma City Symp 1941, National Symp, Washington, D.C. 1946, U S Air Force Symp 1948–54. Va Phila Orch summer 1954, NY Philhar 1954–57. Taught New Sch of Mus (asst to Max Aronoff) 1945–46; Prof of Va Oberlin Coll 1957–77; Calif Mus Center, summers 1975, 76. Oberlin Q 1957–77, group toured widely incl Germany. Va New Zealand Symp 1977–. Had end pin removed from 20″ vertical tenor made by Carleen Hutchins; has played it for 5 years "under the chin without chinrest."

BERNARD, ALBERT, b 1903 Colombes (Paris), France. Stud
Paris Cons 1922–25, Va with M. Vieux; first prize 1925. Va in Obern-
dorfer Q 1920. Va in Boston Symph 1925–68. Boston Symph Q 1927.
Played Va d'Amore and Treble Viol in Boston Society of Early Insts
1946–58. Pre Pf Boston: *Allegro Appasionato* by Joseph Jongen, 1925;
Handel (Casadesus) *Va Concerto*, 1929; *Sonata for Va d'Amore and
Organ*, by Frank Martin with Donald Willing, 1963. Tch Va 25 yrs
Boston Cons; New England Cons of Mus 1964–.

BLUM, RICHARD, b 1929 Oak Park, Ill. Stud Chicago Cons.,
Ludwig Becker; Eastman Sch. of Mus. B.M. (viola, pf. cert.), Samuel
Belov. Found Mbr 1951–53 7th Army Symp. Va Rochester Philh 1947–
50, Grant Park Symp, 1954–58; Pr. Va San Antonio Symp 1953–56;
Dallas Symp 1956–57, St. Louis Symphonette 1953–57. Pro Arte Str.
Q, 1957–, Prof. Va. U. of Wisc. 1957–. Pre Pf Andrew Imbrie *4th Q.*,
Samuel Adler, *5th Q.*, Hilmar Luckhardt, *4th Q.*, Seymour Stuffrin,
5th Q. 1971 and 1974 Pro Arte Q. So. Am. tours. Many other concerts.
Also str instr and bow repairs.

BODMAN, LYMANN, b 1915 Bement, Ill. Stud Oberlin Cons
Raymond Cerf; Eastman Sch of Mus, Jacques Gordon; New York,
Milton Katims; Colorado Col, Ferenc Molnar. Prof Vn-Va, Mich State
U 1947–. Pr Va Lansing Symp 1947–71. Beaumont Q 1947–73. With
wife Virginia, pianist, Pf Va lit and contemporary works, concerts,
radio, television.

BONAFOUS, JEAN-LOUIS, b 1935 Montpellier, France. Stud
Cons Regional de Montpellier, 1st Prize Vn, Va, solfedge; 1st Medal
clarinet, piano. Prize of Minister of Education National at Cons Nat'l
Superieur de Paris, 1st Prize Va Leon Pascal class, 1st Prize Chmb
Mus Jean Hubeau and Joseph Calvet classes. Pr Va Concerts Colonne.
Va Société des Concerts of Cons 1962, l'Orchestre National de France
1962, l'Opera de Paris, l'Orch de Paris 1975. Q of France 1963–65, Q
of Paris 1965–. Participant in many fest and world tours with French
Orch and ens. Va soloist Patick Marcland's *Triple Concerto for Va,
Flute, Harp, and Orch*, Paris 1978.

BONFIGLIOLI, JOSE, b 1851 Bologna, Italy; d 1916 Buenos
Aires, Argentina. See Appendix II.

BOON, KLAAS, second half 20th century. Pr Va Concertgebouw
Orch of Amsterdam. Teaches Conservatorium at Amsterdam. Still

active (1978) in his sixties, particularly in a Piano Q he founded with his second wife.

BORISOVA, VERA, b 1954 Moscow, USSR. Stud Moscow Cons, Fyodor Druzhinin, Dimitri Shebalin. Pr Va and soloist Moscow Chmbr Orch.

BORISSOVSKY, VADIM, b. 1900 Moscow, d. 1972 Moscow. His great contributions to the Va are partially indicated by the title of his biography: *The Founder of the Soviet Viola School*, pub. 1977. See Chapter XIV.

BRIDGES, ROBERT, b 1957 Milwaukee, Wisc. Stud Gerald Stanick 1972–74, Karen Tuttle, Peobody Insti 1975–79, B.M. 1979. Pr Va Annapolis, Md Symp 1977–. Trans Stravinsky *Suite Italienne.*

BROOS, FRANÇOIS J., b 1903 Brussels. Stud Conservatoire Nationale de Musique de Paris 1919–24, Vincent d'Indy, Maurice Emmanuel, Lucien Capet, Maurice Vieux (1st prize in M. Vieux Va class). Va Theatre de l'Opéra-Concerts Colonne; Orchestre Symphonique de Paris (Pierre Monteux), Concerts Bruno Walter. Krettly Q (Columbia, H.M.V.). Prof Va Conservatoire Royal de Bruxelles 1930–48; La Chapelle Musicale de la Reine Elisabeth and Chmb Mus 1938–44. Str Trio of Brussels; Queen Elisabeth Q; Belgium Ancient Instruments, played Va d'Amore. Played Qs with Queen Elisabeth and Albert Einstein. Pr Va Orch Symphonique de Bruxelles (Desiré Defauw); Radio I.N.R. (Franz André). Moved to Portugal 1948–: Prof of Va Conservatoire National, Lisbon 1978–. Pr Va l'Orchestre National de Lisbonne (Emissora). Pre Pf and dedicated works in Paris: Jean Rivier, *Concertino*, Concerts Pasdeloup (A. Wolff) 1936; Belgium: from Ms of Bibliothèque du Cons de Bruxelles, *Concertos* by Zelter, Stamitz, Hoffmeister; works dedicated to Broos by Martin Lunssens, Francis de Bourguignon, Artur Meulemans (1940–43). Portugal: Pre Pf and dedicated works by: Joly Braga Santos (1960), Fernando Lopes Graca (1963), Raphael Frubeck de Burgos, Claudio Carneyro. Honors incl Order of Couronne (Chevalier). Member of juries in Paris and Belgium.

BRUNI, BARTOLOMEO, b 1751 Coni, Piedmont, Italy, d 1821. Stud with Pugnani. Comp one of the standard pedagogical works for Va "25 *Etudes*," written between 1795 and 1805, which has gone through many editions. Comp 3 *Solo Sonatas for Va*, Op. 29 and numerous duets for Vn and Va. See Chapter IX.

BUEBENDORF, FRANCIS, b 1912 NYC. Stud New York U, A.B. 1933, Philip James; Juilliard Grad Sch 1933–37 Composition; Columbia U, A.M. 1938; D. Ed. 1947. Prof Va Kansas City Cons 1947–49. Prof Va U of Missouri (Kansas City Div) 1949–77. Va Kansas City Philh 1959–60. Much conducting in Kansas City area. Many compositions incl *Three Pieces: Spring, The Shepherdess, Autumn, for Va and Piano* (1947).

BUNDRA, FRANCIS, b 1927 Northampton, Pa. Stud New Sch of Mus, Sascha Jacobinoff, Max Aronoff; Eastman Sch of Mus, Francis Tursi. Va Rochester Philh Orch, Rochester Civic Orch, Eastman-Rochester Orch 1962–72. Eastman String Q 1960–72; Rackham Trio (founding mbr.) 1976–; Interlochen Str Q 1972–74. Fac U of Mich, Nat'l Mus Camp 1964–, Interlochen Arts Acad 1962–64. Concertized No. Amer., Eur., Asia, and Afr. Record Voice of Americas, Nat'l Ed. T.V. Guest artist, clinician chmb mus fests and clinics. Students have won Nat'l and Int'l competitions, others are members of prof. orch in Eur. and No. Amer.

CAMBINI, GIOVANNI, b 1746 Livorno, Italy; d 1825 Bicêtre, near Paris. Stud Vn with Nardini; comp with Padre Martini. Played Va in Q's with Manfredi, Nardini, and Boccherini. Wrote comp for Va incl Q with 2 Va.

CAMPAGNOLI, BARTOLOMEO, 1751–1827. Stud with Nardini. Concertmaster of Gewanhaus Concerts, Leipzig 1797–1818; Taught Vn and Va; wrote *"41 Capricen for Va"*, c. 1800; one of the classic etude collections for advanced Va students.

CARLES, MARC, b 1933 Castres (Tarn), France. Stud Cons National Superieur de Paris with Etienne Ginot. Pr Va French Radio Orch 1957–60; l'Ensemble Ars Nova 1965–68. French Radio & Television Q 1964–75. Prof Paris Cons 1972–. Dir L'École Municipale de Musique de Castres 1976–. Has composed many works, in 2 Va Concertos, the 2nd commissioned by the French gov't.

CASIMIR-NEY, L. E., probably b. before 1830, a man of mystery. Name may have been a nom-de-plume, suggested as really being Urhan, Paganini, or Vieutemps; but none fit dates of his many publications and transcriptions. Significant for Va: *Fantasie sur la Sicilienne de A, Va and Piano*, pub Costallat & Cie, c. 1850; *Trio for Vn, Va, and Cello*, pub Reichault, 1882; trans for Va and Piano of Charles-Valentin Alkan's *Sonate de Concert for Cello and Piano*, Op. 47, pub Costallat

c. 1850; *24 Preludes dans tous les tons for solo Va*, best known and now widely used of his works, certain similarities to Paganini's *24 Etudes for Vn* but not mentioned in Paganini's compositions catalogues.

CASADESUS, HENRI, b 1879 in Paris, d 1947. Stud of Lavignac and Laforge in Paris. One of first to give whole concerts on Va. Capet Q until 1903. Found and dir of Société Nouvelle des Instruments Anciens, in which he played the Va d'Amore. Toured Europe and USA. Composed *Va Concerto in B♭ Major* attributed to G. F. Handel and *Va Concerto in C Minor* attributed to Johann Christian Bach.

CAUSSE, GERARD, b 1948 Toulouse, France. Stud in Toulouse, France, Lucien Maruë; Cons Nat'l Superieur in Paris, Leon Pascal, Joseph Calvet. Pr Va Orch de Chambre 1977–. Nova Q 1969–72, Parrenin Q 1972–. Pre Pf Griffith Rose, *Second Concerto for Viola*; Jean Yves Boneur, *Picie pour Alto Seul*; Gerard Grisey, *Prologue pour Alto et Materiel* Électronique. Toured with Luciano Berio, playing latter's *Chemins II*. Has done much recording of Chmb Mus.

CERNY, LADISLAV, b 1891 Pilsen, Czech; d 1975 Dobris. Stud vn, va Konservatorium, Praha with Ferdinand Lachner. Koniglichen Opera Orch, Laibach (Ljubljana) 1916–20. Prager Q. Hindemith's *Sonata for Solo Viola*, Op. 25, No. 1 dedicated to Cerny. Prof of Va Konservatorium in Ljubljana 1916–20, Cons. of Praha 1921–52, Musikakademie of Praha 1952–75. Owned and played very large G. B Grancino Va.

CHAILLEY, MARIE-THÉRÈSE, b 1921 Paris. Stud vn with father; Conservatoire National Superieur de Musique de Paris, Va with Maurice Vieux 1935, 1st Prize 1936 age 15, also in solfege; Chmb Mus with Joseph Calvet 1936–37, shared 2nd Prz with Pál Lukács (no 1st Prz); Concours Int'l de Geneve 1948. Pr Va of Concerts Pasdeloup 1961–69. Gilbert Brel Q 1936–39; Chailley-Richez Quintet 1941–49; Marie-Thérèse Ibos Piano Trio 1953–; frequently 2nd Va for Quintets with those of Leon Pascal, Loewenguth, Stross of Munich, Haydn of Brussels. Prof of Va, Conservatoire National Superieur de Musique, asst to Leon Pascal 1950–69, substituted for Pascal during illness 1969. Prof Va l'École Normale de Musique, Paris 1969–76; Cons Nat'l de Boulogne 1963–; l'Universite Musicale Int'l de Paris 1973–; La Schola Cantorum 1968–71; Centre Musical Int'l Annecy 1973–. Mbr of Jury of Cons Paris; Concors Int'l Geneve. Mbr of famous musical family: Father, violinist; Mother Celiny Chailley-Richez, artist-pianist; Brother, Jacques Chailley, prominent contemporary composer, wrote 4 Va works for sister. Selected to give first recital by Va in "Salle Cortot" 1938; Va soloist with principal orchs, Paris, Cologne, Lamoureaux, Pasdeloup, Radio France. Recitals Europe, Israel, USA, Mexico, Central Amer, No Africa. Records, Erato, Decca. Many Va works ded by contemp comps. Has written several Va etude bks, pub by Leduc.

CHAVES, ANABELA, b 1952, Lisbon, Portugal. Stud Conservatoire National de Lisbon, Va with François Broos; chmb mus with Sandor Vegh, Rudolf Baumgartner. Pr Va Philh of Lisbon, 1971–73; Gulbenkian Orch 1973–. Lisbon Q 1972–. 1st Prizes: Conservatoire 1969 Va.; "Guilheriona Luggia" 1971 Va; Int'l Compt of Orense, Spain, 1974; Int'l Compt Geneva, 1977, unanimous by jury. Pf Milhaud *Concerto* in Lisbon; Bartók *Concerto* in Lisbon, Seville, Genebra, Basel, Shafausen, Mulhause, and Stuttgart.

CHIOSTRI, LUIGI (1847–94). Eminent Va virtuoso. Famous Florentine Q 1805–c.80.

CLARKE, REBECCA, b 1887, Harrow, England. Va and comp. Stud Royal Academy of Mus, Vn Hans Wessley; Royal Coll of Mus, Comp Sir Charles Sanford; Va Lionel Tertis. Played Chmb Mus with Thibaud, Heifetz, Elman, Rubenstein, Schnabel, Casals, Szigeti, Myra Hess, Hubermann, etc. d'Aranyi Q. Composed *Sonata for Va and Piano* which won second prize, Coolidge Festival, 1919 (1st prize Ernest Bloch's *Suite*); *Two Pieces for Va and Cello*, 1930; *Suite for Va and Clarinet*, the latter one of 3 works to receive recognition ISCM Festival, Berkley, Calif. 1942. Married 1944 James Friskin, composer and pianist on Fac of Juilliard. Walter Leigh, English comp wrote a *Va Sonata* for her. She wrote article on Va in *Cobbett Cyclopedia of Chamber Music* 1929; "The History of the Va In Quartet Writing," *Mus and Letters*, IV, 1.

CLEM, FREDERICK D., b 1932, Ft. Scott, Kans. Stud U of Texas, B.M., 1956; Indiana U M.M., 1960; David Dawson, Nathan Gordon. Pr Va Milwaukee Symp 1963–.

COLETTA, HAROLD, b 1917, New York City. Stud Juilliard Grad Sch of Mus, Joseph Kovarcik, Hans Letz, Lionel Tertis, Raphael Bronstein, D. C. Dounis. Pr Va All-Am. Youth Orch (Stokowski) 1941, Va St. Louis Symp 1941, N. Y. Philh 1942–44, NBC Orch (Toscanini) 1945–54, Symp of the Air 1955, Casals Fest Orch, Puerto Rico, 1958.

Phoenix Q, Amer Str Q 1958. Tch: Master Classes for Professional Violists, Stockholm, Swe., 1967; Cong of Str U of Cincinnati, 1970–72; Assoc Prof Yale U, 1972–76; Tch & Conc Artist, Int'l Str. Conf & Chmb Mus Wkshp, Immaculata Coll, Pa, 1973–; Affiliate Artist Tch, NY St U-Coll, Purchase, NY, 1972–; Tch Midwest Regional Str Wkshp, U of Minnesota, 1974; Tch & Conc Art, Nat'l Str Conf, U of Utah, Salt Lake City, 1975. Conc & Pr Pf: Heifetz-Piatigorsky Concerts Carnegie Hall, NYC, 1964–66; Solo rectl tour London, Amsterdam, Berlin, Vienna, 1967, Zurich, Bern, Basel, 1971; Hoffstetter Conc, Int'l Viola Congress, Eastman Sch of Mus Rochester, NY, 1977; Bartók, Telemann Conc, U of Va 1977; Pre Pf *Ritratti Articamente*, comp for Coletta by Paul Martin Palombo of U of Cincinnati, and Yale U, 1974. Record: 2 Hindemith Sonatas, Beethoven *Eyeglasses Duo*, Pleyel Duets, Mace Records; Franz Berwald *4 Quartets*, Phoenix Q, Golden Crest, NY.

CONSOLINI, ANGELO, 1859–1934. Artist on Va and Va d'amore. Taught at Cons di Bologna. Bolognese Q. Pub many trans for Va, incl Giorgio Consolini's important *Principi fondamentali per lo studio del Violino.*

COOLEY, CARLTON, b 1889, Milford, N.J. Stud Philadelphia Musical Acad, Frederick Hahn; Insti of Musical Art, NYC, Louis Svcensky. Pr Va Cleveland Orch 1920–1937; N B C Symp 1937–54; Phila Orch 1957–1963. Cleveland Str Q, N B C String Q. Compositions: *Concertino for Viola and Chamber Orchestra, Etude Suite for Viola Solo—4 Etudes*, Pub Henri Elkan, Philadelphia.

COPPERWHEAT, WINIFRED, 1905–1977. Stud with Lionel Tertis. Zorian Q. Prof Royal Acad of Mus 1955–? Championed English composers. Pre Pf of Theodore Holland's *Ellingham Marshes* in Promenade Concert at Queen's Hall 1940. Works written for her by Priaulx Rainier, Frank Stiles, and Roy Slack.

COURTE, ROBERT, b 1910 Brussels, Belgium; d 1979 Ann Arbor, Mich. Stud Cons Royal de Bruxelles, Diplome Superieur, Leon van Hout. Pr Va Bruxelles Opéra Orch. Artis Q, Gertler Q. Prof of Va Cons Royale de Bruxelles until 1946. In USA Paganini Q 1946–51. Stanley Q, Prof of Va U of Michigan 1951–76. With pianist wife has given many concerts on Va and Va d'amore in Europe and USA. *Sonata for Viola and Piano*, Ross Lee Finney, dedicated to him and wife. Pre Pf *Concertino d'Été* 1955, Darius Milhaud, commissioned by Chmb Players of Charleston, W. Va. Arr and trans many works for Va incl Mozart 3 *Sonatinas*; G. F. Handel *Sonata*; Telemann *Concerto in G Major* (pub Henri Elkan, Phila, and Music Press, Ann Arbor). Many of his students occupy prominent positions in Symp and Univ. Owned and played many fine insts, incl a Mathias Albani Va made in 17th century.

CROPPER, PAUL, F.R.M.C.M. b Wallasey, Cheshire, England, 1913. Stud Vn with father 1924–30; Alfred Barker 1930–31; Henry Holst 1933–36; Va with Lionel Tertis 1937–38. Va Liverpool Philh Orch 1934; Halle Orch 1935; Pr Va Liverpool Philh Orch 1939–40; (army duty 1940–45) B.B.C. Northern Symp Orch 1947–. Taylor Q 1937–50; Ad Solem Piano Q 1961–76, Manchester U; assists Lindsay Q in quintets & sextets. Prof of Va, Royal Manchester Col of Mus, 1949–62. Mozart *Concertante* 10 times with L'pool Philh and B.B.C.; *Harold in Italy* 3 times with B.B.C., N.S.O.; *Don Quixote* 7 times with such cellists as Gekdron, Tortellier, and Rostropovich. Pre Pf: Humphrey Procter Gress, *Sonata for Va and Piano* 1975; Ernest Bloch, *Suite for Va and Orch* in Liverpool, 1947. Fellow of Royal Manchester Coll of Mus, 1959.

CREITZ, JAMES P. b 1957 Madison, Wisconsin. Stud Wisconsin Coll Cons, U of Victoria, B.C., Can, Gerald Stanick 1972–75; Yale U, Harold Coletta, Broadus Erle 1976–7; Milton Thomas Summers 1973–4; Nordwestdeutsche Musikaakdemie, Accademia Musicale Chigiana, Bruno Giuranna 1977–. Pr Va Victoria, B.C. Can. Symp 1974–75. Several appearances with orchs incl Milwaukee Symp Orch. Rogeri Trio. 1st prize Milwaukee Symp Orch Young Artists Compt 1974. Semifinalist William Primrose Va Compt 1979. Pre Pf *Poeme for Viola and Orch* by Bruce Campbell. Owns 2 fine Va: Rogeri-Pasta, c. 1690, and Grancino, c. 1700.

CROUSE, WAYNE TURNER, b 1924 Hampton, Va. Stud Juilliard Sch of Mus, Galamian, DeLay, Katims; at Aspen with Primrose. Pr Va Houston Symp 1965–. Lyric Art Q 1965–74, Shepherd Q 1974–. Fac of Rice U 1974–. Perf William Walton *Viola Concerto* (composer cond) Houston Symp, 1969; *Harold in Italy*, Sir John Barbirolli's 70th Birthday Concert, Houston Symp, 1969.

DALI, EDUARDO R., b 1919 Buenos Aires, Argentina. Stud Bueno Aires, Bruno Bandini. Amateur Va and chmb mus. Friend and correspondent for 37 yrs with Lionel Tertis. Author of several books, incl biographical dictionaries, and a comprehensive work on the Va (in preparation). Collaborated with M. Rene Vannes for *Dictionnaire Universel des Luthiers*, 1950. Contributed material on Argentina Va, luthiers, and composers in Appendix II of this book. Argentine comp Felix Ramos Canoura ded *Four Caprices for Va and Piano,* 1971. Plays Va made for him by H. Pinairo (copy of J.B. Guadagnini ex-Leyds); previously had several Va made by E. Petraglia, one a "Tertis model," now used Zagreb Soloists Chmb Orch.

DALTON, DAVID, b 1934, Springville, Utah. Stud Vn Harold Wolf; Eastman Sch of Mus, B.M. 1959; M.M. 1961, Vn Millard Taylor, Va Francis Tursi; Indiana U, D.M.A. 1970, Wm. Primrose. Akademie fuer Musik, Vienna, 1957, Hochschule fuer Musik, München, 1961. Va Utah Symp 1953; Rochester Phil 1957–61; Pr Va Mobile, Alabama Symp 1966. U of So. Alabama Q 1966; Deseret Q Brigham Young U 1970–. Instr Mus Southwestern Col, Winfield, Kan.; Prof of Va, Cond Orchs & Opera Thea Brigham Young U, 1963–66, 1970–. Concertized in Eur 1957, 1967. Pre Pf Marais, *Suite in D for Viola and Continuo* (trans. by D.D., C.F. Peters); Eschig, *Spanish Songs for Viola and Piano* (trans. by D.D., AMP). Articles in *Music & Letters, The Music Review, The Instrumentalist, American String Teacher, Orchestra News,* and others. Collaborator with William Primrose in prep and pub of *Primrose Memoires, Walk on the North Side,* BYU Press; with Dr. Primrose in prep and pub of book on pedogogy of the viola (in preparation). Host Chm Wm Primrose Int'l Va Compt 1979, Snowbird, Utah; also of 7th Int'l Va Congress, Provo, Utah, 1979, Pf with wife, Donna Dalton, works for Va and Soprano, incl Pre Pf of *Reflections on a Hymn,* by Robert Manookin (b. 1918). Morman missionary to Germany 1954–6.

DANKS, HARRY, b 1912 Pensnet, England, into a musical family. Stud Vn, Paul Beard and played in silent film and variety theaters; Birmingham Symp 1935. Stud Va, Lionel Tertis 1935–?. Va BBC Symp of London 1937–46, Pr Va 1946–. Concerts and solos throughout England and Europe. Prof Va Guildhall Sch of Mus 1978–. Dir of Va section of BBC in concerts commemorating Lionel Tertis 1972, 77, 78. Dir and Pf on treble viol London Consort of Viols, and recorded works with Westminister Abbey Choir, 1950–65; believes all violists should study and play Va d'amore. Pf Vivaldi *Concertos* for Va d'Amore in Westminister Abbey. 30 years of research culminated in book, *The Viola d'Amore,* 1975; second enlarged ed., 1979.

DANN, STEVEN, b 1953, Burnaby, B.C., Can. Stud U of Toronto, Lorand Fenyres; Accademia Chigiana, Siena, Italy, Bruno Giuranna; Sydney, Australia, Robert Pikler. Pr Va National Arts Centre Orch., Ottawa, Can. 1977–.

DAVIS, LEONARD, b 1919 Willimantic, Conn. Stud Juilliard Grad Sch, four year fellowship in Va. Asst Pr Va New York Philh 1950–; N Y Philh Chmb Ensmb 1952–60. Metropolitan Str Q, Codiglino Str Q. Fac Brooklyn Coll, C.U.N.Y.; visiting Prof and Master Classes Indiana U 1976–. Record Int'l, World-Wide, incl J. S. Bach 6 *Solo Suites* (1978).

DAWSON, DAVID, b 1913, New Rochelle, N Y; d 1975, Bloomington, Ind. Stud Juilliard Sch of Mus, Hans Letz 1935. Va Metropolitan Opera Orch, Minneapolis Symp, N B C Symp 1948–49. Coolidge Q 1940–43, Gordon Q 1946–47, Berkshire Q 1949–75. Prof Va Indiana U 1949–75. Concertized as Duo with wife Zhanna Arshanskaja, piano, also Frederick Baldwin, piano. Many important concerts and recordings with Berkshire Q. Many of his students hold important positions in Symp, Chmb Mus groups, and as teachers.

DEBUYSÈRE. Stud with Molique. Va of Stuttgart Q found by Edmund Singer in 1861.

DIAZ, MANUEL, b 1933, Madrid, Spain. Stud Excuela Moderna de Musica de Chile, Zoltan Fischer; Conservatorio Nacionale de Musica de Chile, Enrique Iniesta; Indiana U, David Dawson, William Primrose. Fulbright Scholarship, 1966. Ass't Pr Va Chilean Symp; Pr Va Chilean Chmb Orch; Va Atlanta, (Ga. USA) Symp; Chilean Q. Tch Chilean U, Catholic U of USA, Georgia Academy of Mus. 1st Pf in Santiago, Chile of Va Concertos by Walton, Hindemith, Bartók, Berlioz. Works dedicated to and/or premiered: Roque Cordero (Panama), *Tres Mensajes Breves;* Carlos Botto (Chile), *Fantasia;* Juan Orrego Salas (Chile), *Mobili;* Camargo Guarnieri (Brazil) *Sonata for Viola and Piano.*

DOKTOR, KARL, b 1885 in Vienna; d 1949 in NYC. Stud Vn Vienna Conservatory, Diploma 1903. Pr Va Vienna Symp (Ferdinand Lowe, cond) at age of 18, and Va Konzertvereinsquartette; Friend Adolf Busch became concertmaster of same orch and Q 1912; both groups disbanded during WWI. Pr Va of Military Symp 4 yrs during WWI. Found mbr Busch Q 1919 (A. Busch, Andreasson, Vns; Paul Gümmer, Cello—later H. Busch). Busch Q became one of leading ensembles of Europe, performing standard and contemporary works. Busch Q came to USA in 1940, could not return to Europe because of WWII. When A. Busch became too ill to continue, Q disbanded and other 3 mbrs joined Pittsburgh Symp as section leaders (under Reiner). Doktor formed Vienna Trio (Doktor, Vn; Hermann Busch,

Cello; Friedrich Wührer, Piano); Trio flourished from early 1920s until 1933. Pre Va Sonatas written for him by Egon Kornauth and Günther Raphael; and *Solo Viola Suite* by Adolph Busch (in memory of Max Reger). Taught Vn and Va in Vienna, Pittsburgh, Philadelphia Musical Acad. Had a mechanical aptitude, with several important inventions to his credit. Played Bros-Amati Va (now in possession of son Paul); Paganini Stradivari Va (now in Washington, D.C.) and beautiful Amati Va (loaned by his friend, the one-armed pianist, Paul Wittgenstein). Married singer-pianist Georgine Engelman.

DOKTOR, PAUL, b. 1919 Vienna, Austria. Stud with father, Karl Doktor; State Acad of Mus Vienna, Diploma Vn 1938. Vn and Va in Adolf Busch Chmb Orch 1936–38. 2nd Va Busch Q for Quintets (plan to record all 2-Va Quintets abandoned at outbreak of W W II). Va Toscanini's Lucerne Fest Orch 1939. Pr Va Lucerne Symp 1939–47; Paul Sacher's Collegium Musicum, Zurich 1940–47. 1st Prize Geneva Int'l Va Compt (Unanimous decision) 1942. Moved to USA 1947. Va N Y Philh 1948; Stanley Q (found mbr) 1948–51. Prof of Va U of Michigan 1948–51, Mannes Coll of Mus 1952–,Music Division N.Y.U. 1960–, Fairleigh Dickinson U 1968–, Juilliard 1977–. Guest Prof Salzburg Mozarteum, numerous Universities in USA, England, Ecuador, Korea, where he gave master classes, clinics, and lectures. Found mbr The Rococo Ensemble; New York String Sextet; Mannes Trio; New String Trio of NYC; Duo Doktor-Menuhin (Va-piano, Yalta Menuhin, pianist) 1955–63. Many solo perf with orch, and recitals with piano in USA, So America, England, Europe, Orient. World Premier; Quincy Porter, *Va Concerto* Columbia U (American Mus Fest) 1948; BBC Pre Wilfred Joseph *Va Concertante* (Meditato di Beornmundo). Pre record Walter Piston *Va Concerto* Louisville Symp. Many other important record for Telefunken, Westminister, Odessy, ABC Records, Mirrosonic, Basf, CBS Columbia. Ed and trans many works for Va pub by G. Schirmer, IMC, Doblinger, A. Broude, Worldwide, Oxford U Press. Solo recitals at Int'l Va Congress, 1977, 1978. Rec'd ASTA Artist-teacher of the Year Award 1977.

DOLEJSI, ROBERT. Stud with Otakár Ševčik Vienna 1910–14. Published important work: *Modern Viola Technique*, Chicago: Chicago Univ Press, 1939 (also contains section on Va d'amore); Preface states material is based on the Sevcík method.

DROBISCH, ALEXANDER, 1818–1879. "An excellent musician, a cellist who played the Va equally well. Rubinstein dedicated his

Sonata for Viola and Piano, Op. 49 to him 1855 (pub. 1857)." Taken from preface to Russian edition (1960) of *Sonata*.

DRÜNER, ULRICH, b 1943 Thann, France. Stud Strasbourg Cons, E. Kurz 1962–65; Freiburg Musikhochschule, Ulrich Koch 1965–69. Musicology, Institutade Musicologie de l'Universite, Strasbourg, Marc Honegger 1964–65; Musikwissenschaftliches Seminar de Universität, H. H. Eggebrecht 1965–67. Va Stuttgarter Kammerorchester 1969–75; Württembergisches Staatsorchester Stuttgart 1975–. Ed numerous works for Va incl N. Paganini *Grand Sonata*. A leading scholar of Va. Private library of over 3,500 works for Va: c.1300 are printed or MS of 18th and 19th century; remainder are photocopies, microfilm, and printed copies of 20th century works. Now preparing *Das Studium der Viola*, 100 original Viola Etudes of the 19th century in progression from beginning student through concert artist; *Bibliographisches Quellenlexikon der Viola-Literatur* (c.1980). Author of articles on Va in *Dictionnaire de la Musique: Science de la Musique*, Paris, 1976.

DRUZHININ, FYODOR, b 1932 Moscow. Stud Moscow Cons, Va with Borissovsky. When Borissovsky retired, replaced him as Prof of Va, and as Va in Moscow Beethoven Q. Shostakovich's last comp *Sonata for Va and Piano*, Op. 147, is ded to him.

DUNHAM, JAMES F., b. 1950, Washington, D.C. Stud Calif Inst of the Arts, Va David Schwartz, B.F.A. and M.F.A.; Carleton College, Harry Nordstrom; Interlochen Arts Acad, Raymond Stilwell. Va Sequoia Q (found mbr), 1972–; Prof of Chmb Mus, Calif Inst of the Arts, 1972–; Pr Va Calif Chmb Symph, 1972–; Va Los Angeles Chamb Orch, 1973–. Many Pre Pf of works for Q by Sequoia Q; also festival participation. Resident Artist Chestnut Hill Concerts, Madison, Conn., 1972–.

DÚS, RYSZARD, b. 1952 Wroclaw, Poland. Stud with Jan Michalski; Wiemar, Pál Lukács; Raphael Hillyer, 1973. 1st Prize in Va Compt Pozan, 1975. Wilanow Q. Concerts England, Europe; most slavic T V and radio, BBC London.

DVOŘÁK, ANTONIN 1841–1904. At age 16 Prague Organ-Sch. Earned living as violinist in small orch. Graduated in 1862. Va 1862–1873 National Theatre Orch. 1873–1904, full time to composition and organ. Va in chmbr mus groups.

EGGHARD, JULIUS, Va younger Hellmesberger Q, found 1887 by two sons from older Q: Joseph H., leader and F.H., cello.

ELDERING, BRAM, (1865–1943), b Groningen, Holland. Stud Brussels Cons Vn, Jeno Hubay; won Gold Medal. Followed Hubay to Budapest to play Va in newly-found Hubay-Popper Q, c.1886. In 1889 went to Berlin to study with Joachim. Found Meiningen Q 1894. Tch Cons Amsterdam and Cons of Cologne.

ERDÉLYI, CSABA. Only Va to win Carl Flesch Compt 1972. Protege of Yehudi Menuhin, with whom he has pf. Soloist with most Eng orch, incl several Promenade concerts in London. Pr Va London Philh Orch. Pre Pf at 1978 Int'l Va Congress, London, *Sonata for Va and Piano* written for him by and accompanied by Melanie Daiken. Master class Va concertos at Scottish Va Int'l, Glasgow, 1979.

ERRINGTON, C. SYDNEY, b 1905 Leeds, Yorkshire, Eng. Stud Lionel Tertis. Va Halle Orch, Manchester 50 years, Pr Va 21 years. Turner Q, Holst Q. Introduced many new Va works in North England incl Bax, Hindemith, etc. Before retirement played Jacob Rayman Va 1650.

EWALD, KONRAD, b 1936 Basle, Switz. Amateur violist, chmb mus enthusiast. Swiss language teacher. Author of *Musik für Bratsche*, Liestal, Switz: Pub by author, 1975. Contains annotations for each composer.

FERIR, EMILE, b 1873 Brussels, Belg. Stud Brussels Cons: Va with Firket, Vn with Ysaÿe. Pr Va Scottish Orch of Glasgow; Queen's Hall Orch, London; Philharmonic, London; Boston Symp; Philadelphia Orch 1918–19. Kruse Q, London; Arbos Q, Hess Schroeder Q, Boston; Rich Q, Philadelphia. Frequently Pf the Cecil Forsyth *Va Concerto*. Appeared with Nellie Melba in recital.

FERRAGUZZI, RENZO, b 1915 New Haven, Conn., USA. Stud: Venice Cons, Diploma 1937, L. Ferro; Chigiana Acad, Siena, It., Va 1941, A. Bonucci; St. Cecilia Acad, Rome, Chmb Mus Diploma 1941, A. Serato. Chmb Orch "A. Scarlatti" Naples 1950; Pameriggi Musicali, Milan 1948–49, 1951–52; Angelicum, Milan 1953; Orch d'Archi, Milan, 1954–55; Solisti Veneti, Padua, 1959–60. Pre many Va solo works by contemp Italian comp. Prof of Q, Milan Cons 1970–.

FERRIN, RICHARD, b Kansas. Stud Vn Heifetz, Shapiro, Ignatius (Finland); Va Samuel Belov, Sanford Schonbach, Wm. Primrose. Sibelius Foundation Scholarship in Finland 1957. U of Washington Research Grant USSR: To stud rationale of Soviet pedagogy of Vn 1962. Pr Va Seattle Symp cond by Milton Katims. Va Chicago Symp 1967–; Chicago Symp Trio; found and 1st Vn Landolfi Q. Visiting Prof Va U of Southern Calif., U of British Columbia, Calif State U at Northridge, U of Wisconsin at Madison, Congress of Strings of AFM. Chmb Mus with many of the world's premier string players. 1st Pf in Chicago Shostakovich *Viola Sonata*, Op. 147, 1978.

FIELD, RICHARD, b 1947 Wilmington, Delaware. Stud Eastman Sch of Mus, B.M. 1969, Francis Tursi; Juilliard Sch of Mus, M.S. 1971, Walter Trampler; privately Ernst Wallfisch, Emanuel Vardi, Abriham Skernick. Assoc Pr Va Denver Symp 1971–74; Pr Va Buffalo Philh 1974–. Pf concertos: Bartók, Eastman 1968; Mozart *Duo Concertante*, Rochester Philh 1972; Bartók 1976; Michashoff 1976; Handel 1977; Walton, Buffalo 1978.

FINGER, ALFRED, Va Winkler Q, Venice early 20th century.

FINE, BURTON, b 1930, Phila., Pa. Stud Curtis Insti 1943–48, Ivan Galamian; U. of Penna. B.A. 1951; Ill. Insti. of Technology, Ph.D. (Chemistry) 1955. Pr Va Boston Symp Orch 1964–; Va Boston Chmb Players 1964–. Fac Berkshire Music Center, New England Conservatory, 1964–. New England Cons Q 1964–68. Also Pf Va d'amore. Pre Pf Boston, Georg Benda *Viola Concerto in F Major*, 1976. Participant 3rd Int'l Va Congress, Ypsilanti, Mich., 1975.

FIORILLO, FEDERICO, b Brunswick, Ger.; d after 1823. Composer, violinist, violist. Va in Salomon's Q in London, c.1790. Appeared as Va soloist playing *Va Concerto*, Hanover Square, London, 1794. Author of celebrated *36 Caprices for Vn.*

FIRKET, LÉON, b 1839. Tch Vn, Va Brussels Cons. Comp and trans works for Va. Leopold Wallner ded *Fantasie de Concert for Va and Orch* 1879. Authored *Méthode Pratique*, Bk I and II 1873; same method published in U.S. as *Firket's Conservatory Method for the Viola* (Boston: Jean White, 1879).

FORBES, WATSON, Va and Cond, b 1909, St. Andrews, Scotland. Stud Royal Academy of Mus, London, 1926–32, Albert Sammons, Otakar Ševčik. Pr Va London Symp Orch 1939–45. Aeolian Str

Q, 1932–64. London Str Trio, 1942–64; London Piano Q 1944–64. Prof of Va and Chmb Mus R.A.M. 1954–64. Many first Pf of Bax, Bliss, McEwen, etc. Chosen by Elgar to record Q and Quint 1932, H.M.V.; Record chmb and Va solos for Decca, World Records, & British Council. Concertized extensively in G.B. and Eur Head of Mus B.B.C. in Scotland 1964–72. Honorary Dir of Mus, Glascow U, 1970. Pub many arr for Va for O.U.P., Peters, Hinrichen, Schott, Chester, etc. Wrote *A History of Music in Scotland*, pub by B.B.C.; also *Catalogue of Chamber Music*.

FROELICH, HERBERT, b 1901 Danzig, Germany. Stud Vn, Heinrich Davidsohn. Pr Va Danzig Opera Orch 1922–24. Pr Vn: Berlin Philh (Furtwängler) 1924–26, Hamburg Philh (Muck) 1926–29, Freiburg Opera 1929–33, Sinfonica of Bogota, Columbia 1936–46. Va Lerner Q 1954–64. Prof of Vn and Va Cons Nat'l de Bogota 1936–46. Prof of Va Mexico Cons of Mus 1946–.

FUCHS, LILLIAN, b 1910, NYC. Stud Insti of Musical Art, NYC, Franz Kneisel, Louis Svecenski. Prof of Va Juilliard Sch of Mus; Manhattan Sch of Mus; Aspen, Colorado. Concertized and recordings with brother, Joseph Fuchs, Vn. 1st to record all 6 Bach *Suites*, Decca label. Martinu, De Menasce, Quincy Porter, Ernest Bloch, and other composers wrote Va works for her. Has composed solos, ensembles, and etudes for Va, incl *15 Characteristic Studies* (Oxford U Press; *16 Fantasy Etudes* (I M C); *12 Caprices* (Boosey & Hawkes); *Sonata Pastorale for Unacc Va* (A M P). She owns and performs on a Gasparo da Salò Va. Has many distinguished Va students. Rec'd A.S.T.A. Artist Teacher Award for 1979.

GAMBUZZI, EDGARDO, Buenos Aires, Argentina. See Appendix II.

GARCIA, GILBERTO. Pr Va Mexico Symp Orch. Va of Mexico Q (1979).

GATES, CECILIA. Stud at R.A.M., London, Vn, Sainton. Va of Shinner Q (founding mbr 1886). Also excellent pf on Vn and cello.

GIBSON, GEORGE, 1849–1924, Va, Vn, and Cond. Stud with father, also Henry Farmer. Vn, Va, Prince of Wales Theatre, Drury Lane, and Covent Garden. Leader of the Queen's Private Band 1893, led this orch at the Coronations of King Edward VII and King George V. Va in Joachim Q. Prof Royal Acad of Mus and Guildhall. Owned and played the famous viola which now bears his name, the "Gibson" Stradivarius 1734.

GILLIS, ALBERT, b NYC. Stud Juilliard, B.M. 1940; Yale U M. M. 1948; Aspen, William Primrose, 1951. Prof Va U of Texas, 1948–58; U of Calif: Santa Barbara 1959–65, San José 1965–69, San Diego 1972– 73, Fresno 1969–. U of Texas Q 1948–58; Paganini Q 1958–66. Pre Paul Pisk's Va trans of Enesco's *3rd Violin-Piano Sonata* (NYC), Bartók's *2nd Violin-Piano Sonata* (St. Louis), *Ballade for 6 Violas* by Pisk (Carnegie Hall) 1957. Ed of "Viola Forum," in *American String Teacher* since 1978. Since 1950 owns and plays J. B. Guadagnini Va, 1774.

GIORGETTI, FERDINANDO (1769–1867). Wrote Va tutor in 3 pts, the 3rd being a "Dramatic Scene," with piano acc.

GINOT, ETIENNE, b 1901, St-Etienne, France. Stud Cons of St-Etienne; Paris Cons, Maurice Vieux. Pr Va Concerts Lamoreau, 1923–40, Opéra Comique, 1925–. Prof of Va Paris Cons 1951–c.1970. Trans more than 20 Vn Concertos for Va as *Classiques de l'Alto* (Jobert), because he believed violists should know the violin repertoire. Wrote several method books for Va.

GIURANNA, BRUNO, b 1933, Milano, It. Stud Cons di St. Cecilia, Rome, Vittorio Emanuele, Mario Corti, Remy Principe. Va I Musica 1954–60, Italian Str Trio (Deutsche Gramaphone) 1963–68. Pre Pf G. F. Ghedini's *Viola Concerto*, Rome, H. von Karajan 1954. Solo pf with London Philh, Concertgebow, Berliner Philh, Südwestfunk, Bayerishe Rundfunk, Academia di St. Cecilia, Teatro alla Scala Orchs. Prof of Va: Cons G. Verdi, Milano 1959–64; Cons St. Cecilia, Rome 1965–; Nordwestdeutsche Musikakademie, Detmold, W. Gr 1968–; Accademia Chigiana, Siena, Italy 1966–. Recorded Mozart *Concertante* with H. Szerying; Vivaldi complete *Viola d'amore Concerti*. Also see Chapter XIV.

GLICK, JACOB, b 1926 Philadelphia. Stud New Sch of Mus, Philadelphia, Max Aranoff; Yale Summer School; Kneisel Hall, Maine, Lillian Fuchs; NYC, Valentin Blumberg. Over 200 first performances as soloist and ensemble of new works. Many new works with tape. Specializes in contemporary works.

GLINKA, MICHAIL, 1804–1857. One of the founders of the Russian School of composition, played both Va and piano. Wrote an unfinished *Sonata in D Minor for Va and Piano* between 1825 and 1828, which is available in modern edition.

GLYDE, ROSEMARY, b 1948 Auburn, Alabama. Manhattan Sch of Mus B.M. 1971, Juilliard Sch of Mus M.M. 1973, D.M.A. 1975, Lillian Fuchs, Gustave Reese, dissertation *"The Concerto pour l'Alto Principale" of Johann Andreas Amon, c. 1800.* Soloist and Chmb Va. Manhattan Str Q 1976–. Fac Manhattan Sch of Mus 1974–. 1st Prize, Juilliard Va Comp 1974; Aspen Va Compt 1974.

GOHRING, L. Va of Dresden Q, one of outstanding Q of late 19th century. Also artist on Va d'amore.

GOLAN, RON, b 1924, Gladbach, W. Germany. Stud Düsseldorf Acad of Mus 1934–38 Julian Gumpert; Jerusalem Acad of Mus 1939–41 Emil Hauser, Hanoch Jacoby; Thos. Matthews 1942; Oedoen Partos 1945–50; Wm. Primrose 1951. Pr Va Middle East Int'l Symp (Cairo) 1943–45; Tel-Aviv: Israel Chmb Players 1945–47, Israel Philh Orch 1948–52; Orchestre de la Suisse Romande 1952–78; Instrumentarium Ensemble 1974–. Fac Cons of Mus Geneva 1953–. Mbr Jury Int'l Mus Compt, Geneva 1953–. Hindemith helped launch career as solo violist in 1957–8 by endorsing Golan's interpretations of Hindemith viola works. Pre Pf B. Martinú *Rhapsody Concerto* in many European capitals; F. Martin's *Ballade.* Int'l soloist, master classes.

GOLANI-ERDESZ, RIVKA, b 1946 Tel-Aviv, Israel. Stud Israel Acad of Mus, and Tel Aviv Univ., Oedoen Partos. Va, Tel-Aviv Chmb Orch, 1968; Israeli Philh 1969–74; Recitalist and chmb perf for C.B.C. Radio, Canada, 1975; Prof of Va U of Toronto, Canada, 1978–. Pre Pf of works written for her: *Va Concerto* by Andrea Spirea (Zubin Meta Cond) Israeli Philh, 1978; Howard Gerhard ded *Viola Sonata;* in preparation: *Viola Concerto* by Ezekiel Braun and Morriss Surdin—Pre Pf in 1979. World Pre Pf and record 1979 of *Trio for Va, Harp and Flute,* Oedoen Partos, his last comp (d 1977).

GOLDBERG, LOUISE, b 1937 Chicago. Stud Smith Coll B.A., Louise Rood; U of Chicago, M.A., George Perlman; Eastman Sch of Mus, Ph.D., Francis Tursi; privately with Wm. Primrose. Tch New Trier Twp High Sch, 1961–67; Hobart & William Smith Col 1972–74; Librarian Reference & Rare Books, Sibley Mus Library, Eastman Sch of Mus, 1974–. Research and Ed mus for Va and Va d'amore. Vice-President Va Research Society 1976–78.

GOLDSMITH, PAMELA BRAND, b 1941, Houston, Texas. Stud UCLA; Mannes Coll of Mus; George Peabody Coll, B.M., 1965, M.M., 1966; Stanford Univ, D.M.A., 1969. Privately, Sanford Schonbach, Paul Doktor, William Kroll, and William Primrose. Pr Va of Nashville Symp, 1963–65; Carmel Bach Festival, 1967–70; San Jose Symph, 1967–71; Hollywood Chamb Orch, 1975–78; Va in Casals Festival Orch, 1976–78. Camerata Q, Nashville Q, Sartori Q, Goldsmith Q. Pre Pf of Lee Holdridge *Va Concerto,* 1977; Michael Isaacson *Two's Company but Three's a Trio, for Va, Oboe, and Harpischord,* 1978; Donal Michelsky *Duo for Vn and Va,* 1974; Daniel Kessner *Trio for Va, Bass Flute and Percuss,* 1976; *Pastorale for Solo Va,* 1977. Lecturer Va and Chmb Mus: Stanford U 1970–72; Calif State U Fullerton, 1972–74; Calif State U Los Angeles 1974–78. Also plays Va d'amore. Recorded Roy Harris *Soliloquy and Dance,* Orion Records.

GORDON, NATHAN, b NYC. Stud Vn Herman Rosen; Cleveland Inst of Mus, Charlotte DeMuth Williams, Andre de Ribaupierre; Juilliard Grad Sch of Mus, (double scholarship Vn Va) Hans Letz; privately with Wm Primrose. Va Metropolitan Opera Orch; First Desk Va N.B.C. Symp, Pr Va Chautauqua Symp, Pittsburgh Symp, Detroit Symp, present. NBC Q, Mischakoff Q, Kroll Q, Guest Budapest Q. Prof of Va Dalcroze Sch, NYC; Chatham Coll; Duquesne U; Carnegie Insti; Indiana U; U of Mich; Interlochen Arts Academy and Music Camp; Oakland U. Pre Pf Hindemith's *Trauermusik* NYC; Alan Shulman's *Theme and Variations;* Clark Eastham's *Concerto,* Int'l Congress, Ypsilanti, Mich., 1975. Int'l soloist. Many Master classes. Cond, Detroit Women's Symp; Dearborn Orch; Duquesne U; Carnegie Insti.

GRIFFIN, JUDSON, b 1951, Lewes, Delaware. Stud Mischakoff; Eastman Sch of Mus, B.M., Francis Tursi; Juilliard Sch of Mus, M.M., D.M.A., Lillian Fuchs. Va Rochester, N. Y. Philh 1970–3; Pr Va Aspen Chmb Symp 1977– Ass't Prof Mus, U of N. Carolina 1977–79. Fac Aspen Mus Sch 1979–. Record Nonesuch, Columbia. Dissertation: *A Guide to American Va Mus.* Presently researching for book on American Va Mus. Winner Juilliard Va Compt 1976; Aspen Va Compt 1977.

HARSHMAN, ALLAN, b 1920, Los Angeles. Stud with father, Mischa Gluschkin, Julian Brodetsky. Brodetsky Q; Los Angeles Q (sponsored by Elizabeth Sprague Coolidge). Va, Los Angeles Chmbr Orch; "Big Bands" of Artie Shaw and Tommy Dorsey; Heifetz-Piatigorsky concerts, Los Angeles, San Francisco: incl L. Spohr

"Double" *Q in D Minor,* Op. 65; frequently in informal Q sessions at homes of Heifetz and Piatigorsky. Pre Pf and rec Dorothy Chandler *Palivior Q* for RCA, 1968. Now free-lance Va, motion picture, recording, and TV.

HEISSLER, C. Joined elder Hellmesberger Q as Va in 1849.

HERMANN, FRIEDRICH, 1828–1907. Eminent soloist and teacher. Pr Va Gewandhaus Orch. Tch Cons of Lipsia. Arr and trans for Va numerous comp. One of the most prolific of all editors and transcribers of music for Va.

HERSH, PAUL. Stud Va with WM. Primrose. Va Lenox Q (c. 1965–71); also excellent pianist.

HILL, HENRY (1808–46), English Va, son of Henry Lockey Hill, member of family which, at least since 1740, sold and produced str instr in famous London store, now known as "William E. Hill & Sons." London Pre Pf *Harold en Italie,* 1848, Berlioz, cond.

HILLYER, RAPHAEL, b 1914 Ithaca, N.Y. Stud Moscow Cons, Leningrad Cons, Vn Serge Korgueff, theory Dmitri Shostakovich; Curtis Insti of Mus 1930–32; Dartmouth U 1932–36 B.A.; Harvard U 1936–38 M.A., theory Walter Piston. Va Boston Symp 1942–46 (Koussevitsky), NBC Symp 1950–51 (Toscanini). Stradivari Q 1942–45; Juilliard Q 1946–69 (found mbr). Pre Pf of Camargo-Guarneri *Va Concerto* (dedicated to Hillyer). Prof of Va and Chmb Mus Longy Sch of Mus 1938–41; Juilliard Sch of Mus 1946–69; Temple U 1967–71; Yale Sch of Mus Grad Sch 1974–. Distinguished Fulbright Prof in Brazil (1974) taught and Pf at Us of: Sao Paolo, Brasilia, Bahia, and Cons of Music of Rio de Janeiro. Taught in Japan, Korea, Taiwan, Indonesia, Singapore, Dartington Hall, England, Aspen. First American to teach in Ger Democratic Republic at Franz Liszt Hochschule für Musik. Has coached many young Qs that have gained prominence incl: Tokyo Q; Panocha Q of Prague; Eder Q of Budapest; Varsovia Q of Warsaw; Kreutzberger Q of West Berlin. Recording of many major works with Juilliard Q; Va solo recordings of Bartok *Va Concerto* and Hindemith *Der Schwanendreher* with Japan Philh (Watanabe). Member of juries of Int'l Compt for Va Budapest 1976; also Int'l Compt for Qs Munich 1977. Pf 7th Int'l Va Cong Provo, Utah 1979 incl Prem U S Pf *Sonata for Va Alone* (1961) by Fyodor Druzhinin.

HINDEMITH, PAUL, b 1895 Hanau, Gr, d. 1963. Frankfurt, Gr. Composer, conductor, author. Played several instruments quite well, incl the Va, on which he was a virtuoso. Wrote over 20 significant works for the Va. See Chapter XIV.

HOBDAY, ALFRED, b 1870 Faversham, Eng.; d 1942 Tarkerton, Kent, Eng. Stud at R. A. M., London. By 1900 considered one finest Eng. Va. Pr Va of Philh, London Symp, and Covent Garden. Equally famous as ensmb player. Owned and played the ex-Villa J.B. Guadagnini viola, made in Turin, 1781.

HOFFMAN, TOBY ALEXANDER, b 1958 Vancouver, B. C., Canada. Stud Esther Glazer (mother) 1964–76, Paul Doktor, Juilliard Sch 1976–79. Pr Va Juilliard Orch 1976–9. Hoffman Str Q 1975–, Hoffman Family Players 1975–. Winner of first William Kapell Memorial Award. Appearances as soloist incl N Y Youth Symp and Florida Gulf Coast Symp. From a musical family. Semi-finalist William Primrose Va Compt 1979.

HOFFSTETTER, ROMAN, 1742–1815. Benedictine monk, also a composer and virtuoso violist. Friend of Joseph Haydn. Recent research has prompted several musicologists to reassign the Haydn, Op. 3 *Quartets* to Hoffstetter. Composed 3 *Va Concertos* (E♭, C, and G). The E♭ and C are available in modern editions. Also wrote *Concertante for Va and Cello.*

HORNER, JERRY, b 1935 in Los Angeles. Stud Indiana U with David Dawson, Wm. Primrose. Va in Qs: New Arte 1952–63, Toledo 1964–7, Claremont 1969–71, Berkshire 1975–76. Va Houston Symp; Pr Va: Dallas Symp 1968–69, Piedmont Chamb Orch 1969–73, Pittsburgh Symp 1973–75. Teach Va: U Toledo 1964–67; North Carolina School of the Arts 1969–73; U of Pittsburgh 1973–75; Assoc. Prof. Indiana U 1975–. Soloist in more than 30 concerts with leading orchs including Houston, Dallas, Piedmont Chmb, Pittsburgh; and Va experience with most of the outstanding conductors worldwide. Has cond many workshops lectures, and seminars on Va. Has many outstanding students now in symp orch and teaching in colls and U.

HUMPHREY, GEORGE, b 1904 Bellaire Ohio. Began stud of Vn at age of 21, self-taught; New England Cons grad 1929 1st Va ever; Curtis Insti 1930–31. Va Minneapolis Symp 1929–30; Gaylord Yost Q, Pittsburgh 1931–32; Zimbler Str Q 1932–35; Boston Symp Orch 1934– (Special place made for him by Koussevitzky); Tanglewood Str Q

1939–; Research team at M.I.T. (brain research through music) 1961–66. Pre Pf *Flos Campi*, V. Williams; *Trauermusik*, Hindemith; *Piano Q*, Piston; *2nd Str Q*, Randall Thompson; World Pre Pf *Three Counterpoints*, Walter Piston, written for Humphrey. Exchange Va with Japan Philh, 1967–68, where he Pf *Romantic Phantasy for Vn and Va with Orch*, with Ronald Knudsen, Vn (Watanabe cond).

HYBER, KARL (late 18th Century), mentioned by Hanslick as a fine violist who lived and performed in Vienna. Cf Edward Hanslick, *Gesichte des Konzertwessens in Wien* (1869).

ILMER, IRVING, Vn in Indianapolis and Chicago Symph. Concertmaster of San Antonio Symph. Va in Fine Arts Q until 1967. Played Gasparo da Salò Va formerly owned by Germain Prevost of the Belgian Pro Arte Q. Prof of Va at U. of Wisc., Milwaukee, until 1967.

IKEDA, EIJI, b 1948 Japan. Stud Anna Ono; Musashino Mus Academy, Tokyo, Toshiya Eto; Northern Ill U., Shmuel Ashkenasi, Nobuko Imai. Assoc Pr Va Florida Symp 1973–74. Pr Va Indianapolis Symp 1974–. Pf *Flos Campi*, Ralph Vaughn Williams, Indianapolis Symp 1977.

JACOBACCI, CHEVALIER. Va of Roman Q, which in 1893 was appointed as official Q of Queen Margharite.

JACOBS, ALBRECHT, b 1912 Kassel, W. Ger. Pr Va Stadtischen Orch, Berlin 1936–44. Founder, mbr Spohr Q of Kassel 1948–. Prof Va, Vn, Chmb Mus, Kassel Musikakademie 1948–75. Va soloist Rundfunk San Luis. Pre Pf Richard Gress, *Sonata for Va*.

JACOBY, HANOCH (20th century). Va Israel Philh Orch many years. Taught Va in Jerusalem Academy: students incl Ron Golan, Daniel Benjamin, and others.

JAKOWSKI, JAN. Stud Vn Warsaw Cons with Gorski until 1885, then with S. Barzewicz until 1888. Va in Warsaw Q under Barzewicz from 1888–?

JAMES, MARY ELLIOTT, b 1927 Long Beach, Calif. Stud San Francisco Cons of Mus, B.M. 1956; U So. Calif, William Primrose, Philip Burton, Sanford Schonbach, Milton Thomas; Lionel Tertis; State Acad of Mus, Vienna, Austria, Ernest Morawec; Pittsburg State U, Kansas, M.M. 1975. Fac Va, San Francisco Cons of Mus; Ass't Prof,

Pittsburg State U, Kansas 1968–. Va Vienna Bach Gemeinde, Konzert-haus Kammerorchester, San Francisco Symp and Opera, Los Angeles Philh, Columbia Record Orch, Aspen Fest Chmb Orch, Pittsburg State U Q 1968–, Chmb Mus Conf and Composer's Forum, Benning-ton, Vermont 1975–. Owns and plays Antonio Mariani Va 1666.

JAMIESON, NANNIE, b 1914 Edinburgh, Scotland. Hochschule für Musik, Berlin with Joseph Wolfstahl, Carl Flesch; London Max Rostal. Dartington Hall Chmbr Mus Group 1939–, Robert Masters Piano Q (Robert Masters Vn, Nannie Jamison Va, Muriel Taylor Cello, Kinloch Anderson Piano)—1963. Va Menuhin Festival Orch 1963–. Prof Va Guildhall Sch of Mus, Guest Prof of Va Switzerland, Cam-bridge, and Banff, Canada. Va tch of many artists. Secretary of British Str Teachers Assoc. Co-host and co-chairman of Sixth Int'l Va Con-gress, London, 1978.

Di JANNI, JOHN A., b 1909 NYC. Stud Albino (Pr Va Metropoli-tan Opera), Dounis, Ariam Ariani, Louis Bailly, Wm. Primrose. Va 1931–36, Pr Va 1936–75 Metropolitan Opera Orch (shared 1st chair with father for 9 years); Santa Fe Opera Orch 1960–63; Santa Fe Symp 1976–. LaSalle Q (coached by Flonzaley Q), Santa Fe Symp Q 1976–. Soloist: Saidenberg Symphonette, R.C.A. Recording Symp, Koste-lanetz Orch. Assoc Cond Jersey State Opera. Personnel Manager Metropolitan Opera Orch 1969–75. Tch "Congress of Strings" 1965–69.

JANZER, GEORGES, b 1914 Budapest, Hungary. Stud Franz Liszt Musicakademie, Budapest; Cons de Music, Geneva, Switz; Privately with Oscar Studer. Concertmaster Budapest Symp 1941–46. Vegh Q, 1940–77; Grumiaux Trio 1961–. Prof of Va Musikhochschule, Hannover, W. Ger 1960–63; Robert Schuman Acad, Düsseldorf, W. Ger 1963–; Indiana U 1972–; Aspen 1976–. Many recordings with Q and Trio: Grand Prix's for Mozart, *Clarinet Quintet;* 6 Bartók-Q; Mozart *Divertimento.* "Best Chambermusic Recording of the Year" in USA—Beethoven *Str Trios,* 1971–72.

JEANNERET, MARC, b 1938, Valence, France. Stud Nat'l Con-servatoire de Musique de Paris, Va with Leon Pascal, Pierre Pasquier, Andre le Metayer, 1st Prz at Cons 1961; Indiana U with Wm. Prim-rose, Performer's Certificate 1971. Won "Medaille avec Distinction," Geneva Int'l Compt 1962 and as result played Bartók *Concerto* with Suisse Romande Orch. Va Theatre Nationale de l'Opéra Orch, Paris. Pr Va Collegium Musicum Chambre Orch, 1968–70; Indianapolis

Symp 1970–71; Baltimore Symp 1971–72; Asst Pr Va Pittsburgh, 1973–75; French Nat'l Orch of Paris 1976–77; Va Boston Symp 1977–.

JOHNSON, MAXINE-KAREN, b 1919, Tacoma, Wash. Stud Arthur Palman, Francis Armstrong, D.C. Dounis, J. Albert Fract. Pr Va Tacoma, Wash., Philh and Opera Orch; Charleston, S.C. Symp; Saidenberg Symp; Columbia Recording Symp; Metropolis, Conducting, Compt Orch, NYC; American Symp Orch (Stokowsky), "Mass" Orch (Bernstein); Honolulu Symp Orch 1972–77. Amati Str Q (founder- Va) 1955–65. Artist Fac UCLA. Founder: "Music for Young Listeners." Numerous recordings with Contemporary, Columbia, Everest, Capitol, Esoteric, and motion pictures. Pre Pf Lazarof, *Tempi Concertati;* Menotti, *Triple Concerto;* Van de Vate, *Trio for Va, Piano, and Percussion;* Kashanski, *A Passionate Lament and Exultation* for Va, Str, and Percussion; M-K Johnson, *Music-Color Meditation Improvisation in Concert Form.* Founder: New Musical Purposes Foundation 1971 NYC, incorporated Hawaii, 1974 for Music-Color Therapy, for use in institutions, hospitals, schools, and private therapy healing—an additional area of professional work for musicians; concerts USA, Canada, England.

JONES, ROBERT W., b 1935, Shadyside, Ohio. Stud Cleveland Inst of Mus, Vn with G. Ciompi, Ma Si Hon, W. K. Kellerher, G. Poinar; Va with Abraham Skernik. Pr Va 7th Army Symp 1960–62. Va Houston Symp 1962–63, Cincinnati Symp 1963–68. Pr va Atlanta Symp 1968–.

KAMASA, STEFAN, b 1930 Bielsk, Podlaski, Poland. Stud State Mus Acad in Poznan, Jan Rakowski, 1953; Warsaw Mus Acad, Tadeusz Wronski; Paris Cons, Pierre Pasquier. Debut with Poznan Philh 1950. 1st Prize Va Compt Warsaw, 1957. Winner of "Prize of Critics Orpheus," Warsaw, 1970. Warsaw Q. Prof of Va State Mus Acad in Warsaw 1958–. In 1970, 71, 73, and 76 member of Jury of Int'l Mus Compt in Munich. Many solo Va record on Muza, Electrola label. Many arr and editions: pub by Polish Music of Cracow, Poland.

KAMNITZER, PETER, b 1922 Berlin, Ger. Stud Juilliard with Milton Katims, Ivan Galamian. Pr Va San Antonio Symp and Str Q 1944–47. LaSalle Q, U of Cincinnati 1949–. Fac Colorado Coll 1949–53; U of Cincinnati 1953–.

KARGES, FRANZ. Stud Cologne Cons. Va of Robert Heckman Q found 1872.

KATIMS, MILTON, b New York City, 1910. Stud Columbia U, Vn Herbert Dittler, B.A. 1932. Switch to Va guided by Leon Barzin. Pr Va and Ass't Cond Mutual Broadcasting Co. 1935–. 2nd Va with Budapest Q for Quintets by Mozart, Beethoven, Dvorak, etc. 1940–. Pr Va and Staff Cond of N.B.C. Symp (Toscanini) 1943–. Prof of Va Juilliard Sch of Mus 1942–. New York Piano Q (Alex Schneider, Frank Miller, M. Horszowski, record all of Brahms, Fauré, Copland, etc.). Pf with Elman, Heifetz, Milstein, Morini, Stern, Szeryng, Zukerman: Mozart *Concertante* and other works. Pf and record, with Casals, Prades and Puerto Rico, along with Myra Hess, Szigeti, Tottelier; and with Stern, Schneider, Horszowski. Pre Pf many works for Va by Bax, Bloch, Gould, Hindemith, Rolla, Ruygrok, Serly, Steiner, Tchemberdehy, and Turina. Ed and Arr over 25 works for Va (I.M.C. pub). Cond Seattle Symp many years. Guest cond many of the world's great orchs. Now Fac U of Houston.

KATZ, MARTHA STRONGIN, b 1943 NYC. Stud Ronald Murat, Raphael Bronstein, Ivan Galamian, Lillian Fuchs, Wm. Primrose. 1st Prz Geneva, Switzerland, Va Compt, 1968; Max Reger Award, 1968. Found mbr Cleveland Q 1969, many tours and recordings with this group, played at White House for Jimmy Carter. Tch Va and Chamb Mus: Cleveland Insti of Mus 1968–71, State U of N Y at Buffalo 1971–76, Eastman Sch of Mus 1976–.

KAWAHITO, MAKIKO, b 1956, Tokyo, Japan. Stud Tokyo U of Arts (Geijutsu Daigaku) with Yoshiaki Nakatsuka. Semi-finalist William Primrose Va Compt 1979.

KIEVMAN, LOUIS, b. 1910 Naugatuck, Conn. Stud Juilliard Sch of Mus, Franz Kneisel, Sascha Jacobsen, D.C. Dounis. Va Musical Art Q 1931–37 (found mbr); Styvesant Q 1937–42; Sosson-Kievman Posella Trio 1949–59. Va (at founding) NBC Symp (Toscanini) 1937–42, Westwood Musical Artists 1960–65. Fac Westwood Music Centre 1949–59; Calif. Insti of the Arts 1959–64; Calif State U Long Beach 1973–; Calif State U Northridge 1978–; Immaculate Heart Coll of Los Angeles 1977–. Prominent in Calif str activities as Clinician, Lecturer and President of Los Angeles Chapter of A.S.T.A. Editor of "Viola Forum" of *American String Teacher* magazine 1972–78. Author of several widely used str methods. Owns and performs on a beautifully ornamented Gasparo da Salò Va.

KIRCHNER, EDUARD, b in Verden, Ger. Hänflein Q of Hannover from 1893.

KLATZ, HAROLD D., b 1914, Milwaukee, Wisc. Stud U of Wisc B.M.; Vn Maurice Kypen, Joseph Hoffman, Cecil Burleigh, Leon Sametini; Va Henri Karol Hayza, Wm. Primrose. Pr Va Nat'l Symp 1943–44, Grant Park Symp 1965–8, Dallas Symp 1967–68, Lyric Opera of Chicago 1970–73. Member Casal Festival Orch, 1960–73, Chicago Symp Assoc. Va soloist with Grant Park, Dallas, Chicago Chmb Orchs. Assisting artist for Pro Arte Q, Berkshire Q, Vermeer Q. Founding Mbr Chmb Mus Guild of Chicago. Prof. Va and Chmb Mus Northwestern U, 1960–1966; Prof of Va Congress of Strings; USC 1968–69. Active in record and trans field. Currently Cond and Mus Dir Hyde Park Chmb Orch.

KLEMMSTEIN, EBERHARD, b 1941 Berlin, Ger. Stud Hochschule für Musik, Emil Seiler; privately with Takis Ktenaveas. Reger Q 1965–76. Va tch Shawnigan Summer Sch of the Arts, Can. 1973, 74, 77, 78. Ed works for Va.

KLENGEL, PAUL, 1854–1935 in Leipzig. Vn, Va, pianist. Comp for Va. Brought out modern ed of K. Stamitz *Va Concerto in D* (Breitkopf & Härtel) shortly after Clement Meyer had ed same work (Peters). Arr, Ed, and trans many wks for Va.

KOCH, ULRICH, one of Europe's most outstanding Va soloists and recording artists. Presently (1979) Pr Va Berlin Philh.

KONDAKS, STEPHEN, b 1919 Salonika, Greece. Stud Juilliard and Insti of Musical Art, Sascha Jacobsen, Hans Letz; Cons de Musique, Montreal, Que., Can., Louis Bailly; Oscar Shumsky, NYC. Va McGill U Str Q 1940–41, Pr Va McGill Chmb Orch 1947–; CBC Symp 1947–. Fac McGill U 1940– Prof Va & Chmb Mus 1940–. Pre Pf Bartók *Viola Concerto* in Canada, 1953, CBC.

KORGUEFF, S. Va in St. Petersburg Q, with L. Auer, Kruger, and Werzbilowitch. Later the membership changed and was called the Imperial Russian Q with L. Auer, and Jean Pickel, Vns; Weichmann, Va; and Charles Davidoff, cello.

KOSMALA, JERZY, Krakow, Poland. Stud Krakow Sch of Mus, Uminsha; Eastman Sch of Mus, Francis Tursi; Indiana U, Wm. Primrose, D.M.A. Pr Va in Polish Orchs, Akron, Ohio, Symp. Krakow Q, Eastman Q. 1st Prize All-Poland Va Compt, Warsaw, 3rd Moscow Int'l Compt. Concerts in Poland, USSR, Europe, Canada, USA. Tch Va Krakow U, Indiana U, Peabody Coll, So Florida U, Akron U, Brevard

Mus Center, No Carolina. Scholarly Ed Carl Stamitz' *Concerto in A Major* (original in B Major) *for Va and Orch*, 1975. Article on Stamitz Va concertos, *Polskie Wydawnictwo Muzyczne*, Krakow. Pre Pf Maurice Gardner's *Rhapsody for Va and Orch*, with USAF Symp Orch, 7th Int'l Va Congress, Provo, Utah 1979.

KOVARCIK, JOSEPH, early 20th century. Came to USA in 1892 with his teacher, Antonin Dvorák. Pr Va N. Y. Philh until c.1935.

KRAMER, TOSCA BERGER (1900–1976), student of Ysaÿe; D.M.A. from Eastman School of Music. Pr Va in Tulsa, Okla. Orch. Prof of Va Oklahoma U.

KREUZ, EMIL (1867–1932). Va and comp of numerous works for Va. Gomperte Q. Many trans and ed for Va. Several important étude bks for Va.

KROYT, BORIS, b 1897 Odessa, Russia, d 1969 NYC. Vn prodigy, first concert in Odessa at age 9. At 10 sent to Berlin to study at Stern'sches Conservatorium, Vn with Alexander Fidemann, graduating at age 11, winning the Gustav Hollander Gold Medal. Va in Fiedmann's Q at age 12. Concerts in Europe and So Am 1912–35. Vn and Va soloist under Richard Strauss, Eric Kleiber, etc. Found Kroyt Q 1921 as Vn I, Vn in original Guarneri Q. Played Chmb Mus with Artur Schnabel, Pablo Casals, Artur Rubenstein, etc. Replaced Isvan Ipoli as Va in Budapest Q 1936, remaining until Q disbanded in 1967. Assisted with other members of Budapest Q in coaching the new Guarneri Q. Owned and played a Deconet Va. After World War II Library of Congress loaned all members of Budapest Q Stradivari instruments to play.

KUECHLER, FERDINAND (1867–1937). Stud Frankfort a/M Cons, Vn with W. Hess and H. Heermann. Va in Heermann Q, 1898–. Pr Va Basle Symph 1910–. Tch Vn and Va at Laudes Cons in Leipzig 1927–?.

LAFFOON, R. LARRY, b 1945. Stud Nick Stamon, San Diego, Ca., William Lincer, Walter Trampler. Va San Diego Symp 1963–65, Sherwood Hall Chmb Orch 1964–66, Clebenoff Strings 1965–66; Ass't Pr Va U S Air Force Band: Strolling Strings 1966–, U S A F Symp, Str Orch 1966–; Q at 3rd Int'l Va Congress, assisting Dr. Wolfgang Sawodny lecture-recital, "Q for Vn, 2 Va, and Cello,"; Ass't Pr Va U S A F Orch pf at Int'l Va Congresses 1975, 1977, 1979. Str Trio winning

Coleman Audition, Calif, judged by Budapest Q. Numerous recitals with U S A F in USA and Europe.

LAFORGE, THÉOPHILE, b c.1860; d 1918. One of the first teachers at the Paris Conservatoire to have the title, "le Professeur d'Alto." Tch of Louis Bailly, Henri Casadesus, Paul-Luis Neuberth, Maurice Vieux, and many other prominent French violists.

LALO, EDOUARD (1823–92). Although better known as a composer, Lalo was also a fine violist. Played Va in Armingand Q 1848–9.

LeBEAU, MARTIN, b 1938 Alexandria, Va. Stud Northwestern U, B.M.E., U of Virginia, M.A., Temple U, D.M.A. with Rolf Persinger, Harold Klatz. Va Chicago Chmb Orch 1959. Ass't Pr Va Trenton N.J. Symp 1969–. String teacher Arlington, Va. Sch 1960–66; Music Coordinator Pittsburgh Pa. Sch 1967–8. Ass't Prof of Mus Trenton N.J. State Coll 1969– Dissertation *A Pedagogical Analysis of 20th Century Unaccompanied Viola Literature.*

LEBERMANN, WALTER, b. 1910 Karlsruhe, Ger. Moved to Frankfurt-am-Main, 1929. Pr Vn teacher was Adolf Rebner; at early age switched to Va. After WWII Va in Radio Symp, Frankfurt a/M until 1964. Ed of over 80 previously unpublished Baroque and Classical compositions, of which 24 are for his chosen instrument, the Va. Has authored numerous articles related to his research in early works for the Va (see Bibliography of this book). Vice President of VFG 1973–75. Still active editing and publishing significant additions to Va literature. See article: Maurice W. Riley, "The Contributions of Walter Lebermann to Viola Literature." *American String Teacher,* XXVII, No. 2 (1977), p. 19. Also see Chapter XIV.

LECHNER-BAUER, Madame N. Soldat-Roeger Q, composed entirely of ladies. Found in London about same time as Shinner Q, early 20th century.

LEHNHOFF, SHEPPARD, 1902–1978. Stud Curtis Insti of Mus, Louis Bailly. Va Philadelphia Orch. Fac Murray State Coll, Ky. Pr Va National Symp 1945–54, Va Chicago Sym 1930–45, 1954–78. Found Mbr Fine Arts Q 1939.

LEQUIEN, COLETTE, b 1920 Versailles. Stud Conservatoire National de Versailles: Premier Prix de violon 1938, Prix d'Honneur d'Alto 1940, Premier Prix d'Harmonie 1941; Conservatoire National Superieur de Musique de Paris: Premier Prix d'Alto Classe Maurice

Vieux 1942, Premier Medaille de Musique de Chambre Class Pierre Pasquier 1943. Also stud with Joseph Calvet, Norbert Dujourcq, and Georges Enesco. Soloist: Pr Va O.R.T.F. Radios in Espagne, Suisse, Belgique, Germany, Turkey, England, Holland, etc. Soloist of Festivals: Aix-en-Provence, Menton, le Marais, Bordeau, Avignon, Strasbourg, Stuttgart. Sonia Louis Q 1944–47; Feminin de Paris Q 1949–53; M. Claire Jamet Quintet; Trio de Versailles, etc. Prof Va and Musique de Chambre and Member of Juries: l'École Normale de Paris; Conservatoire Regional de Versailles; and since 1971 Conservatoire National Superieur de Musique de Paris. Record: Pathé, Harmonia Mundi, Philips, Columbia, Valois, Erato, Ducretet, Club Français du disque. Won Grand Prix du disque in 1961 and 1970.

LIFSCHEY, SAMUEL. Pr Va Philadelphia Orch 1925–55. Author of important scale and etude books for the Va.

LINCER, WILLIAM, b 1907 NYC. Stud Insti of Musical Art, Leopold Lichtenberg, Samuel Gardner, Eric Morini. Pr Va Cleveland Symp 1941–42, N Y Philh 1942–73. Va Gordon Q 1935–41. Prof Va Manhattan Sch of Mus 1960–69, Juillard Sch of Mus 1969–, New York U (Adjunct) 1974–. First Pf with N.Y. Philh of *Va Concertos:* Klenner, Starer, Rivier, Hovaness *(Talin),* and Bloch *Suite for Va and Orch,* and discovered and played Mozart *Unfinished Triple Concerto for Vn, Va, Cello, and Orch.* Recorded with N. Y. Philh *Harold in Italy* and *Don Quixote.* Ed of new series of "Repertoire for the Concert Violist," pub by Viola World, 1978.

LOCKYER, JAMES, b late 19th century. Stud in London, Vn with Hans Wessely; Va scholarship at R.A.M. with Lionel Tertis. Pr Va in Beacham Orch c.1912–. Prof of Va at R.A.M. Played Maggini Va.

LOWENBERG, MICHAEL. Va in Bargheer Q and Hamburger Q, both early 20th century.

LOWENTHAL, DAGOBETT, b 1840 in Konigsberg. Stud in Berlin with Joachim. Va in Waldemar-Meyer Q toward end of 19th century.

LUKÁCS, PÁL, Va virtuoso. Prof of Va Franz Liszt Zenemuveszeti Foiskola, Budapest, Hungary. His students have won many honors in contests. Va soloist throughout Europe, and eminent recording artist.

McCARTY, PATRICIA, b 1954 Wichita, Kans. Stud with Joshua Missal; U of Mich, B.M. 1974, M.M. 1976, Francis Bundra. Va Fac U of Mich 1975, summer 1978; Nat'l Mus Camp, Interlochen, Mich, 1976, 1979; Ithaca Coll 1977–79. Ass't Pr Va Boston Symp, & Pr Va Boston Pops 1979–. Ithaca Str Trio, Lenox Q. Music from Marlboro 1976–77. Recital, Int'l Va Congress, Ypsilanti, Mich 1975; entire *Potpourri* by Hummel, Houston Symp 1975; NYC Pre Pf B. Britten's *Lachrymae* with Orch 1978; Tibor Serly Memorial Conc, Chicago, 1979. Winner: First Silver Medal and Prix Radiophonique, Geneva Int'l Compt 1972; Civic Orch of Chicago Soloist Compt 1978; Augusta Symp Str Compt 1979; 3rd Prize, Primrose Int'l Compt 1979.

McINNES, DONALD, b San Francisco, 1939. U of Cal. (Santa Barbara), B.M.; U of So. Cal., M.M., Stud Walter Trampler, William Primrose. Stud chmb mus with Jascha Heifetz, Gregor Piatigorsky, Gabor Rejto, Eunice Shapiro. Pr Va Santa Barbara Symp 1955–61, Seattle Symp 1966–68, Marlboro Festival 1970–71, Pittsburgh Symp 1972–73. Prof. of Va U of Wash. 1966–. Banff 1976–. Va Clinician & Master Classes: Int'l Va Congress, 1975, 1978; M.E.N.C. Convention 1976; Congress of Strings, 1975; and others. World Pre Pf of William Schuman, *Concerto on Old English Rounds for Va, Women's Chor., and Orch,* a Ford Foundation Grant, Boston Symp, cond by Michael Tilson Thomas (1974); William Bergsma, *Variations and a Fantasy,* Va and Orch, Seattle Symp, Rainer Miedel, cond (1978), commissioned by Seattle Symp for Mr. McInnes; John Verrall, *Concerto for Va and Orch* C.B.C. Chamber Orch, John Arison, cond (1969); Paul Louis Fink, *Fantasy for Solo Va,* dedicated to D.M., Pf Palo Alto, Ca. (1974); Vincent Persichetti, *Parable for Solo Viola,* at Int'l. Va Congress. Ypsilanti, MI (1975). Record: (among many) Wm. Schuman, *Concerto with Camerata Singers,* N. Y. Philh, Leonard Bernstein, cond, Columbia; Hector Berlioz, *Harold in Italy,* Orchestre Nationale de France, Leonard Bernstein, cond, Angel. Performed Bartók *Va Concerto,* Duets with Menuhin, and gave Master Class at 6th Int'l Va Congress, London, England, 1978. Pf 7th Int'l Va Congress, Provo, Utah, 1979; Panel mbr.

McKELLAR, CHRISTOPHER, b 1948, Salt Lake City, Utah. Stud U of Utah, Sally Peck. Va Utah symp 1966–70. Pr Va Spokane Symp 1970–71; Utah Symp 1974–. Meridian Str Q 1970–.

MADDY, JOSEPH, b 1891, Wellington, Kans., d 1967, Interlochen, Mich. Stud Wichita Coll of Mus 1906, Theodore Lindberg; Metropolitan Cons, Chicago, Harry Diamond; Columbia Sch of Mus,

Chicago, Ludwig Becker. Va, Minneapolis Symp 1909 at age of 17. Entered teaching as Supervisor Public Sch Mus, Rochester, N.Y. 1918; became pioneer in promotion of instrumental mus in American public sch; Richmond, Ind 1920–25; Ann Arbor, Mich, and U of Mich 1926– Prof of Mus Education. Founder and President Nat'l Mus Camp at Interlochen, Mich, 1928–1967. There he promoted Va on high sch level when there were very few high sch Vas in the US. Required all student Vns to take a turn at the Va. Maddy, himself an avid Va, promoted interest in chmb mus among adults through the annual post-season sessions at Interlochen.

MAJEWSKI, VIRGINIA. Stud Ferdinand Schaefer, Indianapolis; Eastman Sch of Mus; Curtis Insti of Mus, Va with Louis Bailly. Pr Va M.G.M. and Universal Motion Picture Studios, Hollywood, Calif. Trio Classique (Vn, Fl, Va); Marianne Kneisel Q. Founding Mbr American Q. Played concert with Artur Schnabel. Soloist Indianapolis and LaJolla Symps. Ancient Instru Trio: Alice Ehlers Va d'amore, gamba, harpsichord. Pilgrimage Concerts with Heifetz, Piatigorsky, Primrose (and recorded). Private chmb mus with above, also with Rubenstein, Rostropovich, Milstein, Szigetti, Toscha Seidel, Elman, Menuhin, Emanuel Bay, Leonard Penarrio. Tch Phila Settlement Sch. Record Va and Va d'amore with Larnindo Almeida, guitar; Mozart *Clarinet Quintet*, Benny Goodman. 1962 nominee for Naras Awards for best classical Pf: *The Intimate Bach* (with Larnindo Almeida and Vincent DeRosa). With Arthur Guyhorn, Shiburg Boyes, for Coleman Series in Pasadena Pf Paul Creston *Trio for flute, Va, and piano.*

MANCILLA, RAFAEL. Pr Va of Mexico City Opera Orch (1979).

MATTEUCCI, GIUSEPPE, 1893–1952. Pr Va La Scala, Colon, Opera di Roma, Augustero Orchs. Quartetto Italiano. Taught Va Cons di Roma.

MATTIS, KATHLEEN, b 1955, Berkeley, Calif. Stud Vn Eudice Shapiro, George Kast, Charles Castleman; Va Milton Thomas, Heidi Castleman; U of Southern Calif, Magna cum laude, Outstanding String Player Award. Va, Pasadena Symp., Pr Va New York Str Orch 1977, Acting Pr Va St. Louis Symp 1977–. USC Str Q. Fac St. Louis Cons.

MAXINSAK, J. Followed Bachrich as Va in Vienna Hellmes-berger Q.

MAYER, URI, b in Roumania. Stud Academy of Music of Tel-Aviv, Oedoen Partos; Juillard Sch of Mus, Walter Trampler. Prominent as Cond and Va in Montreal, Canada, also U of Mich, and Natl Mus Camp. Gave Lect-Rectl on Va comp of Partos at 5th Int'l Va Congress, Ypsilanti, 1975.

MEYER, CLEMENS, b 1868 Oberplanitz; d 1958, Schwerin, Mecklenburg. Stud Hermann Ritter on Va and Va d'amore c. 1888–1892. Va Bremen Orch 1892. Pr Va Opera Orch, Schwerin, Mecklenburg 1893–1928; many years at Bayreuth, also at Wagner Festivals, Munich. Ed first modern edition of K. Stamitz *Viola Concerto in D Major*, 1900; Ed *Alte Meister der Viola*, 1900, which contains 4 Baroque Va d'amore *Sonatas* by X. Hammer, and the K. Stamitz *Va Concerto*. Played Ritter designed *Viola alta*.

MICHALAKAKOS, CHRISTOS, b. 1926 Athens, Greece. Stud Cons of Athens, 1st Prize Va, José de Bustinduy, Chmb Mus Leda Kouroukeis; diploma of proficiency U of Athens; Cons of Paris, Etienne Ginot, Chmb Mus Pierre Pasquier, Joseph Calvet. Va Titulaire de l'orchestre Symphonique de l'Etat a Athenes and l'Orchestre Symphonique de la Radio d'Athens 1948–53; Colonne Symphonique 1958–60; Lamoureaux Symphonique 1961–63. Pr Va l'orchestre de Chambre Paul Kuentz 1958–61; Symphonique Pasdeloup 1968; l'Orchestre de Chambre J. F. Poullard 1961–72. Altiste di Quatier Serge Blanc 1958–63; Trio Söelle Bernard 1963–65; Duo en Sonates with Pianist Ricardo Zugaro 1967–. Prof Va Conservatoire de Chatou 1968–; l'École Normale de Paris 1976–; l'Academie International D'Été de Nice 1976–;—and Chmb Mus and Str Orch Conservatoire National d'Amiens 1965–. Performer of all the standard Va literature, many concerts in France and abroad. Music critic of *le Soir*, wrote Sept. 21, 1977: "He is the Oistrakh of the Viola."

MIRY, PAUL, b Gand, Belgium. Stud Vn Brussels Cons; first prize. Va in Brussels Q, early 20th century.

MISCHAKOFF, ANNE, b 1942 NYC. Stud Mischa Mischakoff, Lillian Fuchs; Smith Coll A.B Magna Cum Laude, Louise Rood; U of Iowa M.A.; U of Illinois, D.M.A. 1978, Guillermo Perich. Pr Va Evansville Philh and Q 1965–66. Chicago Contemporary Chmb Players and Lexington Q 1966–68; Detroit Symp 1968–72. Prof of Va U of the Pacific 1975– Research in Russia on Va, dissertation: "Ivan Evstaf'evich Khandoshkin and the Beginnings of Russian String Mus" (includes discussion of *Duo for Vn and Va* and authenticity of

Khandoshkin *Viola Concerto).* Pre Pf on West Coast of USA of Shostakovich *Va Sonata;* S.R. Beckler *Va Sonata* (1978); Philip Ahern *Duo for Va and Percussion* (1975); Joseph Olive *7 Episodes for Va and Piano* (1968); David Itkin *Piece for 4 Va* (1978).

MOGILL, LEONARD, b 1911, Philadelphia, Pa. Stud Curtis Insti of Mus 1929–36, Louis Bailly. Musical Fund Q. Philadelphia Orch 1936–. Prof of Va Philadelphia Coll for the Performing arts, 1934–; Temple U 1958–. Four students in Phila Orch; other students in most of USA major orchs. Ed and Arr of many important works for Va, pub by G. Schirmer, Theo. Presser, and Henri Elkan.

MOLDAVAN, NICOLAS, b 1891 Odessa, Russia. Stud Vn at Odessa Cons with Alexander Fiedelman; scholarship St. Petersburg Cons, 1906–12, Vn with Korguef, graduated with highest honors. Founding mbr of Trio for pf at the palace of Grand Duke Boris 1912–18. Migrated to USA in 1920. Stud with Franz Kneisel, who advised switch to Va. Joined Lenox Q as Va 1921–24; Elman Q 1924–5; Flonzaley Q 1925–8; Stradivarius Q of NYC 1929–35. Also taught Va in NYC.

MOLO, CAYENTANO, Buenos Aires. See Appendix II.

MOLNAR, FERENC, b 1896 Budapest, Hungary. Stud at Royal Hungarian Liszt Acad of Mus, Diploma; Univ of Technology, Budapest, Diploma. Capt in Austro-Hungarian Army WWI, 4½ yrs in Siberian Prison Camp. Tours as solo Va in Europe, 1923–26. Pr Va San Francisco Symph (Monteux, Dir) 1944–64. Roth Q (found mbr), worldwide tours 1926–39; San Francisco Q 1939–45; summers June Festival Q, Albuquerque, N. Mex., and Colorado Springs Fest Q. Founder-Dir of Chmb Mus Center and Artists' Series, San Francisco State U, 1952–70. Prof of Mus and Prof of Mech Engineering at Stanford Univ; taught engineering to armed forces during WWII, and participated in design of 100-kv electronic microscope, 1942–4. 21 compositions written and dedicated to him, incl Alan Hovhaness, *Viola Concerto;* Ernst Krenek, *Sonata for Va and Piano;* and Ellis Kohs, *Nocturne.* Record, Columbia, Victor, and Argo. Plays ex-Primrose Bros-Amati Viola, c.1600.

MONTEUX, PIERRE, 1875–1964. Internationally famous conductor. Began career as violist. Played Va in the prestigious Geloso Q. Later sponsored Louis Bailly's viola career.

MORAWEC, ERNST (20th Century). Pr Va Vienna Philh. Prof Hochschule für Musik Vienna; Musikakademie Zürich. Has reputation of being a Va master teacher.

MÜLLER, ADOLPH. Stud Vn with Joachim. Va in Halir Q, founded in 1893.

MÜLLER, BERNARD (b. 1825) Va of second Müller Q, all brothers and sons of Karl Friedrich Müller (1797–1873), leader of the first Müller Q. Second Q organized in 1855 upon death of Theodore, Gustav, and Georg of parent Q.

MÜLLER, THEODORE (1799–1855). Va of the famous Müller Q, composed entirely of brothers.

NANIA, SALVATORE b 1915 Catania, Sicily. Stud Cons di Musica, Bari, Italy, Gioconda de Vito; Deutches Musikinstitut für Ausländer, Berlin, Vasa Prihoda. Pr Va Catania and Palermo Opera Orch 1938–41, Orch Sinfonica Bari 1949–71, Radio Televisione Italiana 1974, Orch Sinfonica Sassari 1974–. Catanese Q 1938–40, Napoletano Q 1962–70.

NARET-KOENIG, J. Frankfort Q (Hugo Heermann, F. Bassermann, Vns; Hugo Becker, cello) which was compared favorably with Joachim Q.

NEDSAL, OSCAR. Bohemian Q, early 20th century.

NEL, RUDOLF, b Berlin 1908. Stud Gustav Havermann, Willy Hess, Karl Flesch. Pr Va Deutsches Opernhaus Berlin 1928–45 (cond Bruno Walter); Festspiele in Bayreuth (cond Furtwängler, Toscanini, Richard Strauss); Bayerischer Ründfunk München 1949–58 (cond Eugen Jochum, Raphael Kübelik). Breronel Q, Lore-Fischer Trio: Lore Fischer (Mrs. Nel) Soprano, Nel, Va, Hermann Reütter, piano. Pre Va works by Hermann Reüetter, Armin Knab, Armin Schibler, Giselher Klebe, Werner Haentjes, Frank Martin, etc. Prof of Va and Chmb Mus at Konservatorium der Reichshauptstadt, Berlin. Also plays viola d'amore and viola pomposa. Taught Va and chmb mus in many countries. Wife is Prof of Voice Musikhochschüle, Stüttgart.

NEUBERTH, PAUL-LUIS, b 1881 in Paris. Stud at Paris Cons with Laforge. Pr Va of l'Orchestra Colonne for 20 years. Aware of the backing given to Hermann Ritter by Wagner, Liszt and others, he went to Würzburg to meet Ritter. Neuberth, greatly impressed by Ritter, returned to France an early exponent of the *Viola-alta*. The large viola he played was made by Paul Kaul (1875–d. after 1935) of Mirecourt and Paris.

NICKRENZ, SCOTT, b 1937 Buffalo, N.Y. Stud Curtis Insti of Mus. Founding Mbr Lenox Q, Vermeer Q, Claremont Q, Orpheus Trio. Prominent Cond and Va. Prof Va New England Cons of Mus, Boston. Owns and plays ex-Bailly ex-dePasquale da Salò Va. Active in festivals for bi-centennial of Schubert's birth 1979.

NOVÁČEK, OTTOKAR, b 1866, Fehertemplum, Hungary; d 1900, New York. Pr Va Damrosch Orchestra, NYC, 1892–93. Brodsky Q 1889–91, 1894–99. Played large Gasparo da Salò viola.

OPPELT, ROBERT L., b 1925 Lorain, Ohio. U of Illinois B.S. 1949, M.S. 1950, Paul Rolland; Eastman School of Mus, D.M.A. 1957, Francis Tursi; privately with David Dawson; William Primrose. Iowa Str Q 1951–53, Kentucky Str Q 1960–68. Va Indianapolis Symp 1950, North Carolina Symp 1951. Pr Va Brevard Mus Festival 1976. Prof of Va and Orch Cond, Eastern Kentucky U 1956–68; Illinois State U 1968–72; Lehman Coll, NYC U 1973–1977. Author of *Graded and Notated List for the Student Violist*. President A.S.T.A. 1973–74.

PAGELS, LUDWIG LUIS, b.1861. Numerous arr and trans for Va. His *Orchesterstudien*, 1902, was one of earliest collections of difficult selections from Symph Overtures, and Suites for Va.

PARNAS, RICHARD, b 1929 St. Louis, Mo. Stud Curtis Insti of Mus, William Primrose. Va St. Louis Symp 1954–55; Pr Va Nat'l Symp Orch, Washington, D.C. 1955–; Nat'l Symp Str Q 1972–. Fac Vn, Va George Washington U, 1969–. Pre Pf Andreas Makris *Va Concerto* with Nat'l Symp Orch 1972.

PARTOS, OEDOEN, b 1907 Budapest; d Israel, 1977. Stud Franz Liszt Acad of Mus, Vn Hubay, Studet; comp Kodály. Concertmaster of Orchestras in Hungary, Germany, and Switzerland. Partos Q (founded 1931 in Berlin) specialized in contemporary music. Taught Comp in Baku, USSR 1936–7. Pr Va Palestine Philh (later named Israel Philh Orch) 1938–. Appeared frequently as Va soloist Israel, London, Paris, playing his own comp (4 Va concertos). Named Dir Israeli Rubin Acad of Mus Tel-Aviv 1951–also taught Va and Comp. Toured USA 1964–5 playing his *Agada for Va and Piano*. Member of Jury for Int'l Vn and Va Compt Munich on 3 occasions. Pf career came to an end with paralysis in 1972, but continued tch and comp until death.

PARTRIDGE, HUGH, b. 1939 Jacksonville, Fla. Stud Indiana U, David Dawson, William Primrose, B.M.; Butler U., M.M.; also John P. Koscielny, Eric Rosenblith, Paul Doktor, Kato Havas. Va Jacksonville Symp 1955–58, Miami Symp 1955–58, Atlanta Symp 1959–60, Indianapolis Symp 1965–66. Pr Va Indianapolis Symp 1966–70, Wichita Symp 1970–76, Asst Cond North Carolina Symp 1976–, Santa Fe Opera (Summers) 1974–. Meridian Q 1966–70, Wichita State U Fac Str Q 1970–76, North Carolina Symp Principals Q 1976–. Prof Va Butler Un Indiana 1966–69, Indiana Central U 1969–70, Wichita State U 1970–76. Pre Pf Daniel Minter, *Sonata for Va and Celeste;* John Biggs, *Inventions for Va and Tape;* Walter Mays, *Five Halucinations for Va Collective;* Michael Baker, *Counterplay for Va and Str Orch, "Point No Point" for Va and Str Orch, Duo Concertante for Vn, Va, and Str Orch*. Creator and Dir of "Va Collective," ensmb of 12 va that pf works with multiple Va parts.

de PASQUALE, JOSEPH, b Philadelphia, Pa. 1919. Stud Curtis Insti of Mus, Louis Bailly, Max Aronoff, William Primrose. 4 yr Marine Band; 4 yr Amer Broadcasting Orch. Pr Va Boston Symp 1947–64, Phila Orch, 1964–. Pre Pf Walton *Va Concerto*, and Walter Piston *Va Concerto* (written for and dedicated to him, Mar. 7, 1958) Boston Symp (Charles Muench, cond); Darius Milhaud *Va. Concerto No. 1*, Boston Symp. De Pasquale Q, all brothers: William, Robert, Joseph, & William Stokking (deceased), replaced by George Harpham, cellist. Pf in Boston and Phila. of Mozart *Concertante;* Strauss, *Don Quixote;* Handel *Concerto;* Bach, *Brandenburg VI;* Vaughan Williams *Flos Campi*. Tch Va Curtis Insti of Mus.; Temple U; Haverford Col.; Phila. Col. for the Performing Arts. Master class and recital at 7th Int'l Va Congress, Provo, Utah, incl Pre Pf of *Sonata* by George Rochberg (b. 1918), a work ded to Wm. Primrose. Mbr jury William Primrose Int'l Va Compt, Snowbird, Utah, 1979.

PASQUALI, GUILIO 1884–1943. Tch Va at Conservatori di Palermo and also Florence. Member Quartetto Veneziano. Artist on the Va d'amore.

PASQUIER, BRUNO, b 1943 Neuilly sur Seine, France. Son of Pierre Pasquier. Cons de Paris, Va with Etienne Ginot, Chmb Mus Pierre Pasquier, Str Q, Joseph Calvet. Prz for Str Q at Munich.

Nouveau Trio á Cordes Pasquier, found 1970–. Pr Va Orch de l'Opéra de Paris. Yeuakis Q (recording).

PASQUIER, PIERRE, b 1902 Tours, France. Stud Cons de Paris, Maurice Vieux. Trio Pasquier (very famous) with two brothers, Jean Vn and Etienne, cello. The quality of their performances brought world acclaim and inspired the writing of many new works dedicated to these artists, including *Trios* by Roussel, Jean Français, Martinu, Hindemith, Milhaud, Rivier, Martinon, Jolivet, Pierné, Florent Schmidt, and Villa Lobos. These compositions gave the Va an added dimension in 20th century ens literature. Prof of Chmb Mus at Paris Conservatoire.

PENCOFF, CHARLES N. b 1933 Chicago, Ill. Stud Chicago Cons of Mus, Ludwig Becker; Chicago Musical Col, Hans Basserman; U of Illinois, Paul Rolland, John Garvey; New Sch of Mus, Philadelphia, Max Aronoff; American U, Washington, D.C., Raphael Hillyer; Alan de Veritch. Pr Va U S Air Force Band: Strolling Strings 1955–, U S A F Symphony, Str Orch, 1965–. Q at 3rd Int'l Va Congress, assisting Dr. Wolfgang Sawodny lecture-recital, "Q for Vn, 2 Va, and Cello," member of U S A F Orch pf at Int'l Va Congresses 1975, 1977, 1979.

PERICH, GUILLERMO, b 1924 Havana, Cuba, now USA citizen. Stud Havana Cons of Mus graduate Vn 1948, Raoul G. Anckermann; Boston U 1956, Va, Joseph de Pasquale. Pr Va Havana Philh 1956–59, Havana Chmb Orch 1956–59, Baltimore Symp 1960–68, St. Louis Symp Orch 1968–71, Champaign-Urbana, Ill. Symp 1971–; Summers: 1963 Chautauqua Fest Orch, 1967–69, Aspen Fest Orch. Concert Society Q (Havana) 1956–59, Baltimore Q 1963–68, St. Louis Q 1968–71, Mischakoff Q 1963 Summer, Walden Q U of Illinois. Prof of Va & Str Mus Literature, U of Illinois 1971–, Chairman Str Division, Sch of Mus, U of Illinois 1974–. Pre Pf Paul Chihara's *Concerto* for Va & Orch, Baltimore 1965; Robert Kelly's *Concerto for Va & Orch* Champaign-Urbana, Ill 1978; Pre Pf in USA Karel Husa's *Poem* for Va & Orch, Baltimore 1966; Juan Orrego-Salas' *Mobili for Va & Piano;* in Spain Aurelio de la Vega's *Soliloquy for Va & Piano,* Herbert Brun's *Sonatina for Va,* Barcelona 1978. 1st Prize Vn of Havana Philh Orch. Author *Annotated Course of Study for Va,* pub Continuing Ed in Mus, U of Illinois. Gave lecture-recital "Music for Va by Spanish and Latin-American Composers," 7th Intl Va Cong, Provo, Utah, 1979.

PERINI, MARIO, b 1911 Buenos Aires, Argentina. See Appendix II.

PERSINGER, ROLF, b San Francisco. Stud Juilliard Sch of Mus. Town Hall Debut 1954. NBC Symp, Toscanini. Assoc Pr Va Chicago Symp, Reiner 9 yrs; Pr Va Minneapolis Symp 4 yrs, San Francisco Symp, Aspen Symp.

PETTINI, ALFREDO, 1865–1927. Pr Va Augusteo Orch. Tch Cons di Roma.

PIETIKÄINEN, MAURI OLAVI, b 1944, Riihimäki, Finland. Stud Sibelius Acad, Helsinki with Aarno Salmela; Gösta Finnström, Stockholm. Ass't Pr Va Finnish Nat'l Opera Orch 1963–5; Va Finnish Radio Symp Orch 1966–73, Helsinki Philh 1973–74, Pr Va 1975–. Tulindberg Q 1963–67, Segerstam Q 1967–, Voces Intime 1973–. Concerts throughout Finland. Owns and plays rare J.B. Guadagnini Va c.1770.

PICHL, WENZEL, b 1741 Bechyně, Bohemia; d 1805 Vienna. Vn, Va, and comp of over 700 works, many for the Va. Va comp not yet available in modern editions.

PIRSCHL, RAIMUND, b 1873 in Brun, Austria. Duesberg Q in Vienna from 1895.

PISENDEL, JOHANN GEORG (1687–1755). German Vn, stud Torelli, Vivaldi. Reputed to have been one of first to play J. S. Bach *Cello Suites* on Viola Pomposa.

POLO, ENRICO b 1868. Comp *Sonatas for Solo Viola*. Author of numerous étude bks and technical studies for Va.

PRAGER, MADELINE EVE, b 1952 Oakland, Calif. U of Calif, Berkley with Detlev Olshausen, Isidore Tinklemann, BA in Mus 1974; Nordwestdeutsche Musikakademie, Detmold, W Germany 1975–9 with Bruno Giuranna: highest German pf honors exam "Konzertexamen" 1979. Pr Va Rhenish Chamber Orch, Cologne W Ger 1976–7. Ass't Giuranna, Nordwestdeutsche Musikakademie, 1976–8. Hertz Memorial Scholarship, U of Calif, Berkeley 1976–7. 2nd Prize German Nat'l Mus Acad Compt for Va, 1979. Semifinalist William Primrose Va Compt, 1979. Va Marlboro Mus Fest 1978. Solo conc, recitals, chmb mus USA & Eur.

PREUCIL, WILLIAM W. b 1931, Joliet, Ill. Stud Eastman Sch of Mus B.M., M.M. with Abram Boone. Pr Va Detroit Symp 1956–58.

Stradivari Q (Found Mbr) 1960, pf 5 years on Paganini Strad, on loan from Corcoran Gallery of Art, Washinton, D.C. Prof Va U of Iowa 1958–. NYC solo recital debut 1960. Va Master Class in Leningrad Cons 1978. Wife, Doris, and 4 children active as family ens. Wife, Doris, active in Suzuki-Va. Panel mbr 7th Int'l Va Congress, Provo, Utah, 1979.

PREVES, MILTON, b. 1909 Cleveland, Ohio. Stud entirely in Chicago: Chicago U; Chicago Mus Coll, Sametini; Bush Cons, Czerwonky; Metropolitan Cons, Diamond; Insti of Mus and Allied Arts, Girvin; American Cons, Mischakoff. Va Chicago Little Symp 1930–34; Chicago Symp 1934; Pr Va Chicago Symp 1939–. Mischakoff Q, Chicago Symp Q 1940–. Pf many Chicago pre of Va works. Pf Ernest Bloch's *Suite for Viola and Orchestra* at Chicago Music Festival, commemorating composer's 70th birthday, Dec. 1950. Bloch in appreciation comp and ded his *Meditation and Processional* to Preves, 1951. Alan Shulman also ded work to Preves. Prof of Va at Roosevelt U, Northwestern U, DePaul U. Cond Orchs: Chicago North Side 1952–; Oak Park River Forest; Wheaton; Gary, Ind.; Gold Coast Ch; Chicago Symp 1967–68. Awards: Myrtle Wreath; Steinway; Library of Congress of Human Dignity; city of Glenview; Chicago South Side. Plays a Montagnana Va, dated 1723, donated to Chicago Symp by Ralph Norton.

PRIMROSE, WILLIAM, b. 1923 in Glasgow, Scotland. The dean of 20th century violists. His many accomplishments have greatly influenced the present and future trends of viola playing. See Chapter XV.

RAMPELMANN, WALTER. Hollander Q of Berlin, found by Gustav Hollander c.1895.

RHODES, SAMUEL, b 1941 Long Beach, N.Y. Stud Mannes Sch, Sydney Beck; privately with Walter Trampler. Galimir Q 1961–69; Juilliard Q 1969–. Marlboro Fest 1960–68, '78, Aspen Fest 1969–77. Fac Juilliard Sch 1969–. Artist in Residence, Mich State U 1977, in residence Library of Congress, Washington, D.C. Commissioned and Pre Pf of Claudio Spies *Viopiacem* for Va and Piano, NYC 1969. Many recordings and Pre Pf with Juilliard Q. Also a composer, writes own cadenzas, e.g., Wanhal's *Concerto in C Major* and Rolla's *Concerto in Eb Major.* Plays an extremely rare Peregrino Zanetto Va c. 1570.

RIDDLE, FREDERICK, b Liverpool, Eng. 1912. Stud, Royal Coll of Mus 1928–1933, Vn Scholarship with Maurice Sons. London Symp Orch 1932–1938; London Philh Orch. 1938–1953; Pr Va Royal Philh Orch 1953–1977. Chmb Mus: Philharmois Ens and Str Trio 1933–39; Wigmore Ens and Str Trio 1945–66; Robles Harp, Fl & Va Trio 1976–; Pougnet, Riddle, Pini Str Trio 1950–65. Prof Va Royal Col. of Mus. 1948–. First record Walton *Viola Concerto*, London Symp Orch, Walton cond, 1937; Pre Pf Dalby and Connolly *Va Concertos* written for him, Royal Philh Orch. "With the RPO Sir Thomas Beecham did about once a season a concert in which I could play any viola concerto I chose, from 1953 until he died. He was the greatest influence on my life as a musician."

RITTER, HERMANN, b 1849 Wismar, E. Ger; d 1926 Würzburg, Ger. Designed the large *Viola-alta*. See Chapters X, XI.

ROCHA, AGUSTÍN. Pr Va of Estado de Mexico Phil Orch (1979).

ROLLA, ALESSANDRO, 1757–1841. Eminent Va and comp of many works for Va. See Chapters X, XI.

ROOD, LOUISE, b 1910 Easton, Pa; d 1964 Northampton, Mass. Stud U of Wisconsin, B.M. 1929; M.A., Thesis "The Viola as a Solo Instrument," vn Cecil Burleigh; Juilliard Graduate Sch 1929–34, Eduoard Dethier, Hans Letz. Marianna Kneisel Q 1932–33. Tch Va, vn, chmb mus, theory U of Iowa, Summers 1930–36; Sweet Briar College 1934–37; Va Smith Coll 1937–64. Benning Q, Smith Coll Q. Visiting Lecturer U of Mich summers 1945-6: Pf K. Stamitz *Va Concerto* (Gilbert Ross, Cond); Chmb Mus, Guest Artist U of Mich, Summer 1956 with Stanley Q: Pf Mozart Quintets and as soloist *Brandenberg Concertos* 3 and 6. Chairman of New Valley Mus Press which pub historical eds; works by contemporary composers. Ms Rood owned and played a Gian Paolo Castagneri viola.

ROSENBLUM, MYRON, b 1923, NYC. Queens Coll, B.A. 1956; New York U, M.A. 1969, Ph.D. 1976 (Performance/Education: Viola d'amore); Vienna Acad of Mus (Fulbright Grant) 1964–65. Privately with Vn Harold Berkley; Va Lillian Fuchs, Margaret Pardee, William Primrose, Walter Trampler; Chmb Mus Joseph Fuchs, Lillian Fuchs, Raphael Hillyer. Pr Va 7th U.S. Army Symp Orch 1957–58. Greenwich Q 1963–64. Assoc Prof Queensborough Comm Coll 1969–. Adjunct Prof Va-Vn Jersey City State Coll 1975–, New York U, 1978–. Ed C. Graupner *Concerto in D for Viola d'amore and Viola* with strings, and gave Pre Pf in U.S. (with Jacob Glick, Va) 1964, Pre Pf in Pöllau, Austria, 1965 (Franz Zeyringer Va). Pre Pf Richard Lane *Trio for Piano, Clarinet and Va*, 1964. Pf Va d'amore Int'l Va Congress 1975, 1977. Found and Pres of American Va Society; also a new Society for Viola d'Amore. Ed of *Newsletter* AVS.

ROSTAL, MAX, b 1905, Teschen, Austria. Stud Schwarzwaldsche Schulanstalten, Vienna, Arnold Rose; State Acad of Mus, Berlin, Carl Flesch (recognized as authority of Carl Flesch's teaching method). Has great interest in Va, which he teaches, and plays as soloist and in Chmb Mus groups.

RUZITSKA, ANTON. Stud Vn with J. Grun. Followed Steiner as Va of Rosé Q. Also Va of Vienna Prill Q.

SABATINI, RENZO, b 1905 in Cagliari, Italy; d 1973. Stud Vn Remy Principe, Goffredo Petrassi. Early career Vn soloist. Prof of Vn at Inst Musicale Pareggiato "Boccherini" in Lucca 1938–41. Career as virtuoso of Va and Va d'amore began with appointment as Prof of Va at Acad Santa Cecilia in Rome 1941. Found mbr Virtuosi di Roma and Quintetto Boccherini. Concertized 1938–53; record artist. One of the great Va teachers of 20th century. Wrote *Concerto for Viola; Esercizi preparatori alle corde doppie*, 1936; revised many works for Va and Va d'amore. Pres of Italy decorated him for achievements and contributions as teacher and artist. Also see Chapter XIV.

SAHLA, RICHARD, 1855–1931. Virtuoso vn of Prague School. Soloist in Könliechen Kapelle in Hannover 1882–88; Hofkapell-meister at Bückeburg 1888; Prof at Orchesterschule 1895–. In his later years he became increasingly interested in Va, prompting Max Reger to ded to him *Suite in D Major for Solo Viola*, op. 131, No. 2.

SAINT-GEORGE, HENRY, b 1841 in Dresden; d 1924 in London. Pf on Va, Va d'amore, and viols; also made these insts. Ed and trans music for these insts. Author of *The Bow, its History, Manufacture, and Use*, 1896.

SALTARELLI, DOMENICK, b 1917 Roseto, Pa. Stud Philadelphia, Mastbaum Sch, Vn Maier Levin; Settlement Mus Sch, Vn Emanuel Zetlin; Va New Sch of Mus, Max Aronoff. Pr Va New Orleans, La. Symp and Opera Orchs; Houston Symp; Austin, Abilene, San Angelo, Corpus Christi Symp Orchs; San Antonio Symp 1951–. Tch and Clinician U of Tex; Trinity U (Tex.) 1960–.

SAWODNY, WOLFGANG, b 1934 Reutenhau, Germany. Amateur violist and musicologist. Ph.D. in Chemistry, U of Stuttgart. Prof of Inorganic Chem at U of Ulm. Extensive research into 18th cent Va Mus. An authority on Q Mus with Vn (Fl or Ob), 2 Va's, and Cello (Bass). Ed numerous pub for Va. Pres of VFG 1974–76; presently mbr of Int'l Executive Board of VFG.

SCHIDLOF, PETER, b 1922 Vienna, Austria. Stud Max Rostal. Amadeus Q 1947–, touring England, Europe, and USA; has recorded most of standard Qs. Many honors which include Doctorate degree from York U, England; Order of British Empire; Grosse Verdienst-Kreuz, W. Ger.; Austrian Cross of Merit for Arts and Letters. Has Pf the standard Va Concertos with many leading orch in Eng and Europe. Plays famous "MacDonald" Stradivarius Va, 1701.

SCHILL, O. Dannreuther Q, which toured Europe, England, and United States in early 20th century.

SCHMID, GEORG, b 1907, München. Stud Staat Akademie der Tonkünst, München, 1927–34, Vn Valentin Härtl, Va Philipp Haass; privately with Karl Freund, Rudolf Hindemith (brother of Paul). Pr Va Orch das Reichssenders, Stüttgart, 1934; Staatsoper München 1940; Sinfoni Orch des Bayerischer, München 1949–76. Freund Q 1950–60; Kehr Trio 1960; Strop Q 1965–76; Müncher Q and Quintet. Prof Va Staat Hochschule für Musik, München 1946–; many of today's finest violists were his students. Played all of major Va concertos as soloist, or with Henryk Szeryng, Tortellier, Fournier, and other artists, under dir of Jochum, Kübelik, Kempe, and others. Concertized extensively throughout Europe. Record many works for Va with orch, chmb mus, and with piano. His wife, Ruth Danz, is also virtuoso Va. They frequently perform J. S. Bach's *Brandenburg VI*, and K. Stamitz *Viola Duo Sonatas.*

SCHNEIDER, F. LOUIS. Prominent London performer on Va and Va d'amore in late 19th century. Wrote articles about Va for the *Strad* magazine as early as 1893.

SCHOEN, WILLIAM, b Czechoslavakia, reared in Cleveland, Ohio. Stud Eastman Sch of Mus, George Eastman Scholarship, B.M. and Certificate of Pf; Chicago Mus Coll of Roosevelt U, M.M. with Honors. Va Rochester Philh; All-American Youth Orch; C.B.S. (NYC) Staff Orch, Pr Va for 8 yrs; Pr Va Philadelphia Orch 1963–64; Asst Pr Va Chicago Symp 1964–. Guilet Q, Claremont Q, Berkshire Q, Contemporary Arts Q, Chicago Symp Trio. Solo recitals and Duo-recitals with wife, Mona Reisman Schoen, Vn. Rare viola, Johannes Baptiste Genova, Turin, It. 1770.

SCHOTTEN, YIZHAK, b 1943 Haifa, Israel. Stud U of So. Cal., Indiana U, Wm. Primrose; Manhattan Sch of Mus and Aspen, Lillian Fuchs. Va Pittsburgh Symp; Boston Symp 1967–73. Pr Va Cincinnati Symp 1973–76. Trio d'Accordo 1976–. Concerto appearance Boston Pops, Cincinnati Chmb Orch 1979. Fac U of Washington 1979–. Pf at 7th Int'l Va Congress, Provo, Utah, 1979. Plays Gasparo da Salò Va used by Kneisel and Joachim Qs.

SCHREIBER. Lobkowitz Q (Schuppanzig and Mayseder, Vns; Kraft, cello), for which Beethoven wrote 6 *Quartets*, Op. 18.

SCHWARTZ, DAVID. Stud Vn Joachim Chassman; Va Curtis Inst of Mus, Louis Bailly, Max Aronoff. Pr Va Cleveland Orch at 22 yr of age; Va N.B.C. Orch (Toscanini); Pr Va N.B.C. Staff Orch, Detroit Symp, Puerto Rico Symp (Casals). Paganini Q, Yale Q (found mbr). Assoc Prof Va & chmb mus Yale U. Record Vangard (nominated for Grammy Award: Beethoven, Op. 132). Soloist, Mozart Fest at Lincoln Center. Pr Va Festival Casals, Puerto Rico. Festival Casals Q. Fac Mus Acad of the West, Santa Barbara, Ca.; U of Calif., Santa Barbara. Lecturer, Swarthmore Coll; Coe Coll; Lec.-Pf, Brigham Young U; Conn. A.S.T.A.; Str Seminar, Hartford U; Hartford U Chmb Mus Fest. Clinician in numerous A.S.T.A. seminars. Solo-lecture-recitals: NET, New York, Channel 13; New Haven, Conn; Detroit, Mich.; Sarasota, Fla. World Pre Pfs: Mel Powell, *Improvisations;* Arnold Franchetti, *Viola Suite;* Richard Browne, *Trio for Solo Viola;* Peter Schulthorpe, *Teotihuacan;* Frank Lewin, *Concerto for Viola and Orchestra.*

SCHWARZ, JOSEPH. Stud Cologne Cons Vn with G. Japha. Va in Cologne Gurzenich Q, late 19th century.

SCIANNAMEO, FRANCO, b 1942 Maglie (Lecce), Italy. Stud Cons Nazionale di Musica Santa Cecilia, Rome, Lilia d'Albore, Arrigo Pelliccia. Pf several Italian orchs, incl I Solisti di Roma. Q di Nuova Musica. Va Hartford Symp. Fac Hartford Cons, Connecticut, USA. Expert on the numerous Va works by A. Rolla, has ed several for pub.

SEBALD, ALEXANDER. Felix Berber Q of Leipzig, early 20th century.

SEILER, EMIL, b 1906 Nürnberg, Ger. Stud Hochschule für Mus, Berlin, Joseph Wolfsthal, Paul Hindemith, Curt Sachs, Georg Schünemann. Va Edwin Fischer Chmb Orch, Michael Taube Chmb Orch. Pr Va Orch des Deutschland Senders (Radio), Berlin 1935–42; Mozarteum 1945–46. Prof Va, Chmb Mus, Va d'amore Hochschule für Mus, Freiburg; Prof Va Breisgau 1947–55; Hochschule für Musik, Berlin 1955–74. Many recordings entitled "Emil Seiler Baroque Ensemble," Deutschen Grammophone.

SERLY, TIBOR, b 1901, Losonc, Hungary. d 1978, London, England. Stud Royal Acad of Mus, Budapest, Vn, Jeno Hubay; comp, Zoltan Kodaly. Va Cincinnati Orch, 1927–28; Philadelphia Orch, 1928–37; NBC Symph, 1937–38 (charter member). Retired from Pf in 1938 to devote full time to comp, condt, writing, and teaching. *Va Concerto* given premier by Milton Katims and ABC Symph, 1935, Pf and record by Emanuel Vardi, Serly cond, Vienna, 1964; Pf by Vardi at Intl Va Congress, Provo, Utah, 1979. Other comp for Va: *Rhapsody for Va; La Bandoline;* and *David of the White Rock;* all recorded by Vardi on Musical Heritage Label. Reconstructed Bartók *Va Concerto,* Pre Pf by Primrose, Minneapolis Orch, 1949; record by Primrose, Serly cond, London, 1950, Bartók Records. Tragically killed by auto in London, Oct. 8, 1978, while enroute to Budapest, Bartók Festival.

SHEBALIN, DIMITRI. Stud Moscow Cons, Vadim Borissovsky. Va of Borodin Q.

SHIN, DONG-OK (Mrs. Clara Whang M.M.), b 1935 Seoul, Korea. Stud Coll of Mus, Seoul U, Va with Kyung-Soo Won; Graduate Sch, Coll-Cons of Mus, Cincinnati, Ohio, Henry Meyer. Taught in Cleveland Public Sch 1962–66. Prof of Va Seoul U, 1969–. Va soloist Seoul Chamb Orch 1976–. Active in promoting interest in Va in Korea.

SHORE, BERNARD, Va, Cond, Auth., b London, 1896. Stud at St. Paul's Sch London; Royal Coll of Mus 1919–22; Va Arthur Bant, Lionel Tertis 1922–? Queen's Hall Orch 1922; Pr Va B.B.C. Symp 1930–40. Spencer Dyke Q; Cotterall Q. Prof of Va Royal Acad of Mus 1935–40; Royal Coll of Mus 1959–76. Mus Edu Inspector 1946–59. Pre Pf: Gordon Jacob, *Va Concerto* (Promenade Conc 1925) Queen's Hall, London; Philip Sainton, *Serenade Phantasque* (Prom conc); Felix Weingartner, *Triple Concerto for Vn, Va, & Cello* (Royal Philh Society); Arthur Benjamin, *Conc for Vn & Va;* Played Wm. Walton *Va Conc* with Concertgebow, Amsterdam, Van Beinum, cond 1947. Toured major cities of Australia playing Vaughn Williams' *Suite for Va and Orch,* 1956. Pres of first Intl Conf of Mus & Edu, Brussels,

1953. Author: *The Orchestra Speaks* (1937); *Sixteen Symphonies* (1947).

SIEGL, OTTO, 1896– Va and Comp of many works for Va. In the preface of his *Duo-Sonatine in F for Vn and Va*, Op. 138 (1944) he stated, "The role of the violist as a lazy middle part player is passé."

SILLS, DAVID L., b 1953, San Luis Obispo, California. Stud U of Calif, Santa Barbara, Stefan Krayk Vn, Peter Racine Fricker, Edward Applebaum, Comp 1971–76 B.A.; Manhattan Sch of Mus, Lillian Fuchs M.A. in Va, D.M.A. program 1977–; Josef Marx, private. Pr Va Brooklyn Philharmonia 1978–, Manticore 1978–, Resonance 1977–, Ars Novae Musicae (co-founder) 1977–. Tch Fellowship Manhattan Sch of Mus 1979. Pre Pf: *Fantasy-Music, Affirmation* by Robert Martin; *Duo for 2 Violins* by Stefan Wolpe; *3 Rounds for 6 Violas, Images from Stillness, Secrets of the Heart* by Robert Kyr; *2 Pieces for Viola and Piano* by Raoul Pleskow; *Ululare, Chamber Concerto for Viola* by Daniel Rothman; *3 Canons* by Matthew Greenbaum; *3 Movements for Viola Solo* by Peter Racine Fricker; Revivals of 18th and 19th century works: Q Sonatas of Johann Gottlieb Janitsch; *Concerto for 2 English horns, 2 Violas, 2 Bassoons, and Basso Continuo* by Johann Friedrich Fasch; *Sechs Stucke*, Op. 3 by Amadeus Maczewski; *Le Songe* by Jacque Fereol Mazas. Comp: *Confession Amantis* (Contata for Soprano, Alto Flute, and Viola; texts by Dante, Maeterlinck, and Dowland), and *Stagioni D'Amore* (Concerto for Viola, Flute, English Horn, and Harp). Compts: George Schick award; 1st Concerto compt, both Manhattan Sch of Mus 1978; semi-finalist, William Primrose Int'l Va Compt, 1979.

SITT, HANS, b 1850 in Prague; d Leipzig 1922. Stud Prague Cons. Eminent concert career throughout Europe as Vn. Va in Brodsky Q. Composed works for Va incl well known *Concerto in G Minor*, Op. 46, 1905; *Viola Concerto in A Minor*, Op. 68; *Praktische Violaschule*, 1915.

SKERNICK, ABRAHAM, b 1923, New York City. Stud Vn John King Roosa; Va Emanuel Vardi, Nicholas Moldavan; Brooklyn Coll. Pr Va Chautauqua Symp, Casals Fest, Aspen Fest, Baltimore Symp 1948-9, Cleveland Orch 1949–76. Fac, Va, Chmb Mus, Peabody Cons 1948–9; Cleveland Insti of Mus 1963–76; Indiana U 1976–. Mischakoff Q, Cleveland Orch Q, Berkshire Q. Record Chmb Mus with George Szell, Rafael Druian, John Mack, Eunice Poois.

SLAUGHTER, ROBERT W., b 1926, Weehawken, N.J. Stud Norman Goldblatt; Oberlin Coll, B.M., M.M., Reber Johnson; U of Mich, Robert Courte. Asst Pr Va Dallas Symp 1952–55; Pr Va Houston Symp 1955–56, Dallas Symp 1957–65. Professional playing in Chicago: Opera, Symp, String Qs. T.V., etc. Prof Va Ball State U, Muncie, Ind. 1973–.

SOLOMON, STANLEY, b 1917 Toronto, Ont. Can. Stud Louis Bailly, Max Aronoff, Oscar Shumsky. Pr Va Toronto Symp and Canadian Opera Orch 1946–, Hart House Chmb Orch, also Manager. Kathleen Perlow Q for 12 years. Owns and plays one of few existing Andrea Amati violas, c.1580.

SPELMAN, SIMON, English Va who Fl late 19th century. Pr Va of Hallé Orch, dir by Sir Charles Hallé. Pf Mozart *Concertante* and Berlioz *Harold in Italy* many times before 1895. Was a favorite of Manchester audiences. Va of Hess Q. Described as one of finest Va of his time.

STAMITZ, ANTON, b 1754 Mannheim, Ger; d Paris c.1809. Son of Johann Stamitz. Virtuoso Pf on Vn, Va, and Va d'amore. Comp works for Va. See Chapter VI.

STAMITZ, KARL, b 1746 Mannheim, Ger; d 1801 Jena, E. Ger. Virtuoso of Vn, Va, and Va d'Amore. Composed works for Va. See Chapter VI

STANICK, Gerald, b 1933 Winnipeg, Manitoba, Canada. Stud Indiana U, David Dawson 1954–58. Pr Va Winnipeg Symp, CBC Radio Orch 1958–63. Corydon Trio, U of Manitoba Q 1958–63, Fine Arts Q 1963–68, Q Canada 1977–. Prof of Music U of Wisconsin Milwaukee 1963–68, U of Victoria, B.C. 1974–77, U of Western Ontario 1977–. Fac Banff Sch of Fine Arts 1974–77, Courtenay Youth Music Centre, Montreal Cons, Summer U of Wyoming, 1974–77. Mus Director Wisconsin Coll-Cons, Cond Ars Musica Chmbr Orch 1968–74. Tours with Q Europe, Asia, Japan, Korea, Hawaii.

STERN, VICTOR, b 1923 Philadelphia, Pa. Stud Manhattan Sch of Mus; Chattham Square Mus Sch; Va privately with William Primrose; Vn D. C. Dounis. Pr Va Miami Philh 1952–72. Prof Va and Chmb Mus U of Miami 1952–. Fac and Pr Va Eastern Mus Fest, North Carolina 1974–. Found Stern-Mercadal Duo (Va and guitar).

STECK, FRANCISCO, b Lieja. Prominent in Cordoba. See Appendix II.

STEINER, H. Va in Rosé Q (founding mbr, 1883).

STILWELL, F. RAYMOND, b 1932, Harrisburg, Pa. Stud American Cons, Chicago, Scott Willits; Eastman Sch of Mus, B.M. and Pf Certificate, Francis Tursi; Indiana U, M.M. and work toward Doctorate, David Dawson, Wm. Primrose 1969–71; Privately with Milton Preves, Leonard Mogill. Fac Interlochen Arts Acad 1965–69; Prof of Va Cincinnati Cons of U of Cincinnati. Pr Va Chicago Little Symp 1965–69, Cincinnati Symp 1971–.

STOCK, FREDERICK, b 1872, in Jülich, West Germany; d. 1942 in Chicago. Stud at Cologne Cons, Vn with G.Japha. Pr Va in Chicago Symphony, 1895–1905, before becoming Cond of this world famous Orch.

STRAUSS, LUDWIG, b 1835 in Pressburg; d 1899 in Cambridge, England. Prominent Vn, Va, and cond in Europe and England. Va in Mayseder Q 1856–7; Va in Popular Concerts Q in London 1888–.

STREET, MARNA, b 1949 Tulsa, Okla. Stud Tosca Berger, Tulsa Okla. Juilliard Sch of Mus, Walter Trampler; Eastman Sch of Mus, Francis Tursi; Hungarian Q, Colby Coll, Waterville, Maine. Vilas Master Q, U of Wisc 1971–73. Va Pittsburgh Symp 1977–. Fac Texas Tech U 1975–77. Also Pf on Va d'amore: Pre Pf Huberty Va d'amore works at V R S Congress, Bonn, Ger 1976; Found mbr Pittsburgh Baroque Players 1977–. Advanced research in conjunction with the Hindemith Insti on 3 unpub Va sonatas. Secretary of American Va Society 1977–.

SUGAREV, STEPHAN, b 1907 Samakov, Bulgaria; d 1958 Sofia, Bulgaria. Pioneer of solo Va Pf in Bulgaria. Tch Acad of Mus in Sofia 1947–58. Great influence on Bulgarian Va.

SVECENSKI, LOUIS, 1862–1926; b and trained in Ger. Moved to USA to join Boston Symp 1885–1903. Kneisel Q 1885–1917. Ed J. S. Bach Suites for Va; wrote 25 *Technical Exercises for Va*.

SZEREDI-SUAPE, GUSTAV, b 1909 Budapest, Hungary. Stud Stadtischen Oberschule für Musik, Budapest, Dozent Maria Zipernovszky; privately Va and Va d'amore with Nándor Zsolt. As a youth played for Paul Hindemith who said, "You are a fine fiddler and an equally fine violist!" Pr Va Budapest Konzertorchester; Melles-Kammer-Orch. Solo Va and Va d'amore Handel Festival Orch at Halle. Tch Va Cons, Székesfehérvár; Dir Martin Luther U, Halle-Wittenberg; presently Istvan Musik-Oberschule, Budapest and privately. Presently Hungarian Harp Trio with Maria Vermes, vn, and his wife Anna Molnar, harp, concertizing throughout Europe. Plays Ruggieri-Testore Va 42.8 cm. (16 7/8 in.).

TAKAHIRA, JUN, b 1960 Graduate Japan U Tsuragauka High Sch. Switched from Vn to Va by himself following 2 week workshop with Milton Thomas, 1977. Stud with William Primrose 1978–, who wrote, "the greatest Va talent to come my way." Debut Sydney, Australia, 1979. 2nd Prz William Primrose Int'l Va Compt 1979. Pre Pf of Marrill Bradshaw's *Homages for Va and Orch* at 7th Int'l Va Cong, Provo, Utah, 1979. Donald McInnes: "The greatest viola talent I've ever heard."

TATTON, THOMAS JAMES, b 1943 Santa Monica, Calif. Stud Calif State U at Northridge with Manuel Compinskyi, B.A. Kansas State Teachers' Coll with Myron Sandler M.M., U of Illinois with Guillermo Perich, D.M.A., Disseration: *English Viola Music, 1897–1937*, Urbana, Ill., 1976. Prof of Va Whittier Coll, Calif. Pr Va Springfield (Calif) Symp and Rio Hondo (Calif) Symp. Ed of pub for ensembles of multiple Va. Music for multiple Vas at Int'l Va Congresses 1976, 78, 79.

TCHAVDAROV, ZAHARI, b. 1930 Jambol, Bulgaria. Stud Vn with father; Va Acad of Mus Sofia 1947–51, S. Sugarev; Budapest Cons 1955, Pál Lukács. Bulgarian State Q 1952; Pr Va Bulgarian State Radio Orch 1957; Stockholm Philh 1970–. Prof of Va Academy of Mus Sofia 1957. Pre Pf in Bulgaria Bartók *Va Concerto* 1965, in Sweden Shostakovich *Sonata* 1976. Recorded for Radio Sweden Label. Arr and Ed works for Va and Piano. Owns and plays Storione Va 1767.

TERTIS, LIONEL, b 1876 West Harterpool, England; d 1975 London. One of the pioneers and early protagonists who elevated the Va from its role as a lesser sibling of the Vn and Cello to an accepted position of musical prominence. See Chapters XII, XIII.

THOMAS, MILTON, b 1920, Washington, Pa. Stud with Ralph Lewando, Pittsburgh, Pa.; Juilliard Grad Sch, vn Fellowship. Became Violist 1940. Stud Pablo Casals, Prades Festival 1949. Stokowski's

Youth Orch, 1940–1; Cleveland Orch 1940–4. Has appeared as soloist with orch in Europe, Israel, USA; radio pf for BBC and in Italy, France, Germany, Scandinavia; Festival Casals, Puerto Rico; Summer Mus Fest Sitka, Alaska. Pre Pf Ingolf Dahl: *Divertimento for Va and Piano* (written for him) in Los Angeles; Henri Lazarof: *Viola Concerto* in Israel, Paris, Turin; *Viola Concerto "Volo"*, in Los Angeles (dedicated to him); *Cadance II* for Va and recorded tape, in Los Angeles; Paul Chihara: *Redwood* for Va and Percussion (dedicated to him). Cond Va Brandenburg Players, Town Hall 1960, Carnegie Hall, 1967. Pf in concert and recordings with Casals, Myra Hess, Heifetz, Piatigorsky, and Stern. Recordings for Columbia, Desto, Everest, Klavier, Orion, Protone, RCA. Now teaching at U.C.L.A., U.S.C., and Santa Barbara Mus Acad. Pf and Master Classes in Japan 1977,8,9. Master Class and Pf at 7th Int'l Va Congress, Provo, Utah, 1979. Owns and plays a Mattio Goffriller viola, Venice, 1699.

THOMPSON, MARCUS, b 1946 Bronx, NY. Stud Juilliard Sch of Mus, Louise Behrend, Walter Trampler, B.M. 1967, M.S. 1968, D.M.A. 1970, Abraham Skernick, Aspen. Prof of Va Juilliard (Preparatory) 1969–70, Oakwood Coll 1970–71, Mount Holyoke Coll 1971–73, Wesleyan U 1971– and including Dir Chamb Mus 1973–, Prof of Humanities Mass. Institute of Technology 1979–. Recitals USA and Central America. Concertos with Nat'l Symp, St. Louis Symp, Boston Pops, Symp of New World, Cypriot Radio Orch, Chmb Orch of San Salvador. World premiers of Barry Vercoe's *Synapse for Va and Computer* 1976; T. J. Anderson's *Variations on a Theme of Alban Berg* 1978. Record for Vox Turnabout. Pf "Mus for Va by USA Composers" 7th Int'l Va Cong, Provo, Utah, 1979. Owns and plays 1798 G B Ceruti.

TICHAUER, THOMAS, b 1943 Buenos Aires, Argentina. See Appendix II.

TÖSZEGHI, ANDRAS von, b 1945 Debrecen, Hungary. Stud Lucerne Cons, Switz. with Rudolf Baumgartner; Privately with Bela Katona, London; Indiana U, William Primrose. Va soloist and Cond "Kammerorchester 1965"; Lucerne Str Q 1966; Hungarian Str Trio Zurich 1977; Melos Trio Zurich 1978. Tch No Carolina Sch of the Arts 1973–74. Recorded 8 Va solos. Pre Pf of Va works by Peter Benary, H. Haller, A. Pitsillides, J. Tamas, R. Vuataz, F. Reizenstein, P. Mieg; World Pre Benjamin Britten posthumous *Va Concerto*, Holland Festival 1977. Special distinction at Swiss B.A.T. modern Chmb Mus Compt; Edwin Fischer Memorial Prz.

TRAMPLER, WALTER, b 1915 Munich, W. Gr. Early training with father. State Acad of Mus Munich with Theodore Kilian. Pr Va Deutschland Radio Orch, Berlin 1935–38; Va Boston Symp 1942–44; Pr Va City Center Symp and Opera Orch; Chmb Mus Society of Lincoln Center, solo recital with 1970. Strub Q 1935–9, New Music Q 1947–56. Pre Pf of Wolfgang Fortner's *Concerto,* 1936 in Ger.; H. Overton' Sonata 1958, Ralph Shapey's *Duo for Va and Piano* 1958, Vincent Persichetti's *Infanta Marina for Va and Piano* 1959, Luciano Berio's *Seguenza VI.* Fac Juilliard 1962–72, Peabody 1968–70, Yale U 1970–72, Boston U —. Works commissioned and Pre Pf Luciano Berio's *Chemins II* (Juilliard) 1968; *Chemins III* (Paris) 1969; Simon Bainbridge, *Concerto* (London) 1977; Mark Neikrug *Concerto,* pending. Soloist 5th Intl Va Congress, Rochester, 1976. Annual concert tours in U.S., England, and Europe. Many significant record of works for Va. Plays and owns beautiful Va by Hieronymous and Antonius Amati, c.1620.

TREE, MICHAEL, b 1934 Newark, N.J. Stud Vn Samuel Applebaum (his father); Curtis Insti of Mus Lea Luboshutz, Veda Reynolds, Efrem Zimbalist. Concert career as Vn soloist incl appearances with Phila Los Angeles, Baltimore, New Jersey, and other orchs; festivals Spoleto, Casals, Marlboro, Israel. Found mbr as Va Marlboro Trio and Guarneri Q. Fac Curtis Insti of Mus.

TRÖTZMÜLLER, KARL, b 1908 Vienna, Austria. Stud Va Acad of Mus 1924–32, also Vn, Mus Theory. Pr Va Wiener Symphoniker 1945–63. Pf Bach Brandenburg VI, in which Hindemith cond and played Va I part 1952; since 1962 owns Hindemith's Va, the composer's wish, according to the Hamma Certificate, an old example of the Milano School. Recording artist on both Va and Flute. Ed of works for Va for Doblinger Publisher of Vienna, incl Johann B. Wanhal *Concerto in F Major* (1978).

TURSI, FRANCIS, b 1922 Camden, N.J. Stud Alfred Lorenz; Eastman Sch of Mus, Samuel Belov; Curtis Insti of Mus, Max Aronoff. Va Eastman Q 1949–60, 1965–. Pr Va Rochester Philh 1966–67. Prof of Va Eastman Sch of Mus 1949–. Has graduated many artist violists into symphonies and teaching profession. Prof of Va summers: Interlochen 1959-60; U of Maine 1971–73; and Dir of Chmb Mus Southern Vermont Arts Center 1975–. Many Pre Pf of Va works by contemporary composers incl Verne Reynold's *Sonata for Va and Piano* (1975), dedicated to Tursi and Barry Snyder. They repeated this *Sonata* on Tursi's recital concert at Int'l Va Congress, Rochester, N.Y., 1977.

TUTTLE, KAREN, Stud at Curtis Inst of Mus; Va with William Primrose. Taught Va and Chmb Mus at Curtis Insti succeeding Primrose. Head Str Dept Philadelphia Mus Acad. Academy Trio. Schneider Q; Galamir Q; Gotham Q. Master Classes, and/or Perf at Yale, Eastman, Orono, U of Utah, Prades, Casals Festivals. Recording and concert artist. Now Fac Va and Chmb Mus at Peabody Cons, also tch Curtis Inst, Mannes Sch of Mus. Recital and Primrose Tribute Pf at 7th Int'l Va Cong, Provo, Utah, 1979.

UGARTE, RAFAEL MANCILLA, b 1937 in Mexico D.F. Stud Vn, José F. Vasquez, Gloria Torres de Vasquez; Mex. Nat'l Cons, Va Herbert Froelich. Pr Va Mexico Opera Orch. Bellas Artes Q.

URHAN, CHRÉTIEN, b 1790 Montjoie near Aix-la-Chapelle; d 1845 Paris. Virtuoso of the Va and Va d'amore. See Chapter XI.

VAN HOUT, LEON, b c.1885 in Liège, Belgium; d after 1940. His dedication and artistry influenced an entire generation of Belgian violists to higher standards of peformance, and inspired Belgian composers to write for the viola. See Chapter XIV.

VANCOILLIE, ANDRES, b Menen, Belgium; d 1974 Buenos Aires, Argentina. See Appendix II.

VARDI, EMANUEL, b 1917 Jerusalem. Stud with his father; Joseph Borisoff; NYC Inst of Mus Art, Constance Seeger; Juilliard Fellowship, Edward Dethier; privately William Primrose; Emanuel Feuermann (Bach *Solo Suites*); Mario Vitetta. Pr Va NBC Symp incl solos 1939–42, 1952–54; Pr Va ABC Radio Symp 1946–49, Symp of the Air. Stuyvesant Q 1940–41, Guillet Q 1953–55; Friedman, Vardi, Silberstein Trio 1976–. Solo concerts: Town Hall debut 1941; Carnegie Hall 1946, Chicago Orch Hall 1946, Los Angeles Phil 1948. Town Hall Critics Award: "Recitalist of the Year" 1943. Helped promote Va works of Tibor Serly. Pre Pf: Tibor Serly: *Rhapsody*, South Dakota Symp 1977; George Kleinsinger: *Prelude, Lament, and Jig for Brendan Behan*. Recordings: Paganini *24 Caprices* (for Va); all Va works by Tibor Serly incl *Concerto, Rhapsody* with Pauline Vardi, piano; Arnold Bax *Sonata for Va and Piano*, Abba Bogin, piano, *Sonata for Va and Harp*, Margaret Ross, harp; Arthur Bliss *Sonata*, Frank Weinstock, piano; Vaughn Williams, *Suite*, Frank Weinstock, piano; Mozart and Stamitz *Duets* (Vardi both parts); many others planned and in preparation under Musical Heritage label. Presently Mus Dir, & Cond South Dakota Symp.

DE VERITCH, ALAN, b 1947, Montclair, N.J. Stud Father Victor de Veritch, Sanford Schonbach, Vera Barstow, William Primrose at Indiana U, Paul Doktor, Ivan Galamian. Co-Pr Va Los Angeles Philharmonic 1970–79. Aldanya Q 1965–70; White House Q 1966–70; An die Musik 1978–. Fac: (Tch Ass't) Indiana U 1965–66; Calif State U at Northridge; U of So Calif 1972–3; Calif Insti of the Arts 1973– Head Va Dept. Pre Pf *Va Concerto* by Robert Parris, Washington Nat'l Symp. Toured USA & Eur Zubin Mehta, L. A. Philh. Rec *Brandenburg # 6* with Pinchas Zukerman, Deutsche Grammophon.

VIELAND, JOSEPH, d 1972. Asst Pr Va N.Y. Philh in 1920's and 30's. Ed and trans many significant works for Va, pub by I.M.C. Ed the widely used *Orchestral Studies,* 5 Vols, I.M.C., 1951/53.

VIEUX, MAURICE, b 1884 in Vieux Conde Nord, Fr; d 1957 Paris. "The father of the modern French Viola School." See Chapter XIV.

VIEUXTEMPS, HENRI, 1820–1881. Famous Belgian Vn. Played Va in cham mus. Wrote several important works for Va, incl *Sonata for Viola and Piano,* Op. 36.

VOLLNHALS, LUDWIG. Va in Walther Q of Munich 1887 – ?.

VOLMER, BERTA. b 1908 in Saarbrücken. Stud Karl Flesch. Va Van Essen Q for 22 yrs; concerts in Germany and abroad. Prof of Va State Acad of Mus Cologne 1958–; Dir of Master Class for Va 1971–. For 20 yrs worked in collaboration with Max Rostal. Pub *Bratschenschule* in 3 pts: 1955, 56, 57. Reputed to be one of Europe's finest viola teachers.

WAEFELGHEM, LOUIS van, b 1840 Bruges, Belgium; d 1908 Paris. Stud Brussels Cons, Vn Meerts. After successful career as Vn in Germany, moved to Paris in 1863 to pursue career as Pf on Va and Va d'amore. By c.1870 his reputation as a superb Va brought opportunities to play Q with Joachim, Auer, Vieuxtemps, Sivori, Sarasate, etc. Pr Va Lamoreaux Orch 1881–95. 1895, full-time Va d'amore, reviving works by Flemish composers of 16th century. With Louis Diemer (harpsichord), Jules Delsaert (Va da gamba), Laurent Grillet (hurdygurdy), found *Société des Instruments Anciens,* 1895.

WALDBAUER, JOSEPH. Followed Bram Eldering, 1889 as Va in the Hubay-Popper Q of Budapest.

WALLFISCH, ERNST, b 1920, Frankfurt, W. Gr. d 1979, Northampton, Mass, USA. Stud Vn at 8 years, switched to Va at 14. Royal Acad of Mus, Bucharest, Roumania, Cecilia Nitzulescu-Lupu, Michail Jora, Michail Andricu, Ionel Perlea. Pro Musica Q 1938 until World War II. Va Bucharest Philh 1944–46; Asst Pr Va Dallas Symp 1947–49; Va Cleveland Orch 1949–53; Pr Va Detroit Symp 1953–55. Prof of Va Mozarteum, Salzburg, Austria and Lucerne Cons, Switz. 1960–64; Smith College, Northampton, Mass 1964–. Many concert tours in USA, Eng, and Europe. Pre Pf G. Fr. Malipiero's *Viola Concerto* ("Dialogue V") with Paris Radio Orch 1958. Prades Casals Fest 1955–60, 1976; Yehudi Menuhin Gstad Fest, 1957–; Int'l Fest at Edinburgh, York, Besancon, Menton, Venice; Yehudi Menuhin 60th Birthday, Carnegie Hall 1976; Int'l Viola Congress, 1975,76,78. Frequent Duo-Recitals with wife, Lory, virtuoso pianist and harpsichordist. Record for Odeon, Fonti, DaCamera, Vox Turnabout, Musical Heritage Society, EMI, Philips, Advance, and Opus One. Also played viola da Gamba; many significant recordings of works for Va. Ed of Baroque mus.

WALTHER, GERALDINE, b.1951 Stud Manhattan School of Mus, Lillian Fuchs; Curtis Institute, Michael Tree. Asst Pr Va Pittsburgh Symp; Now Pr Va San Francisco Symp, soloist under Edo de Waart. Recipient of "Outstanding Musician Award" at Tanglewood. Winner First Prize in Primrose Int'l Va Compt, 1979.

WEBER, FRITZ von, 1761–183?. Older brother and early teacher of Carl Maria von Weber. Leading Va of Hamburg Opera. Carl Maria wrote *Andante und Rondo Ungaresse* for his brother in 1809. Fritz' artistry as a violist may have also influenced Carl Maria in selecting the viola for the obligato part to Aennchen's "Romance und Arie" in the third act of *Der Freichütz*, 1821.

WEISS, ABRAHAM, b 1905 NYC. Stud Vn San Francisco Cons 1930. Va with William Primrose 1942–44; Vn Dounis 1945–47. Immaculate Heart Coll, B.A. 1961. Abos Q 1934–36, Pre Pf Schoenberg Qs 1,2,3; Coriolan Q 1949–67. Va Los Angeles Philh 1937–47: Ass't Pr Va 1944–46, Pr Va 1947. Va United Artist Motion Picture Studio 1968–. Had 17 1/8 inch Gasparo da Salò Va which was stolen in 1967, no trace.

WEISS, FRANZ, b Silesia 1778, d Vienna, 1830. Rasoumowsky Q, Schuppanzig Q. These Q's played most of Beethoven's Chmb Mus from Ms with the composer present.

WERTHEIM, SIEGFRIED, b 1873 in Amsterdam. At age 16 rec'd scholarship from Queen of Holland, Vn with Joseph Cramer. Vn, Concertgebouw Orch, 1890. Pr Va, Philadelphia Orch, 1891, Queen's Hall Orch in London 1904–? Played a Maggini Va which had been cut down from a Va da gamba.

WHITE, JOHN, b 1938, Leeds, England. Stud on scholarship at R.A.M., Watson Forbes, Harry Danks. Albertini Q; Stadler Trio; London Philh Orch. Tch Hockerill Coll of Edu, Bishop's Stortford 1975–; Faculty of R.A.M. 1976–. Frequent concerts and rctls in London area. Gordon Jacob ded *Sonatina for 2 Va* to Harry Danks and John White (1974), and *Variations for Unacc Va* to John White (1975). Alan Richardson ded *Rhapsody for Va and Piano* (1977). Also plays rebec and Va d'amore. Co-found of British Branch of VRS; and co-host of 6th Int'l Va Congress, London, 1978. Ed of British VRS Newsletter. Author of articles in *Strad* on Va. Research in tch of Va all ages.

WIEN, KARL. Prof of Vn at Stuttgart Cons. Succeeded Debuysère as Va in Stuttgart Q in late 19th century, under Edmund Singer's leadership.

WILLIAMS, MICHAEL, b 1942 Buffalo, N.Y. Stud Northwestern U, B.M.E. 1964, M.M. 1966, Harold Klatz; Indiana U Ph.D. 1973 (Musicology) "Violin Concertos of R. Kreutzer." Assoc Prof of Mus U of Houston 1970–. Researching *Music for Solo Viola: An Annotated List of Music for Unaccompanied Viola, Viola and Keyboard Instrument, Viola and Non-Keyboard Instrument, Viola and Chamber Ensemble, and Viola and Orchestra,* Detroit Studies of Mus Bibliography, Detroit: Information Coordinators, forthcoming. *A History of Viola Music to 1820.* Research underway.

WIRTH, EMANUEL, 1842–1923. Outstanding Vn, Tch, Cond. Va many years in famous Joachim Q.

WOODWARD, ANN, b 1940 Cincinnati, Ohio. Stud Oberlin Coll 1958–60, William Berman; Curtis Insti of Mus 1961–65, Max Aronoff; Fontainbleau, France 1963; Yale Sch of Mus 1965–67, David Schwartz, D.M.A. 1973 (first recipient). Prof of Va North Carolina U 1967–. North Carolina U Q. Va works ded to and written for : Roger Hannay, *Fantome for Va, Clar, and Piano* 1968; Thomas Brosh *Innerchange for Va and Electronic Piano* 1974; Henry Woodward *Suite for Va and Piano* 1961, *Eight Pieces for Va and Piano* 1969; Phillip Rhodes, *Partita for Solo Va* 1978. Secretary American Va Society

1967–. Owns and plays ex-Courte Mathais Albani viola made in 17th century.

WRIGHT, DONALD. b 1927, Harrisburg, Pa. Stud D. Harold Jauss; Eastman Sch. of Mus. B.M., M.M., Francis Tursi; U. of Texas Institute Grant in Eng. 1966. Rochester, Houston, Peninsula Mus Fest Orchs. Pr Va Brevard Mus Center; Va Marlboro Mus Fest. Recital Wigmore Hall, London, 1966. Prof of Va U of Texas 1958–. Pre Pf Samuel Adler, *Song and Dance for Va. and Orch*, Commis by Maurice Peress for Wright, Corpus Christi Symp, 1969. Wm. Doppmann, *Shadows: A Journey for Va and Orch*, Pf at Philipps Gallery, Washington, D.C., 1971. Many recitals throughout Texas incl Mozart *Concertante*, Hindemith *Der Schwanendreher*. Chmb Mus with Andor Toth, Leonard Posner, George Neikrug, Robert Sylvester, Paul Olefsky, Stewert Saukey.

von WROCHEM, ULRICH, b 1943, Dippoldiswalde, Ger. Stud Berlin Cons, Kirchner; Hochschule für Musick, Detmold, George Niekrug. Pr Va Nordwestdeutsche Philharmonie 1966, Bayerisches Radioorchester 1967–70, Deutsche Opera, Berlin 1970–72, Bamberger Symphoniker 1972–74, Teatro la Scala, Milan 1974–77. Berlin Str. Trio 1965–. Tch summer Hochschule f. Musik, Karlsruhe 1977. Numerous solo pf with piano, orch, chmb mus groups throughout Europe, Israel, U.S.

ZASLAV, BERNARD, b 1926 Brooklyn, N.Y. Stud Juilliard Sch of Mus, Sascha Jacobsen, Mischa Mischakoff; Yale U, Lillian Fuchs. Va Cleveland Orch 1949–51. Kohon Str Q 1958–63, Composers Str Q 1963–68 (founding member), Fine Arts Str Q (resident Q), U of Wisconsin 1968–. Distinguished Prof U of Wisc Milwaukee. Many concerts Va-Piano Duo with wife Naomi. Latest recording: *French Music for Va and Piano* (Orion ORS-75186), incl 2 *Sonatas* by Darius Milhaud and *Vn Sonata* by Cesar Franck trans for Va and Piano. Owns and plays "ex Villa" J.B. Guadagnini Va, Turin 1781.

ZERBST, OTTO. Stud Vn J. Grun, Vienna. Va Fitzner Q (founding mbr 1894).

ZEYRINGER, FRANZ, b 1920. Va, soloist, tch, author of many books and articles for Va. Founding mbr and Pres. of VFG. Musikdirektor of Musik Hochschule in Pöllau, Austria. Collaborator of IVFG Archives at Mozarteum, Salzburg. Research into measurements for Va. Recitals, lectures, Pf Int'l Va Congresses 1975, 76, 77, 78, 79.

Author of the definitive *Literatur für Viola*, 1963, 1965, 1976. See Chapter XIV.

ZOELLER, CARLI, b 1849 Berlin; d 1889 London. Stud at R.A.M., London, Vn Hubert Ries. Pf on Va and Va d'amore. Wrote *New Method for the Viola d'Amore*.

ZUKERMAN, PINCHAS, b 1948 Israel. Stud Juilliard Ivan Galamian. Since 1967 internationally famous Vn and Va. Concertized and recorded with Isaac Stern. Record Brahms *Sonatas* with Daniel Barenboim. Va with Itzhak Perlman and other artists. Fac and cond at Aspen Festival.

APPENDIX II

ARGENTINE VIOLISTS, VIOLA MAKERS, AND COMPOSERS OF VIOLA MUSIC

Contributed by

Eduardo R. Dali
of
Buenos Aires, Argentina

Outstanding Viola Players of Argentina

BANDINI, BRUNO, b 1889 Faenza, Italy; d 1969 Buenos Aires. Emigrated to Argentina as a child. Stud H. Galvani, A Cattaneo, C. Troiani. Va Opera Theatre Orch 1906 (Toscanini, Cond). 1st rctl on Va as a solo instru in Argentina 1909. Pr Va Theatre Colon Orch, Asociacion de Profesorado Orquestal, 1914–d. Wagnerian Assoc Q; Cattelani Q; found mbr Str Q Society. 25 years Cond Sch of Orch Playing Miguel Gianneo. Dir State Broadcasting Orchs 1955–d. Fac Va St Cons of Mus 1924–d; Municipal Government Cons of Mus 1930. Comp *Prelude for Solo Va* (Pub Ricordi, Buenos Aires), made many orch trans. An eminent figure in the musical field of Argentina and teacher of many Va and orch players.

BONFIGLIOLI, JOSE, b 1851 Bologna, Italy; d 1916 Buenos Aires. Stud C. Berardi. Emigrated to Argentina. Pr Va Theatre Colon Orch. Outstanding Chmb Mus player. 1st leading Va of his time in Argentina. Owned and played Frencesco Stradivarius Va, preserved in Str Instru Museum of Theatre Colon.

GAMBUZZI, EDGARDO. Pr Va Theatre Colon Orch. Tch Va Fine Arts Sch of La Plata. Renacimiento Str Q 1934–48. Now in retirement. Owned and played G. P. Maggini 1585, and Tertis Model by E. Petraglia.

MOLO, CAKETANO, b Argentina. Stud Lyon, France. Va and Pr Va Theatre Colon Orch 1924–? Pessina Q 1932–?; Diapason Q. Found, playing Va d'amore Argentine Ens of Ancient Instrus. Now in retirement. Played Pietro Giov. Mantegazza Va.

PERINI, MARIO, b 1911 Buenos Aires. Stud B. Bandini, comp J. F. Giaccobbe. Pr Va Buenos Aires Symp Orch, Cordoba Symp Orch. Tch Va and chmb mus U of Cordoba. Perini Q. Composer and Va of distinction. Plays 16½ in. (41.9 cm.) E. Petraglia Va.

STECK, FRANCISCO, b Lieja. Stud J. Rogister, vn Massart. Emigrated to Argentina 1911. Pr Va Cordoba Symp Orch. Tch Va Cons of Mus of Cordoba. Comp *Concerto for Va and Orch.* Amateur vn maker.

TICHAUER, TOMAS, b 1943 Buenos Aires. Stud Va, vn H. Weil, L. Spiller; comp E. Wolff, G. Graetzer; Scholarship Yehudi Menuhin, Academia Internazionale di Musica da Camara in Rome and Switz; chmb and old mus N. Boulanger, R. Clemencic. Pr Va "Camerata Bariloche" Orch. Chmb Mus rctls with Yehudi and Hepzibah Menuhin, E. Wallfisch, M. Gendron, and others. Record: Schubert's *Arpeggione Sonata*, Arizaga's *Ciaccona*, Eccles' *Sonata*. Va player of int'l caliber and most promising figure in Argentina at present.

VANCOILLIE, ANDRES, b Menen, Belgium; d 1974 Buenos Aires. Stud Leopold Piery, Belgium. Migrated to Argentina. Va Theatre Colon Orch. Pr Va State Nat'l Orch, Philh Orch of Buenos Aires. Pro Arte Q (Argentina). Tch Va and chmb mus State Cons of Mus, Cons of Mus of La Plata. Played under principal conductors, incl Hindemith *Concerto*, Hindemith cond. Responsible for wide awakening of solo possibilities of Va in Argentina and introduced there works of world's Va repertory.

Viola Music by Argentine Composers

ARIZAGA, RODOLFO, b 1926. *Ciaccona per viola* (1969), ded to and record by Tomas Tichauer, Qualiton Records SQ1–4022, Buenos Aires. An interesting and important work.

BANDINI, BRUNO. (1889–1969) Va pf and tch. *Preludio for Solo Va* (pub Ricordi, Buenos Aires).

CANOURA RAMOS, FÉLIX, b 1921. Spanish comp and Va pf. *Four Caprices for Va and Piano* (1971): 1. *Erinnerung* Op. 33, 2. *Auf Wiedersehen* Op. 34, 3. *Klugelied* Op. 38, 4. *Einleintung und Keltetanz* Op. 39, all ded to Eduardo Dali, unpub.

CASTRO, WASHINGTON, b 1909. Cellist and cond. *Elegiac Concerto for Va and Orch.* Pre Pf 1958. Unpub.

DUBLANC, EMILIO ANTONIO, b 1911. *Sonata for Va and Piano* (1942). Pub by Cuyo U, Mendoza, Argentina.

FICHER, JACOBO, b 1896. Russian comp settled Argentina. *3 Pieces for Va and Piano* Op. 76. *Sonata for Va and Piano* Op. 80 (1953). Pre Pf by Andrés Vancoillie.

KOHAN, CELINA, b 1931. *Concertino for Va and Orch* (1951). Pre Pf 1959. 1st Prz Argentine Culture Commision, 1957, unpub.

PERINI, MARIO, b 1911. Comp and Va. *Three Argentine Themes for Va and Piano* (1948). *Creole Suite for Solo Va* (1951). *Argentine Concerto for Va and Orch* (1952). *Concerto for Four Va and Orch* (1951), 1st Prz Biennal Contest 1948/49 of Argentine Culture Commission, unpub. Perini's style of comp is genuinely based on native folk-lore and he makes frequent use of rhythms, dances, and melodies of Argentina.

STECK, FRANCISCO. Comp and Va of Belgian origin. *Concerto for Va and Orch.* Pre Pf 1941, Cordoba. Unpub.

Viola Makers in Argentina

PETRAGLIA, EMILIO, b 1897 Italy, d 1967 Buenos Aires. Stud J. Capalbo. Adopted Argentine citizenship. Curator str instr collection (Guarneri del Gesu, Gobetti, Guadagnini, F. Stradivari, Norman, etc.) Museum Isaac Fernandez Blanco, 1937–d. Experimented with Argentine woods in vn construction. Made over 200 str instrus. Vas have excellent tone. Made first Tertis model Va in So Amer (commissioned by E. Dali).

PIÑEIRO, HORACIO. Stud Pierre Gaggini of Nice. Leading Argentine luthier, now settled in NYC. Many instrus incl Vas patterned after: Andrea Amati (16½ in, 41.9 cm.); Paganini Antonio

Stradivarius; G. B. Guadagnini Turin 1784 ex-Leyds (15 3/16 in., 40.16 cm.).

VIUDES, ANTONIO, b 1883 Alicante, Spain, d 1961 Buenos Aires. Migrated to Buenos Aires 1909. 1st leading vn maker in Argentina. Made several Vas of magnificent construction and sonority on his own model, 16¼ in (41.27 cm.). Disapproved the Tertis Va model.

GLOSSARY I

Names for the Viola used by German Writers (1618–1756)

Praetorius (1618): Tenor Geig
Hizler (1623)   : Alt-Geig
Kircher (1650)   : Alto di Viola
Herbst (1658)   : Viola di Braccio, and Brazzo
Falck (1688)   : Viola da Braccio
Merck (1695)   : Hohe Alto, Violetta, Viola prima vel
                   segunda, soprano Viola Cantus, and
                   Franzosisch Haut Contre
Speer (1697)   : Viol-braccio, and Braz
Mattheson (1713): Viola, Violetta, Viola da Bracchio, and
                   Brazzo
Eisel (1738)   : Viola, Violetta, and Viola da Braccio
Majer (1741)   : Viola, Violetta, Viola da Braccio, Brazzo,
                   Alt-Viola, and Arm-Geig
Quantz (1750)   : Bratsche
L. Mozart (1756): Bratsche

The multiplicity of terms and spellings in the above list illustrates the etymological evolution that eventually resulted in the crystallization of the word *Bratsche* as the German equivalent for the Italian *viol da braccio*. The German term *Bratsche* has now gone full circle and in the year 1980 the official title for the International Viola Research Society is *Internationale Viola-Forschungsgesellschaft;* articles in MGG are listed under *Viola* not *Bratsche;* several German publishers, e.g., Bärenreiter, Schott, and others are replacing the word, *Bratsche,* with the term, *Viola,* on their covers and in their catalogues. This does not imply that the word *Bratsche* will be dropped from the German vocabulary. It will probably be a part of the language for many years to come. There is, however, a world-wide trend to use the word, *viola,* in all languages.

GLOSSARY II

20th Century Viola Terminology

Danish—Bratsch
English—Viola, Tenor
Estonian—Wiola
Finnish—Alttoviulu
French—Alto
German—Bratsche
Greek—Bioaa
Hungarian—Bracsa
Italian—Alto, Viole
Latvian—Brahtscha
Lithuanian—Broczia
Netherlands—Alt
Norway—Bratsj

Polish—Altowka
Portugese—Violeta
Rhaeto-Romanic—Giun
Rumanian—Vioara Mare
Russian—Braca and
  Alta (Альт)
Ruthenian—Vtorvka
Serbian—Guslina
Spanish—Viola
Swedish—Altfiol
Walloon—Medgrwth
Yiddish—Viole

The list above will continue to have value for the musician or scholar who peruses manuscripts or printed music from any of the indicated countries or ethnic groups. There is a definite trend, however, to change the name in all countries, for better interchange of ideas, to the one most commonly used in printed music, namely *viola*. German usage in music and reference works printed since World War II constitutes a prime example.

BIBLIOGRAPHY

Altmann, Wilhelm and Borissovsky, Vadim, *Literaturverzeichnis für Bratsche und Viola d'amore*, Wolfenbüttel: Verlag für musikalische Kultur und Wissenschaft, 1937.

Altmann, Wilhelm, "Zur Geschichte der Bratsche und der Bratschten," *Allgemeine Musikzeitung*, Vol. 56 (1929), pp. 971–72.

Andrews, Robert E., *Gasparo Bertolotti da Salò*, Berkeley, California: Pub. by the author, 1953.

Anthony, James R., *French Baroque Music*, New York: W. W. Norton, 1974.

Arcidiacono, Aurelio, *Gli Instrument Musicali: La Viola*, Milano: Berben, 1973.

Arnold, F. T., "Die Viola Pomposa," *Zeitschrift für Musikwissenschaft*, Leipzig, 13 (Dec. 1930), pp. 141–45.

Baines, Anthony, *Musical Instruments Through the Ages*, New York: Walker and Co., 1961 [Kenneth Skeaping author of article, "The Viola," pp. 122–6].

Barrett, Henry, *The Viola: Complete Guide for Teachers and Students*, Birmingham: University of Alabama Press, 1972; Second enlarged edition, 1978.

Baudet-Maget, A., *Guide du Violoniste, oeuvres choisies pour violon ainsi que pour alto et musique de chambre*, Lausanne: Foetisch Frères. 1920

Beaumont, Dr. François, *Viola Discographie*, Kassel: Bärenreiter, 1973, [Second Ed., 1975].

——————— *L'Alto et ses Interpretes: Discographie 1920–1976*, [Third Ed.] Auvernier: Pub. by Author, 1976.

——————— *Lionel Tertis (1876–1975) Discographie*, Auvernier: Pub. by Author, 1975.

Beck, Carl Thomas, *Four Recitals and Documents: Performance Problems in Selected Compositions for Solo Viola by Paul Hindemith*, Mus. A.D. Boston University, 1968.

Beckman, Gustav, *Das Violinspiel in Deutschland vor 1700*, Leipzig, Simrock: 1918.

Bender, Hans, "The Tenor Violin, Past, Present, and Future," *The Instrumentalist* (November 11, 1969), pp. 37–42 [The same article appeared in *The American String Teacher* (Fall, 1969)].

Berlioz, Hector, *Memoirs*, Trans. by Rachel and Eleanor Holmes, London: Macmillan & Co., 1884 [Revised by Ernest Newman, and Pub. by Alfred A. Knopf, 1932].

——————— *Treatise on Instrumentation, Enlarged and Revised by Richard Strauss*, Trans. by Theodore Front, New York: Edwin F. Kalmus, 1948.

Berner, Alfred, "Viola," *Diè Musik in Geschichte und Gegenwart*, Vol. 13, Kassel: Bärenreiter, 1966.

Bessler, Heinrich, *Zum Problem der Tenorgeige*, Heidelberg: Müller-Thiergarten, 1949.

Bloch, Suzanne and Heskes, Irene, *Ernest Bloch: Creative Spirit*, New York: Jewish Music Council, 1976.

Bonetti, Carlo, *La Genalogia degli Amati-Liutai e il Primato della Scuola Liutis lica Cremonese Bollettino Storico Cremonese*, Series II, Anno III (Vol VIII), Cremona, 1938.

Boyden, David D., *The History of Violin Playing from its Origins to 1761*, London: Oxford University Press, 1965.

——————— *The Hill Collection*, London: Oxford University Press, 1969.

——————— "The Tenor Violin: Myth, Mystery, or Misnomer," *Festschrift Otto Eric Deutsch zum 80 Geburtstag*, Kassel: Bärenreiter, 1963, pp. 273–79.

——————— *Monteverdi's Violini Piccoli alla Francese and Viole da Brazzo*, Extract des Annales Musicologiques, Tome VI, Neuilly-sur-Seine: Société de Musique d'Autrefois, 1958–63.

Die Bratsche, No. 1–5 (1929–30), Ed. by Wilhelm Altmann, Leipzig: Carl Mersenburger.

The Breitkopf Thematic Catalogue, The Six Parts and Sixteen Supplements, 1762–1787, New York: Dover Publications, 1966 [Edited and with an introduction and indexes by Barry S. Brook].

Bruni, Bartolomeo, *Méthode d'Alto*, Paris: Janet et Cotelle, c.1805.

Campagnoli, Bartolomeo, *41 Capricen*, Leipzig, c.1805.

Carse, Adam, *The History of Orchestration*, London: Kegan Paul, Trench, Trubner & Co., Ltd., 1925 [Dover Reprint, 1964].

Clarke, Rebecca, "The History of the Viola in Quartet Writing," *Music and Letters*, IV, 1, pp. 6–17.

————— *Cobbett's Cyclopedic Survey of Chamber Music*, London: Oxford University Press, First Ed., 1929; Second Ed., 1963 [Material related to viola by Rebecca Clarke].

Complete Instructions for the Tenor . . . , London: Longman and Broderip, c.1795.

Corrette, Michel, *Méthodes pour apprendre à jouer de la Contre-Basse à 3, à 4, et à 5 cordes, de la Quinte ou Alto et de la Viole d'Orphée . . .* , Paris, c.1782 [Reprint, Genève: Minkoff, 1977].

de Coury, Geraldine I. C., *Paganini, the Genoese*, Norman, Oklahoma: University of Oklahoma Press, 1957.

Creitz, Lowell, "The New and the Old Violin Families," *The Catgut Acoustical Society Newsletter* (November 1978), No. 30, pp. 1–5.

Cupis, Jean B., *Méthode d'Alto*, Paris: Janet et Cotelle, c.1788.

Dalton, David, *Genesis and Synthesis of the Bartók Viola Concerto* (Doctoral Dissertation), Bloomington: Indiana University, 1970.

————— "The Genesis of Bartók's Viola Concerto," *Music and Letters*, (April, 1976), pp. 117–129.

Doktor, Paul, "J. S. Bach's Three Viola da Gamba Sonatas: Their Adaptability for Viola," *Journal of the Violin Society of America*, Vol. II, No. 3 (1976), pp. 6–10.

Doring, Ernest N., *The Amati Family*, Chicago: William Lewis and Son, n.d.

————— *The Guadagnini Family of Violin Makers*, Chicago, 1949.

Duckles, Vincent, "Willam F. Herschel's Concertos for Oboe, Viola and Violin," *Festschrift Otto Eric Deutsch zum 80 Geburtstag*, Kassel: Bärenreiter, 1963, pp. 66–74.

Einstein, Alfred, *Mozart, His Character, His Work*, Trans. A. Mendel and N. Broder, New York: Oxford University Press, 1945.

Eisel, Johann Philipp, *Musicus Autodidaktos, oder der sich selbst informirende Musicus . . .* Erfurt: J. M. Funcken, 1738.

Ewald, Konrad, *Musik für Bratsche*, Liestal: Pub. by the Author, 1975.

Falck, Georg, *Idea boni cantoris . . .* , Nürnberg: W. M. Endter, 1688.

Farish, Margaret K., *String Music in Print*, New York: R. R. Bowker, 1965.

————— *Supplement to String Music in Print*, New York: R. R. Bowker, 1968.

Garnault, Paul, "Chrétien Urhan (1790–1845)," *Revue de Musicologie*, XI (1930), pp. 98–111.

Gebauer, Michael Joseph, *Méthode d'Alto*, Paris: Janet, c.1800.

Geiringer, Karl, *Brahms His Life and Work*, New York: Oxford University Press, 1947.

Geiser, Brigitte, *Studien zur Fruehgeschichte der Violine*. Berne: Paul Haupt, 1974.

Gerber, Ernst Ludwig, *Historisch-biographisches Lexikon der Tonkünstler*, 2 Vols., Leipzig, 1790–92.

————— *Neues Historisch-biographisches Lexicon der Tonkünstler*, 4 Vols., Leipzig, 1812–14.

Glyde, Rosemary, *New, Revised Edition of the Concerto pour l'Alto Viola Principale of Johann Andreas Amon, c.1800*. Score, solo viola part, arrangement for viola and piano, text. (D.M.A. Dissertation) New York, Juilliard School of Music, 1975.

Goodkind, Herbert, *Violin Iconography of Antonio Stradivari, 1644–1737*, New York: Pub. by the author, 1972.

Griffin, Judson, *A Guide to American Viola Music*, D.M.A. Dissertation, Juilliard School of Music, 1977.

Hajdecki, Alexander, *Die Italienische lira da Braccio*, 1892.

Henley, William, *Universal Dictionary of Violin and Bow Makers*, 5 Vols., Brighton, Sussex: Amati Pub., Co. Ltd., 1959–60.

Herbst, Johann Andreas, *Musica moderna prattica*, Franckfurt am Mayn: G. Müller, 1658.

Hill, W. Henry, Arthur F., and Alfred E., *Antonio Stradivari, His Life and Work (1644–1737)*, London: Wm. Hill & Sons, 1902, Reprint: Dover, 1963.

——————— *The Violin Makers of the Guarneri Family*, London: Wm, Hill & Sons, 1931, Reprint: Holland Press, 1965.

Hizler, Daniel, *Extract auss der Neuen Musica oder Singkunst . . .*, Nürnberg: Abraham Wagenmann, 1623.

Hoffmeister, Franz Anton, *12 Viola-Etuden*, Leipzig: Bureau de Musique, c.1800.

Hutchins, Carleen Maley "The Physics of Violins," *Scientific American* (Nov. 1962), pp. 79–93.

——————— "The New Violin Family," *American String Teacher* (Spring, 1965), pp. 42–44.

——————— "Founding a Family of Fiddles," *Physics Today* (Feb. 1967), pp. 23–34.

——————— *The Catgut Acoustical Society Newsletter* (Mrs. Hutchins is the Editor of this semiannual publication).

Jahn, Otto, *Life of Mozart*, 3 Vols., Trans. by Pauline D. Townsend, London: Novello, 1891.

Jambe de Fer, Philibert, *Epitome musicale*, Lyon: Michael du Bois, 1556.

Juzefovitsch, Viktor, *V. Borissovsky, the Founder of the Soviet Viola School*, Moscow: State Publishing Co., 1974.

Kaiser, Friedrich Carl, *Carl Stamitz Biographische Beiträge. Das Symphonis Werk . . .*[Dissertation], Marburg: Phillips Uinversität, 1962.

Kircher, Athanasius, *Musurgia universalis sive ars magna consoni et dissoni*, 2 Vols., Rome: Corbelletti, 1662.

Kleefeld, William J., *Das Orchester der ersten deutschen Oper Hamburg (1678–1738)*, Berlin: Druck von R. Bell, 1898.

Kolneder, Walter, *Das Buch der Violine*, Zurich: Atlantis, 1972.

Kunitz, Hans, *Violine/Bratsche*, Leipzig: Breitkopf & Härtel, 1960.

Kushner, David Z., "A Commentary on Ernest Bloch's Symphonic Works," *The Radford Review*, XXI, 3 (Sept., 1967), pp. 100–37.

Laborde, Jean-Benjamin de, *Essai sur la musique ancienne et moderne*, 4 Vols., Paris, 1780.

Lebermann, Walter, "Apokryph, Plagiat, Korruptel oder Falsifikat?" *Die Musikforschung*, XX, 4 (1967), 413–25.

——————— "Ignaz Joseph Pleyel: Die Frühdrucke seiner Solokonzerte und deren Doppelfassungen," *Die Musikforschung*, XXVI, 4 (1973), pp. 481–86.

——————— "Das musikalische Würfelspiel des Iwan Jewstafjewitsch Chandoschkin," *Die Musikforschung*, XXVII, 3 (1974), 332–34.

——————— "The Viola Concerti of the Stamitz Family," *Viola Research Society Newsletter*, (1974), p. 3.

——————— "Georg Philipp Telemanns kühne Stimmführung—ein orthographischer Lapsus des Autors oder Johann Christoph Graupners?" *Musica*, XXXI (1977), p. 50 f.

—————— "Zur Autorschaft dreier Violakonzerte von 'Frederico' Benda," *Die Musikforschung* (Jan., 1979), pp. 289–91.

Leipp, Émile, *The Violin*, Toronto: University of Toronto Press, 1969.

Letz, Hans, *Music for the Violin and Viola*, New York: Rinehart, 1948.

Majer, F. B. C., *Neu-eröffneter theoretisch- und pracktischer Music-Saal*, Nürnberg: Johann Jacob Cremer, 1741. Facsimile reprint, *Documenta Musicologica*, I, Kassel und Basel, 1954.

Martinn, Jacob J. B., *Methodé d'Alto*, Paris: Frey, c.1815.

Mattheson Johann, *Das neu-eröffnetes Orchester oder grundliche Anleitung...*, Hamburg, 1713.

McCredie, Andrew D., *Instrumentarium and Instrumentation in the North German Baroque Opera* [Doctoral Dissertation], Hamburg: University of Hamburg, 1964.

Menuhin, Yehudi, and Primrose, William, *Violin and Viola (Music Guides)*, London: MacDonald and Jane's, 1976.

Merck, Daniel, *Compendium Musicàe Instrumentalis Chelicae...*, Augsburg: J. C. Wagner, 1695.

Mersenne, Marin, *Harmonie Universelle...*, Paris: S. Cramoisy, 1636–37.

Millant, Roger, *J. B. Vuillaume, His Life and Work*, London: W. E. Hill & Sons, 1972.

Mischakoff, Anne, *Ivan Evstafevish Khandoshkin and the Beginnings of Russian String Music* (Doctoral Dissertation), Urbana: University of Illinois [Includes discussion of *Duo for Violin and Viola*, and authenticity question of the Khandoshkin *Viola Concerto*].

Moser, Andreas/Hans-Joachim Nösselt, *Geschichte des Violinspiels*, 2 Vols., (second corrected and supplement edition), Tutzing: Hans Schneider, 1966.

Mucchi, Antonio Maria, *Gasparo da Salò, la Vita e l'Opera 1540–1609*, Milano: Ulrico Hoepli, 1948 [Reprint, Milano: Institute Editoriale Cisalpino-Goliardica, 1978].

Muffat, Georg, *Florilegium primum*, Augsburg 1695; —————— *Florilegium secundum*, Passau, 1698 [Both volumes reprinted in *Denkmaler der Tonkunst in Oesterreich*, Vienna, 1894 and 1895].

Nelson, Sheila, *The Violin Family*, London: Dennis Dobson, 1964 [Section II "The Viola"].

—————— *The Violin and Viola*, New York: W. W. Norton, 1972.

Nettl, Paul, *Forgotten Musicians*, New York: Philosophical Library, 1951.

Otto, Irmgard and Adelmann, Olga, *Katalog der Streichinstrumente, Musikinstrumenten-Museum, Berlin*, Berlin: H. Heenemann, 1975.

Pasqualini, Dr. Gioacchino, "Referendum internazionale sulla viola moderna," *Saint Cecilia*, 8 (April, 1959), pp. 81–3.

—————— "Risultat sul referendum internazionale A.N.L.A.I. sulla viola moderna," *Saint Cecilia*, 9 (1960), pp. 73–4.

Perich, Guillermo, *Annotated Course of Study for Viola*, Urbana, Illinois: University of Illinois Press, 1974.

Petzold, Richard, *Georg Philipp Telemann*, Leipzig, 1967, English Ed. Trans. by Horace Fitzpatrick, New York: Oxford University Press, 1974.

Pierre, Constant, *Histoire du Concert spirituel 1725–1790 (Publications de la Société Française de Musicologie)*, troisième série, tome III, Paris: Heugel, 1975.

Playford, John, *An Introduction to the Skill of Music*, London: W. Godbid [appeared in 19 numbered and 5 unnumbered editions between 1654 and 1730].

Praetorius, Michael, *Syntagma Musicum*, Vol II *De Organographia*, Wolfenbüttel: E. Holwein, 1619. English trans. by Harold Blumenfield, New York: Bärenreiter, 1962.

Primrose, William, *Technique is Memory*, London: Oxford University Press, 1960.

—————— *Walk on the North Side: Memoirs of a Violist*, Provo, Utah: Brigham Young University Press, 1978.

Puccianti, Anna, *Antonio Stradivari: I Grand Liutai Cremonese*, Collana di monografie autorizzato dal Ministero della Scuola Internazionale di Liuteria Cremona, 1959 [English Trans. by Salvatore Coco, 1959].

Quantz, Johann Joachim, *Versuch einer Anweisung die Flöte traversiere zu spielen.* Berlin: Johann Friedrich Voss, 1752. English Trans. by Edward R. Reilly, *On Playing the Flute*, New York: Macmillan, 1966.

Rigby, Stanley, "Memoirs," *Music and Letters* (April, 1954), pp. 140–3.

Riley, Maurice W., "From Violin to Viola," *Educational Music* Magazine (Jan.-Feb., 1951).

————— *The Teaching of Bowed Instruments from 1511 to 1756 [Doctoral Dissertation]*, Ann Arbor: University of Michigan, 1954.

————— "18th Century Concertos for the Viola," *Journal of the Violin Society of America*, III, 2, (Spring, 1977), pp. 88–90.

————— "The Contributions of Walter Lebermann to Viola Literature," *American String Teacher*, XXVII, 2, (Spring, 1977), p. 19.

————— "Louis Bailly (1882–1974)," *Journal of the Violin Society of America*, III, 3, (Summer, 1977), pp. 33–49.

————— "Louis Bailly's Gasparo da Salò Violas," *Journal of the Violin Society of America*, III, 3, (Summer, 1977), pp. 50–57.

————— "A Visit with Alexandra de Lazari-Borissovsky, Russia's Mother Viola," *Journal of the Violin Society of America*, IV, 2 (Spring, 1978), pp. 32–42.

Ritter, Hermann, *Die Viola alta.* Heidelberg, 1876.

————— *Die Geschichte der Viola alta und die Grundsätze ihres Baues.* Leipzig, 1877.

————— Reprint of 1877 edition, Wiesbaden: Dr. Martin Sändig, 1969.

————— *Die Viola alta oder Altgeige*, Leipzig, 1885.

————— *Die fünfsaitige Altgeige Viola alta*, Bamberg, 1899.

Roda, Joseph, *Bows for Musical Instruments*, Chicago: William Lewis & Son, 1959.

Rood, Louise, *The Viola as Solo Instrument*, Master's Thesis, Smith College, 1942.

————— "Bach for Violists," *Repertoire* (Jan., 1952), pp. 169–71.

————— "A Welcome Viola Concerto," *Repertoire* (Oct., 1951), pp. 47–9.

Rosen, Charles, *The Classical Style: Haydn, Mozart, Beethoven*, New York: W. W. Norton, 1972.

Rosenblum, Myron, "Vadim Borissovsky—Violist, Teacher, Scholar," *American String Teacher*, XXIV, 3 (1974), p. 46.

————— *Newsletter of the American Viola Society* [as Editor Dr. Rosenblum has written numerous significant articles on the viola, its music, and its players, 1973–].

Rubinstein, Arthur, *My Young Years*, New York: Alfred A. Knopf, 1973.

Sachs, Curt, *Handbuch der Musik instrumentenkunde*, Leipzig: Breitkopf & Härtel, 1930.

————— *History of Musical Instruments*, New York, W. W. Norton, 1940.

Serly, Tibor, "A Belated Account of the Reconstruction of a 20th-Century Masterpiece," *College Music Symposium*, Vol. XV (Spring, 1975), pp. 7–25.

Schenk, Erich, *The Italian Trio Sonata*, Köln: Arno Volk, 1955.

Sciannameo, Franco, "Allesandro Rolla," *Viol*, No. I (Nov. 1975), pp. 16–18.

Skelton, Geoffrey, *Paul Hindemith, the Man Behind the Music*, London: Victor Gollancz, 1975.

Speer, Daniel, *Grund-richtiger kurtz leicht und nöthiger . . . der musicalischen kunst. . .*, Ulm: G. W. Kühnen, 1697.

Straeten, E. van der, "The Viola," *The Strad* [continued from issue to issue, 1912 to 1916].

Street, Marna, *Annotated Bibliography of Unaccompanied Viola Music (Originally for Viola)*, [DMA Dissertation (date ?)], Eastman School of Music.

384   The History of the Viola

Strunk, Oliver, "Haydn's Divertimenti for Baryton, Viola and Bass," *Musical Quarterly*, XVIII (1932), pp. 216–51.

Tatton, Thomas James, *English Viola Music, 1870–1937* [Doctoral Dissertation], Urbana: University of Illinois, 1976.
Torri, Luigi, *La Construzione ed I Costruttori degli Istrumenti ad Arco: Bibliografia Liutistica*, Padova: G. Zanibon, 1920.
Tertis, Lionel, *Cinderella No More*, London: Wm. Carling & Co. Ltd., 1953.
—————— *My Viola and I*, London: Elek Books, Ltd., 1974.
—————— *Beauty of Tone in String Playing*, London: Oxford University Press, 1946.

Vatelot, Etienne, *Les Archets Français*, 2 Vols., Nancy: Sernor-M. Dufour, 1977.
Vieux, Maurice, "Considération sur la technique de l'alto," *Courrier Musical et Théatral*. XXX, 7 (1928), p. 216.

Wagner, Richard, *On Conducting,—Treatise on Style in the Execution of Classical Music*, Trans. by Edward Dannreuther, London; 1885 [Modern Reprint, London: William Reeves, 1940].
Walther, Johann Gottfried, *Musikalisches Lexikon oder Musikalische Bibliothek* (Leipzig, 1972).
Watson, J. Arthur, "Mozart and the Viola," *Music and Letters* XXII (1941), pp. 41–53.
Websky, Wilhelm, *Versuch eines moglichst vollständigen thematischen Katalogs der Duo-Literatur für Bratsche und Violoncello*, Kassel: Violaforschungsgesellschaft, n.d.
Weertman, Roelof, *Violin Building My Way*, Falmouth, Mass.: Published by the author, 1974.
Weingartner, Felix, "Das Ritter Quartet," *Die Musik* 4 (1904/5), p. 169.
Whistling, C. F., *Handbuch der musikalischen Literatur*, 1828.
Wilkens, Wayne, *Index of Viola Music*, Magnolia, Arkansas: Pub. by Author, 1976 [with annual supplements].
Winternitz, Emanuel, *Guadenzio Ferrari: His School and the Early History of the Violin*, Milano: Verallo Sesia, 1967.
Woldemar, Michel, *Méthode d'Alto*, Paris: Sieber, c.1795.
Wolff, Hellmuth Christian, *Die venezianische Oper in der zweitens Hälfte des 17 Jahrhunderts, Ein Beitrag zur Geschichte der Musik und des Theatres in Zeitalter des Barock*, Berlin: Verlagsgesellschaft, 1937.

Zeyringer, Franz, *Literatur für Viola*, Hartberg, Austria: Verlag Julius Schönwetter, 1963.
—————— *Literatur für Viola* Ergänzungsband (Supplement), 1965.
—————— *Literatur für Viola, Neuausgabe 1976*, Hartberg, Austria: Julius Schön- wetter, 1976.
—————— *The Problem of Viola Size*, New York: The American Viola Society, 1979.

INDEX